Keynes's *General Theory*

Keynes's *General Theory*

Seventy-Five Years Later

Edited by

Thomas Cate

Northern Kentucky University, USA

Edward Elgar

Cheltenham, UK • Northampton, MA, USA

Published by
Edward Elgar Publishing Limited
The Lypiatts
15 Lansdown Road
Cheltenham
Glos GL50 2JA
UK

Edward Elgar Publishing, Inc.
William Pratt House
9 Dewey Court
Northampton
Massachusetts 01060
USA

A catalogue record for this book
is available from the British Library

Library of Congress Control Number: 2011932877

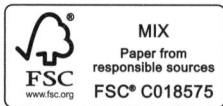

MIX
Paper from
responsible sources
FSC
www.fsc.org   FSC® C018575

ISBN 978 1 84542 411 4

Typeset by Servis Filmsetting Ltd, Stockport, Cheshire
Printed and bound by MPG Books Group, UK

Contents

Contributors

Angel Asensio Associate Professor of Economics, Centre d'Economie de Paris Nord, University of Paris 13, France

Roger E. Backhouse Professor of the History and Philosophy of Economics, Department of Economics, University of Birmingham, UK and Erasmus Institute of Philosophy and Economics, Erasmus University Rotterdam, the Netherlands

Bradley W. Bateman Provost and Professor of Economics, Denison University, USA

Alcino F. Camara-Neto Dean, Law and Economic Sciences Center, Federal University of Rio de Janeiro, Brazil

Thomas Cate Professor of Economics, Northern Kentucky University, USA

Michel DeVroey Professor of Economics, Department of Economics, Université Catholique de Louvain, Belgium

Robert W. Dimand Professor of Economics, Department of Economics, Brock University, St Catharines, Ontario, Canada

Peter Docherty Associate Professor, Economics Group, UTS Business School, University of Technology, Sydney, Australia

Gilles Dostaler Professor of Economics, Department of Economics, Université du Québec à Montréal, Canada

Omar F. Hamouda Department of Economics, Glendon College, York University, Canada

M.G. Hayes Fellow and Director of Studies in Economics, Robinson College, University of Cambridge, UK

Matthew N. Luzzetti Graduate student, Department of Economics, University of California, Los Angeles, USA

Elke Muchlinski Economist, Visiting Professor, and Philosopher, has held teaching positions at the Free University of Berlin, the University of Halle (2010–11), the University of Trier (2009), and the University of Hamburg (summer 2008) and at the time of publication held a temporary appointment at the University of Saarland, Saarbrücken, in International Economics and Philosophy

Lee E. Ohanian Professor of Economics, Department of Economics, University of California, Los Angeles, USA

Lall Ramrattan Instructor, University of California, Berkeley, USA

Louis-Phillippe Rochon Director, International Economic Policy Institute and Associate Professor, Department of Economics, Laurentian University, Canada

John Smithin Professor of Economics, Department of Economics and the Schulich School of Business, York University, Canada

Michael Szenberg Distinguished Professor of Economics, Department of Finance and Economics, Lubin School of Business, Pace University, New York City, USA

Matías Vernengo Associate Professor of Economics, Department of Economics, University of Utah, USA

L. Randall Wray Professor of Economics, Department of Economics, University of Missouri-Kansas City, USA

In memory of Gilles Dostaler

Gilles Dostaler, Keynes scholar, bon vivant, professor of economic science at the Université du Québec à Montréal (UQAM) and member of research centres at the Universities of Paris-1, Paris-8, and Toulouse, passed away on 26 February 2011. Sustained by his partner Marielle Cauchy, Gilles remained active in research and in life to the very end of his battle with cancer: in the last week before his death, we exchanged e-mails about a CEA (Canadian Economics Association) session we were organizing to mark the 75th anniversary of the publication of Keynes's *General Theory*. An internationally-renowned economist and historian of economic thought, Gilles Dostaler published ten books, a dozen edited books, more than 30 journal articles, more than 30 papers in edited volumes, and 16 published interviews (three of them in Japanese newspapers), and was on the editorial boards of seven journals – and was as much at home waist-deep in a salmon stream in Gaspé as in a library.

After teaching mathematics at Collège Jean-de-Brebeuf and graduating from McGill University (MA in economics, 1972) and the Université de Paris-8 (PhD in economics, 1975), Gilles joined the faculty of UQAM in 1975, initially in sociology and then from 1979 in economics (associate professor 1982, full professor 1991). As a student at McGill, Gilles had been one of the organizers of the 'McGill français' demonstrations that led to the creation of UQAM. Writing a dissertation on Marxian value theory, his first books were *Marx, la valeur, et l'économie politique* (Paris: Anthropos, 1978) and *Valeur et prix: histoire d'un débat* (Paris: Maspero, Grenoble: Presses Universitaires de Grenoble, Montréal: Presses de l'Université du Québec, 1978; revised and expanded edition Paris: L'Harmattan, 2010; Spanish translation, 1980). Subsequently the focus of Gilles's scholarship was the ideas of John Maynard Keynes. He stressed the continuing relevance of Keynes's insights and analysis to the understanding of economic crisis and stabilization, notably in his last books, *Keynes par-delà l'économie* (Paris: Thierry Magnier, 2009) and *Keynes y el desemple* (Madrid: Abada, 2011). As an historian of ideas, Gilles explored the role of the Bloomsbury Group in the origins of Keynes's social, political, and aesthetic ideas, the relation of Keynes's thought to that of Freud, and comparing and contrasting Keynes's vision of how the economy works with those of Karl Marx, Friedrich Hayek, Milton Friedman, and Gunnar Myrdal, a comparative focus evident of the titles of many of his articles: 'The debate between Hayek and Keynes' (1991), 'Hayek contra Keynes' (1997), 'Keynes and Friedman on money' (1997), 'Friedman and Keynes: divergences and convergences' (1998), 'Freud and Keynes on money and capitalism' (2000), 'Freud et Keynes: un combat commun' (2009), 'Bloomsbury, Freud et Keynes' (2010), '*The General Theory*, Marx, Marxism, and the Soviet Union' (2011).

Gilles Dostaler's scholarship reached a world-wide audience, published on five continents and in nine languages. His invaluable reference work with Michel Beaud, *La pensée économique depuis Keynes* (Paris: Seuil, 1993), was not only published in English as *Economic Thought since Keynes* (Edward Elgar, 1995, revised paperback Routledge, 1997) but also appeared in Arabic, Portuguese, Romanian, and Vietnamese translations. Gilles's magnum opus was *Keynes et ses combats* (Paris: Albin Michel, 2005, expanded edition 2009), translated as *Keynes and his Battles* (Edward Elgar, 2007, paperback 2009) and also translated into Japanese, Portuguese, and Spanish. His *Le libéralisme de Hayek* (Paris: La Découverte, 2001) was translated into Italian and Vietnamese. His book with Bernard Maris, *Capitalisme et pulsion de mort* (Paris: Albin Michel, 2009), drawing on Keynes's concept of a morbid desire for liquidity and on Freud's ideas to understand the world financial crisis, will appear in Italian and Portuguese editions.

Robert W. Dimand

Robert Dimand is also a contributor to this volume. He wrote this obituary for publication in the *Canadian Economics Association Newsletter*, in August 2011.

Editor's introduction

Thomas Cate

In a letter to George Bernard Shaw dated 1 January 1935, Keynes wrote:

> To understand *my* state of mind, however, you have to know that I believe
> myself to be writing a book on economic theory which will largely revolutionize
> – *not*, I suppose, at once but in the course of the next 10 years – the way the
> world thinks about economic problems.
>
> J. M. Keynes, *Collected Writings*, Vol. XIII, p. 492 (emphasis in original)

While the question of a revolution in the Kuhnian or Lakatosian
sense has yet to be completely resolved, the economic profession has
experienced a dramatic transformation since the publication of *The
General Theory of Employment, Interest, and Money* (Keynes 1936).[1] As
Samuelson notes: 'The *General Theory* caught most economists under
the age of 35 with the unexpected virulence of a disease first attacking
and decimating an isolated tribe of south sea islanders' (Samuelson
1966, p. 1517).

At least three differences distinguish *The General Theory* from some
of Keynes's earlier books. First, there is the difference in audience: *The
Economic Consequences of the Peace* (Keynes, CW, vol. I) and *A Tract
on Monetary Reform* (Keynes, CW, vol. IV) were written for a much
larger audience: Fellow economists, policy makers and sophisticated
readers who were aware of the issues being raised in each book; whereas
The General Theory was written for his fellow economists. Second, there
is the difference in tone and style of writing: *Economic Consequences*
and the *Tract* are much more engaging, lively, and literary; whereas
The General Theory is a very difficult read. Third, there is the difference in the plan of the book: *Economic Consequences* and the *Tract*
may be divided into three distinct parts: a statement of the problem,
a thorough examination of the problem and a specific public policy
proposal designed to resolve the problem; whereas *The General Theory*
revolved around several versions of a simple macroeconomic model of
the English economy.[2]

KEYNES'S SIMPLE MODEL[3]

The economics of Keynes is distinctly different from Keynesian economics, otherwise known as bastard Keynesianism, the term coined by Joan
Robinson for the neoclassical synthesis (Robinson 1962, 1980). While
both theories investigate the macroeconomic implications of decision
making in the face of uncertainty, the crucial difference between them lies
in their respective definitions of uncertainty. So . . . what is meant by the
term uncertainty?

Formal Logic and Uncertainty

Formal logic is a process associated with the calculus of probabilities, and
relies on equivalent certainties – the weighted average of each potential
outcome by its objective probabilities. In this process uncertainty is objective, the variance of some probability distribution, as illustrated by Hicks
in 'The Theory of Uncertainty and Profit' where he states that

> The co-operating parties are divided into two groups, only one of which
> receives a remuneration depending on the firm's success (that is to say, receiv-
> ing a share of profits). The members of the other group receives a remuneration
> which is not directly contingent on the results of the operations in which they
> collaborate, but which is fixed before the act of collaboration is performed. The
> first group receives profit; the second group receives wages, interest, or rent.
> (Hicks 1931, p. 176)

Thus, Hicks's theory of profit, which can be traced to Cantillon through
Cannon, does not resort to metaphysical foundations to explain the existence of profit. Unlike Knight (1921) who defines uncertainty as being not
measurable and associated with estimates, Hicks uses a frequency theory
of probability and defines uncertainty as an increase in the variance in a
share of the expected net return on an investment position taken by an
entrepreneur in an on-going collaborative business operation (Hicks 1931,
pp. 176–83).[4] Entrepreneurs' reward for making decisions in the face of
Hicks's uncertainty is profit.

   This approach to uncertainty can easily be incorporated into a mathematical model, as illustrated by the quants who borrowed a concept from
physics – Brownian motion, to model the prices of stocks and structured
financial instruments (Patterson 2010, pp. 28–9). However, as the Great
Recession spread to Main Street from Wall Street, at least three sources
of systemic error are revealed in these models: trivial contradictions are
rooted in the core of mathematics and logic (Godel 1931), the act of measurement alters the physical properties of the system (Heisenberg 1927) and

a system of well-defined and well-behaved equations may exhibit over time movements that cannot be predicted (Lorenz 1972).

Human Logic and Uncertainty

Human logic is a process associated with heuristics and unknown unknowns. In this process human knowledge of future events is spread along an ordinal continuum, the end points being known and unknown. Along this continuum,

> Fundamental uncertainty refers to situations in which at least some essential information about future events cannot be known at the moment of decision because this information does not exist and cannot be inferred from any existing data set. (Dequech 1999, pp. 415–16)

Fundamental uncertainty may have epistemological or ontological origins, and clearly there is a lack of objective knowledge, a key variable for formal logic. Keynes's uncertainty is an example of fundamental uncertainty and can be explained by either epistemological uncertainty or ontological indeterminacy because either approach captures the spirit of Keynes's position (Skidelsky 2009, pp. 83–8). Keynes made his position on uncertainty quite clear. In *The General Theory*, when he defined the term 'very uncertain' Keynes referred the reader to *The Treatise on Probability*: 'By "very uncertain" I do not mean the same thing as "very improbable." See my *Treatise on Probability*, chapter 6, on "The Weight of Arguments"' (Keynes 1936, p. 149, note 1). He repeated this definition in his 1937 *Quarterly Journal of Economics* article

> By 'uncertain' knowledge, let me explain, I do not mean merely to distinguish what is known for certain from what is merely probable . . . The sense in which I am using the term is that in which the price of copper and the rate of interest twenty years hence, or the obsolescence of a new invention are uncertain. About these matters there is no scientific basis on which to form any calculable probability whatever. We simply do not know. (Keynes 1937, p. 214)

When confronted with a decision in the face of Keynes's uncertainty, what does an individual do?

We have devised for this purpose a variety of techniques, of which the most important are the three following:

- We assume that the present is a much more serviceable guide to the future than a candid examination of past experience would show it to have been hitherto. In other words, we largely ignore the prospect of future changes about the actual character of which we know nothing.

- We assume that the *existing* state of opinion as expressed in prices and the character of existing output is based on a *correct* summing up of future prospects, so that we can accept it as such unless and until something new and relevant comes into the picture.

- Knowing that our own individual judgment is worthless, we endeavor to fall back on the judgment of the rest of the world, which is perhaps better informed. That is, we endeavor to conform with the behavior of the majority or the average. The psychology of a society of individuals each of whom is endeavoring to copy the other leads to what we may strictly term a *conventional* judgment (ibid.; emphasis in original).

That is, in the face of fundamental uncertainty the decision maker uses heuristics. What is a heuristic? It is not an optimization rule like the least cost rule or the utility maximization rule: the decision maker is not seeking the best possible outcome. No, the decision maker is making a constrained choice, the constraint being Keynes's uncertainty. The decision maker is a satisficer seeking an outcome that is good enough (Simon 1955). In this process decision makers use heuristics, rules of thumb, for example a 'tit for tat' strategy.

The process of human logic can be modelled *ex post*. For example a mathematical model of Keynes's marginal efficiency of capital (MEC) schedule can be developed, and while the mathematical symbols used to represent the decision variables in the resulting formula give the appearance of a mathematical model of a formal logic process, a reification of human logic into formal logic has taken place. Ignoring the process (human logic) whereby the numbers that are dropped into the MEC formula are created is just asking for trouble: one should not expect humans to exhibit the same behaviour as Brown's pink fairies (Patterson 2010, pp. 291–3; Wilmott 2000).[5]

Uncertainty, Confidence and Future Events

One of the roles played by humans is that of entrepreneurs, and as Schumpeter has shown, entrepreneurs are the driving force of capitalism (Schumpeter 1934) or as Dequech states, they '. . . possess the ability to see and do things in a novel way' (Dequech 1999, p. 422). That is, entrepreneurs possess creativity, a key variable in developing expectations, the other two being knowledge and the optimistic disposition to face uncertainty. Together with the confidence that the entrepreneur has in a set of expectations, a state of expectation for a plan of future events can be developed and decisions in the face of Keynes's uncertainty can be undertaken and implemented.

Having implemented her or his plan the entrepreneur compares the ex post results to the ex ante expected results for the purpose of closing the planning cycle loop. This comparison has three possible outcomes: the ex post results are greater than, equal to, or less than the ex ante expected results. These outcomes lead to the following questions: What did you learn? What went right? What needs to be fixed? What can be done with the windfall profits? How to cover the unexpected losses? Given Dequech's state of expectation scheme (Dequech 1999, p. 418), both confidence and expectations may be revised in light of two of the possible outcomes: windfall profits and unexpected losses. In the case of windfall profits, expectations may be upgraded because the optimistic disposition to face Keynes's uncertainty may improve, and the entrepreneur's confidence in the revised set of expectations may increase because he or she may become less adverse with respect to uncertainty and/or have a better perception of uncertainty. While these adjustments to confidence and expectations occur at the entrepreneurial (microeconomic) level, a herd mentality could come into play resulting in a wave of optimism at the macroeconomic level (Bateman 1996, pp. 71–140; Marshall 1890/1953, pp. 119–20; Pigou 1920/1952, p. 773). A similar explanation can be developed for a wave of pessimism.

MACROECONOMIC IMPLICATIONS OF KEYNES'S UNCERTAINTY

There are two macroeconomic implications of decision making in the face of Keynes's uncertainty. The first implication is that business cycles are endogenous not exogenous as postulated by real business cycle theory. As Keynes explained, it is '. . . important to understand the dependency of the marginal efficiency of a given capital stock on changes in expectation, because it is chiefly this dependency which renders the marginal efficiency of capital subject to the somewhat violent fluctuations which are the explanation of the Trade Cycle' (Keynes 1936, pp. 143–4). The second implication is that monetary economies are prone to liquidity crises because of the potential conflict between private sector liquidity demanders and private sector liquidity suppliers.

In a monetary economy both enterprise and speculation play a role. Enterprise involves '. . . the activity of forecasting the prospective yields of assets over their whole life' (ibid., p. 158). Speculation, on the other hand, involves '. . . the activity of forecasting the psychology of the market' and is '. . . largely concerned, not with making superior long-term forecasts of the prospective yield of an investment over its whole life, but with forecasting changes in the conventional basis of valuation a short time ahead of the general public' (ibid., pp. 158, 154). Both enterprise and speculation are associated with decision making in the face of Keynes's uncertainty and affect the operation of a monetary economy's financial markets (liquidity preference) through three categories of risk. First, there is borrower's risk: '. . . doubts in the borrower's mind as to the probability of his actually earning the prospective yield for which he hopes' (ibid., p. 144). Second, there is lender's risk: '. . . this may be due either to moral hazard, *i.e.* voluntary default or other means of escape, possibly lawful, from the fulfillment of the obligation, or to the possible insufficiency of the margin of security, *i.e.* involuntary default due to the disappointment of expectations' (ibid.). Third, there is system risk: '. . . a possible adverse change in the value of the monetary standard which renders a money-loan to this extent less secure than a real asset' (ibid.). Keynes's warning is ignored: '. . . speculators may do no harm as bubbles on a steady stream of enterprise. But the position is serious when enterprise becomes the bubble on a whirlpool of speculation' (ibid., p. 159). The 'numbers' developed in response to human logic and dropped into the MEC formula, itself an example of the reification process, take on a life of their own. With each success, the downside effects inherent in the three categories of risk are discounted or forgotten in the euphoria of the expansion.

Bursting bubbles may be associated with a decline in business confidence (enterprise and speculation), or a decline in the state of credit, or both. For a revival to occur both business confidence and the state of credit must be revived. However, cutting money wages as a means of reviving business confidence is not revival strategy because of the adverse effect on consumer income and spending. Also, when bubbles burst and individuals begin to implement their risk management policies in an attempt to achieve some position of liquidity their actions expose the economic system to another problem: the potential conflict between money demanders for whom time is more important than price (they need cash now) and money suppliers for whom price is more important than time (they can wait for a better price) becomes a reality and the system may seize up: a liquidity crisis occurs, the price of financial assets decline, and further pressure is placed on organizations' cash flows, margins of safety and balance sheets. If the private money suppliers are unable or unwilling to meet the needs of the private money demanders, and if the public money suppliers, the Central Bank and the Treasury, are ideologically opposed to supplying the requisite liquidity, The Slump is the only result.

If the two macroeconomic implications of decision making in the face of Keynes's uncertainty are that business cycles are endogenous and that monetary economies are prone to liquidity crises, then what macroeconomic policies could be implemented to mitigate their adverse effects? The answer to that question is linked to the answer to another question: What is the purpose of economic growth? Keynes would say that the purpose of economic growth is, first to solve the economic problem, and second, to '. . . allow people to learn to live wisely, agreeably, and well' (Keynes, CW, vol. XXVII, p. 322).

In the case of liquidity crises, when private money demanders need cash now and private money suppliers are willing to wait for a better price, the public money suppliers must realize that it may be in their self-interest to meet the demands of the private money demanders. A triage system could be implemented: solvent and liquid; solvent and not liquid; and not solvent and not liquid. The second group may have a good case for an injection of money; whereas the third group must be dealt with on a case-by-case basis, just in case some are 'too big to fail'. Thus, sometimes the central bank must play the role of supplier of money of last resort.[6]

The case of endogenous business cycles is more complicated because they cannot be eliminated: the best that can be done is for the government to design a macroeconomic risk management plan designed to reduce their adverse effects.[7] To that end, Keynes noted that gross domestic investment is the sum of gross private and gross public domestic investment. On occasion, gross private domestic investment declines because of a decline in business confidence (enterprise and speculation) and/or the state of credit. Keynes's proposal for restoring business confidence and the state of credit involved a three-part macroeconomic risk management proposal. Three institutions would play an important role in this risk management proposal: the Bank of England, the central government, and the public corporations that at that time controlled approximately two-thirds to three-quarters of Britain's capital stock.[8] The first part of Keynes's plan requires that the Chancellor of the Exchequer modify the government's budget accounting system along the following lines. The total budget should be divided into two sub-budgets, current and capital expenditures, with the proviso that the current budget always be balanced.

The capital budget would be sub-divided into four sections: The Exchequer Capital Budget tracks the capital expenditures made by the central government; the Public Capital Budget tracks the capital expenditures made by Local, Borough, and County Authorities; the Investment Budget tracks the total capital expenditures, private and government; and the Remnant Budget tracks the liquidation of war expenditures. The capital budget may be in deficit or surplus, and is countercyclical.

The second part of Keynes's plan involves the creation of a Board of Public Investment. In conjunction with the first part of the plan, this Board develops and implements an investment inventory/needs assessment mechanism whereby the government identifies what investments are scheduled or currently in progress, by whom, for what purpose, and how they are funded. From this data the government is able to develop and modify as needed plans for future self-liquidating capital expenditures undertaken by the government; and, when, for whatever reason, gross private domestic investment declines, the government would *encourage* the public corporations to increase their capital expenditures.

The third part of Keynes's plan has the Bank of England implementing a policy of stable low long-term interest rates. Such a policy is designed to encourage gross private domestic investment, and would lower the cost to the various levels of government and the public corporations when undertaking their capital expenditures, for example constructing and maintaining a national system of highways, electrical transmission, and port facilities. These investment projects would benefit not only emerging industries like automobiles and consumer electronics but also existing industries like cotton textiles and coal.

The three keys for the effective implementation of this proposal are associated with the quality of the individuals chosen to lead these institutions. First, they should be knowledgeable about the finer points of economic theory and day-to-day business operations and practices. Second, because the financial markets are highly interconnected and new products are being developed, they should take a holistic approach to decision making. These two points are captured by Keynes in his description of requisite skills of an economist (Keynes 1951, pp. 140–1). Third, they must possess the political will to act.

Thus the principal difference between the economics of Keynes and modern macroeconomic theory – either the New Classical or the New Keynesian version – lies in their respective views on uncertainty: epistemological or ontological indeterminacy vs. the variance in an objective probability distribution. The former cannot be modelled mathematically whereas the latter can be with the result that the economics profession has decided to train generations of economists who believe that Brown's pink fairies provide a solid foundation for modelling human behaviour. The Great Recession exposed the fallacy of that assumption. Economics is a difficult discipline because it is intimately linked not only to Keynes's theory of uncertainty but also requires knowledge of a wide variety of other disciplines (ibid.). Unless the profession is willing to change the way it produces future generations of economists, we should expect more of the same (Cate 2011).

THE RESEARCH AGENDA

This simple model contained an immense research agenda:

- To develop a method for measuring the stream of output: Richard Stone's (1947) work on the system national income accounts earned him a Nobel Prize in 1984;
- To verify and, if necessary, revise Keynes's consumption hypothesis: Modigliani's (1963) work with Ando on the life-cycle saving model earned him a Nobel Prize in 1985;
- To verify and, if necessary, modify Keynes's investment hypothesis: Tobin's (1969) work on the investment function earned him a Nobel Prize in 1981;
- To explore the growth implications of this model: Solow's (1956) work in the area of economic growth earned him a Nobel Prize in 1987; and
- To explore the model's public policy implications: Lucas's (1976) work on the implications of the rational expectations hypothesis earned him a Nobel Prize in 1995.

Work on each of these agenda items continues to this day.

ENTRIES IN THIS VOLUME

The entries in this volume are divided into four categories. What follows is a brief description of the entries in each of the four categories.

The General Theory and Fundamental Uncertainty

Asensio argues that Keynes's seminal innovation and hence key contribution to economic theory is the concept of fundamental uncertainty – the absence of any objective anchor for expectations. A competitive model with fundamental uncertainty would be subject to violent instability which could be constrained and restricted but not eliminated by the use of heuristics and social forces and regulatory institutions.

Hayes explores three aspects of *The General Theory*: the meaning of competitive equilibrium in a monetary economy, the central role and nature of expectation, and the meaning of liquidity. Hayes argues that these aspects have been unduly neglected by theorists and suggests that there needs to be far reaching change in economic theory and policy making.

Muchlinski defends Keynes against the charge that he constructed an imprecise and therefore a non-scientific economy theory. Muchlinski argues that Keynes's approach to economic theory was influenced by contemporaneous debates between Wittgenstein and Russell, Keynes and Moore, and Ramsey and Johnson. The influences of these debates are seen in three specific characteristics of Keynes's theoretical reasoning: the concept of vagueness, the idea of a state of confidence and the demand that a model's assumptions be grounded in the world of contemporary facts. Keynes's models and theories are examples of the art of economics – models and theories designed with policy makers in mind.

The General Theory **and the History of Macroeconomics**

DeVroey uses two main but conflicting conceptions – defending the free market and defending economic liberalism, to describe the emergence of and the rise to prominence of Keynesian macroeconomics and the subsequent successful attacks by Friedman and Lucas which brought about its fall. DeVroey then examines the three phases of the dynamic stochastic general equilibrium (DSGE) approach to macroeconomics – Lucas and New Classical macroeconomics and the vain attempt by the new Keynesian macroeconomics to address the issues posed by New Classical macroeconomics, Kydland and Prescott and real business cycle theory which transformed Lucas's qualitative approach to modelling into a quantitative approach and the emergence of what may be called New neoclassical synthesis or New Keynesian Phillips Curve models. DeVroey concludes his examination of the history of macroeconomics since *The General Theory* with the suggestion that the injunctions of Skidelsky and Krugman will not impact the future development of macroeconomic theory.

Dimand, building on historical studies, examines the recurrence of certain approaches, problems, and debates in macroeconomics, how they are transformed in their later guises, and how theoretical innovation occurs within a background of earlier contributions. The recurrence of problems in macroeconomics, combined with both cycles and innovation in approaches to analysing these problems, accounts for the saying that it is easier to set graduate comprehensive exams in macroeconomics than in microeconomics: in macroeconomics, the questions can be kept the same from year to year, only the answers change. Because of the pattern of recurrent concerns, themes, and analyses (such as whether the source of instability is government intervention or volatile expectations of the profitability of investment), developments in postwar macroeconomics are not only the consequence of new empirical evidence and policy experience and of advances in formal technique, but are also to be understood in light of the discipline's prior evolution. Macroeconomics has a useful past, and macroeconomists would have a better understanding of what they do if they knew more about what macroeconomists have done in the past.

Docherty reviews the evolution of macroeconomic theory from Keynes to the New Keynesian synthesis and explores the implications for modellers of interest rate rules and the assumptions of endogenous and exogenous money supply. Docherty concludes that care must be taken when comparing any of these models to the model developed by Keynes in *The General Theory*.

Luzzetti and Ohanian discuss why *The General Theory* had such a long-lasting impact on economic theory and policymaking: Keynes was in the right place at the right time. They then detail the reasons for the decline of *The General Theory* among research economists, the principal one being the problems posed by stagflation and identify the theoretical innovations in equilibrium macroeconomics that helped supplant *The General Theory* as the primary macroeconomics paradigm, in particular the impact of Kydland and Prescott's paper. They conclude that *The General Theory*'s model, as viewed through the lens of neoclassical economics (the idea of the inflation-unemployment tradeoff and the policy prescription of aggregate demand management) remains alive and well at most Central Banks.

Ramrattan and Szenberg review Keynes's writings, identify his critical train of thought and the central ideas contained therein. They propose that these ideas may be nested into Smith's vision of capitalism, a novel way of linking these two great English political economists.

The General Theory and Friedman, Kaldor, Marx and Sraffa

Backhouse and Bateman note deep-seated differences between Friedman and Keynes – Friedman believed that economics is a positive science and that the market can regulate the economy; whereas Keynes believed that economics is a moral science and that the market, by itself, cannot regulate the economy. They examine the similarities – both believed in the dangers posed by inflation, the importance of monetary policy and their informal approach to modelling. They conclude that both developed models and policies that were consistent with their individual albeit different visions of capitalism.

Camara-Neto and Vernengo analyse to what extent Keynes was successful in showing that the economic system tends to fluctuate around a position of less than full employment. They argue that a successful extension of Keynes's principle of effective demand must be based on an understanding of Sraffa's dismissal of the natural rate of interest and Kaldor's work on the super multiplier and Verdoorn's Law.

Dostaler relates the debate between Keynes and Shaw over Marx and Stalin to the 'Ricardian foundations of Marxism'. Dostaler uses this expression to show a contradiction – Marx as a non-classical economist and a precursor of the theory of effective demand, and to demonstrate that Keynes's 'monetary theory of production' is borrowed from Marx. Dostaler argues that Keynes, Marx and Freud are in the same camp relative to the questions of the nature of money, the love of money and the drive to accumulation. Dostaler then examines the impact of *The General Theory* on Marxism in Western countries and the Soviet Union and its satellites and identifies the reasons for the evolution of Keynes's perception of the Soviet Union.

The General Theory and New Interpretations

Hamouda develops his version of Keynes's model of a monetary economy as set forth in *A Treatise on Money* and *The General Theory* and describes how his version differs from the models advocated by the Post Keynesians and Marshallian/Walrasian economists. Hamouda forcefully argues that those writers did not – and still do not – take the time to master the master's original model.

Rochon examines the question – In *The General Theory*, did Keynes have a theory of endogenous money or did he merely assume the money supply as exogenous and under the control of the Bank of England? Rochon begins by reviewing the debate on endogenity succinctly summarizing the positions taken by the participants, the circuitists, the horizontalists, and the structuralists and restates his 'revolutionary' definition of endogenous money. Rochon then examines passages from *The General Theory* and two *Economic Journal* articles for textual evidence that Keynes had a theory of endogenous money and concludes that Keynes's theory of endogenous money is incomplete.

Smithin argues that the distinction between interest and profit is not always very clear. To that end he examines four theories of interest and profit (classical, neoclassical, Keynesian/Kaleckian and Marxian). He develops a synthetic theory of profit, one that avoids the problems identified in the previous theories and shows that his theory provides a reasonable explanation of the empirical evidence associated with the operation of the modern economy.

Wray provides an overview of alternative approaches to money, then focuses in more detail on two main categories: the orthodox approach to money that views money as an efficiency-enhancing innovation of markets and the Chartalist approach that sees money as a creature of the state. Wray then examines the implications of viewing money as a public monopoly and links that view back to Keynes, arguing that extending Keynes along these lines would bring his theory up to date.

NOTES

1. While Klein asserted the existence of a revolution in economics (*The Keynesian Revolution* (Klein 1966)) a huge body of literature has been generated on this issue. The interested reader may begin with Kuhn (1970) and Lakatos (1969, 1970).
2. In his remarks about the *Tract*, Schumpeter notes:

   He knew for certain that it would soothe and that return to a gold system at pre-war parity was more than *his* England could stand. If only people could be made to understand this, they would also understand that practical Keynesianism is a seedling which cannot be transplanted into foreign soil: it idles there and becomes poisonous before it dies. But in addition they would understand that, left in English soil, this seedling is a healthy thing and promises both fruit and shade. Let me say at once and for all: all this applies to every bit of advice Keynes ever offered. (Schumpeter 1969, p. 275, emphasis in original).

3. See Robinson (1933) for one of the first public articulations of this simple model.
4. Haavelmo (1944) formalized the integration of objective probability and econometrics.
5. 'The flexibility of the human to consider as-yet-unforeseen consequences during critical decision making, go with the gut when problem-solving under uncertainty and other such abstract reasoning behaviours built up over the years of experience will not be readily displaced by a computer algorithm' (Schmorrow 2010).
6. It is necessary to distinguish between two aspects of a liquidity crisis. The first aspect is associated with short-run cash flow problems that are confined to a few businesses and financial institutions. Black Monday would be an example of this aspect. The second aspect is associated with a potential collapse of a nation's financial system stemming from the failure to price a wide variety of financial instruments, the existence of questionable and unregulated financial practices and the intimate interconnection among financial institutions and their counterparties. The solution to this aspect of a liquidity crisis involves more than an injection: the actions taken by the Fed and the Treasury to prevent the systemic failure of financial institutions in the United States would be an example.
7. What follows is a brief summary of one of Keynes's many plans for the socialization of investment.
8. The specific references for the items in Keynes's risk management plan are: Memorandum to Sir Richard Hopkins and others dated 15 May 1942 'Budget Policy' pp. 277–80; Letter to James Meade dated 25 April 1943 pp. 319–20; Memorandum to Sir Wilfred Eady dated 10 June 1943 'Maintenance of Employment: The Draft Note for the Chancellor of the Exchequer' pp. 352–7; and Memorandum to Sir Richard Hopkins dated 21 June 1945 'National Debt Enquiry: The Concept of a Capital Budget' pp. 403–15. These documents may be found in Keynes, CW, vol. XXVII. See Cate (2011) for additional comments on this proposal.

BIBLIOGRAPHY

Ando, A. and F. Modigliani (1963), 'The life cycle hypothesis of saving: (I) aggregate implications and tests', *American Economic Review*, **53**(1) (March), 55–84.

Bateman, B. (1996), *Keynes' Uncertain Revolution*, Ann Arbor, MI: University of Michigan Press.

Cate, T. (2011), 'Uncertainty and the policy analyst', *The American Economist*, **56**(1) (Spring), 13–19.

Dequech, D. (1999), 'Expectations and confidence under uncertainty', *Journal of Post Keynesian Economics*, **21**(3) (Spring), 415–30.

Fama, E. (1965), 'The behavior of stock market prices', *Journal of Business*, **38**(1) (January), 34–105.

Friedman, M. (1968), 'The role of monetary policy', *American Economic Review*, **58**(1) (March), 1–17.

Godel, K. (1931), 'On formally undecidable propositions of *Principia Mathematica* and related systems', *Monatshefte für Mathematik und Physick*, **38**, 173–98.

Haavelmo, T. (1944), 'The probability approach to econometrics', *Econometrica*, **12** (supplement), July, pp. 1–118.

Heisenberg, W. (1927), 'Über den anschaulichen Inhalt der quantentheoretischen Kinematik und Mechanik', *Zeitschrift für Physik*, **43**, 172–98.

Hicks, J. (1931), 'The theory of uncertainty and profit', *Economica*, **32**(2) (May), 170–89.

Keynes, J. M. (1936), *The General Theory of Employment, Interest, and Money*, London: Macmillan.

Keynes, J. M. (1937), 'The general theory of employment', *Quarterly Journal of Economics*, **51**(2) (February), 209–23.

Keynes, J. M. (1951), 'Alfred Marshall', in *Essays in Biography*, New York: W. W. Norton, pp. 125–217.

Keynes, J. M. (1971–1989), *The Collected Writings of John Maynard Keynes*, London: Macmillan/Cambridge University Press for the Royal Economic Society.
  Vol. I: *The Economic Consequences of the Peace*
  Vol. IV: *A Tract on Monetary Reform*
  Vol. VIII: *A Treatise on Probability*
  Vol. XIII: *The General Theory and After Part I, Preparation*
  Vol. XXVII: *Activities 1940–1946 Shaping Post-war World Employment*

Klein, L. (1966), *The Keynesian Revolution*, New York: Macmillan.

Knight, F. (1921), *Risk Uncertainty and Profit*, Chicago, IL: The University of Chicago Press.

Kuhn, T. (1970), *The Structure of Scientific Revolutions*, Chicago, IL: Chicago University Press.

Lakatos, I. (1969), 'Criticism and the methodology of scientific research programmes', *Proceedings of the Aristotelian Society*, **69**, 149–86.

Lakatos, I. (1970), 'Falsification and the methodology of scientific research programmes', in Imre Lakatos and A. Musgrave (eds), *Criticism and the Growth of Knowledge*, Cambridge: Cambridge University Press, pp. 91–196.

Lorenz, E. (1972), 'Predictability: does the flap of a butterfly's wings in Brazil set off a tornado in Texas?', presentation to the American Association for the Advancement of Science Annual Meeting, Washington, DC.

Lucas, R. (1976), 'Econometric policy evaluation: a critique', in K. Brunner and A. H. Meltzer (eds), *The Phillips Curve and Labor Markets*, Amsterdam: North-Holland, pp. 19–46.

Marshall, A. (1890; 1953), *Principles*, 8th edn., 5th printing, Macmillan: New York.

Minsky, H. (1986), *Stabilizing and Unstable Economy*, New Haven, CT: Yale University Press.

Muth, J. (1961), 'Rational expectations and the theory of price movements', *Econometrica*, **29**(3) (July), 315–35.

Patterson, S. (2010), *The Quants*, New York: Crown Publishers.

Pigou, A. (1920; 1952), *Economics of Welfare*, 4th edn., 5th printing, Macmillan: London.

Robinson, J. (1933), 'The theory of money and the analysis of output', *Review of Economic Studies*, **1**(1) (October), 22–6.

Robinson, J. (1962), 'Money, trade and economic growth by H. G. Johnson', *Economic Journal*, **72**(287) (September), 690–2.

Robinson, J. (1980), 'The age of growth', in J. Robinson (ed.) *Collected Economic Papers*, vol. 5, Cambridge, MA: MIT Press, 120–9.

Samuelson, P. A. (1966), '*The General Theory* 1946', in Joseph E. Stiglitz (ed.), *The Collected Scientific Papers of Paul A. Samuelson*, vol. 2, Cambridge, MA: MIT Press, 1517–33.

Schmorrow, D. (2010), 'Handling the cornucopia', *The Economist*, 25 February, p. 18.

Schumpeter, J. (1934), *The Theory of Economic Development*, New York: Oxford University Press.

Schumpeter, J. A. (1969), 'John Maynard Keynes (1883–1946)', in *Ten Great Economists*, New York: Oxford University Press, pp. 260–91.

Simon, H. (1955), 'A behavioral model of rational choice', *Quarterly Journal of Economics*, **69**(1) (February), 35–55.

Skidelsky, R. (2009), *Keynes: The Return of the Master*, New York: Public Affairs.

Solow, R. (1956), 'Contribution to the theory of economic growth', *Quarterly Journal of Economics*, **70**(3) (June), 65–94.

Stone, R. (1947), 'Definition and measurement of the national income and related totals', in *Appendix to Measurement of National Income and Construction of Social Accounts*, Geneva: United Nations.

Tobin, J. (1969), 'General equilibrium approach to monetary theory', *Journal of Money, Banking and Credit*, **1**(1) (February), 15–29.

Wilmott, P. (2000), 'The use, misuse, and abuse of mathematics in finance', *Philosophical Transactions of the Royal Society*, **358**(1765) (January), pp. 63–73.

PART I

The General Theory and fundamental uncertainty

1. On Keynes's seminal innovation and related essential features: revisiting the notion of equilibrium in *The General Theory*

Angel Asensio

INTRODUCTION

While econometrics has been a powerful instrument of the mainstream academic domination, it is becoming a major source of its weakening, as clearly attested in the exploding literature on 'time varying' relations, 'shifting'/'switching' regimes and structural change. This involves heavy methodological consequences (Hendry 2002; Kurmann 2005; Hinich et al. 2006), especially as concerns the predictive capacity of agents. Edmund Phelps, winner of the 2006 Nobel Prize, accordingly could claim that '. . . if an economy possesses dynamism, so that fresh uncertainties incessantly flow from its innovative activities and its structure is ever-changing, the concept of rational-expectations equilibrium does not apply and a model of such an economy that imposes this concept cannot represent at all well the mechanism of such an economy's fluctuation' (Phelps 2007, p. 548).[1]

According to Kregel (1976) and Chick (1983), *The General Theory* provides a method of thinking about such an intrinsically dynamic, continuously changing, uncertain economy. The method rests on taking expectations as given, in spite of the fact that they are subject to endogenous change. Therefore, in 'the static model of a dynamic process' (in Chick's words), expectations influence the individual economic decisions and thereby, the aggregate solution, while the aggregate solution influence over expectations is provisionally ignored. Neutralizing the feedback effects of the system on expectations makes it possible to draw a temporary solution, the motion of which can be analytically assessed as a function of the state of expectations.[2]

Keynes's 'static model' is essential to the study of any dynamic aspect of the theory, for it provides the equilibrium value of the key variables *at any time* as a function of the set of given variables (expectations, but also capital stock, productivity, income distribution . . .), so that the functional relations involved in the determination of effective demand can be considered in a tractable way. Once those relations have been identified, and the related equilibrium solution is determined, it becomes possible to consider the dynamics of equilibrium by considering the effects of a change in such and such variable which had been taken as given until then. This is the way Keynes goes about things in *The General Theory*, especially in Chapter 18 in order '. . . to discover what determines at any time the national income' (Keynes 1936, p. 247).

The nominal wage is another important variable that Keynes's 'static model' takes as given in spite of the fact that it is subject to endogenous change. Until Chapter 19, the money wage is taken as constant (Chapter 13) or independent (Chapter 18) 'to facilitate the exposition of *The General Theory*' (p. 27), the case for endogenous changes in wages being properly discussed in Chapter 19. In Chapter 19 Keynes then explores the reasons why decreases in wages caused by unemployment could harm effective demand and depress the economy even more, instead of clearing the labour market. According to Chick, this '. . . feature constitutes the vital difference between Keynes's model and neoclassical models which loop back and alter real wages until both employment and profit expectations are met. The absence of such a loop is the essence of Keynes's model' (Chick 1983, p. 246). Accordingly, authors that attempted to formalize Keynes's static/short run equilibrium (Chick 1983; Palley 1996) admit that Keynes's statement that nominal wages rigidity is stabilizing, in the sense that there would be no equilibrium in the absence of such a rigidity (but a cumulative depression). Their formal statement of the model therefore takes the nominal wage as given.[3]

Now, insofar as the theory is concerned with the question of equilibrium, it must deal with the determination of both expectations and wages in terms of the equilibrium outcome of some endogenous forces. This is an aspect of his theory Keynes did not discuss extensively and to which little attention has been paid in spite of its crucial importance for the theory of equilibrium. The question actually is related to the stabilizing role of conventions and institutions. The notion of stability is however often ambiguous, since it is scarcely specified whether it is to be taken as the equilibrium outcome of some offsetting forces at a point in time (say static stability/instability) or as the dynamic outcome of such forces (dynamic stability/instability).

Authors like Minsky (1986) and Cornwall and Cornwall (2001) emphasized how institutions can durably repel or limit dynamic instability and support macroeconomic performances through the control they have on some factors that influence the succession of the short-run equilibrium positions (for example, financial regulation, 'socialization of investment' . . .).[4] But institutions cannot be considered only from a dynamic point of view, for they also play a crucial role in the determination of the equilibrium solution at any point in time, before the dynamics of equilibrium can even be considered.[5] This is implicit in those works that have pointed out that fundamental uncertainty would lead to indeterminacy or chaos in the absence of institutions and conventional behaviours (Lawson 1985; Hodgson 1989; Rotheim 1993; Crotty 1994). Institutions and conventions, according to these authors, provide the foundations failing which uncertainty would make the system inherently chaotic and untheorizable. This suggests that institutional stabilizers (including conventions) must be introduced for an equilibrium solution to be an outcome, which amounts to say that some institutional stabilizers behave endogenously in such a way that the equilibrium solution is reached.[6] It is the purpose of the present contribution to emphasize the two main channels through which, in *The General Theory*, institutions and conventions do contribute endogenously to economic stability in the 'static' sense (that is, to the determination of equilibrium): the formation of expectations and the stabilization of wages. This entails a wider role for institutions and a richer definition of Keynes's equilibrium than usually admitted.

The discussion starts by arguing that fundamental uncertainty is Keynes's seminal innovation which allowed for a general theory, non-neutral money, effective demand, equilibrium unemployment. Attention then is paid to those institutional stabilizers which, although it is sometimes only implicit in *The General Theory*, must behave endogenously if an equilibrium is to be the logical outcome of the individuals' decisions in the face of uncertainty. Some policy implications of these essential features of Keynes's theory are also discussed.

KEYNES'S SEMINAL INNOVATION

Taking fundamental uncertainty seriously is the critical innovation Keynes introduced in economics. This allowed him to get rid of three restrictive classical axioms (see Davidson (2007) for a recent appraisal): (1) ergodicity, (2) money neutrality and (3) gross substitution. Ergodicity basically denies fundamental uncertainty, since it is defined by the dynamic stability, hence predictability, of a stochastic process.[7] As for the reasons why uncertainty provides money with non-neutrality, they were discussed extensively in *The General Theory* Chapters 13, 15 and 17, the latter also discussing why 'gross substitution' could not be assumed in a true monetary economy.

Because of uncertainty, that is, in the absence of any objective anchor for expectations, decisions have to be made according to the subjective feelings about what the future will be, which implies that the collective outcome of such decisions continuously depends on the changing views about the future. Consequently, in a competitive system, Keynes's theory delivers a different equilibrium for every state of the 'views concerning the future', while the mainstream only reckons the Pareto-optimal equilibrium as a result of optimal intertemporal choices. This is why *The General Theory* is basically more general than the mainstream's theory.

Giving a Role to the State of Confidence in Economic Theory

Keynes's uncertainty does not imply that individuals cannot try to predict the value of such and such decisive variable, but the meaning and usefulness of forward looking expectations is much weaker than the one which is supposed in the mainstream approach. Keynes's rational expectations admit that people make use of all available information of course, but whatever the kind of probabilistic or non-probabilistic tools they use, true uncertainty makes it possible for expectations to be eventually systematically wrong: the past events never give enough information about what the future will be. That is the reason why Keynes thought that decisions actually '. . . also depend on the confidence with which we make this forecast, on how highly we rate the likelihood of our best forecast turning out quite wrong' (Keynes 1936, p. 148).

Interestingly, non-Keynesian theorists admit larger definitions of uncertainty more and more, with the result that adaptive learning and expectations no longer look irrational nowadays (Sargent 1999; Farmer 2002; Evans and Ramey 2006; Preston 2006; Hansen 2007). Epstein and Wang showed in a general equilibrium model of asset price determination that 'uncertainty may lead to equilibria that are indeterminate, that is, there may exist a continuum of equilibria for given fundamentals. That leaves the determination of a particular equilibrium price process to "animal spirits" and sizable volatility may result'[8] (Epstein and Wang 1994, p. 283). There are also dynamic models based on the Rational Beliefs Equilibrium theory (RBE; see Kurz 1994; Kurz and Motolese 2001; Wu and Guo 2003), a theory of nonstationary (therefore nonergodic) systems, where people's expectations change according to their (rational) changing beliefs/theory about the economic system functioning. This approach unquestionably improves the role of uncertainty by allowing for nonergodicity, but it assumes that individuals always are confident about their expectations in spite of the fact that their theory is likely to change in the future, which looks not that rational. This is an unfortunate assumption which dispossesses uncertainty of its venom, for it has been suggested at least since Knight in 1921 that the 'degree of confidence' is a key concept of decision theory in uncertain contexts.

The point is formally attested in the modern theory of decision under uncertainty, in general (see Chateauneuf et al. 2007) as well as in specific fields. In their job search model, Nishimura and Ozaki (2004) showed that, while an increase in risk ('mean preserving spread of the wage distribution the worker thinks she faces') increases the reservation wage, an increase in Knightian uncertainty ('a decrease in her confidence about the wage distribution') reduces the reservation wage. Although their analysis is not about financial decisions, the intuitive reason strongly recalls Keynes's arguments on liquidity preference and inducement to invest: when uncertainty increases, people aim at reducing it by accepting a job and cancel a future search (that is by preferring a certain amount of money today, rather than an uncertain amount tomorrow). The authors also showed in a more recent paper on investment that '. . . an increase in Knightian uncertainty makes the uncertainty-averse decision-maker more likely to postpone investment to avoid facing uncertainty', in a way similar to Keynes's views about the effects of a state of confidence decrease on the inducement to invest (Nishimura and Ozaki 2007, p. 671). In the same vein, Gomes found that 'an uncertainty averse agent saves more than a risk aversion agent and this gap increases with the degree of uncertainty aversion' (Gomes 2008, p. 274).

By refuting the mainstream's restrictive definition of uncertainty and considering the decisive role of the 'state of the confidence', Keynes revolutionized macroeconomics, providing it with new concepts such as the liquidity preference and the marginal efficiency of capital, which allowed him to emphasize the crucial role of the financial market 'convention' and the 'animal spirits'. But as *The General Theory* consequently caused so much trouble within the classical way of thinking, orthodox economists provided a (degenerated) rationale for Keynes's critical concepts, based on a restrictive definition of uncertainty. For example, when Keynes put forward the speculative motive of the demand for money, empirical evidence against the single transaction-money theory called for a theoretical response of the mainstream economics, but Tobin's (1958) response only consisted in justifying the speculative demand for money in terms of some optimal portfolio trade-off between interest and risk (not uncertainty). Another crucial example is given by the marginal efficiency of capital, whose meaning was cautiously distinguished by Keynes from the marginal productivity of capital precisely because of uncertainty. But Keynes's theory of the inducement to invest, which proved to be better than the traditional function of the interest rate, was translated in terms of 'Tobin's Q'

deviations from the equilibrium value (that is 1) within a stationary model (Brainard and Tobin 1968, p. 105). Yet, Keynes's Q clearly departed from the ergodic vision of the world, as attested in *The General Theory* Chapter 11 (section 2) and Chapter 21 (section 1).

From Uncertainty to the Theory of Effective Demand

The spectacular result of Keynes's innovations was a transmutation of the standard four macro-markets articulation of the competitive equilibrium analysis, and, as a matter of consequence, the non neutrality of money, the leading role of 'effective demand' and the failure of competitive forces to remove unemployment. In order to see how introducing uncertainty led to such a result, let us first remember that, according to the mainstream, an insufficient aggregate demand of goods, or, equivalently, an excess of full-employment saving over investment could not be a stable situation, for it would trigger a decrease in the rate of interest, thereby clearing both the market for goods and the market for saving simultaneously (Say's law). As the supply of goods therefore cannot be constrained by the demand side, firms can freely hire until the marginal product of labour is equal to the real wage.[9] Hence, in the mainstream view, unemployment simply cannot result from a deficient aggregate demand.

In the presence of strong uncertainty on the other hand, the long-term interest rate decrease caused by a depressed aggregate demand, and the real balance effect as well, may meet some obstacles.[10] First, if the money supply decreases endogenously along with the demand for money, the rate of interest does not decrease.[11] Second, it may be that the depressive forces harm the state of confidence in such a way that people increase the liquid-assets share in their portfolio, which could inhibit both the Keynes and Pigou effects even if the authorities were prepared to let the interest rate decrease by means of a weaker decrease in the money supply. Hence the equilibrium interest rate involves the money market instead of the loanable funds market. Why cannot the mainstream theory consider these obstacles? The answer is that uncertainty is never considered as anything but 'risk' in the mainstream view, with the result that, when a depression arises, the portfolio strategies remain unchanged insofar as the depression is supposed to be a 'white noise', a temporary phenomenon that will be removed spontaneously provided the monetary authorities do not hinder the adequate interest rate decrease. And in the same spirit, a depression does not change the long run expected return on capital.

Uncertainty finally impacts dramatically the macro-markets interaction: the forces that influence the rate of interest do not ensure that the saving amount that would prevail at full employment would be automatically absorbed by the firms' investments; this in turn impacts the goods market by preventing the operation of Say's Law, and the labour market, since firms cannot but decide their production and employment levels in accordance with the expected aggregate demand. As for the equality between aggregate investment and saving, it is the output adjustment to effective demand which simultaneously ensures the adjustment of saving to aggregate investment, given the equilibrium rate of interest.

INSTITUTIONAL STABILIZERS AND EQUILIBRIUM THEORY

As far as it is the level of expected demand which drives the economy, there is an additional question the theory has to deal with, for the effective demand depends both on the individual's views about the future (that have no objective anchor) and on the level of wages (that market forces alone would not tend to anchor either). Should it therefore be considered that there is an inherent indeterminacy in *The General Theory*? Of course not, because Keynes put forward strong arguments that allowed him to develop the theory of a system which, 'whilst it is subject to severe fluctuations in respect of output and employment, [it] is not violently unstable' (Keynes 1936, p. 249). These arguments are based on the meaningful idea that institutions and conventional behaviour provide powerful devices aimed at anchoring the system in spite of potential indeterminacy. As stated in Crotty (1994) a stable set of conventions and institutions allows for stability in Keynes's theory.

The General Theory deals with 'conditions of stability' much more extensively from the dynamic point of view (Keynes 1936, pp. 250–4) than from the 'static' point of view, but it nevertheless deals with static stability or instability/indeterminacy when it refers to both the role of conventions and 'animal spirits' as a way to anchor expectations and make decisions (Chapters 12 and 15),[12] and the role of trade unions and wage rigidity as an hedge against potential cumulative depression, which is another kind of indeterminacy (Chapters 19 and 21).[13] Rotheim (1993, p. 215) accordingly noticed that '. . . given the conventional behaviors that followed from the social interactions of individuals, Keynes sought not indeterminacy . . .' while Hodgson (1989, p. 116) pointed out that in Keynes's theory '. . . markets function coherently *because* of institutional rigidities and "imperfections", and not *despite* them as neoclassical theorists presume'.

Now, insofar as market forces would produce 'violent instability' in the absence of institutional stabilizers but do not show indeterminacy most of the time, one is led to the conclusion that the system itself generates endogenously the institutions/conventions stabilizing response, for otherwise there would be no equilibrium solution. This point maybe has not been emphasized enough yet, although it appears to be a necessary condition in Keynes's equilibrium theory. Two topics in *The General Theory* deal with that important question, more or less explicitly.

Endogenous Equilibrium Wage

In Chapter 19 Keynes discusses why flexible wages do not remove unemployment necessarily and might even increase it through negative effects on the effective demand. As a matter of consequence, there could not be, strictly speaking, any flex-price competitive equilibrium with Keynesian unemployment, for, with flex-prices, either competitive wages would effectively adjust to full employment, or unemployment would increase continuously, thereby putting a continuous pressure on wages. The alternatives, accordingly, are either full employment or cumulative depression. As Keynes stated:

> If . . . money-wages were to fall without limit whenever there was a tendency for less than full employment, . . . there would be no resting-place below full employment until either the rate of interest was incapable of falling further or wages were zero. In fact we must have *some* factor, the value of which in terms of money is, if not fixed, at least sticky, to give us any stability of values in a monetary system. (Keynes 1936, pp. 303–4)

Of course, the fact that rigidities are required for an equilibrium with unemployment being a possible solution is not to say that rigidities cause unemployment, by contrast with the Benassy–Malinvaud (Benassy1984; Malinvaud 1980a and b) range of models, where it was argued that flexible prices would eventually lead the economy toward the Walras outcome.[14] Money-wage rigidity in Keynes's theory expresses a form of endogenous resistance to further wages decreases when it becomes clear that wage flexibility do not reduce unemployment. It is the necessary stabilizing response of institutions like trade unions, regulation, wage bargaining to the cumulative depressive forces, a response failing which no equilibrium would even exist. In Keynes's theory, wages rigidity involves a richer definition of equilibrium, where institutional stabilizers endogenously take part of the markets adjustment to equilibrium at any time.

Such endogenous stabilizers may anchor the system in a more or less unfavourable position, according to the level where the various factors that influence the 'resistance' of wages does effectively anchor wages. The equilibrium position also depends on whether or not some policy tool supports the effective demand, thereby reducing unemployment and alleviating the downward pressure on wages. This is what authorities use to demonstrate in the periods of violent turmoil, when is not assured that the prevailing institutional routines alone could enforce stability.

These considerations offer a way to explain heterogeneity in macroeconomic performances which might usefully complete the existing literature, where performances are rather related to some deliberate institutional and policy arrangements aimed at improving efficiency, but where little attention is paid to the defensive actions aimed at countering cumulative depressive forces. Fighting against indeterminacy and destabilizing forces is not necessarily the same as promoting efficiency. Wage resistance and/or public support in case of a depressing private demand are not the same as public demand stimuli aimed at increasing the effective demand. This type of institutional stabilizer, we have been referring to in terms of 'static stability', differs from the one that, endogenously or exogenously, is involved in the dynamic performances of an economy.

The Equilibrium Interest Rate as a 'Highly Conventional Phenomenon'

Chapter 15 of *The General Theory* also deals with such endogenous stabilizing forces when it puts forward the conventional nature of the rate of interest, thereby allowing for an equilibrium solution to emerge in spite of fundamental uncertainty and potential indeterminacy. Actually, there are two approaches to the equilibrium interest rate in the book, which are reconciliated when Keynes argues that the convention finally commands the market equilibrium rate. In terms of the Post Keynesian endogenous money approach, the long-term rate of interest is determined by the banking sector and money demand interaction,[15] but no discussion is made as to whether this rate meets the 'conventional expectation of the future' (Keynes 1936, p. 204). Yet Keynes's theory suggests that if the current market rate is higher/lower than the convention and the rate of interest therefore is expected to decrease/increase, the demand for money alters so that the current rate eventually meets the convention. The long-term rate of interest therefore

> is a highly conventional [. . .] phenomenon. For its actual value is largely governed by the prevailing view as to what its value is expected to be. *Any* level of interest which is accepted with sufficient conviction as *likely* to be durable *will* be durable; subject, of course, in a changing society to fluctuations for all kinds of reasons round the expected normal (Keynes 1936, p. 203, emphasis in original).

This questions the ability of monetary authorities to really control the long-term interest rate, especially in the case of interest rate reductions.[16]

In order to make this clear within the Post Keynesian approach to endogenous money, let us suppose that the monetary base is increased as a result of a cheap refinancing policy, and that, as a matter of consequence, banks reduce the long-term rates so that the demand for credit is stimulated. If, at the same time, the liquidity preference increases because of a loss of confidence or because a future increase of interest rates is expected, then banks may be able to sell more credit without reducing their interest rates substantially, for bonds and other non-bank loan rates tend to rise in this case, in order to compensate for the increasing liquidity preference. Even if '. . . the monetary authority were prepared to deal both ways on specified terms in debts of all maturities, and even more so if it were prepared to deal in debts of varying degree of risk . . .', there would be '. . . limitations on the ability of the monetary authority to establish any given complex of rates of interest for debts of different terms and risk' (Keynes 1936, pp. 205, 207). Some of these limitations (ibid., pp. 207–8 for a detailed discussion) can be considered purely theoretical, insofar as they would only arise in extreme circumstances (virtually absolute liquidity preference when rates are considered too low; breakdown of stability in the rate of interest – owing to a flight from the currency or other financial crisis); but others apply in normal circumstances (the intermediate cost of bringing the borrower and the lender together, the 'allowance for risk' required by the lender, including liquidity risk).

Policy Implications

In the absence of any objectively predictable equilibrium rate of interest, the convention may anchor the system in a more or less unfavourable position, depending on the market's views about the future. Authorities may or may not influence the equilibrium rate, depending on whether they are able to change the 'views as to what its value is expected to be'. Keynes deals with that problem quite explicitly in Chapter 15, in a way that could still be helpful with regard to the Post Keynesian debate on interest rate rules (Asensio 2009). The challenge for monetary policy does not amount merely to set the short-term rate at some desired level; it is necessary, in addition, to have some influence on the convention so that the long-term interest rate changes as well. The task is difficult because the state of confidence is volatile and makes the liquidity preference and inducement to invest shifting variables, with the result that both the control over the long-term interest rate and the final effect on effective demand are erratic. The problem is all the more difficult as the short-term rate variations may themselves influence the state of confidence, thereby making uncertainty endogenous to the monetary policy itself and producing shifts in the demand for money. As Keynes put forward,

> a monetary policy which strikes public opinion as being experimental in character or easily liable to change may fail in its objective of greatly reducing the long-term rate of interest, because M_2 may tend to increase almost without limit in response to a reduction of r below a certain figure. (Keynes 1936, p. 203)

According to Bateman successful policies therefore have to 'take into account the unpredictable reactions of businessmen to those policies' (Bateman 2003, p. 82). This is a matter of confidence which requires from authorities to be able to move long-term expectations and the related conventional interest rate into line with a feasible employment target. The concept of policy credibility is irrelevant here. In the face of uncertainty, it makes little sense to wonder whether or not the authorities will honour their commitment. The right question is whether the authorities are pursuing feasible objectives that have been pragmatically defined in accordance with circumstances, and whether these objectives have been widely understood and accepted. In this case, it may be possible for a prudent monetary policy to take advantage of the conventional nature of the interest rate:

> if it appeals to public opinion as being reasonable and practicable and in the public interest, rooted in strong conviction, and promoted by an authority unlikely to be superseded. [. . .] Public opinion can be fairly rapidly accustomed to a modest fall in the rate of interest and the conventional expectation of the future may be modified accordingly; thus preparing the way for a further movement – up to a point. The fall in the long-term rate of interest in Great Britain after her departure from the gold standard provides an interesting example of this; – the major movements were effected by a series of discontinuous jumps, as the liquidity function of the public, having become accustomed to each successive reduction, became ready to respond to some new incentive in the news or in the policy of the authorities. (Keynes 1936, pp. 203–4)

Notice that if the central bank acts to decrease the long-term interest rate gradually, the expected reductions may have a negative impact on the marginal efficiency of capital (Keynes 1936, p. 143)[17] and if, on the other hand, the central bank attempts a sharp adjustment in the long-term interest rate, the liquidity preference may rise and the marginal efficiency of capital may decrease.[18] Hence, there are conditions for the success of a monetary policy (see Asensio (2009) for further discussion). The key element is that, at any time, the policy which is being implemented meets the market convention, so that the pernicious effects on the liquidity preference and on the marginal efficiency of capital are avoided.

CONCLUSION

While everyone can agree that things do not go unbridled in our uncertain world, one can hardly rely on any mystic force which would deliver socially optimal outcomes spontaneously. According to *The General Theory*, competitive systems *alone* would be subject to 'violent instability', owing to the deleterious effects of fundamental uncertainty, but the continuous adaptation of conventions, institutions and all kinds of social forces drives the effective demand so that the system at the end of the day exhibits some stability.

The Post Keynesian literature puts forward that institutions do provide the economy with a set of structural stabilizers, such as laws and regulations, monetary contracts, lender of last resort . . ., some of which are subject to endogenous changes in the long run. As they influence the economic processes, these structures also influence the economic performances. The present contribution extends the discussion by showing that, in *The General Theory*, the role of institutions and conventional behaviours is first of all to repel endogenously the potential indeterminacy and to anchor the economy on an equilibrium solution at any point in time. This anchoring works mainly through the attraction of the market interest rate towards the conventional expected rate, through the resistance of wages to further decreases in case of unemployment and through the public support to the aggregate demand that use to accompany the private demand depression (even in countries where macroeconomic policy is usually supply-side oriented).

The General Theory accordingly involves both a wider role for institutions and a richer concept of equilibrium: in a competitive system, the wage and interest rates do not adjust so that markets clear; they adjust in such a way that the induced response of institutions and conventional expectations to the potentially destabilizing competitive forces does stabilize the system at any given time. Their equilibrium value therefore is influenced by the endogenous response of institutions and conventional views. Nevertheless, nothing ensures that such defensive reactions ought to push the system to the level of full employment. Endogenous stabilizers alone do not necessarily solve the economic policy problem, although they certainly interact with it.

NOTES

1.   Experimental economics also attests that, 'when the environment changes continually, including the behavior of other investors, the learning process may never reach a stationary point' (Sunder 2007).

2. As Kregel (1976) pointed out, Keynes refers to three (distinct but related) notions of equilibrium in his *General Theory*, depending on whether the short run expectations, the long run ones, or both remain stable (which supposes they are fulfilled). The three notions are of analytical interest to study some specific aspect of the whole theory: if long run expectations are stable, it is possible to consider the dynamic effects of changing short run expectations (as in *The General Theory* chapter 5); if long run and short run expectations are stable, we have Keynes's static model, and if short run expectations are stable while long run expectations are allowed to vary, we have Keynes's 'shifting equilibrium'. It is of course the latter which is the primary object of the theory.

3. Palley (1996) Chapter 4 discusses several possible wage-adjustment processes. In those special cases there is an endogenous equilibrium wage of course, but in Chapter 13, where the full macro model is stated with the higher degree of generality, the nominal wage is taken as given.

4. Minsky for example argued forcefully that massive liquidity pumping and public deficit are the necessary/endogenous responses to the intrinsic bias of capitalism towards 'financial fragility'. See Delli Gatti et al. (1994) for an attempt at modelling the dynamics that may emerge from this approach.

5. Though dynamic models deal with changes in variables, they start necessarily from a point in time, with initial values: X_0, Y_0, Z_0 ... the consistency of which requires a theory of equilibrium values at date (0). The dynamics actually considers the effects on equilibrium of the changing technology, income distribution, expectations, institutions ... This is the reason why the 'static' model is of paramount importance.

6. This is distinct from the dynamic approaches mentioned above, where the institution's endogenous responses refer to something quite different.

7. See Vercelli (1991), pp. 40, 154 and Davidson (2002), pp. 39–69.

8. These results were obtained with Knight's definition of uncertainty, which remains narrower than the one adopted by Keynes and, therefore, does not fully capture Keynes's view. See Davidson (1996).

9. In the (pseudo) monetary version of the theory, the fourth market, namely the money market, also contributes to the support of aggregate demand through the real balance effect and the (not Keynesian) 'Keynes effect'.

10. Notice that even if the rate decreases, the worsening business climate can deter investments (if the marginal efficiency of capital schedule goes down) in such a way that unemployment does not decrease (and may even increase, as Keynes put forward in *The General Theory*, Chapter 19, p. 263).

11. It is of interest to notice that monetary authorities are necessarily involved in the adjustment process, for the central bank decides whether or not it makes it easier for banks to accommodate the money demand in order to activate more or less the interest rate adjustment.

12. 'We are merely reminding ourselves that human decisions affecting the future, whether personal or political or economic, cannot depend on strict mathematical expectation, since the basis for making such calculations does not exist; and that it is our innate urge to activity which makes the wheels go round, our rational selves choosing between the alternatives as best we are able, calculating where we can, but often falling back for our motive on whim or sentiment or chance' (Keynes 1936, pp. 162–3).

13. '[It] would be much better that wages should be rigidly fixed and deemed incapable of material changes, than that depressions should be accompanied by a gradual downward tendency of money-wages, a further moderate wage reduction being expected to signalise each increase of; say, 1 per cent in the amount of unemployment' (Keynes 1936, p. 265).

14. In Malinvaud (1980a) nevertheless prices flexibility could produce a cumulative depression in case of unemployment, but that result was obtained within a two-market economy (labour and goods) where the cumulative process resulted from the assumption that the decrease in prices produced by the supply excess of goods is stronger than the decrease in wages (hence the real wage does increase, so that firms reduce the

production level). That is, the stabilizing (not that Keynesian) 'Keynes effect', that would have been triggered if the money market had been considered in a complete model of the economy, was simply ignored.

15. Fontana and Setterfield's (2009) 'teachable model' assumes pure horizontalism (total accommodation) for the sake of simplicity. In Palley's (1996) model on the other hand, the supply curve may be positively sloped in both the 'accommodationist' and the 'structuralist' case, but the rationales of course differ (see Palley 1996, p. 111). For accommodationists, a positively sloped money supply curve requires partial accommodation by the central bank. Palley suggests a wider 'endogenous finance' approach which aims at considering the demand and supply of 'liquid finance' (Palley 1996, p. 152).

16. Indeed, a 'dear money' policy can always get an increase in the long-term interest rates.

17. The argument is also developed in relation to expected money-wage decreases in Keynes (1936, p. 263), where monetary policy also is considered.

18. 'Just as a moderate increase in the quantity of money may exert an inadequate influence over the long-term rate of interest, whilst an immoderate increase may offset its other advantages by its disturbing effect on confidence' (Keynes 1936, pp. 266–7).

BIBLIOGRAPHY

Asensio, A. (2009), 'Between the cup and the lip – on Post Keynesian interest rate rules and long-term interest rates management', paper presentation, the IEPI-Laurentian University conference The Political Economy of Central Banking, Toronto, ON, May.

Bateman, B. W. (2003), 'The end of Keynes and philosophy?', in Jochen Runde and Sohei Mizuhara (eds), *The Philosophy of Keynes's Economics: Probability, Uncertainty, and Convention*, London and New York: Routledge, pp. 71–84.

Benassy, J. P. (1984), *Macroéconomie et théorie du déséquilibre*, Paris: Dunod.

Brainard, W. C. and J. Tobin (1968), 'Pitfalls in financial model building', *American Economic Review*, **58**(2) (May), 99–122.

Chateauneuf, A., J. Eichberger, and S. Grant (2007), 'Choice under uncertainty with the best and worst in mind: neo-additive capacities', *Journal of Economic Theory*, **137**(1) (November), 538–67.

Chick, V. (1983), *Macroeconomics after Keynes*, Cambridge, MA: MIT Press.

Cornwall, J. and W. Cornwall (2001), *Capitalist Development in the Twentieth Century: An Evolutionary Keynesian Analysis*, Cambridge; Cambridge University Press.

Crotty, J. (1994), 'Are Keynesian uncertainty and macrotheory compatible? Conventional decision making, institutional structures, and conditional stability in Keynesian macromodels', in R. Pollin and G. Dymski (eds), *New Perspectives in Monetary Macroeconomics*, Ann Arbor, MI: University of Michigan Press, pp. 105–39.

Davidson, P. (1996), 'Reality and economic theory', *Journal of Post Keynesian Economics*, **18**(4) (Summer), 479–508.

Davidson, P. (2002), *Financial Markets, Money and the Real World*, Cheltenham, UK and Northampton, MA, USA: Edward Elgar.

Davidson, P. (2007), 'Keynes and money', in P. Arestis and M. Sawyer (eds), *A Handbook of Alternative Monetary Economics*, Cheltenham, UK and Northampton, MA, USA: Edward Elgar, pp. 139–53.

Delli Gatti, D., M. Gallegati, and H. Minsky (1994), 'Financial instability, economic policy and the dynamic behavior of the economy', Levy Economics Institute of Bard College working paper no. 126, Annandale-on-Hudson, NY.

Epstein, L. G. and T. Wang (1994), 'Intertemporal asset pricing under Knightian uncertainty', *Econometrica*, **62**(3) (March), 283–322.

Evans, W. G. and G. Ramey (2006), 'Adaptive expectations, underparameterization and the Lucas critique', *Journal of Monetary Economics*, **53**(2) (March), 249–64.

Farmer, R. E. A. (2002), 'Why does data reject the Lucas critique?', *The Annals of Economics and Statistics*, 67–68 (June), 111–29.

Fontana, G. and M. Setterfield (2009), 'A simple (and teachable) macroeconomic model with endogenous money', in G. Fontana and M. Setterfield (eds), *Macroeconomic Theory and Macroeconomic Pedagogy*, New York: Palgrave/Macmillan, pp. 144–68.

Gomes, F. A. R. (2008), 'The effect of future income uncertainty in savings decision', *Economic Letters*, **98**(3) (March), 269–74.

Hansen, L. P. (2007), 'Beliefs, doubts and learning: valuing macroeconomic risk', *American Economic Review*, **97**(2) (May), 1–30.

Hendry, D. F. (2002), 'Forecast failure, expectations formation and the Lucas critique', *The Annals of Economics and Statistics*, **67–68** (June), 21–40.

Hinich, M. J., J. Foster, and P. Wild (2006), 'Structural change in macroeconomic time series: a complex systems perspective', *Journal of Macroeconomics*, **28**(1) (March), 136–50.

Hodgson, G. (1989), 'Post-Keynesianism and institutionalism: the missing link', in J. Pheby (ed.), *New Directions in Post Keynesian Economics*, Aldershot, UK and Brookfield, VT, USA: Edward Elgar, pp. 94–123.

Keynes, J. M. (1936), *The General Theory of Employment, Interest, and Money*, London, Macmillan.

Knight, F. H. (1921), *Risk, Uncertainty and Profit*, New York: Harper.

Kregel, J. A. (1976), 'Economic methodology in the face of uncertainty: the modelling methods of Keynes and the Post-Keynesians', *Economic Journal*, **86**(342) (June), pp. 209–25.

Kurmann, A. (2005), 'Quantifying the uncertainty about the fit of a new Keynesian pricing model', *Journal of Monetary Economics*, **52**(6) (September), pp. 1119–34.

Kurz, M. (1994), 'On the structure and diversity of rational beliefs', *Economic Theory*, **4**(6) (November), 877–900.

Kurz, M. and M. Motolese (2001), 'Endogenous uncertainty and market volatility', *Economic Theory*, **17**(3) (May), 497–544.

Lawson, T. (1985), 'Uncertainty and economic analysis', *Economic Journal*, **95**(380) (December), pp. 909–27.

Malinvaud, E. (1980a), *The Theory of Unemployment Reconsidered*, Paris: Calman Levy.

Malinvaud, E. (1980b), *Profitability and Unemployment*, Cambridge: Cambridge University Press and Editions de la Maison des Sciences de l'Homme.

Minsky, H. P. (1986), *Stabilizing an Unstable Economy*, New Haven, CT: Yale University Press.

Nishimura, K. G. and H. Ozaki (2004), 'Search and Knightian uncertainty', *Journal of Economic Theory*, **119**(2) (December), 299–333.

Nishimura, K. G. and H. Ozaki (2007), 'Irreversible investment and Knightian uncertainty', *Journal of Economic Theory*, **136**(1) (September), 668–94.

Palley, T. (1996), *Post Keynesian Economics: Debt, Distribution, and the Macro Economy*, New York: Palgrave Macmillan.

Phelps, E. S. (2007), 'Macroeconomics for a modern economy', *American Economic Review*, **97**(3) (September), 543–61.

Preston, B. (2006), 'Adaptive learning, forecast-based instrument rules and monetary policy', *Journal of Monetary Economics*, **53**(3) (April), 507–35.

Rotheim, R. (1993), 'On the indeterminacy of Keynes's monetary theory of value', *Review of Political Economy*, **5**(2) (April), 197–216.

Sargent, T. J. (1999), *The Conquest of American Inflation*, Princeton, NJ: Princeton University Press.

Sunder, S. (2007), 'What have we learned from experimental finance?', in Sobei Oda (ed.), *Developments on Experimental Economics: New Approaches to Solving Real-world Problems*, pp. 91–100, published as lecture notes in economics and mathematical systems, 590, Berlin: Springer.

Tobin, J. (1958), 'Liquidity preference as behavior towards risk', *Review of Economic Studies,* **25**(2) (February), 65–86.

Vercelli, A. (1991), *Methodological Foundations of Macroeconomics: Keynes and Lucas*, Cambridge: Cambridge University Press.

Wu, H. M. and W. C. Guo (2003), 'Speculative trading with rational beliefs and endogenous uncertainty', *Economic Theory*, **21**(2–3) (March), 263–92.

2. Keynes, the Neglected Theorist

M.G. Hayes

Notwithstanding Keynes's reputation, very little of his magnum opus, *The General Theory*, has been received into modern economics. The investment-saving identity is perhaps the only original concept which has been fully accepted into the canon and, while his name is most closely associated with aggregate demand and the multiplier, neither of these really originated with Keynes (Laidler 1999). Furthermore, 'Keynesian' economics was rightly criticized for its lack of explanation of its assumption of sticky prices, including wages.

In this chapter, I will argue that Keynes's theoretical contribution, neglected by followers and opponents alike, was to restate the Marshallian theory of value (based on competitive, *flexible* prices) in a form which took full account of the nature of time and incorporated the theory of money. Keynes showed that perfect competition could not deliver full employment and that sticky wages were the consequence, not the cause of this failure. In doing so, he introduced some highly original concepts, which still have not been fully appreciated and should be, if macroeconomics is ever to progress beyond the Classical orthodoxy to which it has currently reverted. This theoretical neglect has also limited the impact of Keynes on policy, notably in the areas of labour markets, the international monetary system and financial regulation.

Underlying Keynes's approach is an awareness that money plays no essential role in the Classical theory of value and that a proper treatment of a monetary economy (meaning any industrialized economy) requires a theory in which the nature of time and money are taken seriously. There are three key areas in which *The General Theory* offered new insights which require far-reaching change in economic theory and policy: the meaning of competitive equilibrium in a monetary economy, the central role and nature of expectation and the consequent meaning of liquidity. All of these insights have been unduly neglected, even by Post Keynesian theorists, and are now addressed in turn.

COMPETITIVE EQUILIBRIUM IN A MONETARY ECONOMY

Income in a productive market economy, characterized by a division of labour, is intrinsically monetary. Both output and capital are heterogeneous and it is an error to treat vectors of 'incommensurable collections of miscellaneous objects' as scalar variables: an index will not serve for causal analysis. Yet this is precisely the approach, not only of Classical, but also of most Post Keynesian macroeconomists. Despite Keynes devoting 38 pages (nearly 10 per cent of *The General Theory*) to the problem of defining income and its relation to saving and investment (pp. 37–40, 52–85), Hansen states: 'The section on Income is of no great importance for an understanding of the *General Theory* and may quite well be omitted if the student so wishes' (Hansen 1953, p. 54). Then he, and nearly everyone else since, proceeds to write Y for real income, without realizing that they are thereby committed to a 'corn model' in which, under perfect competition, involuntary unemployment is impossible. This is entirely different, of course, from deflating money-income by the wage-unit as numeraire to give a measure of real income 'in some sense' (Keynes, *Collected Writings* (CW), vol. VII, p. 91).

If output were truly homogeneous, the central argument of *The General Theory* would fail. Keynes's principal policy aim was to discredit the prescription of wage-cuts as a remedy for unemployment and his argument hinges on the distinction between money and real wages. If employers and workers bargain in real terms, for example over quantities of corn, there can be no denying that if workers are prepared to accept their marginal production of corn as their wage, they can all be profitably employed. The corn might pile up in the employers' granaries rather than being eaten by landlords, but since there can be no difference between saving and investment, there can be no failure of Say's Law.[1] Keynes's point is that employers and workers bargain in money terms and that, even under perfect competition, the real wage is not determined in the labour market. When output is heterogeneous, the real wage is not a causal variable, it is simply the resultant of the money-wage and an arbitrary index of product prices.

Under what conditions might the assumption of homogeneous output be a harmless abstraction in a monetary economy? All firms would have to be producer co-operatives, in which labour was paid according to the sales value of its output. In a co-operative or self-employed economy, given competitive product markets, the exertion of labour to produce saleable output will generate revenue. If the product price is low, the revenue may not be worth the effort and leisure may be preferred. The difference between an economy of self-employed households in perfect competition and Robinson Crusoe lies only in the division of labour.

By contrast, what we observe in practice is the existence of a wage-dependent labour force. Employment in this context means wage labour, the hire of labour for a sum of money, and not merely occupation or self-employment. A theory of employment is then a theory of the decisions of employers to hire labour and of employees to offer their services. In a theory of self-employment, there is no hiring decision. The payment of a money-wage under an employment contract brings money directly into the production process so that it becomes more than a medium of exchange for finished output.

The General Theory does not consider the weighty question of why a wage-dependent labour force exists. For Keynes, the distinction between entrepreneurs (employers) and workers (employees) is essential, as in Marx, Marshall and Pigou, but not in Walrasian general equilibrium models. Entrepreneurs alone, and not workers, sell to product markets and decide what, and how, to produce. It is tempting to argue that the division between employers and workers is a consequence of uncertainty but Keynes does not claim this directly: aware, no doubt, that there are many other human, technical, social and political factors that consign most of us to the status of employees.

In a 'monetary production economy' labour cannot insist on being employed, even if its marginal revenue product and real wage exceed the marginal disutility of that amount of employment (Keynes, CW, vol. VII, p. 291). Entrepreneurial firms exist, not to hire labour, but to make profit. By definition, wage-labour does not make the hiring decision, and the primary purpose of *The General Theory* is to explain how firms can find it unprofitable under competitive conditions to employ more labour, even though unemployed labour is for hire at the going rate. At the root of this problem is that both workers and employers are necessarily concerned with income, in the form of money wages and profits respectively. Neither workers nor shareholders can be paid in kind.

This discussion of the nature of income has been necessary in order to address Keynes's use of equilibrium analysis. In summary, Keynes's definition of competitive equilibrium in terms of the choices of entrepreneurs, investors and consumers, which he calls the principle of effective demand, is radically different from the Classical concept of the preferred allocation of factor services. The owners of factors *per se* do not make hiring decisions. The principle of effective demand is therefore a concept of the equilibrium of industry as a whole which supersedes the Classical full-employment equilibrium. Since the term 'general equilibrium' has become inextricably linked to the Classical concept, it may be better to use the term 'system equilibrium' as the still more general case, encompassing both Walrasian general equilibrium and Keynes's equilibrium of industry as a whole, with or without full employment.

Keynes's concept of system equilibrium is superior to the Walrasian, partly because it reclaims the use of equilibrium analysis for the explanation of the level of employment at any time, whether or not there exists involuntary unemployment. The Walrasian concept is applicable only to full employment, and either involuntary unemployment must be denied (as in New Classical theory) or if unemployment is admitted (as in New Keynesian theory), it is a matter of disequilibrium or departure from full-employment equilibrium. The very concept of disequilibrium implies corrective forces working to restore equilibrium, if they are not impeded. Keynes, by contrast, offers a theory of employment as in equilibrium at any time, even if the position of equilibrium may change from day to day.

Keynes's formal device for expressing this is the employment function $N = F(D_w)$, which relates the level of employment to the level of effective demand (expected money-income, expressed in wage-units). Any given level of aggregate employment may be associated with an indefinitely large number of distributions of employment across industries. This idea is captured by the concept of a production possibility surface, defined for any given set of factors of production including labour. For Keynes, there are many production frontiers nested inside one another, like electron shells, each representing all the possible distributions of employment that correspond to any given level of aggregate employment offered by entrepreneurs, while by contrast the Walrasian model considers only the full employment frontier. In Walrasian terms, the employment function introduces the preferences of households contingent upon any given level of income, thus picking out the point on the particular production possibility shell for any given level of employment that entrepreneurs expect to be preferred by consumers and investors: the point of effective demand.

It is worth noting, as an important aside, that Keynes's neglected employment function is the answer to Sraffa's critique (1926) of the Marshallian theory of value and is the key to a Marshallian macroeconomics. Just as the Walrasian general equilibrium approach does not consider the distribution of output between individual firms but considers the production possibilities of the economy as a whole, so Keynes works 'top down' from the aggregate supply and demand functions of industry as a whole. Having established the point of aggregate effective demand, the distribution of effective demand between industries and firms is then endogenous, based on the physical conditions of supply, consumer and worker preferences and (of course) aggregate income. An important implication (which has not generally been understood by the Post Keynesian school) is that Keynes's construction depends on – not merely accommodates – perfect competition: imperfect competition cannot be introduced at the aggregate level without indeterminacy (Keynes, CW, vol. VII, p. 281). The degree of monopoly cannot be derived from the demand curve. The theory of monopolistic competition is necessarily an exercise in partial equilibrium analysis.[2]

Thus both Keynes and the Walrasian school offer expressions of competitive system equilibrium in which preferences, technology and endowment combine to determine a set of prices and quantities. The difference is that in the Walrasian system the resource constraint is the endowment alone, while in Keynes's, the endowment may not be fully employed: his system is over-determined, by an additional constraint in the form of the level of effective demand (Ambrosi 2003). An important corollary is that in Keynes's system, factor prices are not market-clearing prices, as are the prices of new goods. The money-wage and the money-rents of land and other existing capital-goods: none of these are equilibrium prices in that sense. The Classical reader may be reluctant to accept Keynes's definition of an equilibrium excluding factor markets, yet it is the inevitable consequence of involuntary unemployment: in the Classical system, factors in excess supply are free goods and their prices should drop to zero. Only if we are prepared to let go of the Classical concept of equilibrium, can we release equilibrium analysis to explain a monetary economy.

It is interesting (revealing?) that the early Hicks refused to accept aggregate income as a causal variable, arguing that income is an unnecessary concept and that economic theory can do quite well without it (Hicks, 1939, p. 180). It is true that modern general equilibrium theory (unlike macroeconomic theory) has, at one level, accepted Keynes's critique of the concept of homogeneous real income and manages to construct an equilibrium of heterogeneous prices and quantities without once referring to aggregate income. Yet our argument has shown that it can do so only by ignoring the possibility that effective demand may constrain the employment of the endowment; the use of effective demand requires the proper definition and recognition of money-income as a causal variable in a monetary economy.[3]

THE STATE OF EXPECTATION

The General Theory extends Classical competitive equilibrium analysis so as to incorporate money into the theory of value. This extension of Marshallian analysis falls into two main areas, the definition of system equilibrium appropriate to a monetary economy, and the understanding and treatment of time. Keynes takes time seriously, as a one-way, irreversible sequence of historical events, and recognizes that decisions are always made in the present, based on the unchangeable past and the unknown future. It is time which gives money its 'essential and peculiar' character, and makes a monetary economy

> ... one in which changing views about the future are capable of influencing the quantity of employment and not merely its direction. But our method of analysing the economic behaviour of the present under the influence of changing ideas about the future is one which depends on the interaction of demand and supply, and is in this way linked up with our fundamental theory of value. We are thus led to a more *general theory*, which includes the Classical theory with which we are familiar, as a special case. (Keynes, CW, vol. VII, p. xxii)

The understanding of time as irreversible has profound implications for equilibrium analysis. If today's decision to produce, consume or invest is to be described as an equilibrium outcome, the competitive forces bringing about this equilibrium must also act today, in the present. Past decisions and future outcomes are strictly irrelevant.

For Marshall, the present corresponds to the market period, during which a given stock of finished goods and endowment of factor services are traded, and the supply and demand for the product of each industry are held in equilibrium by competition. However, most production takes time. The decision to employ labour or invest in a capital-good today depends on the market prices that are expected to rule in the future (the 'expectations'), when the final output resulting from these decisions is finished and ready for sale.

One formal Walrasian response to time is to postulate the existence of complete markets, so that the price of future finished output at any date and in any state of the world can be determined today by the balance of supply and demand. Under these strong conditions the future is reduced to the present, time disappears, and equilibrium remains a meaningful, but ideal, concept. No one disputes that not all futures and insurance markets exist, so the real question is whether competitive equilibrium theory can explain any important aspect of the world as we find it.

In the absence of a forward contract, decisions must be made on the strength of an expectation, something which already plays an important part in Marshall's system. Marshall's market prices are qualitatively different from his Normal prices, the expectation of which in the short period, induces firms to produce goods in a particular quantity, and in the long period induces investors to order new capital equipment. Marshall does not suggest that Normal prices as such are directly observable, but he does assume that competition tends to bring market prices into line with Normal prices in both the short and long periods, and conflates this process of convergence through time with the determination of Normal prices as equilibrium prices. Keynes accepts for theoretical purposes that market prices tend to converge towards Normal prices; but he changes the definition of the equilibrium periods in terms of calendar time, as well as the concept of a stationary or steady state that is necessary for this process of convergence also to generate Normal values as equilibrium prices. While Marshall's stationary or steady state refers to a physical allocation of resources, Keynes will allow only a given *state of expectation* that is independent of the physical parameters. Furthermore, Keynes makes an important distinction between short-term expectation, which governs the level of production and employment, and long-term expectation, which governs the investment decision.

Walrasian general equilibrium theory denotes as a 'temporary' equilibrium (not to be confused with Marshall's usage, to mean market-period equilibrium), an equilibrium based on expectations rather than complete markets. In terms of realism, this is an improvement over the complete markets assumption, since it limits knowledge to the present configuration of endowment, technology and preferences, all of which are open to change. Today's temporary equilibrium may be superseded tomorrow, given change in the parameters. However, no distinction is made in Walrasian models between short- and long-term expectations, between on the one hand, expectations of the prices of goods producible today and on the other, expectations of the future goods producible in turn with the capital-goods producible today. This amounts to making the state of expectation endogenous and postulating some nexus (Keynes, CW, vol. VII, p. 21) that co-ordinates expectations in such a way as to ensure full employment of the endowment.

Post Keynesian theorists have placed great emphasis on the state of long-term expectation and this will be addressed in the next section. However, the consensus interpretation of the state of short-term expectation, stemming mainly from Kregel (1976), needs revision. It has become common to assert that Keynes tacitly assumes the fulfilment of short-term expectations in *The General Theory* Chapter 3. By this assumption, it is argued, he avoids the need to model the formation of expectations as a process over time. On the contrary, there is no need to read in extra assumptions and implicitly disparage Keynes's capacity for theoretical reasoning. The principle of effective demand is itself a theory of the formation of short-term price expectations by the equilibrium of supply and demand.

In order to substantiate this claim, first consider again Keynes's conception of system equilibrium. He offers a theory of the level of employment at any time as an equilibrium value. His method of equilibrium analysis is static, but forward-looking. The analytical framework is a direct extension of Marshall's supply and demand apparatus for use at the macroeconomic level. The aggregate demand function (D) relates the total money-income expected by industry as a whole to the total level of employment (N), where the direction of causation runs from employment to income. The aggregate supply function (Z) relates the total expected money-income to the total level of employment (N), where the direction of causation runs from expected income to employment. The intersection of the aggregate demand and supply functions determines as equilibrium values the effective demand (let us call it D^*) and the level of employment (let us call it N^*).

The principle of effective demand is part of the theory of value and, in moving from the consideration of the individual industry to industry as a whole, there is no suggestion by Keynes that supply and demand have ceased to determine the prices and quantities of each product. Apart from improvements such as the introduction of user cost to deal with the element of supply price attributable to the use of existing capital-goods, Keynes's theory of value remains essentially that of Marshall and Pigou. However, the principle of effective demand solves the problem that supply and demand in each industry depend on the output and income of industry as a whole, and brings precision to Marshall's claim that short-period and long-period *expected* prices, and not only the spot prices of the market period, can realistically be treated as determined by the equilibrium of supply and demand.

There are major difficulties with Marshall's treatment of time and his theoretical distinction between periods, which Keynes refers to in his biography of Marshall (Keynes, CW, vol. X) as unfinished business and takes pains to address in *The General Theory*. The principal difficulty resolved by Keynes is how the equilibrium periods should relate to real or calendar time. In *The General Theory*, both the market and short periods correspond to the same period of calendar time, the 'day'. Whereas Marshall distinguishes between them in terms of the length of time ('several months or a year') over which production and employment can adjust so that market prices become equal to Normal short-period supply prices, for Keynes the difference between the market and the short periods is that between realized and expected prices: between income and effective demand.

The production and employment decision involves two separate units of calendar time, which Keynes defines as the *day* and the *period of production*, which is a number of *days*. The day is Keynes's quantum unit of time, 'the shortest interval after which the firm is free to revise its decision as to how much employment to offer. It is, so to speak, the minimum effective unit of economic time' (Keynes, CW, vol. VII, p. 47, footnote 1); the primary concern of *The General Theory* is the employment decisions of firms. This definition of a day is also the definition of the technical short period, in which entrepreneurs adjust the aggregate employment of labour associated with a given aggregate capital equipment to maximize their expected profits. The correspondence of the day with the market period again follows from the definition of the day, since it is the maximum interval for which the supply of finished output is limited to the stock on hand or producible on demand. Keynes's day need not correspond to a terrestrial day, but it does no harm to think of it as such, if only because the hours of over-time working can be, and often are, varied at such short notice. The *period of production* is the number of *days* 'notice of changes in the demand for [a product that] have to be given if it is to offer its maximum elasticity of employment' (ibid., p. 287). This definition is the macroeconomic counterpart of the period between starting and finishing an individual production process (ibid., p. 46), or production period.[4]

Keynes defines the long period in a unique and strictly *short-term* technical sense, to define the equilibrium on which the employment of labour and capital-goods will in theory converge if a new state of expectation persists for the full length of the period of production, allowing in particular for the production or depletion of raw materials and work-in-progress in line with the new pattern of production. This is very different from Marshall's concept of the long period ('of several years'), during which capital-goods are accumulated to the point where no new capital-good (and not only the marginal investment on a given day) yields more than the rate of interest, in a stationary state (or at least in a steady state of growth in line with secular growth in population and territory).

It is perhaps helpful to follow Joan Robinson in thinking of the terms market-period, short-period and long-period mainly as adjectives rather than substantives (Harcourt 1995). That is not to deny the importance of their connection with intervals of calendar time. Each equilibrium period refers to a different type of adjustment: the market period mainly to market clearing, and income; the short period to the employment of labour and the other factors of production (including existing capital-goods), and effective demand; the long period to the employment of new capital goods, and the capital stock. Thus we need to distinguish the nature of the adjustment from the interval of time in which it takes place, as well as from the time horizon of the relevant expectations which prompt adjustment. The market-period adjustment of the demand for and supply of current output and existing stocks takes place 'instantaneously', on a single day, cleared by spot market prices – this is fairly standard. The short-period adjustment of employment also takes place on a single day but refers to short-term expectations of income that will arise at the end of the various production periods for different goods. The long-period adjustment of the capital stock takes place as a dynamic process over the period of production, and is contingent upon a given state of expectation.

Many have been puzzled by the definition of aggregate demand as 'the proceeds which *entrepreneurs* expect to receive from the employment' (Keynes, CW, vol. VII, p. 25, emphasis added; see also pp. 28–9, 89), rather than in terms of the expenditure of consumers and investors, the aggregate demand of 'Keynesian' economics. Yet this paradox is already implicit in Marshall's claim that Normal prices, which are prices expected by entrepreneurs *today*, are determined by the equilibrium of supply and demand. The answer is that Keynes's entrepreneurs must be understood as fulfilling two separate functions on either side of the market, as employers of labour on the one hand, and as wholesale and retail dealers on the other (see Marshall 1920, p. 283; Keynes, CW, vol. XIII, p. 616). Employers are specialized in managing the risks of production, and dealers in managing the risks of marketing finished goods; a division of enterprise commonly observed in practice. In this construction, production takes place when an employer receives an order, usually from a dealer or another employer. Production to order implies, under perfect competition, the existence of a set of forward markets, for each good that is producible today, for delivery at the end of its production period. Competition between employers establishes a unique supply price for any given quantity, and competition between dealers, whatever their individual expectations about future spot prices, establishes a demand-price at which each dealer's demand is in equilibrium. If any speculation about future spot prices by employers is treated as a dealer activity, the equilibrium forward prices of current output become shared short-term expectations, which permits unique definition of 'the' state of expectation.[5]

The point of effective demand is a short-period equilibrium position, meaning that entrepreneurs as a whole adjust their employment of labour to maximize their expected profit with a given aggregate stock of capital-goods. Since Keynes's short period relates to his day, and the day is the quantum unit of time, this means that aggregate demand and supply are in static equilibrium at all times (every day); the equilibrium process of finding the point of effective demand described on p. 25 of *The General Theory* takes place on a single day, the present day. The equilibrium price of the output of each industry corresponding to *today's* aggregate employment is determined *today* as the price which clears the supply offers by employers and the demand bids by dealers in the forward market for delivery at the end of the production period. Each day employment moves directly to the equilibrium position corresponding to the set of forward prices, so that within the quantum limit of the day as the unit of time, employment is in continuous equilibrium.

The set of equilibrium expected prices that determines effective demand corresponds to the state of short-term expectation (Keynes, CW, vol. VII, p. 46), so that it can properly be said that expectation determines output and employment, the title of Chapter 5. In modern terms, Keynes's short-term expectations are 'rational expectations', or in his own words, based on 'judicious foresight'. Although he recognizes that in practice expectations may be formed by trial and error, from the perspective of economic theory 'the main point is to distinguish the forces determining the position of equilibrium from the technique of trial and error by means of which the entrepreneur discovers where the position is' (Keynes, CW, vol. XIV, pp. 182–3).

By contrast, the state of long-term expectation is an entirely different matter. Keynes does not assume long-term expectations are fulfilled even in his long-period equilibrium (where they are merely unchanged), and indeed considers disappointment more than likely when expectations are not based on the rents of natural resources or monopoly. The problem is the durable nature of capital-assets: if the expectations upon which the investment was based prove mistaken, it is not possible, either to reverse the investment today, or to go back in time, adjust the original investment decision, and then check the revised results in the present, in order to find the equilibrium position. It is only in a stationary or steady state that adjustments made today might (given stable dynamics) be expected to have the same effect in the future as the same adjustments, made in the past, would have had today. So, the convergent feedback mechanism, which would be necessary to generate in practice a set of long-term equilibrium prices as the basis of prospective yield, is absent in any economy subject to unforeseen change, such as the one we inhabit. The period over which competitive equilibrium analysis is of scientific value relates directly to the time horizon within which expectations can reasonably be treated as determinate. The method cannot be applied to the long term, thus wholly undermining the Classical concept of long-period competitive equilibrium, whether static or dynamic.[6]

To assume 'rational expectations' in the long term is heroically to assume a very unheroic world, in which the future can reliably be predicted from knowledge of the present and the past. The state of long-term expectation is as exogenous in *The General Theory* as the endowment and other Classical system parameters, meaning that it is beyond the reach of equilibrium analysis. It is a close cousin to the propensity to consume and the preference for liquidity, both of which also reflect the historical nature of time. These three psychological states represent rational (by which here

I mean reasonable, not optimal in some objective sense) responses by purposeful individuals to the problems of time, in the real world where the Classical long-period equilibrium is logically unattainable, and therefore an objectively optimal response is physically impossible.

LIQUIDITY

Much has already been written by Post Keynesian economists about the state of long-term expectation, including the notion of conventional valuation represented by the famous beauty contest of Chapter 12. The inescapable fact that there is no such thing as 'fundamental value' (except with hindsight) has been driven home forcibly by recent events. Yet less attention has been given to what Keynes means by 'liquidity' and indeed most Post Keynesians accept the common understanding of liquidity as ease of conversion into money. Most have missed that Keynes wrote about something quite different, perhaps encouraged, once again, by Hansen's statement that 'not much would have been lost if [Chapter 17] had never been written' (1953, p. 159).

Keynes distinguishes between the attributes of convertibility and liquidity; there is more to his conception of liquidity than convertibility. In principle, an asset with low convertibility may have high liquidity, and *vice versa*, however counter-intuitive this may now seem. Liquidity is intimately related with expectation in *The General Theory*, and its meaning is fundamental to the understanding of the book as a whole. Kaldor notes that

> Mr Keynes, in certain parts of *The General Theory* appears to use the term 'liquidity' in a sense which comes very close to our concept of 'perfect market-ability'; ie goods which can be sold at any time for the same price, or nearly the same price, at which they can be bought. Yet it is obvious that this attribute of goods is not the same thing as what Mr Keynes really wants to mean by 'liquidity'. Certain gilt-edged securities can be bought on the Stock Exchange at a price which is only a small fraction higher than the price at which they can be sold; on this definition therefore they would have to be regarded as highly liquid assets. In fact it is very difficult to find satisfactory definition of what constitutes 'liquidity' – a difficulty, I think, which is inherent in the concept itself. (Kaldor 1939, p. 4, footnote 5)

The paradox of *The General Theory* is that Keynes so emphasizes the liquidity of money within a theoretical framework, based on perfect competition, in which *all* assets are equally marketable or convertible. Why does he then discuss *degrees* of liquidity (Keynes, CW, vol. VII, p. 226) and, furthermore, suggest that in certain historic environments *land* has 'ruled the roost' in the hierarchy of liquidity (ibid., p. 241)? If the assumption of perfect competition is to be qualified in practice so that differences in the liquidity of assets are allowed, as a function of their degree of convertibility, this suggestion is startling. Land can never have been preferred for its convertibility, let alone as the medium of exchange. Keynes claims that historically it has possessed high liquidity, despite low convertibility. Conversely, in his discussion of organized investment markets, which come closest in practice to the ideal of perfect competition in terms of transaction costs and uniformity of price, he treats their 'liquidity' (note the inverted commas) as an illusion and something distinct from true liquidity. Listed equity securities have high convertibility, but low liquidity.

Keynes's implicit definition of liquidity is the degree to which the value of an asset, measured in any given standard, is independent of changes in the state of expectation. Liquidity risk is therefore the possible (*not* probable or expected) loss of value as a result of a change in the state of expectation, which includes the state of confidence. In *The General Theory*, there is a hierarchy of liquidity risk, in which bonds are superior to capital-goods, and money is superior to bonds. This hierarchy is of crucial importance to Keynes's division between consumption and different types of investment decisions, which later theory has neglected. Keynes's conception of liquidity is intimately bound up with his conceptions of the state of expectation and of the historical nature of time. Liquidity has value only because the future is unknown, and its value increases with our fear of what might happen that we cannot prevent or insure against. In *The General Theory*, money is *the* liquid asset and dominant store of value, as well as the standard of value, and money's liquidity is the foundation of its non-neutrality.

Keynes comes closest to defining liquidity from first principles in his discussion of a situation where the standard of value (perhaps the goat to which he refers in *A Treatise on Money* (Keynes, CW, vol. V), but certainly not land) does not have the normal character of money:

> In [a non-monetary] economy capital equipments will differ from one another (a) in the variety of the consumables in the production of which they are capable of assisting, (b) in the stability of value of their output (in the sense in which the value of bread is more stable through time than the value of fashionable novelties), and (c) in the rapidity with which the wealth embodied in them can become 'liquid', in the sense of producing output, the proceeds of which can be re-embodied if desired in quite a different form. (Keynes, CW, vol. VII, p. 240)

Liquidity is first a function of the degree to which a capital-asset can be used in the production of different consumables, so that a change in prospective yield based on production in one line can be met by switching to another line. The prospective yield on the second line is lower than originally expected from the first, but higher than now expected from the first after the change in expectations, reducing the impact of the change on the value of the asset. Keynes then refers to the importance of the stability of the value of the consumables produced. Stability in this context means independence from changes in the state of long-term expectation (for example, bread is not a fashion item). The third element of his definition is the 'turnover period', the period over which the asset can be converted through production into consumable output. The shorter the period, the less likely is it that a change in the state of long-term expectation will arise during the life of the asset. Clearly Keynes is here thinking in aggregate terms: although an individual investor can always exchange an asset for money under perfect competition, its convertibility for the community as a whole depends on its conversion into consumption-goods through production and not just exchange.

For the various rather complex reasons set out in Chapter 17, the standard of value tends to be the asset whose value in terms of consumable output is the most stable with respect to changes in the state of long-term expectation. Thus when Keynes refers to liquidity he really does mean money, including short-term bank and state debts whose value is not sensitive to changes in the rate of interest because of the short period to redemption. Keynes treats capital-assets as fully convertible but not liquid, and mentions, almost as a footnote to the above definition (ibid.), the need for a premium to compensate for their liquidity risk relative to bonds. The rate of interest on bonds, where there is no 'risk proper', is entirely compensation for liquidity risk from unexpected changes in interest rates. From this it is clear that Keynes regards capital-assets as less liquid than bonds, in the sense that their value is more sensitive to changes in the state of long-term expectation, since the value of capital-assets depends on expectations of both the interest rate and the prospective yield. On this definition of liquidity, money and bonds dominate capital-assets in terms of both 'risk proper' and liquidity risk. The first step in the portfolio decision is to choose between money and the next most liquid and safe class of assets, that is, bonds; only then does the choice arise between capital-assets and bonds. Thus liquidity risk is the criterion for placing different categories of asset in separate compartments, and the demand for liquidity cannot be satisfied by assets other than money (that is, the set of assets convertible on demand into means of payment at a fixed price in terms of the standard of value).

This 'hierarchy of liquidity' is central to the causal structure of *The General Theory* that Keynes describes in his 1937 summary. Stage 1: 'The rate of interest is the factor which adjusts at the margin the demand for hoards to the supply of hoards'. Stage 2: 'The owner of wealth, who has been induced not to hold his wealth in the shape of hoarded money, still has two alternatives between which to choose. He can lend his money at the current rate of money interest or he can purchase some kind of capital asset . . . This is brought about by shifts in the money prices of capital assets relative to the prices of money loans': so bonds (money loans) dominate capital assets. Stage 3: 'If the level of the rate of interest taken in conjunction with opinions about their prospective yield raise the prices of capital assets, the volume of current investment . . . will be increased': thus the supply price and output of new capital assets rises to meet the demand price. Stage 4: 'The amount of consumption goods it will pay entrepreneurs to produce depends on the amount of investment goods which they are producing': investment determines total employment and consumption through the multiplier relation. 'This that I offer is, therefore, a theory of . . . employment because it explains why, in any given circumstances, employment is what it is' (Keynes, CW, XIV, pp. 112–22).

It is of the greatest importance to realize that in *The General Theory* individuals do not choose between (say) consumption-goods on the one hand and bonds or capital-assets on the other (Fisher and Hicks); nor between money and consumption-goods (Pigou and Friedman), or even money and capital-assets (Minsky). Keynes does not accept the Classical axiom of gross substitution, he insists upon a causal sequence: first, liquidity-preference must be satisfied and the prices of bonds adjust in response; second, the prices of capital assets must adjust to the prices of bonds. Finally, aggregate income, employment and consumption adjust to the rate of investment in new capital assets. Without a clear understanding of liquidity, Keynes's one-way causal sequence appears arbitrary and inferior to a treatment in which direct trade-offs exist between all classes of goods and factor services.

RELEVANCE TO POLICY

After a long period in the wilderness, Keynes is back in fashion. 'Keynesian' demand management policies made an overnight resurgence in response to the 2008 financial crisis and government deficits have been running at levels unprecedented in peace-time. Nevertheless, just as Keynes's impact on academic economic theory has been minimal, three examples will suffice to show that key policy areas remain largely immune to his influence.

Recent developments have so far left intact the doctrine of so-called 'flexible labour markets' as the remedy for unemployment. Underpinning this is the theoretical concept of the 'natural rate' of unemployment, which corresponds to the rate consistent with frictional and voluntary unemployment (on Keynes's definitions in Chapter 2). These are matters of great importance, of course, and of particular relevance to productivity growth and social welfare. There is much to be said for policies that make it easier for workers to retrain and move between occupations and industries as the pattern of demand changes. Equally, it is important that employment and welfare policies do not create perverse incentives, preventing a rational reallocation of labour in the long-term interests of both workers and the economy as a whole. However, the flexible labour market is often simply a euphemism for an attack on organized labour, employment protection rights and welfare benefits. Leaving aside the partisan motives of the business class, the public interest case for such policies is based on the Classical theory of employment and

> . . . the conclusion, perfectly logical on their assumption, that apparent unemployment (apart from the admitted exceptions) must be due at bottom to a refusal by the unemployed factors to accept a reward which corresponds to their marginal productivity. A classical economist may sympathise with labour in refusing to accept a cut in its money wage, and he will admit that it may not be wise to make it to meet conditions which are temporary; but scientific integrity forces him to declare that this refusal is, nevertheless, at the bottom of the trouble. (Keynes, CW, vol. VII, p. 16)

Thus the doctrine of flexible labour markets, in the form in which it is generally promoted, wholly ignores Keynes's careful demonstration that it is the level of employment which determines the real cost of labour and that not only does the opposite not hold, the real cost of labour is not a causal variable and certainly not proxied by money wages or benefits. Wide movements in the 'natural rate' are interpreted as having their roots in shifts in productivity or labour practices, based on a partial reading of the empirical evidence (Galbraith 1997; Nickell 1997), and no credence is given to the idea that these variations in the unemployment rate reflect, in great part, movements in the level of effective demand.

The second area of policy is the reform of the international trading and monetary system. Although Keynes is often given credit for the Bretton Woods system, the institutions which emerged were a pale imitation of his own proposals and were empowered and have survived only insofar as they have served the interests of Anglo-American hegemony. The downfall of the pegged exchange rate system and the end of 'Keynesian' demand management in the 1970s coincided with the counter-reformation in economic theory and was followed by the era of financial liberalization. Yet even during the 'Keynesian' era, policy-makers failed to distinguish between aggregate and effective demand and sought to maintain full employment by demand management with insufficient attention to the need for demand to become effective, that is, matched by supply. The most important aspect of this is the balance of payments constraint on employment and growth which plagued countries, such as the UK under Bretton Woods, that tended towards full-employment trade deficits. Keynes had offered two alternative approaches to this problem: managed trade and surplus country adjustment. The idea of managed trade was anathema and the idea that payments and exchange rate adjustment should fall on surplus countries, as embodied in Keynes's original plans for an International Clearing Union, has always been opposed by large surplus countries (the US in the 1940s, West Germany and Japan in the later 1960s and early 1970s, China today). Since in political terms it is these surplus countries that determine the outcome in negotiations over the international monetary system, it is unsurprising that no progress has been made.

So we find that global demand is still constrained by an excessive propensity to save, in the form of trade and payments surpluses intended to promote domestic employment, combined with a propensity to hoard in the form of central bank reserves to protect exchange rates from the depredations of international speculation. The era of 'financial liberalization' sold an image of smoothly adjusting capital and foreign exchange markets allocating capital efficiently across the globe, diversifying risk, promoting stability and freedom. The reality has been a massive loss of democratic sovereignty over domestic policy, forcing states either into monetary union or into amassing war chests against the next financial crisis. The natural linkage between monetary and political union, perhaps desirable in itself, combined with an inability to regulate an independent exchange rate, has forced states into premature membership of the European Union and the euro-zone. The Union has been enlarged hastily, without putting in place an adequate political or fiscal mechanism for dealing with intra-union regional imbalances, placing severe strains on peripheral countries that may yet break the union and in any case quite likely to leave generations of unemployed in the poorer regions. The choice faced by Keynes, between the fetters of the Gold Standard and the anarchy of the inter-war period, remains before us still, in a new form, and the world remains deaf to pleas for a more rational way of organizing the international financial system.

One of the fundamental obstacles to the reform of international finance has been financial liberalization itself, particularly the free movement of financial capital across borders. Keynes correctly understood such capital movements to be incompatible with an orderly exchange rate system and the world has chosen 'freedom' over order. The removal of cross-border exchange controls on portfolio investment were among the first fruits of liberalization and have been followed down the years by a change in the nature of the regulation of financial institutions from a 'structural' to a 'prudential' approach. Structural regulation makes a link between form and activity, defining different types of financial institution and limiting each to a particular kind of activity and creating 'fire-walls' between them: the Glass-Steagall Act is an example. Structural regulation conflicts with the competitive ethos of liberalization and fire-walls appear to the liberalizer simply as obstacles to competition and enterprise. Prudential regulation, by contrast, is intended to allow integrated financial institutions the freedom to pursue any activity provided they meet various conditions, notably capital adequacy. While the intention of the new approach was to promote competition and innovation at the same time as protecting the system from risk, regulators have proved no match for the larger financial institutions and have imposed an increasingly oppressive compliance burden on smaller ones, while the Basle II regime itself has proved pro-cyclical and destabilizing. The implicit acceptance by the state of responsibility for the effectiveness of this kind of regulation has led to the almost universal government guarantee of retail deposits in the face of the failure of the regulatory system in 2008. It has not escaped public notice that bank shareholders and managers have thereby succeeded in transferring the cost of their failure to the state.

As in the case of unemployment and the 'natural rate', underpinning financial liberalization is another theoretical concept, the 'efficient markets hypothesis'. Based in turn on the concept of long-term rational expectations, this is another example of the refusal of policy-makers to accept the core implications of Keynes's thought. Keynes would, I think, have been horrified by financial liberalization and by the blind faith of policy-makers and regulators in the stabilizing ability of speculative market forces to identify fundamental value. The failure to recognize that there is no such thing as fundamental value (except with hindsight) has left policy-makers wide open to the larger failure to recognize the destabilizing power of speculation when:

> . . . the energies and skill of the professional investor and speculator are mainly occupied . . . not with making superior long-term forecasts of the probable yield of an investment over its whole life, but with foreseeing changes in the conventional basis of valuation a short time ahead of the general public . . . Moreover, this behaviour is not the outcome of a wrong-headed propensity. It is an inevitable result of an investment market organised along the lines described. (Keynes, CW, vol. VII, pp. 154–5)

Furthermore the financial sector has long lost touch with its primary social justification as a source of finance for industrial investment, that is, the production of new capital-goods. It is a commonplace in the City of London that the City does not exist to finance industry, industry exists to finance the City. The hypertrophy of financial instruments over the last decade, fuelled by sophisticated, if theoretically ill-founded, mathematical alchemy and computer technology, converting some underlying piece of lead into gold, exemplifies the elevation of rentier capitalism to an end in itself and has met its Nemesis in the failures of Lehman Brothers and AIG.

The credit crunch itself has been an object lesson in the importance of liquidity preference. With a significant proportion of bank depositors switching to foreign banks or sovereign debt, UK and US banks themselves became reluctant to lend to each other in order to protect their dwindling reserve assets. Each bank was torn between the need to hoard reserves against the possibility of a run and the high cost of doing so. Keynes's definition of money became strikingly relevant:

> Without disturbance to this definition, we can draw the line between 'money' and 'debts' at whatever point is most convenient for handling a particular problem. For example, we can treat as money any command over general purchasing power which the owner has not parted with for a period in excess of three months, and as debt what cannot be recovered for a longer period than this; or we can substitute for 'three months' one month or three days or three hours or any other period; or we can exclude from money whatever is not legal tender on the spot. (Keynes, CW, vol. VII, p. 167, n. 1)

At the height of the crunch, 'money' moved right to the end of this spectrum, as exemplified by the unparalleled spread of inter-bank interest rates over central bank rates (for example, Bank of England 2009, p. 15). The emergency measures (such as guarantees of inter-bank lending, extended discount facilities and quantitative easing) were successful, not because they addressed long-term bank solvency in the sense of capital adequacy, that is, the *probability* of loss (which had been addressed separately), but because they removed the *possibility* of default on short-term inter-bank deposits through further bank runs. Keynes's theory of interest was mainly concerned with interest rates on long-term bonds, since fundamental uncertainty about the spot value of debts is normally a property of long time horizons, yet during the period of the financial crisis, the reality of liquidity preference became scaringly clear, even at the short end.

Yet still, after all we have been through, the conventional wisdom remains that interest rates are determined by the supply and demand for loanable funds and the case for cutting public deficits is partly that an increase in national saving will reduce interest rates:

Shadow Chancellor George Osborne rightly believes cutting spending allows interest rates to remain lower than they would otherwise be. Indeed, this is what textbook macroeconomic models suggest. The Bank of England believes much the same. (*Financial Times*, 19 January 2010)

In darker moments, one is inclined to fear that the conventional wisdom, together with the mainstream macroeconomic theory from which it derives, is impervious to reason or experience.

CONCLUSION

I have argued that Keynes's direct influence on economic theory and policy has so far been minimal. This, perhaps surprising, conclusion does not discount the importance of the policies of demand management associated with his name, it merely emphasizes that he gave cogency, respectability and authority to policies advocated by many others. Nevertheless, while such a conclusion may be disappointing in relation to the hopes that were entertained 75 years ago, it is actually cause for considerable hope for the future. Economic policy is ultimately rooted in economic theory, consciously or not. The first attempts to articulate the Keynesian revolution in theory have failed. In the case of the 'Keynesian' neoclassical synthesis, Keynes's distinctive innovations were rejected so that his message could be assimilated into the mainstream of economics as the economics of rigidity, now represented by a 'New Keynesian' economics that should really be called 'New Pigovian' economics. The Post Keynesians, for the most part, rejected Keynes's Marshallian framework as an attempt to pour new wine into old wineskins and many have moved outside the mainstream of economic theory based on the competitive equilibrium of supply and demand. Keynes himself, by contrast, sought to redefine the very mainstream itself.

The research programme initiated by Keynes has not failed or degenerated, it has barely begun. The history of science suggests that it can take several generations of academic scholarship for truly original ideas to be received. Scientific progress involves many wrong turns and dead ends. I have tried here to show that future theoretical research must start from three key propositions about *The General Theory*:

- A valid macroeconomic theory of a competitive monetary economy cannot begin from the assumption of homogeneous output. Competitive corn models are ineluctably Classical. Production in a monetary economy involves the hiring of labour by the payment of a money-wage. The principle of effective demand represents accordingly the conception of competitive system equilibrium relevant to a monetary economy and supersedes the Classical conception of general equilibrium as the preferred allocation of factor resources. This invariably means that factor markets do not clear and factor prices are not equilibrium values.

- The principle of effective demand is itself a theory of the formation of the state of short-term expectation (which determines employment at any time) by the equilibrium of supply and demand. In short, it is a restatement of the Marshallian theory of value so as to take proper account of time and money. The concept of what we now call 'rational expectations' was well understood by Keynes under the name of 'judicious foresight'. The key distinction he drew was between short-term expectation, relating to currently producible goods, and long-term expectation, relating to the investment decision. While the method of rational expectations can validly be applied to the short term, the long term is an entirely different matter.

- The causal structure of *The General Theory* cannot be understood without the recognition that liquidity for Keynes is far more than a matter of convertibility and is intimately related with the state of expectation. Liquidity means for Keynes stability of value in the face of changes in the state of expectation, so that in certain circumstances an asset such as land can be a liquid asset and stock market securities are generally illiquid for society as a whole.

As for policy, the doctrines of labour market flexibility and efficient markets have their roots in Classical theory. The former leads to cruel and futile attempts to remedy involuntary unemployment by creating insecurity and poverty through cuts in employment rights and benefits. The fruits of the efficient markets hypothesis have been a financial crisis of unprecedented scale and a plunge in global activity which has, perhaps, been countered only by the single-minded application of 'Keynesian' demand management policies in the teeth of an academic orthodoxy that largely denies their potency. Finally, we are unlikely ever to see a world of human flourishing, free from the scourge of involuntary underemployment, without radical reform of the international monetary system in the teeth of an economic and political ideology committed to financial liberalization. Such reform will only become conceivable if and when the intellectual substrate of the conventional wisdom finally comes to terms with the message of *The General Theory*.

NOTES

1. There is also a clear connection between corn models and the under-consumption (i.e. over-production) theories of Malthus, Marx and Hobson, who noted, in effect, that there must be a limit to the accumulation in granaries.
2. This is not to deny that the concept of effective demand can be expressed in quite different terms such as Kalecki's or Sraffa's, by introducing an exogenous mark-up over average cost. In these alternative constructions, prices are not determined by supply and demand. For an explanation of the difference between the degree of monopoly and Keynes's degree of competition see Hayes (2008).
3. The 'fixed-price general equilibrium' approach introduces a similar over-determining constraint on employment of the endowment. The difference is that Keynes's own concept of effective demand retains market-clearing in new goods markets with factor demand as a residual (see Malinvaud 1985, p. 31, footnote 28). The problem is that 'in the long run', if prices are flexible, Malinvaud's conception of equilibrium reverts to the Classical.
4. The consensus about Keynes's use of time periods, from which I depart, is that Keynes's day and production period coincide, and correspond to a Hicksian week (Chick 1983; Amadeo 1989), an equation which tacitly assumes a uniform production period for all goods. Daily employment thus differs, for these authors, from the short-period employment equilibrium in which expectations are fulfilled.
5. Chick (1983, 1992) offers perhaps the most sophisticated development of the received idea that the equilibrium point of effective demand is discovered by the fulfilment of expectations. She distinguishes between D^e, aggregate demand in terms of entrepreneurial expectations (which may be entirely individual to each firm, and thus does not permit definition of a unique and common state of expectation), and D, meaning aggregate demand in terms of expenditure. The point of effective demand is then defined by the intersection of Z and D^e, but equilibrium is not reached in terms of fulfilled expectations until (if ever) D^e coincides with D. A difficulty with her interpretation is that it leaves no room for Keynes's long-period employment, which various other authors have also found problematic.
6. Harrod did not accept that our ignorance of the future made long-term equilibrium theory pointless and regarded the absence of dynamic equilibrium from *The General Theory* as a weakness. He envisaged (and subsequently contributed to) the development of a theory 'concerned not merely with what size, but also what rate of growth of certain magnitudes is consistent with the surrounding circumstances. There appears to be no reason why the dynamic principles should not come to be as precisely defined and as rigidly demonstrable as the static principles' (Harrod 1937, p. 86). This is also the view ultimately embodied in modern Classical dynamic general equilibrium theory based upon the concept of long-term long-period equilibrium that Keynes fundamentally rejected. Theories of accumulation and technical change are possible but they should not be based on competitive equilibrium.

BIBLIOGRAPHY

Amadeo, E. J. (1989), *Keynes's Principle of Effective Demand*, Aldershot, UK and Brookfield, VT, USA: Edward Elgar.

Ambrosi, G. M. (2003), *Keynes, Pigou and Cambridge Keynesians*, Basingstoke: Palgrave Macmillan.

Bank of England (2009), *Inflation Report*, November, London.

Chick, V. (1983), *Macroeconomics after Keynes*, Oxford: Philip Allan.

Chick, V. (1992), 'The small firm under uncertainty: a puzzle of *The General Theory*', in B. Gerrard and J. Hillard (eds), *The Philosophy and Economics of J. M. Keynes*, Aldershot, UK and Brookfield, VT, USA: Edward Elgar, pp. 149–64.

Financial Times (2010), 'UK public spending in an election year', Lex column, 19 January, London.

Galbraith, J. K. (1997), 'Time to ditch the NAIRU', *Journal of Economic Perspectives*, **11** (1), (Winter), pp. 93–108.

Hansen, A. H. (1953), *A Guide to Keynes*, New York: McGraw-Hill.

Harcourt, G. C. (1995), 'The structure of Tom Asimakopulos's later writings', in G. C. Harcourt, A. Roncaglia, and R. Rowley (eds), *Income and Employment in Theory and Practice: essays in Memory of Athanasios Asimakopulos*, Basingstoke and London: Macmillan, pp. 1–16.

Harrod, R. F. (1937), 'Mr Keynes and traditional theory', *Econometrica*, **5** (1), (January), 74–86.

Hayes, M. G. (2008), 'Keynes's degree of competition', *European Journal of the History of Economic Thought*, **15** (2), (June), 275–91.

Hicks, J. R. (1939), *Value and Capital*, Oxford: Clarendon Press.

Kaldor, N. (1939), 'Speculation and economic stability', *Review of Economic Studies*, **7** (1), (June), 1–27.

Keynes, J. M. (1971–1989), *The Collected Writings of John Maynard Keynes*, London: Macmillan/Cambridge University Press for the Royal Economic Society.
   Vol. V: *A Treatise on Money: 1, The Pure Theory of Money*
   Vol. VII: *The General Theory of Employment, Interest, and Money*
   Vol. VIII: *A Treatise on Probability*
   Vol. X: *Essays in Biography*
   Vol. XIII: *The General Theory and After: Part I Preparation*
   Vol. XIV: *The General Theory and After: Part II Defence and Development*
   Vol. XXIX: *The General Theory and After: A Supplement*

Kregel, J. A. (1976), 'Economic methodology in the face of uncertainty: the modelling methods of Keynes and the Post-Keynesians', *Economic Journal*, **86** (342), (June), 209–25.

Laidler, D. (1999), *Fabricating the Keynesian Revolution*, Cambridge: Cambridge University Press.

Malinvaud, E. (1985), *The Theory of Unemployment Reconsidered*, 2nd edn, Oxford: Basil Blackwell.

Marshall, A. (1920), *Principles of Economics* 8th edn, 1949 reprint, London: Macmillan.

Nickell, S. (1997), 'Unemployment and labour market rigidities: Europe versus North America', *Journal of Economic Perspectives*, **11** (3), (Spring), 55–74.

Sraffa, P. (1926), 'The laws of returns under competitive conditions', *Economic Journal*, **36** (144), (December), 535–50.

3. Keynes's economic theory – judgement under uncertainty

Elke Muchlinski[1]

INTRODUCTION

This chapter is an attempt to explain why there is no 'Keynes-rule' to be found in Keynes's economic theory by concentrating on two elements in his writings: 'vagueness' and 'state of confidence'. Both concepts are important per se as signposts to his understanding of judgement under uncertainty. I want to emphasize that Keynes also made economic theory the subject of discussion as conceptual investigation. The concept of 'rule' he introduced in his economic theory, monetary policy, and international monetary relations went beyond rigidly designed propositions and assumptions of certainty and complete knowledge. Furthermore any reference to formal aestheticism or rigidly defined concepts or rules, seems to imply an inadequate interpretation of his work.

The traditional way of asking, what he *really meant* is not the way I have chosen in this chapter since no answer is possible. Any link from Keynes's work to current debates should be as cautious as possible. The reading of Keynes's work is inevitably itself an interpretation (Rorty 1991). In this chapter I intend to provide textual evidence that Keynes's scepticism to rigidly fixed rules as formal description in economic theory is rooted in a view he also shared with some contemporaries and which is related to a common theoretical background and to intellectual upheavals in Cambridge, UK. John Maynard Keynes (1883–1946), Bertrand Russell (1872–1970), and Ludwig Wittgenstein (1889–1951) lived contemporaneously in Cambridge, UK. They created important theories which revolutionized philosophy and economics in the 1920s.

The chapter argues that Keynes's economic thinking was widely influenced by contemporaneous debates between Wittgenstein and Russell, Keynes and Moore, and Ramsey and Johnson among others (see Bateman 1990; Carabelli 1988; Davis 1994, 1996; Dostaler 2005; Hillard 1995; Moggridge 1992; Muchlinski 1996, 1998; O'Donnell 1989). I shall substantiate this claim with textual evidence. The aim of this chapter is not to compare Keynes's, Russell's and Wittgenstein's writings, but rather to support the contention that they had initiated and intensified certain scientific debates and theoretical upheavals in Cambridge. They benefited from discussions and controversies which dominated the agenda of those times. Therefore I propose to consider Keynes's writings within the context of his contemporaries and their debates. In his economic writings, for example, *The General Theory of Employment, Interest, and Money*, he demanded that any theoretical assumptions be linked not to a model's consistency itself but rather to the contemporary world.

It is claimed in the first section of this chapter that Keynes provided new framework for economics with his conceptual investigation. The second section outlines the concept of 'vagueness'. In the third section I pursue the point of exegesis through *The General Theory* in order to outline the concept of 'state of confidence' as crucial to Keynes's economic theory. I will attempt to defend Keynes's economic theory against those authors, for instance Hayek among others, who argue that Keynes constructed an imprecise and hence a non-scientific economic theory.

ECONOMICS AS CONCEPTUAL INVESTIGATION

Keynes deals with the function of concepts or propositions in his early manuscripts (1904–1912), in his book *A Treatise on Probability* (*Collected Writings* (CW), vol. VIII; hereafter *A Treatise*) and in Chapter 13 of *The General Theory*. Keynes followed Kant who abandoned in his 'Copernican revolution' the realist justification of causal principles. Keynes rejected Kant's transcendental deduction of causal principles because Keynes did not support the view that a cause is proportional to a consequence. He did not propose ideal norms or principles for the sake of dignity (Muchlinski 1996). In short, we can discover a common scientific view in the work of Keynes, Russell and Wittgenstein: scientific investigations are conceptual investigations. Conceptual investigations or propositions structure the perception of reality. Concepts can differ from the perceived world as Keynes was expounding in his writings.

Common to the theories of Keynes, Russell and Wittgenstein is their questioning how knowledge can be established.[2] The underlying idea is that everything that refers to reality must be related by concepts or propositions. It is for this reason that Keynes referred in his critique of neoclassic theory to the concepts they used. At this point, three chapters of *The General Theory* are noteworthy: Chapter 2 The Postulates of the Classical Economist, Chapter 13 *The General Theory* of the Rate of Interest, and Chapter 14 The Classical Theory of the Rate of Interest. Here, he investigated whether the neoclassical concepts are based on logical reasoning only, or if they are engaged with the concept of truth and reality. Many other remarkable passages in Keynes's writing give witness to his methodological and epistemological approach to economic theory, in which language and 'vagueness' of meaning and the 'state of confidence' are fundamental. He built up his theory by a distinctive epistemological and methodological approach in which the meaning of concepts and propositions, sentences and words, are linked to their use and not to metaphysical assumptions or formal premises.

ON VAGUENESS

Keynes explained the relevance of *a priori* reasoning as opposed to the dominant empirical paradigm of the British School of Empiricism in *A Treatise*. He also emphasized the limits of Empiricism by developing a theory of knowledge regarding fundamental uncertainty.

Keynes investigated 'vagueness' and the relation between formal language and everyday language. In the preface of *A Treatise* he conceptualized his view on language as a critique on formal language as proposed by Russell in *Principia Mathematica*. Russell, Ramsey, Keynes, and also Wittgenstein, simultaneously worked on the relations between formal language, logic, and everyday language and how to establish knowledge. Keynes focused on the critical assumptions underlying the formal language approach as proposed by Russell at the time when Russell had already started to revise his view. This revision was also impelled by certain criticisms of Wittgenstein and Ramsey among others (Green 2007), Keynes asked whether Russell still remained with his project of 'perfectly exact language' within the realm of reasonable judgements:

> Confusion of thought is not always best avoided by technical and unaccustomed expressions, to which the mind has no immediate reaction of understanding; it is possible, under the cover of a careful formalism, to make statements, which, if expressed in plain language, the mind would immediately repudiate. (Keynes, CW, vol. VIII, p. 20, footnote 1)

The premises Russell put forward are neither linked to thought nor to reasonable judgements because they are taken as granted for logical reasons only. Keynes wrote:

> He concludes with familiar results, but he reaches them from premises, which have never occurred to us before, and by an argument so elaborate that our minds have difficulty in following it. (It) gives rise to questions about the

relation in which ordinary reasoning stands to this ordered system. (ibid., p. 128)

Keynes criticized the scholasticisms of Russell. As a lecturer in Cambridge from 1908–1915 and 1932–1935, Keynes was familiar both with Russell's first positive and then negative views on the acceptability of mathematics and formal language in sciences and with Wittgenstein's first affirmative and later sceptical approach to that same issue (Wittgenstein 1979, 1980). Through the connection with Russell, Keynes came into contact with Wittgenstein (Monk 1990). Russell and Keynes organized the return of Wittgenstein's manuscript of the *Tractatus Logico-Philosophicus* (hereafter *Tractatus*) in the year 1914 while Wittgenstein himself remained in Italian captivity.

In the year 1918 Russell had confessed in his lecture on 'The Philosophy of Logical Atomism' (hereafter *Philosophy*) to insurmountable problems with the formal language approach.

> A moment ago I was speaking about the great advantage that we derive from the logical imperfections of language, from the fact that our words are all ambiguous. . . . In a logically perfect language, there will be one word and no more for every simple object, and everything that is not simple will be expressed by a combination of words, by a combination derived, of course, from the words for the simple things that enter in, one word for each simple component. A language of that sort will be completely analytic, and will show at a glance the logical structure of the facts asserted or denied. The language which is set forth in *Principia Mathematica* is intended to be a language of that sort. It is a language which has only syntax and no vocabulary whatsoever. . . . It aims at being that sort of a language that, if you add a vocabulary, would be a logically perfect language. Actual languages are not logically perfect in that sense, and they cannot possibly be, if they are to serve the purpose of daily life. A logically perfect language, if it could be constructed, would not only be intolerably prolix, but, as regards its vocabulary, would be very largely private to one speaker. That is to say, all the names that it would use would be private to that speaker and could not enter into the language of another speaker. (Russell 1986, p. 176)

The editor remarked that Russell's own criticism on formal language, 'The Philosophy of the Logical Atomism' (1918), which pointed to its inadequacy for scientific work and understanding because it lacks a link to everyday language, was published well after 1918. It was based on Russell's syllabus that he had sent to America before he went to prison. According to the editor the published manuscript is a rewritten and reprinted version, that is, a long time after Keynes had addressed his criticism on Russell in the preface of *A Treatise*.

Vagueness of everyday language is of great importance for Keynes, too.

In *A Treatise* he compared the benefits and risks of the formal language approach to knowledge and probability. What does 'vagueness' mean and imply? Keynes did not define vagueness; rather he provided a description of it.

> There is vagueness, it may be noticed, in the number of instances, which would be required on the above assumptions to establish a given numerical degree of probability, which corresponds to the vagueness in the degree of probability which we do actually attach to inductive conclusions. (Keynes, CW, vol. VIII, p. 288)

Moreover, Keynes maintained that the concepts of vagueness and probability consist of a common ground, that is, inductive reasoning. In contrast to deductive reasoning, inductive reasoning is accompanied by ignorance, incomplete knowledge, and belief. Inductive reasoning is essential to Keynes's theory of probability, hence to his economic writings. Inductive reasoning implies an approach to reasons for supporting the evidence of a sentence. Although probability also indicates a form of logical probability (p), say 1—p, the outcome of probable reasoning is not the proof of a sentence or an assertion. In contrast to inductive reasoning, deductive reasoning provides complete knowledge by applying logical rules within a formal operation.

Keynes not only characterized probability as a pattern of knowledge and rational belief. He also differentiated between ignorance from logic and deductive reasoning on the one hand, and knowledge based on vagueness or probability on the other hand. He underlined the crucial difference:

> As soon as we have passed from the logic of implication and the categories of truth and falsehood to the logic of probability and the categories of knowledge, ignorance, and rational belief, we are paying attention to a new logical relation in which, although it is logical, we were not previously interested, and which cannot be explained or defined in terms of our previous notion. (ibid., p. 8)

Inasmuch as he emphasized categories of knowledge, ignorance and rational belief as elements of the theory of probability, he enlarged this concept in order to also integrate vagueness. Consequently he stated '. . . probability is the study of the grounds which lead us to entertain a rational preference for one belief or another. There are rational grounds other than statistical frequency' (ibid., p. 106). The transformation of categories and concepts is also to be found in his economic theory, in which rational grounds configure market procedures. Judgements under uncertainty imply rational grounds in changing environments (Kahneman 2002). It is for this reason that individual judgement in economic theories should not be restricted to the application of logical symbols – true or (and) false – but to the actual language.

This is also relevant regarding the development of economic theories which cannot be built up by logical symbols or by deductive reasoning only. Such a construction made by logical or deductive symbolism is just an 'empty concept' (Kant) or 'dry bones' (Keynes) (Muchlinski 1996, 2003b). Keynes criticized the constructions of the orthodox theory because it preconfigured certainty, truth and knowledge. Orthodox theory actually eliminates uncertainty, error, and vagueness through its alleged premises and preconditions. By this method it also neglects '. . . the fact that our knowledge of the future is fluctuating, vague, and uncertain' (Keynes, CW, vol. XIV, p. 416). Keynes expounded this statement later on:

> It is reasonable, therefore, to be guided to a considerable degree by the facts about which we feel somewhat confident, even though they may be less decisively relevant to the issue than other facts about which our knowledge is vague and scanty. (Keynes 1936, p. 148)

The constructed economic world of orthodox theory tells a story about how the construction was made by the constructor's chosen methods. It does not tell a story about the world or how economic interactions in markets work. As based on a 'logically perfect language' (Russell) this construction is combined of words, symbols, and formal components and might also be judged as analytically brilliant.

In contradistinction, Keynes's analysis of vagueness, probability, and uncertainty created a new perspective on economic theory and interactions. He provided new concepts for his economic theory, for instance 'vagueness', 'expectations', 'state of confidence', 'animal spirits', 'individual judgement', and 'conventional judgement'. I therefore propose to argue that Keynes was also concerned with conceptual investigations. He criticized the orthodoxy because

> . . . all these pretty, polite techniques, made for a well-panelled Board Room and a nicely regulated market, are liable to collapse. . . . I accuse the classical economic theory of being itself one of these pretty, polite techniques which tries to deal with the present by abstracting from the fact that we know very little about the future. (Keynes, CW, vol. XIII, p. 215)

Even if individual judgement and conventional judgement are replaced by formal symbols this will not lead to a greater understanding and a comprehensive perception of economic problems because the procedure of substitution is only possible by a distinctive method of reduction. This distinctive method of reduction should also be considered by those who construct model views. Keynes wrote: 'Those writers who try to be *strictly* formal generally have no substance' (Keynes, CW, vol. XXIX, pp. 37–8, emphasis in original).

Logical symbols, logic and mathematics, and hence models, are all based on deductive reasoning and should be used as the starting point of reasoning as a cognitive map. Deductive reasoning is not compatible with vagueness and uncertainty. Deductive reasoning also presumes certainty of knowledge in the present and future, since circumstances or context are presumed to be stable or invariantly given. This certainty of deductive reasoning is a result of the pre-arranged, systematic application of pre-determined, fixed rules to a subject. As Keynes commented:

> It is a great fault of symbolic pseudo-mathematical methods of formalising a system of economic analysis . . ., that they expressly assume strict independence between the factors involved and lose all their cogency and authority if this hypothesis is disallowed; . . . [too] large a proportion of recent mathematical economics are merely concoctions. (Keynes 1936, pp. 297–8)

Models should be linked to perceptions of the 'contemporary world'. How is it possible to link mathematics to the contemporary world? This question was also important to Russell and Wittgenstein and a crucial motivation to rebuild their theories (Muchlinski 2006). Both had fundamentally changed their view on mathematics and how it could be applied to social sciences. Russell moved from *Principia Mathematica* (1910) to *Philosophy* and beyond. Wittgenstein moved from the *Tractatus* to a new understanding on logic and its relation to everyday language in the 1920s. His lectures in Cambridge in 1933 to 1934 were dictated as *Blue Book*, his lectures during the session 1934–1935 were dictated as *Brown Book*. Both contributions are important steps in the process of revising the *Tractatus* (Wittgenstein 1979, 1980).

As a contemporary of, and like Wittgenstein, Keynes's scepticism to formal aestheticism in sciences can also be traced back to his view that the scientific process cannot be completely based on a formal approach. Economics is a social science or 'moral science', as Keynes outlined. Economic theory lacks fundamental presumptions which are indeed necessary to construct a hard science, such as mathematics. To describe economic interactions in markets requires inductive reasoning. Otherwise market interaction would have to be treated as a particular rule or as a norm.

Given this view as sketched in the last sentence, economic decisions, individual judgement and actions should be deduced from market interaction as a predefined rule. To conceive of markets as predefined rules implies the view that 'the markets know'. If markets know how to decide, to judge and to act, why should we consider vagueness, uncertainty, state of confidence or expectations of the agents in markets? The next step could be to analyse market interactions as mathematical economics. Furthermore why should we be concerned with failures of markets or with the need for probability judgements about market procedures if we have modelled our contemporary world as sound and coherent mathematic systems? At this point, economics as a social science has to be seen differently: 'In writing economics one is not writing either a mathematical proof or a legal document' (Keynes, CW, vol. XXIX, p. 151). In an earlier draft of *The General Theory* Keynes argued that '. . . much economic theorising to-day suffers, I think, because it attempts to apply highly precise and mathematical methods to material which is itself much too vague to support such treatment' (Keynes, CW, vol. XIV, p. 379).

Keynes also insisted on the need to acknowledge the difference between the present and the future as important guidelines to economic decisions: the present is not a discounted future. Here the concept of expectation fills in the gap. The differentiated view on the present and the future brings our attention again to Wittgenstein who might have completed Keynes's thinking immediately by claiming '. . . we can only foresee what we ourselves construct' (Wittgenstein 1974, No.5.556; 1979, p. 71e).

To apply mathematics to the perceived world and experience requires adjusting the observations, considerations, and sentences of everyday language to make them fit the formal symbols of mathematics. In social science this procedure should be implemented as carefully as possible because

> . . . theoretical economics often has a formal appearance where the reality is not strictly formal. It is not, and is not meant to be, logically watertight in the sense in which mathematics is. It is a generalisation which lacks precise statement of the cases to which the generalisation applies. (Keynes, CW, vol. XXIX, pp. 36–8)

Keynes was not interested in constructed world views composed of market procedures presumed to work on rules or rigidly fixed rules which tend to equilibrium at all times and at all places. Actually he was not at all concerned with economics as presumed mechanisms. The notion that reading and understanding Keynes's economics as a social science enterprise in which language-based interaction configure the economic world seems to be related to the later work of Wittgenstein published posthumously.

Keynes's method of conceptualizing economics as a social science comes to a preliminary fruition in Chapter 12 of *The General Theory* where Keynes considered why economics is a result of language-based actions and interaction surrounded by uncertainty and the need to grasp the 'average opinion' or conventional judgement in markets. Consequently he asked under which conditions the economic decisions and actions lead to particular results regarding vagueness, uncertainty, and incompleteness of knowledge or probability respectively. Against the background of the theory of knowledge which he had developed *A Treatise*, he focused on individual judgement and conventional judgement within the realm of uncertainty and vagueness (Muchlinski 2003a).

Keynes did not adhere to Adam Smith's theory of the 'invisible hand' in order to outline how markets function. In one of his early lectures held in Cambridge, he explained his methodological approach to social science:

> . . . a definition can often be *vague* within fairly wide limits and capable of several interpretations differing slightly from one another, and still be perfectly serviceable and free from serious risk of leading either the author or the reader into error. (Keynes, CW, vol. XXIX, pp. 36–8, emphasis in original)

As Wittgenstein outlined the turning point of his later project on everyday language, words, and sentences are recognizable irrespective of having a sharp boundary or of being defined rigidly regarding the context in which the words and sentences are used. Shortly after the publication of *Tractatus* Wittgenstein started on this project which involved discussions with Keynes, Ramsey, Russell and Sraffa. His objections to the demand of exactness or perfectly defined notions are found in Wittgenstein 1958a, §76 and §88.

Keynes also contended with the demand of exactness and a dominating use of mathematics in social science:

> If an author tries to avoid all vagueness, and to be perfectly precise, he will become so prolix and pedantic, will find it necessary to split so many hairs, and will be so constantly diverted into an attempt to clear up some other part of the subject, that he himself may perhaps never reach the matter at hand and the reader certainly will not. (ibid.)

If one tried to create a perfect exact language with sharp boundaries, one would not reach any conclusion (see Keynes 1936, p. 4). The search for exactness and non-ambiguous words, sentences or propositions is doomed to fail because it would only lead to formal aestheticism. Keynes argued that sentences and propositions are understandable in relation to their use in concrete circumstances, for example, a *corpus of knowledge*:

> To speak of propositions as certain or probable, this expresses strictly a relationship in which they stand to a *corpus* of knowledge, actual or hypothetical, and not a characteristic of the proposition in themselves. (Keynes, CW, vol. VIII, p. 4, emphasis in original)

Economics as a social science uses everyday language to develop theories and hypothesis. Quantitative methods should be implemented carefully.

> Economics is being a moral science. . . . It deals with introspection and judgments of value. I might have added that it deals with motives, expectations, psychological uncertainties. One has to be constantly on guard against treating the material as constant and homogeneous. (Keynes, CW, vol. XIV, p. 300)

It is not surprising that Keynes objected to the demand of exactness and sharp borders of sentences while emphasizing that economic decisions and interactions have their roots not in formal exactness but rather in the habits of everyday life or 'forms of life'. He accused neoclassic economics of focusing only on marginal cost, marginal revenues and marginal yields because of their exactness and measurability. In such an unshakeable and ideal search for formal exactness they overlook the 'whole' and therefore the relevant details of the research.

ON THE STATE OF CONFIDENCE

Keynes created the concept state of confidence in order to describe the situational vagueness and uncertainty in which a person is forced to anchor the decision-making processes and expectations. The state of confidence is not grounded in the application of logic or mathematic symbols, but rather in the fact that the 'justification comes to an end' (Wittgenstein 1969, p. 192; see also Keynes 1936, p. 161). In other words, the infinite regress of justification is brought to an arbitrary end. Keynes emphasized 'uncertainty' and 'conventional judgement' in describing why the language in use and understanding are major factors to consider. Otherwise it would not be possible to anchor the decision-making process. According the uncertainty, and how to create a confident surrounding, Wittgenstein also referred to the situational context as 'forms of life' and 'parts of speech' which are configured by interactions: 'Here the term "language-*game*" is meant to bring into prominence the fact that the *speaking* of language is part of an activity, or of a form of life' (Wittgenstein 1958a § 23, emphasis in original).

This interdependence of concepts, actions, individual judgements, decisions, and everyday language was of great importance for Keynes's work. He proposed conceptual investigations on classical theory to expound his distinctive considerations concerning the interrelations of economic development, hence employment, interest and money. Without a shadow of doubt Keynes opposed rigidly fixed rules in his economic thinking regarding international economics and monetary economics (Moggridge 1986; Muchlinski 2005a, 2003b).

Economics as a social science is an inexact science. It deals with norms, values, motives, judgements, and expectations (Akerlof 2007). Incomplete knowledge and uncertainty surround every decision-making procedure. The decision-making procedure hence needs to be anchored because experience teaches us what *had* happened but not what *will* happen, as both Keynes and Wittgenstein emphasized. Familiarity teaches us after a period of similar experience that we can trust in similar situations. However, a judgement like 'I know how to decide and to judge' is reasonable as linked to other evidence of the agent's knowing within the perceived circumstances. Judgement under uncertainty implies relying on one's own decision and on a '*corpus* of knowledge' which is part of changing contexts. 'We must consider, that is to say, the probability which is relative not to actual knowledge but to the whole of certain kind of knowledge' (Keynes, CW, vol. VIII, p. 318). Changing contexts or circumstances do not have sharp boundaries. The individual has to build up his own judgement and then to connect this knowledge with that of other individuals who are in comparable situations. Keynes pictured this kind of judgement by using a metaphor:

> For it is, so to speak, a game of Snap, of Old Maid, of Musical Chairs – a pastime in which he is victor who says *Snap* neither too soon nor too late, who passed the Old Maid to his neighbour before the game is over, who secures a chair for himself when the music stops. These games can be played with zest and enjoyment, though all the players know that it is the Old Maid which is circulating, or that when the music stops some of the players will find themselves unseated. (Keynes 1936, p. 156, emphasis in original)

Keynes described how we anchor our judgements under uncertainty by creating a connection between the perception of 'the existing market valuation' and 'our existing knowledge' (ibid., p. 152). The individual does not rely on 'arithmetically equal probabilities' to stabilize his own capability to act and to decide. Keynes's considerations are also to be found in cognitive science (Gigerenzer 2004). The individual anchors his decision-making procedure under uncertainty by relying on conventional judgements which '. . . will be compatible with considerable measure of continuity and stability in our affairs, so long as we can rely on the maintenance of the convention' (Keynes 1936, p. 152). In a situation of uncertainty and 'state of ignorance', mathematical probability or mathematical expectations do not provide certainty to make a decision. That is, any mathematical calculation or expectation needs to be supported by individual judgement: '. . . individual initiative will only be adequate when reasonable calculation is supplemented and supported by animal spirits' (ibid., p. 162). We are also forced to rely on our own judgement as perceived in relation to the conventional judgement as presumed correct according to the circumstances. Trust or state of confidence is a prerequisite of action and decision-making within the realm of uncertainty.

Since uncertainty is the landscape of everyday decisions, economic agents create certainty or a state of confidence in order to stabilize the fragile border of the decision-making procedure based on inductive reasoning. This creation is not grounded in logical foundations. Any use of inductive reasoning implies vagueness of judgement. Agents in the markets, either financial or good markets, regularly act on the basis of the assumption that their perceptions of present events and expectations of future events are shared by other agents, no matter whether these expectations are rational or not.

In the light of Keynes's writings, rational expectations are not deductive operations to a mathematical term but rather to individual and conventional judgements (Muchlinski 2003a). Wittgenstein similarly emphasized trust in a particular situation in order to make the 'language game' successful (Wittgenstein 1969, § 509).

Keynes described this reliance on one's own view in relation to the perceived views of other agents as follows:

> Most, probably, of our decisions to do something positive, the full consequences of which will be drawn out over many days to come, can only be taken as a result of animal spirits – of a spontaneous urge to action rather than inaction, and not as the outcome of a weighted average of quantitative benefits multiplied by quantitative probabilities. (Keynes 1936, p. 161)

The metaphor 'animal spirits' implies a particular state of confidence and trust in a particular situation. A necessary condition of creating a state of confidence is that it is perceived and shared by other agents in the market.[3] To say that an individual creates his own private state of confidence makes no sense. A state of confidence cannot be private. This is also true for the use of language as Russell and Wittgenstein stressed.

In Keynes's view agents create certainty as a convention through the use of everyday language interactions. Wittgenstein similarly pointed to agreement in situational contexts: 'That is not agreement in opinion but in form of life' (Wittgenstein 1958a, § 241). Agents directly take possession of the commodity or product, or the option to buy or to sell, without having doubts. In creating a state of confidence heterogeneous agents create a kind of certainty or state of confidence homogeneously. This is comparable to a building and its supporting foundations. The process of constructing a building requires a foundation in the same way that decision-making needs to be based on an 'unmoving foundation of a language game' used by the language of the everyday and not formal symbolism (Wittgenstein 1969, § 403).

The foundation is an indication of trust and provides a reason for the expectations-building procedure. Inasmuch as many agents trust in the foundation, agents try to jump on the bandwagon and to benefit as they think others will. Keynes claimed that in the light of 'average opinion', investors do attempt to succeed unconventionally rather than to fail conventionally (Keynes 1936, pp. 156, 158). In reverse, every agent tries to get off the bandwagon before it crashes. Therefore the action of an individual is in every respect related to the perceived expectations or state of confidence of other agents in the market, or to 'conventional judgement'. Keynes concluded: '. . . it needs more intelligence to defeat the forces of time and our ignorance of the future than to beat the gun' (ibid., p. 157).

He also explained these movements by agents succinctly in Chapter 12: 'The actual, private object of the most skilled investment to-day, is "to beat the gun", as the Americans too well express it, to outwit the crowd, and to pass the bad, or depreciating, half-crown to the other fellow' (ibid., p. 155). This 'battle of wits' is anchored in conventional judgement of market procedures, '. . . it can be played by professionals amongst themselves' (ibid.).

This view on professional play depicts more than just a game for fun. It is a play linked to economic institutions, norms, values, and rules. Decision-making and judgements under uncertainty might be described as a game within a broader context.

> The state of long-term expectation, upon which our decisions are based . . . depends on the *confidence*. . . . The *state of confidence* . . . is a matter to which practical men always pay the closest and most anxious attention. . . . There is, however, not much to be said about the state of confidence *a priori* . . . Since expectations only indicate some aspects a judgment can be based on, uncertainty is the landscape of every action. (ibid., p. 148, emphasis in original)

Consequently Keynes stated, 'by uncertain knowledge let me explain, I do not mean merely to distinguish what is known for certain from what is only probably. . . . *We simply do not know*' (ibid., emphasis in original).

'We simply do not know' is not to be confused with the 'know nothingism' as Blinder in his book on central banks explained (Blinder 1998, p. 6). The literature on central banks and their decision-making procedures under uncertainty has started to consider and revise important concepts (see Blinder et al. 2001; Muchlinski 2005b). Also economics as science changes all the time and hence the economic background also constantly shifts. It is this background as a whole against which we judge upon decisions, actions, regard our concepts, meaning and methods. Therefore concepts, conceptual investigations, meaning, methods, and models must be flexible.

It is a crucial characteristic of scientific procedure to change, to rebuild and to reorient concepts, meaning, methods, and models when they do not fit the contemporary world. Judgements about the market have to be constantly renewed. Only when one lives in a 'panelled-board room' or sees oneself as a representative of the premises of classical or neoclassical world one will be embedded in certainty without any need to change one's perceptions and considerations. In contrast to this artificiality of a constructed world, judgement under uncertainty necessitates the orientation to a common background, Keynes stated: 'In practice we have tacitly agreed . . . to fall back on what is . . . a *convention*' (Keynes 1936, p. 152, emphasis in original). As was argued at the beginning of this chapter the reliance on convention does not eliminate uncertainty or vagueness. We have to acknowledge and deal with them because they cannot be eliminated by mathematical calculation.

The foregoing considerations have already emphasized the importance in Keynes's writings of expectations as embedded in circumstances that surround any decision-making procedure. I would like to add a further aspect. Expectations are part of everyday expressed judgements. Neither judgements nor expectations are mental states or inner processes but rather language-based interaction and hence articulations in concrete circumstances (Muchlinski 2006). Expectations are articulated in decision-making procedures hence expectation can be understood as interpretation of symbols, words and sentences regarding particular circumstances and contexts as well as the perceived conventional judgement of other agents in the market. Expectations or judgements are only perceivable as expressed expectations or judgements. This means that they also function as indicators regarding prospective events. Therefore they are connected with reality. In contrast to that is the expectation to win the lottery. I do not say, 'I expect to win the lottery this Saturday'. As linked with reality any expectation configures our perception and also our methods and concepts (Wittgenstein 1958a, § 445, 1958b, pp. 41–2).

CONCLUDING REMARKS

I have tried to pay particular attention to Keynes's economic theory by concentrating on two elements in his writings: 'vagueness' and 'state of confidence'. Keynes's guiding concern is here to criticize our habit of relying on presupposed concepts such as rigid rules in order to escape from vagueness and uncertainty which are the essential features of changing circumstances and contexts. The attempt to rely exclusively on a formal approach to economics is a complete failure as a solution to economic problems. The constructed economic world of orthodox theory tells a story about how the construction was made by the constructor's preferred methods. It does not tell a story about the perceptions of different circumstances and how economic interactions in markets work. As based on a 'logically perfect language' (Russell) this construction is combined of words, symbols and formal components and might also be judged as analytically brilliant.

In contrast, Keynes's analysis of vagueness, probability, and uncertainty created a new perspective on economic theory and interactions. He provided new concepts for his economic theory, for instance 'vagueness', 'state of confidence', 'animal spirits', 'individual judgement', and 'conventional judgement'. Consequently I argue that Keynes was also concerned with conceptual investigations.

NOTES

1. I wish to thank Susan Hechler for her help in editing the English manuscript.
2. Wittgenstein criticized the system of logic relation to which Russell adhered until 1918 because it lacked a link to the contemporary world and experience. As a result of this criticism Russell abandoned this position. In a similar move, Wittgenstein abandoned a view which he had defended in *Tractatus Logico-Philosophicus* shortly after its publication.
3. The current financial crisis (2007–2010) indicates that expectations are shared, irrespective of being rational or irrational. See Akerlof and Shiller (2009).

BIBLIOGRAPHY

Akerlof, G. (2007), 'The missing motivation in macroeconomics. Presidential address', *American Economic Review*, **96**(1) (March), 3–36.

Akerlof, G. and R. Shiller (2009), *Animal Spirits. How Human Psychology Drives the Economy and Why it Matters for Global Capitalism*, Princeton, NJ: Princeton University Press.

Bateman, B. (1990), 'Keynes, induction, and econometrics', *History of Political Economy*, **22**(2) (Summer), 359–79.

Blinder, A. (1998), *Central Banking in Theory and Practice (The Lionel Robbins Lectures)*, Cambridge, MA: MIT Press.

Blinder, A., C. Goodhart, P. Hildebrand, D. Lipton, and C. Wyplosz (eds) (2001), *How Do Central Banks Talk?*, Geneva Reports on the World Economy no. 3, Geneva and Oxford: International Centre for Monetary and Banking Studies.

Carabelli, A. (1988), *On Keynes's Method*, London: Macmillan.

Davis, J. (1994), *Keynes's Philosophical Development*, Cambridge: Cambridge University Press.

Davis, J. (1996), 'Convergences in Keynes and Wittgenstein's later views', *The European Journal of the History of Economic Thought*, **3**(3), 433–48.

Dostaler, G. (2005), *Keynes et ses combats*, Paris: Albin Michel.

Gigerenzer, G. (2004), 'Fast and frugal heuristics: the tools of bounded rationality', in D. Koehler and N. Harvey (eds), *Blackwell Handbook of Judgment and Decision-making*, Oxford: Blackwell, pp. 62–88.

Green, K. (2007), *Bertrand Russell, language and linguistic theory*, London: Continuum.

Hillard, J. (1995), 'Keynes, interdependence and the monetary production economy', in S. Dow and J. Hillard (eds), *Keynes, Knowledge and Uncertainty*, Aldershot, UK and Brookfield, VT, USA: Edward Elgar, pp. 244–63.

Hilmy, S. (1987), *The Later Wittgenstein. The Emergence of a New Philosophical Method*, Oxford: Blackwell Oxford University.

Kahneman, D. (2002), 'Map of bounded rationality: psychology for behavioural economics', *American Economic Review*, **93**(5) (December), 1449–75.

Keynes, J. M. (1904–1910), *Manuscripts*, The Provost and Scholars of King's College, Cambridge University.

Keynes, J. M. (1936), *The General Theory of Employment, Interest, and Money*, London: Macmillan.

Keynes, J. M. (1971–1989), *The Collected Writings of John Maynard Keynes*, London:

Macmillan/Cambridge University Press for the Royal Economic Society.
  Vol. VIII: *A Treatise on Probability*
  Vol. XIII: *The General Theory and After, Part 1: Preparation*
  Vol. XIV: *The General Theory and After, Part 2: Defence and Development*
  Vol. XXIX: *The General Theory and After: A Supplement (to Vols. XIII and XIV)*

Moggridge, D. (1986), 'Keynes and the international monetary system 1909–1946', in J. Cohen (ed.), *International Monetary Problems and Supply-Side-Economics. Essays in Honour of Lorie Tarshis*, Basingstoke: Macmillan, pp. 56–83.

Moggridge, D. (1992), *Maynard Keynes. An Economist's Biography*, London: Routledge.

Monk, R. (1990), *Ludwig Wittgenstein. The Duty of Genius*, London: Penguin Books.

Muchlinski, E. (1996), *Keynes' Philosophy*, Berlin: Duncker & Humblot.

Muchlinski, E. (1998), 'The philosophy of John Maynard Keynes – a reconsideration', *Cahiers d' Économie Politique. Histoire de la Pensée et Théories*, no. 30-31, Paris/Montreal: L'Harmattan, pp. 227–53.

Muchlinski, E. (2003a), 'Knowledge, knowledge sharing and convention in Keynes' thinking', in E. Helmstädter (ed.), *The Economics of Knowledge Sharing*, Cheltenham, UK and Northampton, MA, USA: Edward Elgar, pp. 115–29.

Muchlinski, E. (2003b), 'Against rigid rules – Keynes's economic theory', discussion paper of the Free University of Berlin, accessed 12 December 2007 at http://econpapers.repec.org/paper/wpawuwpma/0503018.html.

Muchlinski, E. (2005a), 'Controversies in international monetary policy: a retrospective look at Keynes-White-Boughton & IMF', *Intervention. Zeitschrift für Ökonomie*, **2**, 57–73.

Muchlinski, E. (2005b), 'Central banks: reasons to creative ambiguity', in J. Hölscher and H. Tomann (eds), *Globalization of Capital Markets and Monetary Policy*, Basingstoke: Palgrave Macmillan, pp. 130–47.

Muchlinski, E. (2006), *What Does Wittgenstein Mean With "It is in Language That it's all Done"?* in German, Berlin: Logos Verlag.

Muchlinski, E. (2008), 'Keynes', in S. Gosepath, W. Hinsch and B. Rössler (eds), *Handbuch für Politische Philosophie und Sozialphilosophie*, Berlin, New York: Walter de Gruyter, pp. 604–8.

Muchlinski, E. (2011), *Central Banks and Coded Language. Risks or Benefits?*, Basingstoke: Palgrave Macmillan.

O'Donnell, R. (1989), *Keynes: Philosophy, Economics and Politics. The Philosophical Foundations of Keynes's Thought and Their Influence on his Economics and Politics*, Basingstoke: Macmillan.

Rorty, R. (1991), 'Inquiry as recontextualisation: an anti-dualist account of interpretation', in D. Hiley (ed.), *The Interpretative Turn. Philosophy, Science, Culture*, Ithaca, NY: Cornell University Press, pp. 59–80.

Russell, B. (1986), 'The philosophy of logical atomism and other essays 1914–1919', in J. Slater (ed.), *The Collected Papers of Bertrand Russell*, vol. 8, London: George Allen & Unwin, pp. 157–244.

Wittgenstein, L. (1958a), *Philosophical Investigations*, translated by G. Anscombe, Englewood Cliffs, NJ: Prentice Hall.

Wittgenstein, L. (1958b), *Preliminary Studies for The "Philosophical Investigations"*, generally known as The Blue and Brown Books, Oxford: Basil Blackwell & Mott, Ltd.

Wittgenstein, L. (1969), *On Certainty*, G. Anscombe and G. von Wright (eds), translated by Denis Paul and G. Anscombe, New York: Harper & Row.

Wittgenstein, L. (1974), *Tractatus Logico-Philosophicus*, translated by D. Pears and B. McGuiness, introduction by Bertrand Russell, London: Routledge.

Wittgenstein, L. (1979), *Wittgenstein's Lectures, Cambridge 1932–1935. From the Notes of Alice Ambrose and Margaret Macdonald*, Alice Ambrose (ed.), Oxford: Basil Blackwell.

Wittgenstein, L. (1980), *Wittgenstein's Lectures, Cambridge, 1930–1932. From the Notes of John King and Desmond Lee*, D. Lee (ed.), Oxford: Basil Blackwell.

PART II

The General Theory and the history of macroeconomics

4. Dead or alive? The ebbs and flows of Keynesianism over the history of macroeconomics

Michel DeVroey

INTRODUCTION

A fine way to make sense of the history of a given discipline is to bring out the milestones that marked its unfolding. When it comes to macroeconomics, the subject of this chapter, two such milestones come to mind at once. The first is of course John Maynard Keynes's *The General Theory of Employment, Interest, and Money* (1936). While Keynes's book was the fountainhead of the new discipline, the direction that it took was shaped by Hicks when he devised the IS-LM model. The second benchmark is the radical transformation that this discipline underwent in the late 1970s and early 1980s with the overthrowing of Keynesian macroeconomics and its replacement by what later became called dynamic stochastic general equilibrium (DSGE) macroeconomics, under Robert Lucas's leadership. My aim in this chapter is to recount these developments.[1]

I start with describing the emergence of Keynesian macroeconomics and move to explaining its fall under Friedman's and Lucas's successive attacks. Next, I discuss the emergence of new classical macroeconomics, the first instalment of the DSGE approach. I then assess the eventually vain attempts of new Keynesian economists to refute Lucas's claims. I study the real business cycle models initiated by Kydland and Prescott, which transformed Lucas's qualitative style of modelling into a quantitative style. Finally, I examine a further transformation within DSGE approach, models that are labelled either as new neoclassical synthesis or New Keynesian Phillips curve models. The chapter concludes with an examination of the question of the present crisis on the future development of macroeconomic theory. Unfortunately, this is a question to which historians of theory cannot really answer (nor for that matter other scholars). In my concluding remarks, I shall nonetheless make a few observations on this subject in the light of the observations presented in the course of this chapter.

Macroeconomics is a politically-laden field. This follows from its very object, the study of the ideal way of organizing the working of the economy and the policies that need to be taken to achieve this purpose. Two main views on this matter coexist: the defence of what is called the 'free market', i.e. full economic liberalism, and a more moderate conception of economic liberalism, a view which supports the market system but admits to its possible failures and to the need for an active role of the government in remedying upon them. This second view is associated with Keynes, the former with Friedman, Lucas and his followers. Most people hold a firm standpoint on this divide. Perfectly fine with me, except that I think that historians of economics should be the exception here and refrain from taking sides. This is the methodological position that I shall adopt.

THE EMERGENCE OF KEYNESIAN MACROECONOMICS

The emergence of macroeconomics as a specific sub-discipline, and by the same token the emergence of Keynesian macroeconomics, was a three-step process. The first step was Keynes's *The General Theory*, the second was the invention of the IS-LM model by John Hicks and its subsequent transformation by Franco Modigliani, and the third the creation of macroeconometric models under the impulse, first, of Jan Tinbergen and, subsequently, of Lawrence Klein.

Keynes

Keynes was already a towering figure in the economic profession as well as in the world of policy decision-making in the UK and internationally renowned before he wrote *The General Theory*; but, beyond doubt, this book put him definitively in the pantheon of great economists. A versatile personality, Keynes was mainly a monetary economist. Although he had a good foot in academics, his main activity was to be an expert on monetary matters advising the British government and international organizations, formally and informally. But the Great Depression prompted him to tackle more theoretical matters.

Without the Great Depression, *The General Theory* would certainly not have seen the light of day. Keynes's aim when writing it was to elucidate the causes of the phenomenon of mass unemployment that affected all economies in those years and the policy measures that should be taken to solve the problem. This was a time of great disarray with no remedy at hand to fix the ailing economic system. Existing economic theory proved to be of little help both for understanding what was happening and indicating the measures to be taken. In most countries the unemployment rate was soaring and deflationary policies had been met with failure. In contrast, market rationing had no room in economic theory. The notion of frictional unemployment had started to be evoked but it had no theoretical status. Its only policy prescription was that any decrease in real wage that could occur would be a good thing. So economic theory, Keynes realized, was blatantly wanting, and needed to be reformed. He was hardly alone in believing this. A feeling of malaise was widespread in the profession. Academic economists were torn between their expertise and their instinct. According to economic theory, unemployment could not but have been caused by too high real wages and decreasing them was the remedy. Yet their instinct told them that this was untrue and that the remedy lay in state-induced demand activation. In Keynes's words:

> A classical economist may sympathize with labour in refusing to accept a cut in its money-wage, and he will admit that it may not be wise to make it to meet conditions which are temporary; but scientific integrity forces him to declare that this refusal is, nevertheless, at the bottom of the trouble. (Keynes 1936, p. 16)

Keynes's book, which was mainly addressed to his fellow economists, aimed at solving this deadlock by providing a theoretical basis for economists' gut feelings. The first task to be addressed, Keynes believed, was to fill the lacuna of the absence of a notion such as involuntary unemployment in existing economic theory while it looked obvious in the context of the time that the mass of unemployed people had not chosen their fate. He also perceived that this phenomenon should be accounted for in general equilibrium terms (although he did not use the word). That is, involuntary unemployment might well be a labour market phenomenon but its origin had to be looked for in other parts of the economy. Partial equilibrium analysis *à la* Marshall could not do. Finally, Keynes also wanted to exonerate too high wages of being the cause of involuntary unemployment, an exoneration implying that wage decreases could not be the remedy. His diagnosis as to the basic reason of the labour market failure was that it was due to a deficiency in aggregate demand, itself the result of insufficient investment. The remedy he proposed was a state-induced demand activation combined with a policy of low interest rates as well as some dose of income redistribution. To Keynes all these measures were hardly amounting to introducing socialism. On the contrary, their aim was to avoid its arising and to preserve democratic capitalism.

To make his claim, Keynes developed a rich and subtle argument and introduced a series of new concepts in the lexicon of economic theory (effective demand, involuntary unemployment, preference for liquidity, marginal efficiency of capital, etc.). However, it must be admitted, for all Keynes's maestria, his reasoning remained obscure. Not only did he develop his argument at distinct levels of abstraction without bringing them together, but also many passages of his book were almost undecipherable. Several reasons explain. Aiming at generalizing Marshallian theory was a totally new enterprise, and for that matter a daunting one the achievement of which might have required long years of work without guarantee of success. Keynes, in contrast, was pushed by a feeling of urgency. What mattered to him was to pave the way, and he was ready to leave the finessing job for others. Moreover, he was an extraordinarily gifted and inspired writer able to shift from technical argument to pure rhetoric. These factors, combined with the fact that there was a strong demand for a new theory of the kind Keynes proposed, explains that, despite its flaws, *The General Theory* got an enthusiastic reception especially among young economists. Dissatisfied with existing theory, they were crying for a new theory that would justify getting away from the laissez-faire doctrine, and Keynes's work delivered on these two scores. Dissenting views, focusing on the shortcomings of Keynes's reasoning, were expressed but the pressure to produce a new theoretical framework that might account for the obvious dysfunctions in the market system was such that they were hardly listened to. Nevertheless, the perplexity as to the central message of Keynes's book was great, even amongst his admirers. The following extract from Samuelson is a fine testimony:

> *The General Theory* caught most economists under the age of thirty-five with the unexpected violence of a disease first attacking and decimating an isolated tribe of south sea islanders. Economists beyond fifty turned out to be quite immune to ailment. With time, most economists in-between began to run the fever, often without knowing or admitting their condition. . . . And I think I am giving away no secrets when I solemnly aver – upon the basis of vivid personal recollection – that no one else in Cambridge, Massachusetts, really knew what it was about for some twelve to eighteen months after its publication. Indeed, until the mathematical models of Meade, Lange, Hicks and Harrod, there is reason to believe that Keynes himself did not truly understand his own analysis. (Samuelson 1964, pp. 315–16)

The IS-LM Model

As stated by Samuelson, the central message of *The General Theory* was clarified after a session of the Econometric Society Conference taking place in Oxford and which was devoted to the book. James Meade (1937), R. F. Harrod (1937) and John Hicks (1937) gave three distinct papers about it.[2] All three saw it as their first task to reconstruct the classical model in order to assess whether Keynes's claim that his model was more general than the classical was right. They all concluded against Keynes's claim. Their interpretations were also rather similar. The three papers were more than review articles: they offered a reconstruction of Keynes's insights that made them more easily understandable to economists while at the same time cutting off its most unorthodox edges. One of the papers presented at the Oxford Conference was promised to an extraordinary future, Hicks's piece, containing the first version of what was to become the IS-LM model. In order to compare Keynes's views with those of the 'classics', Hicks transformed Keynes's reasoning in prose into a simple system of simultaneous equations. He also conceived of an ingenious way of allowing the joined outcome of three different markets to be represented in a single graph. The IS-LM model became the main benchmark in the development of macroeconomics, to the point that one wonders what would have become of *The General Theory* had Hicks's interpretation not seen the light of day. Eventually, however, it is not Hicks's own model that became the workhorse of the new discipline but a model that resulted from Modigliani's recasting of it (Modigliani 1944).[3]

The third and final stage in the emergence of macroeconomics consisted of transforming qualitative models into empirically testable ones. An author who played an inaugural role in this respect is Jan Tinbergen. Like Keynes, he was a reformer, motivated by the will to understand the Great Depression and to develop policies that would impede its return. Tinbergen's League of Nations study of business fluctuations in the US from 1919 to 1932 (Tinbergen 1939) can be pinpointed as the first econometric model bearing on a whole economy. The main impulse, however, was due to Lawrence Klein. In his book, *The Keynesian Revolution* (Klein 1948), he commented that Keynes's concepts were crying out for a confrontation to the data. Implementing this idea became his life's task. His 1955 monograph co-authored with A. S. Goldberger (Klein and Goldberger 1955), *An Econometric Model of the United States*, introducing the celebrated Klein-Goldberger model, marked the start of a colossal line of works.

It was a 'medium size' model, and was truly intended (at the time) to be an up-to-date working model, applicable to practical economic problems like those encountered in business cycle forecasting. A distinctive feature of the model was that it was not viewed as a 'once-and-for-all' effort. It was presented as a part of a more continuous program in which new data, reformulations and extrapolations were constantly being studied. The model consisted of 15 structural equations, five identities and five tax-transfer auxiliary relationships. It was estimated by the limited information maximum likelihood technique and was based on the annual observations from the split sample period 1924–41, 1946–52. (Bodkin et al. 1991, p. 57)

Several evolutions concurred to make this new development possible: the emergence of the IS-LM model on the theoretical side, new and more rigorous statistical estimation methods, the systematic construction of national data bases, the invention of new calculation methods eventually leading to emergence of computers. Klein took advantage of these innovations. He almost single-handedly created a new sub-discipline, macroeconomic modelling. For the first time, governments had at their disposition a quantitative macrodynamic model concerned with the economy as a whole that they could use to help the elaboration of their policy.

The high technicality involved in the construction of these successive generations of model should not hide their Keynesian nature. In effect, they rested on the unquestioned idea that excess supply was a recurrent feature of both the labour and the goods markets. In other words, they had a disequilibrium substratum.

The Heyday of Keynesian Macroeconomics

The 1950s, the 1960s and the first years of the 1970s were the heydays of Keynesian macroeconomics. It seemed that, thanks to Keynesian precepts, business cycle fluctuations had been tamed to such an extent that many macroeconomists were not afraid to proclaim them a phenomenon of the past. On the theoretical front, the new scientific community of macroeconomics was thriving unified around the Keynesian paradigm while the notion of a neoclassical synthesis, introduced by Paul Samuelson, served as a mantle allowing the avoidance of any deep conflicts between micro- and macroeconomists. That arrangement allowed each of these communities to cultivate its own garden and to keep economics running smoothly. Intellectually, it meant that the concern of Keynesian theory was short-period disequilibrium phenomena while microeconomics was concerned with the long-period state of equilibrium to arise after adjustments have come to an end.

This was also a time where the notion of Keynesianism or being a 'Keynesian' was unambiguous in its bringing together two possible meanings of the term. The first, more ideological (without giving a pejorative connotation to this term) refers to a vision as to how the economy ought to be organized – leaving the supremacy to market forces but having governments ready to act in an auxiliary way when market failures happen to arise. The second refers to the use of a precise conceptual apparatus, the IS-LM model, itself flowing from a Marshall-Keynes-Hicks lineage. Most, if not all, macroeconomists were Keynesians on these two scores. Table 4.1 presents a framework that will enable me to capture the successive splits that will unfold later on, and summarizes this state of affairs.

Table 4.1   *Characterizing Keynesian macroeconomics in terms of the*
             Keynesian/non-Keynesian criterion

	The Marshallian approach *(the Marshall-Keynes-Hicks line)*	The Walrasian approach
The policy viewpoint defended	*Defense of demand activation* *Defense of the free market*	– **Keynes's *General Theory*** – **IS-LM model**

THE FALL OF KEYNESIAN MACROECONOMICS

Keynesian theory had always its opponents but it took time for this opposition to be transformed in a powerful movement. The two names to be
evoked in this respect are those of Milton Friedman and Robert Lucas.
Friedman criticized Keynesian policy conclusions while choosing to
reason in terms of the Keynesian methodology and conceptual apparatus.
In contrast, Lucas led an all-out attack, bearing both on policy conclusion
and method, which changed the course of macroeconomics.

Friedman

Friedman was a fierce opponent of Keynesian theory from the beginning of his intellectual career. Like Keynes, he developed his argument
along two lines, sometimes addressing the wide public – as in his famous
Capitalism and Freedom book – sometimes engaged in advanced academic
work. Over the years, his status in the profession changed from that of
an outlier, whose ideas were often mocked, to that of a highly respected
scholar. Of all his papers, one of the most influential was his Presidential
Address to the 1967 meeting of the American Economic Association
(Friedman 1968) in which he proposed a re-interpretation of the Phillips
curve, the so-called expectations-augmented Phillips curve model.

The Friedman address is a short text which, on examination, can be
judged as confused. Still, it marked a decisive point in the evolution of ideas.
Whereas, on first reading, the criticism he advances seems to be modest and
of limited scope – the conciliatory tone he adopts is not unrelated to this
impression – in fact, it is devastating. Friedman's stroke of genius was to
realize that the Phillips curve, which had become a cornerstone of Keynesian
theory, could actually be used as a weapon against Keynesian policy recommendations, as much from the conceptual point of view as in terms of policy

*Table 4.2   Characterizing monetarism in terms of the Keynesian/non-
Keynesian criterion*

		The Marshallian approach (*the Marshall-Keynes-Hicks line*)	The Walrasian approach
The policy viewpoint defended	*Defense of demand activation*	– Keynes – IS-LM model	
	Defense of the free market	– **Monetarism (Friedman)**	

implications. The received view was that the Phillips curve was stable over time. This allowed Paul Samuelson and Robert Solow (1960) to point out that it offered a policy-menu for governments, a trade-off between unemployment and inflation. Friedman claimed, first, that such a trade-off could exist only as a temporary phenomenon, the result of workers' misperception of the effects of monetary policy and, second, that any attempt to use the Phillips curve for implementing a policy based on an inflation/unemployment trade-off led to its displacement. From the policy viewpoint this amounted to an indictment of the more general view that governments could use monetary policy as a means to durably increase employment. Moreover, Friedman made his claim on the eve of the stagflation years, to the effect that these could be invoked as the demonstration of the rightfulness of his views. This was a severe blow to Keynesian theory, and at the time Keynesian economists were at a loss as how to rebut Friedman's attack.

However, Friedman's contribution should not be viewed as a rejection of Keynes's conceptual apparatus. Keynes and Friedman shared the same methodological viewpoint and a common belonging to the Marshallian framework. Moreover, when requested to put his claim in a broader theoretical perspective, the model on which Friedman fell back was the IS-LM model (Friedman 1974). In short, Friedman should be considered as Keynesian from the methodological viewpoint and as anti-Keynesian from the policy viewpoint.

Lucas

Friedman's anti-Keynesian offensive dealt exclusively with policy. His was an internal criticism led from within the Marshallian–Keynesian conceptual apparatus. This was no longer true for the subsequent attack led by Lucas and his associates. As an external criticism, Lucas's attack led to a change that had all the hallmarks of a Kuhnian scientific revolution: a shift in the type of issues that are addressed, a new conceptual toolbox, new mathematical methods, the coming into power of a new generation of scholars, etc.

As in all scientific revolutions, the new approach combined a criticism of the previous and the emergence of a new direction of research. I will not go into details on the former, contenting myself with mentioning two of Lucas's main indictments. First, he argued against the aim of constructing a theory of involuntary unemployment on the ground of this notion's elusiveness.[4] His second indictment, which became known as the 'Lucas critique', pertained to the inability of Keynesian models to provide a robust basis on which to assess alternative economic policies due to their lack of microfoundations.

As to the new direction of research, the main change concerned the research agenda assigned to macroeconomics. In 1971, in his Presidential Address to the American Economic Association, James Tobin wrote that macroeconomics deprived of the full employment concept was unimaginable (Tobin 1972, p. 1). But this is exactly what was about to happen. In a span of a few years, the unemployment theme – and in a wider sense the search for the malfunctioning of markets – ceased to be an important preoccupation of macroeconomists. It fell out of fashion, macroeconomists being glad to send it back to labour economists. At the top of the agenda we now have issues related to the business cycle and a wider spectrum of themes related to growth and development.

This went along with the introduction of a series of new concepts and methodological perspectives. They were not necessarily Lucas's invention – the obvious example is the notion of rational expectations, introduced by John Muth – nor was he the only person to bring them to the forefront, but he provided the impulse.

Keynesian theory explained variations in employment as resulting from changes in aggregate demand. The underlying picture is that labour suppliers are passive, employment decisions being made unilaterally by firms. Moreover, this theory considers the supply of labour, and the labour force as selfsame, taking for granted that any difference between the total labour force and the level of employment is involuntary unemployment. Lucas's claim (in a joint work with Leonard Rapping, Lucas and Rapping 1969) was that supply of labour played as decisive a role as demand. His basic insight was that labour supply decisions ought to be studied not only as an arbitrage between leisure and participation in the labour market within a period of exchange but also as an intertemporal choice. That is, economic agents ought to be depicted as comparing the condition prevailing over the distribution of labour at one point in time with those they expect to prevail later in time, say today and tomorrow. If the former are more advantageous than the latter, they will decide to work more today and less tomorrow. This phenomenon, it is argued, is a clue for understanding variations in the level of activity over time, such variations being then viewed as grounded on optimizing behaviour.

Against this background and drawing from his renowned 1972 'Expectations and the Neutrality of Money' article (Lucas 1981f), Lucas devised an equilibrium model of the business cycle (Lucas 1981e). In this model, variations in employment are due to two factors: exogenous monetary shocks, on the one hand, and agents' imperfect information, on the other. Let me dwell on the latter factor. Agents face a single signal incorporating two distinct pieces of information, each of which would trigger an opposite reaction, changing or not changing the total hours worked, if available separately. Agents then face a signal extracting problem, which they solve by mixing the two opposite reactions in some weighted way. As a result, the hours worked will depart from what they would have been without imperfect information. Here, Lucas claims, lays the explanation of the variations of employment over the business cycle.

A different vision of the business cycle ensues. Earlier, it was viewed as a disequilibrium phenomenon *par excellence*, the manifestation of a market failure. Lucas's account turns this view upside down. Now, the business cycle expresses the optimizing reactions of agents to outside shocks affecting the economy. In other words, the existence of business fluctuations should no longer be interpreted as market failures, and governments should refrain from trying to prevent their occurrence. Nor is there any rationale for acting upon them.

The change that occurred is clearly multifaceted – a change in the agenda, in the conceptual framework, in the mathematical tools used, and in the vision of the business cycle. It also comprises a methodological dimension – first, the introduction of the microfoundations requirement and, second, a shift from a Marshallian towards a Walrasian perspective. I shall deal with these in turn.

Microfoundations

Keynesian macroeconomics hardly bothered to make explicit the microeconomic foundations of its aggregate variables. To all intents and purposes, microeconomics and macroeconomics were considered two separate universes. This is a state of affairs that Lucas found unacceptable.[5] In this line, macroeconomics ought to start with the description of how agents make their choices, these being made in an optimizing way: an objective function is to be maximized or minimized under given constraints. This microfoundations requirement is decreed to be the *sine qua non* of valid theoretical practice. Models that do not accord with it ought to be rejected.

The same requirement can be expressed differently as the 'equilibrium discipline'. It states that, to be valid, economic models should rest on two postulates: (a) that agents act in their own self-interest and their behaviour is optimal; and (b) that markets clear (Lucas and Sargent 1994, p. 15). The 'discipline' term is used to convey the view that this is a rule that economists impose upon themselves, and which stamps their specific way of looking at social reality. Accepting such a standpoint results in proclaiming that the notion of disequilibrium, which before was widely used, should be banned from the economic lexicon.

Lucas's precept will look odd at first sight. To understand its rationale, two elements ought to be taken into account. First, it makes sense only when realizing that it is accompanied by a radical change in the meaning of the concept of equilibrium. In earlier times, from Adam Smith to Marshall and Keynes, the notion of equilibrium differed little from its common-sense understanding. It was viewed as a standstill position, a centre of gravity. The hallmark of equilibrium was the persistence of the same outcomes over time. The question raised about equilibrium was whether a given market or a given economy was in a state of equilibrium at a given point in time. Lucas's originality was to depart from this traditional conception by adhering to a conception of equilibrium where the model economy could be stated to be in equilibrium while evincing ever-changing outcomes over time. Moreover, and crucially, for Lucas, equilibrium is no longer a feature of reality. The following quotation, drawn from an interview with Brian Snowdon and Howard Vane, illustrates his viewpoint:

> I think general discussions, especially by non-economists, of whether the system is in equilibrium or not are almost entirely nonsense. You can't look out of this window and ask whether New Orleans is in equilibrium. What does that mean? Equilibrium is a property of the way we look at things, not a property of reality. (Snowdon and Vane 1998, p.127)

In other words, it is claimed that the ever presence of equilibrium is a feature of the model economy, the fictive economy created by the economist, but not a feature of reality.

From Adam Smith onwards, equilibrium has been a cornerstone of economic analysis. The distinct contribution of neoclassical theory has been to depict agents as behaving intelligently, i.e. in an optimizing way. At a time where this premise was questioned, Lucas proposed to take it even more in earnest than before, the ground for this being its powerfulness, and he claimed to have made the point. Up to then, it had been taken for granted that the phenomenon of the business cycle was by nature a disequilibrium occurrence and that it would be impossible to account for it theoretically while assuming that at every point of the business cycle the assumption that agents were acting in an optimizing way. Lucas, and later Kydland and Prescott, proved the contrary. An equilibrium model of the business cycle, whose movements mimic those of reality, can be constructed. This shows that, instead of being a hindrance, the equilibrium discipline allows new breakthroughs.

Walrasian Macroeconomics

I now turn to the second aspect, the replacement of Marshallian macroeconomics with Walrasian macroeconomics. In my recent book on the history of macroeconomics (De Vroey 2009a), I claim that this is a central benchmark for understanding the transformation of macroeconomics triggered by Lucas. Keynesian macroeconomics ought to be considered as a simplified Marshallian general equilibrium theory. In contrast, Lucas's work belongs to the Walrasian approach. Different dimensions are involved into which I cannot enter here, except for one, which I find illuminative.[6] The transformation I have in mind can be summarized by stating that a shift occurred from ideas to demonstrations. *The General Theory* was a book full of ideas, often collapsing ones, several of which were arcane. The result is that even now, seven decades after its publication, every year several books are published aiming at reconstructing Keynes's thought, none of which has any chance to raise a consensus. That was the beginning of Keynesian macroeconomics. In contrast, new classical macroeconomics started with a twenty-page mathematical paper, Lucas's 'Expectations and the Neutrality of Money' article. It paved the way for a new research programme without eliciting any hermeneutic discussions.

Underlying this transformation from theory as a set of ideas to theory as a mathematical demonstration lays another difference constantly pointed out by Leijonhufvud.[7] Adopting a Marshallian perspective, as Keynes did, amounts to having the theoretical enterprise evolving at two levels of discourse, the theory and the model. A theory is a set of propositions about reality, aiming at uncovering the truth about it (in the way historians do). A model consists of a reasoning, that is usually mathematical but which can also proceed in prose, zeroing in on a part of the theory with the aim of setting out the underlying mechanism at work in the most consistent possible way. In this vision, the model is clearly subservient to the theory. Again, we have here a startling contrast. Following Walras, Lucas states that the model and the theory are one and the same thing, the model now being limited to a mathematical reasoning, and possibly complemented with meta-theoretical comments. In this light, it is no longer claimed that a theory, made selfsame to a model, consists of propositions about reality. Its object of study is not reality but a fictive construction, the model

Table 4.3   The contrast between Keynesian macroeconomics and new classical macroeconomics

	Keynesian macroeconomics	New classical macroeconomics *à la* Lucas
Top research priority	unemployment	business fluctuations
Core theoretical model	the IS-LM model	dynamic stochastic general equilibrium model
relationship between micro and macro	neoclassical synthesis	equilibrium discipline
Central concepts:		
– expectations	– adaptive expectations	– rational expectations
– studying the labour market	– emphasis on the demand for labour for explaining variations in employment	– emphasis on the supply of labour for explaining variations in employment
– main exchange framework	– short-period analysis	– intra- and intertemporal substitution
Wider basic approach	the Marshallian approach	the Walrasian approach

economy. It is not claimed that the theory/model ought to be realistic. It cannot be so, because wanting to have a realistic model is an oxymoron. Still, according to Lucas, such a theoretical enterprise is far from gratuitous. The purpose of constructing such models is to have an array of analogous models helping economists to think about the efficiency of alternative policy measures.

To summarize, in this new perspective, the task at hand when doing macroeconomics is not to put ideas on paper, as Keynes did brilliantly, but to produce demonstrations and measurement. Any idea that cannot enter into the mathematical language ought to be left aside until further progress makes it possible.

I hope that these remarks have served the purpose of showing the contrast between the two generations of macroeconomic paradigms. Table 4.3 above summarizes its main elements. Instead of having two opposite conclusions drawn from broadly the same paradigm, as was the case with Friedman, now, clearly, we face two distinct paradigms.

Finally, let me return to my taxonomy of macroeconomic theories against the Keynesian/non-Keynesian criterion. With Lucas, a new configuration arises, to be fully non-Keynesian, that is, both from the conceptual apparatus side and from the policy vision side. This is illustrated in Table 4.4.

Table 4.4   Characterizing new classical macroeconomics in terms of the Keynesian/non-Keynesian criterion

		The Marshallian approach (*the Marshall-Keynes-Hicks line*)	The Walrasian approach
The policy viewpoint defended	Defense of demand activation	– Keynes – IS-LM model	
	Defense of the free market	– Monetarism (Friedman)	– **New classical macro (Lucas)**

NEW KEYNESIAN MODELS, GENERATION ONE

Lucas's attack, often uttered in an aggressive language, led to two types of reactions from Keynesians. The first consisted in claiming that he had it all wrong. The following two quotations illustrate.

> I argue . . . that there was no anomaly, that the ascendancy of new classicism in academia was instead a triumph of *a priori* theorizing over empiricism, of intellectual aesthetics over observation and, in some measure, of conservative ideology over liberalism. (Blinder 1997, p. 110)

> To many Keynesians, the new classical program replaced messy truth by precise error. (Lipsey 2000, p. 76)

Such assertions suggest that the direction opened by Lucas and kindred economists was to be radically rejected. In contrast, the other reaction amounted to admitting that many of Lucas's criticisms were well founded and could not be dismissed with a sweep of a hand. This attitude was the hallmark of so-called 'new Keynesian' economics. While wanting to re-habilitate Keynes's insights, they agreed to wage their counter-offensive on Lucas's turf, i.e. to respect the micro-foundations requirement. However, new Keynesian economics was far from being a unified approach. Let me just mention a few of the lines of research taken. Some new Keynesian models – such as efficiency wages models (e.g. Shapiro and Stiglitz (1984)) – made it their priority to demonstrate the equilibrium existence of involuntary unemployment. Others – in particular coordination failures models (e.g. Diamond (1991) – concerned themselves with the less ambitious aim of demonstrating underemployment in a multiple equilibria framework. Thereby, they were able to exonerate wage rigidity as a cause of the phenomenon and to vindicate demand activation. Still other authors (e.g. Hart (1991), Blanchard and Kiyotaki (1991)), also concerned with

Table 4.5   Characterizing new classical macroeconomics in terms of the Keynesian/non-Keynesian criterion

		Marshallian approach		Walrasian approach
		The Marshall-Keynes-Hicks line	The Marshall-Chamberlin line	
Policy viewpoint	Defense of demand activation	– Keynes – IS-LM model	– **New Keynesian models of the imperfect competition type**	– **New Keynesian models of the coordination failures type**
	Defense of the free market	– Monetarism (Friedman)		– New classical macro (Lucas)

underemployment, adopted an imperfectly-competitive framework. This framework was also adopted by Fischer (1991) and Taylor (1991) who conceived staggering contracts models in order to rebut Friedman's and Lucas's claim about the ineffectiveness of monetary policy. Table 4.5 shows how some of these models enter my taxonomy. The reader will observe that the emergence of imperfect competition models prompts the need for an enlargement of my taxonomy, a new sub-category within the Marshallian approach being introduced, the Marshallian-Chamberlin line. The striking point is that these models are Keynesian as far as policy is concerned but are non-Keynesian for what concerns the conceptual apparatus criterion.

New Keynesian economists have succeeded in their retort to Lucas's attack in that they constructed models giving an equilibrium foundation to involuntary unemployment or unemployment. Nonetheless, after a period of fierce debates, it turned out that they were on the losing side. On the one hand, the emergence of search and matching models vindicated Lucas's claim that the topic of unemployment could be send back to labour economists instead of remaining at the center of macroeconomics. On the other, most of the new Keynesian models were framed in a static framework while the stochastic dynamic perspective had become the compelling modelling way. Gradually, new Keynesians realized that they needed to enter into the new language if they wanted to have an effect on the unfolding of macroeconomics.

REAL BUSINESS CYCLE MACROECONOMICS

In his 'Methods and problems in business cycle theory' paper, Lucas (1981b, p. 288) stated that the task ahead was to write a FORTRAN program. As he wrote in a related paper, the macroeconomist's aim must be to construct '. . . a fully articulate artificial economy which behaves through time so as to imitate closely the time series behavior of actual economies' (Lucas 1981d, p. 219). However, Lucas himself contributed little to this enterprise. In contrast, Kydland and Prescott took Lucas's injunction literally and devoted themselves to the task of transforming a qualitative type of modelling into a quantitative one.

The aim of Kydland and Prescott's 'Time to Build and Aggregate Fluctuations' model (Kydland and Prescott 1982) was to show that economic fluctuations could be explained as the result of economic agents' optimizing adjustment to exogenous technological shocks. Their model adopted most of the distinctive features of Lucas's model – in particular, the equilibrium discipline, rational expectations, the Lucasian supply function – but abandoned the idea that the shock was monetary as well as the imperfection information set up. To implement their aim, Kydland and Prescott constructed the most rudimentary conceivable model of an economy comprising a large number of identical infinitely-lived agents. This allows the analysis to be undertaken in terms of a representative agent shouldering both the functions of capitalist and wage-earner.

Kydland and Prescott's starting point was Ramsey's (1928) and Cass's (1965) models of optimal growth, which was extended to the case of a stochastic economy by Brock and Mirman (1972). They also characterized their model economy with stochastic auto-correlated shocks. A positive shock leads the representative agent to increase investment, what in turn leads to a decrease in leisure and an increased labour supply. Finally, they wanted to make their model empirical, in spite of its Robinson Crusoe nature, by confronting its results with real-world data. The field of application chosen was the evolution of the US economy from 1950 to 1975.

I cannot enter into the detailed description of their model and the several technical steps required for making it empirical, which proved to be a titanic task.[8] Its validation occurs by comparing the moments (volatility, correlation and auto-correlation) that summarize the actual experience of the US economy with similar moments obtained from simulating the model economy. The model succeeds if the simulation mimics the empirical observations. To a large extent and somewhat surprisingly, this was the case with the Kydland and Prescott model. Taking the fluctuations of output as reference, the model satisfactorily reproduced both the lower variability of consumption and the higher variability of investment. The same is true for the pro-cyclicity and persistence of most of the variables considered.

Merely asserting that qualitative modelling gave way to quantitative modelling fails to convey the full measure of the change that took place. Behind this contrast lies another, more sociological, difference. Earlier, I have evoked the question of what would have happened to *The General Theory* if its message had not been transposed into the IS-LM model, and if Klein had not extended this model into an econometric framework? The same conundrum arises over the relationship between Lucas, on the one hand, and Kydland and Prescott, on the other. Without Kydland and Prescott, would the seismic change that macroeconomics underwent have occurred? It is far from sure. Lucas's conceptual papers were impressive but too highbrow to generate a huge following. As to Lucas's criticism, its impact on the profession could have been limited to making modellers more cautious when drawing conclusions from their models, and not produced a radical change in method. To have a scientific revolution, an alternative way of doing applied work, providing new grist to the mill for the majority of members of the community, must be made available. This was Kydland and Prescott's main contribution: they were able to set the agenda of macroeconomics. While their model was initially met with scepticism, it grew to become the workhorse for further developments. A large fraction, if not the majority, of the macroeconomic community started working in the direction set out by Kydland and Prescott.

A question worth raising about real business cycle modelling pertains to its scope of relevance. Lucas has recurrently claimed that such models were apt to tackle normal business fluctuations but fell short of explaining a phenomenon such as the Great Depression. After having shared this viewpoint, Prescott changed his mind and argued that the real business cycle methodology was able to come to grips with great depressions – quite a bold claim when it is reminded that such models are based on the premises of optimizing behaviour and market clearing.

Turning to the characterization of real business cycle models in my taxonomy, real business cycle models ought to be put in the same spot as new classical models. They are fully non-Keynesian, both from the policy and the conceptual aspects.

Finally, since I have recounted the drifting away from Keynesian theory that started with Friedman and culminated with real business cycle models, it may be useful to briefly characterize the evolution that took place from Friedman to Kydland and Prescott. Table 4.7 does this job. It brings out that while Friedman started the whole process, at the end of the day, little, except the policy viewpoint defended, is left from Friedman own way of positing issues.

Table 4.6 *Characterizing real business cycle models in terms of the Keynesian/non-Keynesian criterion*

		Marshallian approach		Walrasian approach
		The Marshall-Keynes-Hicks line	The Marshall-Chamberlin line	
Policy view-point	*Defence of demand activation*	– Keynes – The IS-LM model	– New Keynesian models of the imperfect competition type	– New Keynesian models of the coordination failures type
	Defence of the free market	– Monetarism (Friedman)		– New classical macro (Lucas) – **Real business cycle models**

Table 4.7 *The evolution in approach from Friedman's expectations-augmented Phillips curve model to Lucas's and Kydland and Prescott's models*

	Friedman (1968)	Lucas (1981f)	Lucas (1981e, 1981d)	Kydland and Prescott (1982)
Purpose	Demonstrating the inefficiency of monetary policy	Demonstrating the inefficiency of monetary policy	Constructing an equilibrium theory of the business cycle	Constructing an equilibrium theory of the business cycle
Theoretical project	Marshallian	Walrasian	Walrasian	Walrasian
Main assumptions				
(a) the nature of the shock	monetary	monetary and real	monetary and real	real
(b) expectations	adaptive	rational	rational	rational
(c) allocative mechanism	intra-temporal	inter-temporal	intra- and inter-temporal	intra- and inter-temporal
(d) information	imperfect	imperfect	imperfect	perfect

NEW KEYNESIAN MODELS, GENERATION TWO

Of course, real business cycle models are not the final stage of macro-economics. New models gradually emerged at the end of the 1990s, marking a significant departure from the earlier framework. They often go under the DSGE (dynamic stochastic general equilibrium) modelling but the problem with this denomination is that it is too broad as it applies also to new classical and real business cycle models. The change that new Keynesian models (mark II or second generation models) bring about should not be viewed as a revolution overthrowing the earlier paradigm that Lucas's work generated. Rather it constitutes an endogenous evolution in which the two theoretical streams that previously were fighting each other, new Keynesians and real-business cycle theorists, now come to terms about adopting a single model as the common ground for further theoretical discussions – hence the 'new neoclassical synthesis' tag proposed by Goodfriend and King (1997). In effect, these models borrow their ingredients both from the real business cycle and the new Keynesian tool boxes. From the former they take the view that macroeconomics is concerned with the study of the dynamic evolution of the economy in a stochastic context, and ought to be based on microfoundations, rational expectations and intertemporal substitution. From the second, they inherit imperfections – imperfect competition on the one hand, and sluggish prices and wages on the other – with pride of place being given to monetary policy.

The integration of monopolistic competition in these models follows from the borrowing of the Dixit-Stiglitz aggregator from Dixit and Stiglitz's (1977) model of product differentiation. In the canonical model, the economy comprises four types of goods: labour, a final all-purpose good, a continuum of intermediary goods, and money. The final good is a homogeneous good produced using the intermediary goods. It is exchanged competitively. Intermediary goods are each produced by a monopolistic firm using Leontief technology based only on labour. These monopolistic firms are price-makers applying a mark-up on their marginal costs. If, for any reason, they are willing but unable to change their prices, it is in their interest to increase the quantity sold until demand is fully satisfied. The reason invoked for such an occurrence is a price-setting process *à la* Calvo (1983), where it is assumed that at each period only a given proportion of all firms are able to change their prices.

The issue of the real effects of monetary policy, the very topic that Friedman and Lucas had declared to have settled once and for all, is now re-opened with new conclusions. First, it turns out that monetary policy actions can have an important effect on real economic activity, persisting over several years, due to gradual adjustment of individual prices and the general price level. Second, even in settings with costly price adjustment, the model leads to some long-run trade-off between inflation and real activity. Third, significant gains are obtained from eliminating inflation. They stem

Table 4.8   Characterizing new neoclassical synthesis models in terms of the Keynesian/non-Keynesian criterion

		Marshallian approach		*Walrasian approach*
		The Marshall-Keynes-Hicks line	*The Marshall-Chamberlin line*	
Policy view-point	*Defence of demand activation*	– Keynes – The IS-LM model	– New Keynesian models of the imperfect competition type – **New Keynesian models mark II**	– New Keynesian models of the coordination failures type
	Defence of the free market	– Monetarism (Friedman)		– New classical macro (Lucas) – Real business cycle models

from increased transactions efficiency and reduced relative price distortions. Fourth and finally, credibility plays an important role in understanding the effects of monetary policy (Goodfriend and King 1997, p. 232).

The end result of all these developments is that we now find economists who hold opposite policy views agreeing about the conceptual apparatus upon which to base their theoretical conversation. This state of affairs seems to be agreeable to both camps. Macroeconomists from the real business cycle tradition are happy because new Keynesians have yielded by adopting their language and toolbox. New Keynesians are content because they have been able to bring to the merger the concepts they were insisting upon in their more static days. Moreover, the admission that monetary policy can have real effects marks a reversal of the Friedman-Lucas view that had previously held the high ground. In other words, when it comes to policy, new Keynesians seem to be the winners. In terms of my taxonomy, there is a return, however mild, to the Keynesian policy standpoint.

CONCLUDING REMARKS: THE IMPACT OF THE GREAT RECESSION ON MACROECONOMIC THEORY

The issue of the impact of the great recession on the development of macroeconomics ought to be decomposed into two distinct questions.

The first is whether this event raises a challenge to macroeconomic theory as it stood when the crisis was about to break out. The second is whether the course of development of the discipline may change consequently to the crisis.

As to the first question, many commentators have blamed macroeconomists for not having predicted the outbreak of the crisis but, to me, the discussion should rather bear on the ability of present-day macroeconomic theory to come to grips with it. Here, the diagnosis tilts towards the negative. Two factors stand out. The first one, upon which I shall not expand, is that the strategy adopted in DSGE models is one of constructing simple models – a defensible strategy when tractability is taken into account. As a result, little attention has been given to the financial sector, which played a crucial role in the recession.

The second factor pertains to the limits of what can be done with an equilibrium model, that is, models premised on the view that, whatever the situation in which economic agents find themselves, they should be considered as having achieved their optimizing plan. In other words, DSGE models exclude in advance the possibility of any pathology in the working of the market system.[9]

Not that a real business cycle theorist is unable to recast the crisis in the language of his model. The story he could tell is as follows.[10] An exogenous shock, occurring in the financial sector, affects the economy. As a reaction, households fear that future high taxes will be necessary to compensate the bailing out of the banking system by the state. Because of this fear, business, in particular small business, will cut investment and take more cash out of business. Employment will decrease because of a shift in both the demand for and the supply of labour. Households will cut their durable consumption. This should account for the drop in activity. As to the nature of the shock, it is viewed as a government failure, the addition of two mistakes. The first, which goes back to Clinton's presidency, is the US government political pressure on state-controlled mortgage companies to extend mortgages to households that could not afford it. The second, is the Fed's low interest rate policy. Even if there may be some truth in these observations, the main point lays in what this scenario discards, the possibility that markets can fail and that agents may find themselves in a state where they are unable to achieve their optimizing plan. While this neglect is admissible when the economy is in a plain sailing state, it is no longer so when the economy shows signs of erring. As a result, the present-day state of macroeconomics resembles that which Keynes faced: existing theory excludes systemic market failures and involuntary outcomes while everything indicates that the contrary is true in reality. Whatever the virtues of the real business cycle methodology, its limits become blatant. So, it can rather safely be concluded that the great recession presents a strong challenge to present macroeconomic theory.

However, no straightforward answer can be given to the question, in which direction will a change occur? For lack of space, I shall limit myself to making two remarks. The first is that future developments in macroeconomics are an open matter because they depend on theoretical innovations led by scholars, the next Keynes, Lucas, Kydland and Prescott, blazing new directions of research. A race for theoretical innovation is open into which many contenders will enter. But at this juncture it is difficult to conjecture which lines will be taken (and prove feasible) although it may be guessed that a basic aim of these attempts will be to introduce more market failures in the picture.

My second remark is that the crisis has resulted in a shift in visibility between the defenders of the free market and economists with a Keynesian inclination in the policy vision sense. The former are now in the defensive and the latter cheer up after two decades of gloom. Nonetheless, to get the right perspective, a distinction must be drawn between what is going on in the sphere of media and meta-theoretical essays, on the one hand, and in the academic world, on the other. Two prominent defenders of Keynes are Lord Skidelsky, Keynes's biographer and the recent author of *The Return of the Master* (Skidelsky 2009), and Paul Krugman, the 2008 Nobel Prize laureate (see for example Krugman 2010). They share the same simple message: one should return to Keynes! In Krugman's words, 'Keynesian economics remains the best framework we have for making sense of recessions and depressions' (2010, p. 8). My distinction between Keynesianism as a policy vision and as a conceptual apparatus is useful here. Krugman and Skidelsky take up the viewpoint proper to the era of Keynesian macroeconomics that these two aspects are intertwined. I disagree with them. While I think that we shall witness a revival of the Keynesian motivation of bringing out market failures, I doubt that any return to the Keynesian conceptual apparatus will occur. First, claiming that one should return to a theory that was proposed more than seventy years ago amounts to assuming that no progress has been made in between, and that the methodological choices that offered themselves at that time are still worth considering today. On the contrary, I think that the criticism that Lucas made about Keynesian theory were well taken, and that his positive contributions, as well as those of Kydland and Prescott and the many economists who trod in their footsteps, will be overtaken but not written off. Second, as mentioned above, the transformation that took place in macroeconomics took the form of a replacement of mere exchanges of ideas about reality by the requirement to demonstrate propositions pertaining to a model economy (or, in other words, the conflation of the notions of theory and model). I believe that there will be no return on this state of affairs. Any dilemma between the tractability constraint and the real-world direct relevance constraint will be solved in favour of the former. Therefore, in my opinion, Krugman's and Skidelsky's injunctions will have little, if any, impact on academic work.

NOTES

1. Other papers or books on the same topic are Blanchard (2000), Hoover (2003), Leijonhufvud (2006a), Snowdon and Vane (2005) and Woodford (1999).
2. See Young (1987).
3. Cf. De Vroey (2000).
4. 'Involuntary unemployment is not a fact or a phenomenon which it is the task of theorists to explain. It is, on the contrary, a theoretical construct which Keynes introduced in the hope it would be helpful in discovering a correct explanation for a genuine phenomenon: large-scale fluctuations in measured, total unemployment. Is it the task of modern theoretical economics to 'explain' the theoretical constructs of our predecessor, whether or not they have proved fruitful? I hope not, for a surer route to sterility could scarcely be imagined' (Lucas 1981c, p. 243).
5. 'The most interesting recent developments in macroeconomic theory seems to me describable as the reincorporation of aggregative problems such as inflation and the business cycle within the general framework of "microeconomic" theory. If these developments succeed, the term "macroeconomic" will simply disappear from use and the modifier "micro" will become superfluous. We will simply speak, as did Smith, Ricardo, Marshall and Walras of *economic* theory' (Lucas, 1987, pp. 107–8).
6. For a wider comparison, see De Vroey (2009b).
7. See for example Leijonhufvud (2006b, p. 70).
8. To get a taste of what it involved, the reader unacquainted with the nuts and bolts of constructing real business cycle models can turn to Prescott's Nobel lecture (Prescott 2006).
9. Imperfect competition could be labelled a pathological case but it involves no obstacles towards the attainment of equilibrium.
10. This is the story that Prescott told in a conference given in Paris in July 2009 (Prescott 2009).

BIBLIOGRAPHY

Blanchard, O. (2000), 'What do we know about macroeconomics that Fisher and Wicksell did not?', *Quarterly Journal of Economics*, **115**(4) (November), 1375–409.

Blanchard, O. and N. Kiyotaki (1991), 'Monopolistic competition and the effects of aggregate demand', in G. Mankiw and D. Romer (eds), *New Keynesian Economics, vol. 1, Imperfect Competition and Sticky Prices*, Cambridge, MA: The MIT Press, pp. 345–75.

Blinder, A. (1997), 'The fall and rise of Keynesian economics', in B. Snowdon and H. Vane (eds), *A Macroeconomics Reader*, London: Routledge, pp. 109–34.

Bodkin R., L. R. Klein and K. Marwah (eds) (1991), *A History of Macroeconometric Model-Building*, Aldershot, UK and Brookfield, VT, USA: Edward Elgar.

Brock, W. and L. Mirman (1972), 'Optimal economic growth and uncertainty: the discounted case', *Journal of Economic Theory*, **4**(3) (June), 479–513.

Calvo, G. (1983), 'Staggered price setting in a utility-maximizing framework', *Journal of Monetary Economics*, **12**(3) (September), pp. 383–98.

Cass, D. (1965), 'Optimum growth in an aggregative model of capital accumulation', *Review of Economic Studies*, **32**(3) (July), 233–40.

De Vroey, M. (2000), 'IS-LM "*à la* Hicks" versus IS-LM "*à la* Modigliani"', *History of Political Economy*, **32**(2) (Summer), 293–316.

De Vroey, M. (2009a), *Keynes, Lucas, d'une macroéconomie à l'autre*, Paris: Dalloz.

De Vroey, M. (2009b), 'Marshall and Walras: incompatible fellows?', University of Louvain Department of Economics discussion paper, no 200908, forthcoming in the *European Journal of the History of Economic Thought*.

De Vroey, M. and L. Pensieroso (2006), 'Real business cycle theory and the Great Depression: the abandonment of the abstentionist viewpoint', *Contributions to Macroeconomics*, **6**(1), article 13.

Diamond, P. (1991), 'Aggregate demand management in search equilibrium', in G. Mankiw and D. Romer (eds), *New Keynesian Economics, Volume 2, Coordination Failures and Real Rigidities*, Cambridge, MA: The MIT Press, pp. 31–46.

Dixit, A. and J. Stiglitz (1977), 'Monopolistic competition and optimum product diversity', *American Economic Review*, **67**(3) (June), 297–308.

Fischer, S. (1991), 'Long-term contracts, rational expectations, and the optimal money supply rule', in G. Mankiw and D. Romer (eds), *New Keynesian Economics, vol. I, Imperfect Competition and Sticky Wages*, Cambridge, MA: The MIT Press, pp. 215–31.

Friedman, M. (1968), 'The role of monetary policy', *American Economic Review*, **58**(1) (March), 1–17.

Friedman, M. (1974), 'A theoretical framework for monetary analysis', in R. J. Gordon (ed.), *Milton Friedman's Monetary Framework*, Chicago, IL: Chicago University Press, pp. 1–62, 132–77.

Goodfriend, M. and R. King (1997), 'The new neoclassical synthesis and the role of monetary policy', in B. Bernanke and J. Rotenberg (eds), *NBER Macroeconomics Annual 1997*, Cambridge, MA: The MIT Press, pp. 231–83.

Harrod, R. F. (1937 [1947]), 'Mr. Keynes and traditional theory', *Econometrica*, **5**, 74–86.

Hart, O. (1991), 'A model of imperfect competition with Keynesian features', in G. Mankiw and D. Romer (eds), *New Keynesian Economics, vol. 1, Imperfect Competition and Sticky Prices*, Cambridge, MA: The MIT Press, pp. 313–44.

Hicks, J. (1937), 'Mr. Keynes and the "classics": a suggested interpretation', *Econometrica*, **5**(2) (April), 147–59.

Hoover, K. (2003), 'A history of postwar monetary and macroeconomics', in J. Biddle, J. Davis, and W. Samuels (eds), *The Blackwell Companion to the History of Economic Thought*, Oxford: Blackwell, pp. 411–27.

Keynes, J. M. (1936), *The General Theory of Employment, Interest, and Money*, London: Macmillan.

Klein, L. (1948), *The Keynesian Revolution*, New York: Macmillan.

Klein, L. and A. Goldberger (1955), *An Econometric Model of the United States, 1922–1952*, Amsterdam: North-Holland.

Krugman, P. (2010), 'How did economists get it so wrong', *New York Times*

Magazine, 2 September 2009, accessed at www.nytimes.com/2009/09/06/magazine/06Economic-t.html.

Kydland, F. and E. Prescott (1982), 'Time to build and aggregate fluctuations', *Econometrica*, **50**(6) (November), 1345–70.

Leijonhufvud, A. (2006a), 'Episodes in a century of macroeconomics', in D. Colander (ed.), *Post-Walrasian Macroeconomics. Beyond the Dynamic Stochastic General Equilibrium Model*, Cambridge: Cambridge University Press, pp. 27–45.

Leijonhufvud, A. (2006b), 'Keynes as a Marshallian', in R. Backhouse and B. Bateman (eds), *The Cambridge Companion to Keynes*, Cambridge: Cambridge University Press, pp. 58–77.

Lipsey, R. (2000), 'IS-LM, Keynesianism, and the new classicism', in R. Backhouse and A. Salanti (eds), *Macroeconomics and the Real World, vol. 2, Keynesian Economics, Unemployment and Policy*, Oxford: Oxford University Press, pp. 57–82.

Lucas, R. E. Jr. (1981a), *Studies in Business Cycle Theory*, Cambridge, MA: The MIT Press.

Lucas, R. E. Jr. (1981b) 'Methods and problems in business cycle theory', *Studies in Business Cycle Theory*, Cambridge, MA: The MIT Press, pp. 271–96.

Lucas, R. E. Jr. (1981c), 'Unemployment policy', *Studies in Business Cycle Theory*, Cambridge MA: The MIT Press, pp. 240–47.

Lucas, R. E. Jr. (1981d), 'Understanding business cycles', *Studies in Business Cycle Theory*, Cambridge, MA: The MIT Press, pp. 215–39.

Lucas, R. E. Jr. (1981e), 'An equilibrium model of the business cycle', *Studies in Business Cycle Theory*, Cambridge, MA: The MIT Press, pp. 179–214.

Lucas, R. E. Jr. (1981f), 'Expectations and the neutrality of money', *Studies in Business Cycle Theory*, Cambridge, MA: The MIT Press, pp. 66–89.

Lucas, R. E. Jr. (1987), *Models of Business Cycles*, Oxford: Basil Blackwell.

Lucas, R. E. Jr. and L. Rapping (1969), 'Real wages, employment, and inflation', *Journal of Political Economy*, **77**(5) (September/October), 721–54.

Lucas, R. E. Jr. and T. Sargent (1994), 'After Keynesian macroeconomics', in P. R. Miller (ed.), *The Rational Expectations Revolution. Readings from the Front Line*, Cambridge, MA: The MIT Press, pp. 5–30.

Meade, J. (1937 [1947]), 'A simplified model of Keynes's system', *Review of Economic Studies*, **4**, 98–107.

Modigliani, F. (1944), 'Liquidity preference and the theory of interest and money', *Econometrica*, **12**(1) (January), 45–88.

Prescott, E. (2006), 'The transformation of macroeconomic policy and research', *Journal of Political Economy*, **114**(2) (April), 203–35.

Prescott, E. (2009), 'Effective measures against the recession', conference, 6 July 2009, accessed at www.slideshare.net/madridnetwork/effective-measures-against-the-recession.

Ramsey, F. (1928), 'A mathematical theory of saving', *Economic Journal*, **38**(152) (December), 543–59.

Samuelson, P. A. (1964), '*The General Theory*', in R. Lekachman (ed.), *Keynes's General Theory. Reports of Three Decades*, London: Macmillan, pp. 315–31.

Samuelson, P. A. and R. Solow (1960), 'Analytical aspects of anti-inflationary policy', *American Economic Review*, **50**(2) (May), 177–94.

Shapiro, C. and J. E. Stiglitz (1984), 'Equilibrium unemployment as worker discipline device', *American Economic Review*, **74**(3) (June), 433–44.

Skidelsky, R. (2009), *The Return of the Master*, London: Public Affairs.

Snowdon, B. and H. Vane (1998), 'Transforming macroeconomics: an interview with Robert E Lucas Jr.', *Journal of Economic Methodology*, **5**(1), 115–45.

Snowdon, B. and H. Vane (2005), *Modern Macroeconomics. Its Origins, Development and Current State*, Cheltenham, UK and Northampton, MA, USA: Edward Elgar.

Taylor, J. (1991), 'Staggered wage setting in a macro model', in G. Mankiw and D. Romer (eds), *New Keynesian Economics, vol. 1, Imperfect Competition and Sticky Prices*, Cambridge, MA: The MIT Press, pp. 233–41.

Tinbergen, J. (1939), *Statistical Testing of Business Cycle Theories*, 2 volumes, Geneva: League of Nations.

Tobin, J. (1972), 'Inflation and unemployment', *American Economic Review*, **62**(1/2) (March), 1–19.

Woodford, M. (1999), 'Revolution and evolution in twentieth-century macroeconomics', accessed at www.columbia.edu/~mw2230/.

Young, W. (1987), *Interpreting Mr Keynes. The IS-LM Enigma*, London: Polity Press.

5. The roots of the present are in the past: the relation of postwar developments in macroeconomics to interwar business cycle and monetary theory

Robert W. Dimand[1]

INTRODUCTION

The reading lists of graduate courses in macroeconomic theory notoriously focus on articles published within the preceding five years or still circulating as preprints and discussion papers. This reflects the consensus that, this time, the issues and perspectives that agitated economics in the past may safely be discarded as relics of a time when people wrote in prose or in mathematics that did not quite match the notation and assumptions now in use (see Mark Blaug 2001; David Laidler, 2004, Chapter 19). Thus, if the course is being given in the mid-1960s, 'We are all Keynesians now', the future lies with disaggregated structural macroeconometric models of two thousand equations or more, and macroeconomists need not trouble themselves about the quantity theory of money or about the classical side of 'Keynes and the classics'. Similarly, 15 years later, acceptance of the monetary misperceptions version of New Classical Economics as definitive and final meant that there was no need for serious study of Keynesian economics (a single chapter on IS/LM near the end of Robert Barro's intermediate macro textbook or in Thomas Sargent's graduate macro textbook suffices), since the remaining Keynesians were isolated holdovers (like the quantity theorists at the University of Chicago 15 years before) and there was not going to be a New Keynesian macroeconomics. This time is always different, as it also is for optimists discerning a 'New Economy' in each stock market boom (of whom Irving Fisher was neither the first nor the last). Yet as the names New Classical and New Keynesian suggest, all is not made anew with each generation of macroeconomists. It is noteworthy that Michael Woodford (2003), writing about monetary

policy in an economy in which financial innovation has effectively eliminated the need for base money (Woodford 2003, p. 237), selected a title
recalling Knut Wicksell on the dynamics of a pure-credit economy and
significantly discarding Don Patinkin's addition of money to Wicksell's
title (Wicksell 1898; Patinkin 1965).

Historians of economics have studied the relationships between several
important aspects of post-Second World War macroeconomics and
parallels in interwar monetary and business cycle theory. This chapter,
building on these historical studies, examines the recurrence of certain
approaches, problems, and debates in macroeconomics, how they are
transformed in their later guises, and how theoretical innovation occurs
within a background of earlier contributions. The recurrence of problems
in macroeconomics, combined with both cycles and innovation in
approaches to analysing these problems, accounts for the saying that it
is easier to set graduate comprehensive exams in macroeconomics than
in microeconomics: in macroeconomics, the questions can be kept the
same from year to year, only the answers change. Because of the pattern
of recurrent concerns, themes, and analyses (such as whether the source
of instability is government intervention or volatile expectations of the
profitability of investment), developments in postwar macroeconomics are
not only the consequence of new empirical evidence and policy experience
and of advances in formal technique, but are also to be understood in light
of the discipline's prior evolution. Macroeconomics has a useful past, and
macroeconomists would have a better understanding of what they do if
they knew more about what macroeconomists have done in the past.

It would be difficult for most of them to know less about it. Practising
macroeconomists are only imperfectly aware, at best, of the recurrent
themes of their subject because of the easy step from ignorance of the
past to conviction that there is no relevant past to know. Thus Francis
X. Diebold holds in a *Festschrift* for Lawrence Klein that 'A striking and
easily forgotten fact is that, before Keynes and Klein, *there really was no
macroeconomics* . . . Certainly Smith, Ricardo, Mill, Marshall and others
addressed some macroeconomic concerns' but 'Classical economics is
essentially microeconomics' (Dimand 2003, p. 325, emphasis in original).
The theory of the determination of output as a whole dates from Keynes
(1936), yet as Wesley Mitchell (1927, p. 7) remarked, 'Before the end of
the nineteenth century there had accumulated a body of observations and
speculations sufficient to justify the writing of histories of the theories of
crises'. Barnett (1941) devoted a 124-page journal supplement to business
cycle theories in the United States from 1860 to 1900, a period when the
United States was far from being a leader in that field (apart from Fisher
1896 near the end of the era), while histories of theories of economic crises

were published by Eugen von Bergmann in Stuttgart (still a centre of the history of business cycle theory, e.g. Hagemann 2001–2002) in 1895 and Edward D. Jones in New York in 1900.

WHAT IS A MONETARY ECONOMY?

The cover of David Laidler's *The Golden Age of the Quantity Theory* (1991a) shows the faces of three economists, Irving Fisher, Alfred Marshall and Knut Wicksell, who have cast long shadows over modern monetary economics, so that few later developments are unrelated to the work of at least one of them (apart from some purely technical developments, and those that are in the spirit of Louis Bachelier's 1900 dissertation on stochastic processes and financial speculation). The quantity theory of money is the oldest surviving theory in economics (going back beyond David Hume's 1752 essays to the Salamanca School and to Jean Bodin, both in the sixteenth century), but, as Laidler (1991b) has put it, the quantity theory is always and everywhere controversial. It has long been observed that monetary shocks have real effects in the short run (see Humphrey (1986) on Hume and Henry Thornton). Some questions recur repeatedly in the literature of monetary economics since the time of Fisher and Wicksell. Should the money supply be viewed as endogenous or exogenous? How is monetary economics related to general equilibrium analysis of the real economy and real interest (the problem of integrating Fisher's monetary theory of economic fluctuations with his 1892 dissertation on general equilibrium and of bringing together the two volumes of Wicksell's lectures on political economy)? Why does unbacked fiat money have a positive value when other stores of value exist with higher rates of return? Does the fact that the economy in which we live is a monetary economy, rather than a barter economy, have implications for the existence, uniqueness, or global stability of full-employment equilibrium?

Milton Friedman's work in monetary economics was explicitly a revival of the quantity theory tradition, drawing most directly on Chicago sources (most notably Henry Simons on rules versus discretion in monetary policy) but also on the wider tradition going back to Hume, to the young Keynes of *A Tract on Monetary Reform* (1923), and, recognized most clearly in Friedman's later writings, on Irving Fisher, an earlier advocate of a monetary policy rule with a varying exchange rate, of indexation, of adaptive expectations, of expected inflation as the difference between real and nominal interest rates, and of monetary shocks as the primary cause of economic fluctuations (while, beyond monetary economics, Friedman's permanent income hypothesis built on Fisher's two-period consumption diagram). Friedman and Schwartz (1963) explored monetary history, finding that the exogenous policy mistakes of the Federal Reserve System account for the severity of the Great Depression, to which may be added the analysis by Fisher (1935) of how the fixed exchange rates of the gold exchange standard then spread the Depression from country to country (an empirical analysis that was independently rediscovered by several writers from 1980 onwards). Friedman (1968) combined the Phillips curve relating inflation and unemployment (see Fisher 1926) with adaptive expectations (related to Fisher's use of distributed lags to find expected inflation) to argue that, as any constant rate of inflation came gradually to be anticipated, unemployment would return to its natural rate (a term recalling Wicksell's natural rate of interest). Although Friedman had championed Marshall's methodology against that of Walras, he identified the natural rate of unemployment as the number ground out by the Walrasian system of equations for general equilibrium (a surprise to general equilibrium theorists such as Frank Hahn, who were not aware of any proof of uniqueness of equilibrium except under restrictive assumptions). Friedman's very influential contributions to monetary economics were, consciously and explicitly, formalization and synthesis of concepts with long histories.

The work of James Tobin was shaped by John Hicks's 'Suggestion for Simplifying the Theory of Money' (1935) as well as by Keynes (1936), both directly and as interpreted by Hicks (1937). Tobin looked to portfolio choice and to transactions costs to rationalize the positive value of fiat money and the holding of money when other assets had higher returns. He was particularly concerned with Keynes's argument that a monetary economy might not automatically readjust to full employment after a sufficiently large negative demand shock, an issue relating to the call by Leijonhufvud (1981) for models of an economy that normally is self-adjusting, with the adjustment mechanism breaking down under exceptionally severe shocks. Tobin (1980) analysed this question in the spirit of Keynes (1936, Chapter 19) on why flexible money wage rates may be stabilizing and of Fisher (1933) on the debt-deflation process. While the Pigou-Haberler-Patinkin real balance effect showed that a *lower* price level would increase aggregate demand by increasing the real value of outside money (the non-interest-bearing monetary base), Tobin (1980), following Keynes and Fisher, argued that a *falling* price level would have the opposite effect of increasing demand for real money balances, increasing the risk of bankruptcy, and transferring wealth from borrowers to lenders (see also Minsky 1982). If how rapidly prices and wages would fall depends on how far the economy is from its full-employment equilibrium, which effect dominates (that is, whether the economy will move back towards full-employment equilibrium or further away) will depend on how far the initial shock has pushed the economy from equilibrium. As with Friedman, this contribution by Tobin was a formalization and synthesis of earlier concepts.

REAL BUSINESS CYCLES AND CREATIVE DESTRUCTION

Monetary approaches to economic fluctuations, whether in the quantity theory tradition of Hume (1752), Fisher with Brown (1911), Hawtrey (1913, 1932), and Friedman and Schwartz (1963) on the short-run real effects of monetary shocks, or in the Keynesian tradition of Keynes (1936) on effective demand determining the equilibrium level of employment in a monetary economy, look to variations in aggregate demand to explain changes in output, although differing over whether the system is self-adjusting after shocks and whether the source of shocks is public policy or private spending. An alternative of long standing interprets output fluc-tuations as shifts in aggregate supply, due to changes in technology and the capital stock (or to fluctuations in their rates of change). Real business cycle theory, honored by the award of the 2004 Nobel Prize in economics to Finn Kydland and Edward Prescott (see Hoover (1988) for references and an evaluation of the approach), continues this line of analysis.

Charles Goodhart and John Presley (1994) and David Laidler (1999, pp. 90–91) note that, like the real business cycle theorists, Joseph Schumpeter (1912), and, as Laidler mentions, Minnie T. England (1912, 1913), Dennis Robertson (1915, 1926) emphasized the role of sector-specific invention and innovation (rather than changes in money supply or demand) in gen-erating cycles in aggregate investment and output (along with productivity shocks in agriculture due to weather, previously stressed by W. S. Jevons). Like T. N. Carver, C. F. Bickerdike, and Albert Aftalion (reprinted in Dimand 2002, Vol. III), and Ralph Hawtrey (1913), Robertson (1915, p. 125) took account of the accelerator effect of a sectoral increase in invest-ment (Goodhart and Presley 1994, p. 291, suggest that real business cycle theorists still have something to learn from Robertson about the transmis-sion of sectoral changes to the aggregate economy). Although Robertson (1926) allowed for monetary and psychological influences as secondary factors in economic fluctuations, he began with an entirely non-monetary analysis of individual, self-employed producers, remarking that

> the fact that our long, complicated, and perhaps not unfruitful discussion has been conducted so far almost entirely without reference to specifically monetary

> phenomena relieves us of the necessity of a formal refutation of those who, like
> Clement Juglar and Mr Hawtrey [1913], find in monetary influences the sole
> and sufficient explanation of industrial fluctuation. (Robertson 1915, p. 211)

An invention or an exogenous positive productivity shock in agriculture
makes an 'instrumental good' (capital good) or a consumption good
cheaper in real terms. Although Robertson (1915) was concerned with
fluctuations in industrial production, 'an increase, due to an increased
bounty of nature, in the exchange value of industrial products against the
products of agriculture' would stimulate industrial output just as well as
'the increase in the expected future productivity' due to 'some physical
or legal invention' or 'A general increase in the physical productivity of
effort due to the adoption of improved methods, etc. under the stimulus of
depression' (ibid., p. 239). Assuming that demand for that good is elastic
in terms of own-effort, each individual producer will provide more effort,
increasing output not only of the good subject to the positive productive
shocks but also of other goods made by producers who would buy the good
that has become cheaper (see the diagram in ibid., pp. 132, 204; Goodhart
and Presley 1994, p. 282, which shows curves for the marginal utility of all
other goods and the marginal disutility of effort). How long the expansion
lasted would depend on the gestation time, indivisibility, and durability
of the new investment projects (Robertson, in his 1948 introduction to a
reissue of his 1915 book, cited railways, steel, electricity, and oil refining as
areas in which inventions led to major new investments). Robertson, like
the real business cycle school, thus had a theory of fluctuations that did
not depend on imperfect information about prices, labour market failure,
or stickiness of prices and nominal wages. In contrast, Pigou (1927, p. 56)
held that real causes of cycles such as invention and innovation could,
in general, be disregarded in favour of a psychological theory stressing
waves of optimism and pessimism. Like Austrian trade cycle theorists such
as Friedrich Hayek (1931) and like modern equilibrium business cycle
theory, Robertson considered some economic fluctuation as 'Appropriate
Fluctuations of Output' (the title of Chapter II of Robertson 1926), inevitable and perhaps even desirable, declaring on the last page of Robertson
(1915) that 'out of the welter of industrial dislocation the great permanent
riches of the future are generated'. However, 'the temptation to over-
investment may involve a general rupture between the sacrifice involved
in postponing consumption and the future satisfaction procured by means
of that sacrifice (Robertson 1915, p. 200), an Austrian-sounding reference to coordination failure in inter-temporal allocation (deviation from
the inter-temporal equilibrium represented by the celebrated diagram of
Fisher 1907, p. 409) except that, as Laidler (1999, pp. 91–2) points out,

Robertson did not parallel Mises and Hayek in their attribution of such coordination failure to the central bank and the monetary system getting the interest rate wrong. For Robertson, unlike Pigou (1927), 'the temptation to over-investment' occurred in the course of an expansion initiated by a real shock.

Beyond the elements of real business cycle analysis of Robertson (1915), another key feature of real business cycle and endogenous growth theory derives from Schumpeter (1912), a link emphasized by Philippe Aghion and Peter Howitt (1998), whose second chapter is entitled 'The Schumpeterian Approach'. This key feature is Schumpeter's concept of creative destruction, competition among innovating entrepreneurs to find new ideas that will make the physical, human, and intellectual capital of their rivals obsolete. Instead of thinking of competition in static terms as the absence of market power, Schumpeterian creative destruction looks to a competitive quest to create market power and acquire quasi-rents. An indication of how widely this concept has been adopted is that the spell-checker for MS Word recognizes the adjective Schumpeterian. Such recognition does not as yet extend to the work of Minnie Throop England (1912, 1913), even though both Schumpeter and Wesley Mitchell (1927) identified her as the economist whose theory of fluctuations and growth was closest to that of Schumpeter and even though Schumpeter had reviewed a monograph by England as early as 1908 (see Dimand 1999). John Elliott (1980) noted the resemblance of Schumpeterian creative destruction to Marx's vision of capitalism, but it would be asking too much to expect the endogenous growth literature to acknowledge that link.

What do real business cycle and endogenous growth theorists have that would have been unavailable to an earlier theorist with the economic interests and mathematical ability and training of Louis Bachelier or Frank Ramsey or Eugen Slutsky if he or she had read Albert Aftalion (1913), Schumpeter (1912), England (1913), Robertson (1915) and Hayek (1931)? First of all, techniques of time series analysis, heavily used in analysing the dynamics of cycles and growth, have improved greatly in sophistication, advancing far beyond such early methods as the periodogram analysis with which Sir William Beveridge could convince himself that any set of observed fluctuations was truly periodic by simply assuming the existence of a sufficiently large number of superimposed cycles of differing period and amplitude (although, with different statistical methods, quantitative economists have pursued Beveridge's goal of decomposing economic time series into trend, cycles, and irregular fluctuations). These advances in time series analysis began with Slutsky (1937), demonstrating that filtering and averaging of a random series could produce seeming cycles (so that 'business cycles' as the name of a field is now just a synonym for fluctuations, and implies nothing about whether fluctuations are truly periodic), and Ragnar Frisch (1933), showing that cycles could be oscillatory responses to shocks that were not themselves cyclical (freeing economists from searching for cyclical sources of exogenous shocks, such as Jevons's sunspots), but technical progress in the field has gone much further.

The major innovation in real business cycles and growth, however, is a mathematical formalization of a much earlier insight. Surprisingly, the concept that sets modern real business cycle analysis apart from the Schumpeter-England-Robertson-Hayek versions was hiding in plain sight like Edgar Allan Poe's purloined letter in what should have been the most noticeable place: the first three chapters of Adam Smith's *Inquiry into the Nature and Causes of the Wealth of Nations*. That concept is increasing returns to scale: the engine of productivity growth and the stimulus to invention is increasing the division of labour (specialization and exchange), which is limited by the extent of the market. Paul Krugman (1990, p. 4) writes that, 'The long dominance of Ricardo over Smith – of comparative advantage over increasing returns – was largely due to the belief that the alternative was necessarily a mess. In effect, the theory of international trade followed the perceived line of least mathematical resistance'. So too did the theories of business cycles and economic growth. Until simple and elegant ways were found to incorporate increasing returns to scale in formal models, it was ignored. Once such formalization was developed, increasing returns could be linked to creative invention and innovation, creative destruction, and technical progress as an endogenous trend with random shocks, and the trade, growth, and real business cycles literatures took off. Apart from the acknowledgement of Schumpeter by Aghion and Howitt (1998), these literatures often gave scant recognition to the giants on whose shoulders they stood: the quoted passage from the introduction to Krugman (1990) is the only mention of Smith in that volume of collected articles, while Grossman and Helpman (1991, p. 1) cite Nicholas Kaldor only for his 'stylized facts' of economic growth without ever mentioning that he had modelled endogenous technological change, admittedly at a time when doing so was decidedly non-mainstream and even heretical (however, they do quote Schumpeter twice, although not Schumpeter 1912).

Even when a model is presented as a formalization of a past insight, however, acquaintance with the nature of that insight may be perfunctory while still sufficient to recognize a continuity of topic. Even though Paul Beaudry and Franck Portier entitle their article 'An exploration into Pigou's theory of cycles', the only mention of Pigou is in the second paragraph of the introduction, in connection with the difficulty agents have in forecasting the economy's need for capital:

For example, this difficulty was seen by Pigou as being an inherent feature of any economy with technological progress. As emphasized by Pigou (1926) [*sic* – 1927], when agents are optimistic about the future and decide to build up capital in expectation of future demand then, in the case where their expectations are not met, there will be a period of retrenched investment which is likely to cause a recession. (Beaudry and Portier 2004, p. 1183)

The Great Depression of the 1930s has served as the crucial experiment for macroeconomic theories, demonstrating according to Keynes (1936) that the economic system is not self-adjusting to full employment after large negative demand shocks, according to Fisher (1933) and Minsky (1982) the fragility of a financial system that has inside debt of fixed nominal value, and according to Friedman and Schwartz (1963) that a substantial reduction in the money supply will severely affect real output and employment. Schumpeter (1939) explained the Depression as the fortuitous coincidence in three cycles of differing periodicity, exacerbated by misguided government efforts to stimulate the economy. Although Schumpeter (1939) did not persuade his audience, real business cycle theorists have attempted to use total factor productivity shocks in neoclassical growth theory to explain the major depressions of the twentieth century (Kehoe and Prescott 2002). In light of criticism of real business cycle theory as theory ahead of measurement, it is striking to read the editor's introduction (p. 1) summarizing Cole and Ohanian (1999) and Prescott (1999): 'While Cole and Ohanian find that conventional shocks fall far short of a satisfactory explanation' of the Great Depression in the United States, 'Edward Prescott embraces the conclusion that they found themselves unable to reach: Prescott says that Cole and Ohanian's work in this issue has changed his views on the Great Depression, and he predicts that their version of the facts will influence the direction of macroeconomic research. Prescott conjectures that ultimately the Depression will be explained by industrial and labor market policies of the period'.

For the purposes of this chapter, the development of real business cycle theory and the related development of endogenous growth theory (and, outside macroeconomics, the theory of international trade with imperfect competition, market power, and increasing returns) display a striking pattern. The advances in this area in the last twenty or twenty-five years have come, not from new concepts or new ways of looking at the world, but from advances in technique that allowed the formalization and fruitful synthesis of approaches with long and distinguished histories.

INCREASING RETURNS, ENDOGENOUS GROWTH, AND THE CLASS OF 1928

There was a remarkable false dawn of modern growth theory at the end of 1928. Although theorizing about the causes of growth goes back at least to Quesnay and Smith (see Hoselitz 1960; Eltis 1984), three journal articles in November and December 1928 brought the question to a new level of coherence, formalization, and insight. Allyn Young (1928), recently arrived from Harvard to a chair at the London School of Economics, gave a presidential address to Section F of the British Association on 'Increasing Returns and Economic Progress', a bold call for a theory of economic growth built around Adam Smith's concept of increasing returns to scale, anticipating the themes of endogenous growth theory (see Sandilands 2000). This address was much admired and for a long time had no influence whatsoever. This might be because Young (1928) is a presidential address and not a mathematical model (see Paul Romer quoted by David Laidler (2004, pp. 410–11), with the discussion of a diagram in an endnote being the only formal analysis, but the same could be said of Friedman (1968), the most influential presidential address in economics. In the December 1928 issue of the *Economic Journal*, Young (1928) immediately followed a mathematical analysis of optimal capital accumulation by the Cambridge mathematician and philosopher Frank Ramsey (1928), with credit to the journal's editor, his King's College colleague J. M. Keynes, for a helpful discussion of the rate at which people will be willing to give up present enjoyment to approach the bliss point (Ramsey 1928, p. 545). Ramsey's article, also much respected, was, in contrast to Young's paper, too mathematical to have wide influence among economists for several decades. In that same month and the preceding month, G. A. Fel'dman (1928) of Gosplan published a remarkable two-part article in the Soviet journal of economic planning proposing a mathematical theory of the growth of national income and consumption and the relationships among sectoral growth rates, based on Karl Marx's schema of simple and expanded reproduction in Volume II of *Capital* (see Lianos 1979 and Trigg 2002 on the relation of Marx's reproduction schema and conditions for balanced growth to Evsey Domar's growth model).

Young and Ramsey were highly respected and influential scholars, and Gosplan, then at the start of the Soviet Union's First Five-Year Plan, had a desperate need for the mathematical techniques of planning econometric growth that re-emerged after the Stalinist catastrophe as 'planometrics', to which Marx's reproduction schema provided a cloak of respectability (Fel'dman 1928, Ramsey 1928, and Young 1928 are reprinted in Dimand 2002, vol. III). Young had been brought to Britain with the intention that he would dominate economic theory at LSE, while Ramsey could interest the formidable Keynes in formal growth theory. By 1930, however, Young and Ramsey were prematurely dead (Ramsey just short of his twenty-seventh birthday) and Fel'dman had disappeared in the purges that savaged Gosplan, destroyed the internationally-respected economic research institutes headed by N. D. Kondrate'ev and A. Chayanov, and removed planning decisions from the sphere of rational calculation. Nicholas Kaldor, the future proponent of an economic growth model including a technical progress function, attended, and kept from his notes from Young's LSE lectures on increasing returns and economic growth. Marx's reproduction schema reappeared in David Hawkins's 1948 article on what became the Hawkins-Simon conditions for macroeconomic stability (see Hawkins's article and the subsequent note by Hawkins and Herbert Simon, both in Dimand 2002, vol. III), and were echoed, along with Quesnay's *Tableau Economique*, in Wassily Leontief's input-output tables. Otherwise, the contributions to growth theory of November and December 1928 were not followed up. Harrod-Domar growth theory was not concerned with increasing returns to scale, endogenous technical change, or optimal saving. Nonetheless, once the mathematical prowess of economists had advanced to the stage of being able to formalize Young (1928) and to read and understand Ramsey (1928), the 'New Growth Theory' took the form of a formalization and synthesis of concepts advanced in 1928.

THEORY AND/OR MEASUREMENT

In 1947, Tjalling Koopmans, the director of the Cowles Commission for Research in Economics, which was then at the University of Chicago, wrote a hostile review article criticizing Burns and Mitchell (1946) and the entire National Bureau of Economic Research approach to business cycles as 'Measurement without Theory' (Koopmans's article and his subsequent exchange with Rutledge Vining are reprinted in Hendry and Morgan 1995, while Dimand 2002, vol. VII, reprints Koopmans's articles from 1941 and 1949 making a positive case for his econometric approach to business cycles). Among other things, Koopmans's review article was an incident in the intramural feuding of the Cowles Commission and the Chicago School, for it was an affront to Milton Friedman, who had done his doctoral dissertation with Arthur F. Burns, had written a sceptical review of the second volume of Tinbergen (1939), and who was provoked to devote his memorial article on Mitchell to arguing that Mitchell was an economic theorist. It also raised questions of continuing importance about how the relationship can or should be between formal economic and statistical theory and quantitative empirical economics and how each affects the other, highlighting differences in approach between two groups of quantitative economists who hitherto, despite contrasting attitudes to formal theory, cooperated amiably (Wesley Mitchell was one of the first cohort of Fellows of the Econometric Society).

Although Mitchell, who gave a celebrated lecture course at Columbia on types of economic theories and their history, was well read in mainstream neoclassical economics, he and his institutionalist associates at NBER wished to build up generalizations by looking for patterns of leads and lags in time series, rather than starting from *a priori* theory. Mitchell had begun his career as a student of J. Laurence Laughlin at the University of Chicago (then a bastion of opposition to the quantity theory of money), by showing that movements in the US money supply did not explain movements in the price level, a disproof of the quantity theory that did not survive taking account of trends in velocity of circulation and the growing demand for real money balances as the economy grew (see Fisher with Brown 1911). In the 1920s, NBER studies such as Mitchell (1927) questioned the monetary theory of economic fluctuations, reporting that the price level did not seem to explain the level of economic activity or employment, whereas Fisher's studies (such as Fisher 1926) obtained very different results by correlating unemployment or an index of economic activity with a distributed lag of *changes* in the price level.

Koopmans argued that without starting from theory, the empirical researcher will lack means to gauge which observations are relevant to testing a hypothesis, and that facts do not speak for themselves but only, at best, respond to questions posed to them. In particular, in a Cowles monograph that he edited and another that he co-edited in the 1950s, Koopmans argued for the estimation of structural simultaneous-equations econometric models, whose identification (being able to distinguish one equation from a linear combination of the model's equations, to solve for the structural form from the reduced form) depended on prior theoretical arguments that certain exogenous (or predetermined) variables belonging as explanatory variables in some equations but not in others. The model could then be tested for misspecification statistically (as by the Box-Cox transformation, a name recalling a Victorian comic opera but referring to testing linear versus log-linear specification) and by out-of-sample prediction. Specification searches (data mining), however, made it too easy to find some specification that appeared to fit the data well. The growth and disaggregation of such models by the 1960s and early 1970s, although remarkable, did not instil widespread confidence, which was weakened by the influential single-equation methods of the Federal Reserve Bank of St Louis monetarist model and by the warning of Robert Lucas (previously suggested by Jacob Marshak, Koopmans's predecessor as director of Cowles) that changes in policy regime would change the structural equations, making structural models unsuitable for predicting the effects of policy changes. One highly controversial response to this apparent impasse, the vector autoregressions (VARs) or atheoretical macroeconometrics of Christopher Sims (1980, 1996), revives (with more modern technical apparatus) the NBER approach of Wesley Mitchell: investigating the stochastic properties of the observed time series, instead of assuming that one actually has enough *a priori* information about exclusionary restrictions (or enough exogenous variables) to identify structural models. Again, an earlier debate has recurred and a noteworthy contemporary contribution turns out to be an earlier approach developed with a more advanced technical apparatus.

THE LABOUR MARKET IN MACROECONOMICS

A recurring question in economics is whether unemployment should be analysed as a problem of adjustment in the labour market, as Beveridge argued in 1909 and 1930 (Beveridge 1930), or as a macroeconomic problem, as Beveridge argued after his conversion to Keynesianism. It is possible to hold one of these positions on analytical grounds while endorsing the policy implications of the other, so that Pigou (1933) presented a non-monetary analysis of how wage cuts could eliminate unemployment at a time when Pigou, like Keynes, argued for expanding demand through public works and lower interest rates as a response to unemployment (Dimand 1988, pp. 76–7 on Pigou and on Gösta Bagge of Lund). The chapter in Pigou (1927) on 'The Part Played by Rigidity in Wage-Rates' argued that an all-round reduction in money wages would eliminate unemployment (apart from frictional unemployment), because prices would fall by less than money wages. Similarly, in his later articles on the real balance effect in a monetary economy, Pigou insisted that in theory a lower wage rate and price level could restore full employment even with a liquidity trap, while emphasizing that this abstract exercise did not affect what he considered the practical case for expanding aggregate demand instead of waiting for wage cuts to deal with unemployment.

There were prominent economists in the 1920s and early 1930s, such as Gustav Cassel, Jacques Rueff, Sir Josiah Stamp, and Edwin Cannan who attributed high unemployment to trade union policies and subsidized unemployment benefits (see Dimand 1988, pp. 66–9; Casson 1983). In his presidential address to the Royal Economic Society, Cannan insisted that general unemployment is in reality to be explained almost in the same way as particular unemployment . . . General unemployment appears when asking too much is a general phenomenon. . . . So-called 'fixed interest' should be allowed to be eaten away by defaults and stoppages without too much attention being given to the injustices involved. Money-wages and salaries should be allowed to be reduced without resistance to the reductions being backed by the state and public opinion (Cannan 1932, pp. 366–7, 370; see also Sir Henry Clay 1928).

Rueff's 1931 *Revue d'Economie Politique* article on unemployment insurance as a cause of permanent unemployment (reprinted as a booklet with a foreword by Charles Rist and much later in the same journal on the fiftieth anniversary of the article's first publication) was summarized and quoted at length in two articles by Stamp in *The Times* in June 1931, sparking Parliamentary discussion of the analysis. Similarly, Pigou's 1927 *Economic Journal* article on 'Wages Policy and Unemployment' (reprinted in Dimand 2002, vol. VIII) estimated that the unemployment insurance system added five percentage points to Britain's unemployment rate. In 1936–37, Beveridge, the Director of LSE, reacted to Keynes (1936) by presenting 'An Analysis of Unemployment' marshalling quantitative evidence to show that all current British unemployment was frictional, seasonal, or structural, with none left to be explained by demand deficiency (in a series of three *Economica* articles reprinted in Dimand 2002, vol. VIII). The most technically sophisticated contribution to this literature was W. H. Hutt's *Theory of Idle Resources* (1939), a search-theoretic analysis of unemployment anticipating later developments in the field.

Daniel Benjamin and Levis Kochin (1978, p. 315, see also Benjamin and Kochin 1979; Kehoe and Prescott 2002), with full acknowledgement of Rueff and Stamp as predecessors, revived the 'explanation of persistent unemployment in interwar Britain: the dole did it. Although aggregate demand was chiefly responsible for the high unemployment in 1921 and 1930–1932, the million man armies of the unemployed of the late 1920s and the late 1930s were for the most part volunteer armies', adding that the dole was 'an extraordinarily generous poorly safe-guarded system' (although three million applicants were rejected in 1921–1930 as not genuinely seeking work, another 460 000 because of the means test, and from 1930 any married woman who lost a job was held to have left the labour force). Martin Feldstein, as their discussant, pointed out that what had increased the ratio of unemployment benefits to wage rates was the deflation of wages and prices associated with the return to the gold standard at the prewar parity in 1925, and that part of the rise in the recorded unemployment rate would be fuller registration of the unemployed as the deflation increased the real value of benefits.

The contrasting view, epitomized by Keynes (1936), holds that output and employment are determined in the economy as a whole, not just the labour market, and that money wage bargains cannot achieve market-clearing real wages because the price level is endogenous and affected by money wage rates. Edmond Malinvud (1977, 1998–2000) and Jacques Dreze (1991) offer formalization of Keynes's concept of an unemployment equilibrium, in which deficient effective demand causes unemployment: the value of the labour that an unemployed worker is unable to sell in a quantity-constrained labour market is not part of the budget constraint for that worker's demand for goods, so that a suboptimal result occurs even though the firms would be willing to hire the workers if the workers would buy the goods. Jean-Pascal Benassy (2002) develops this approach with emphasis on imperfect competition, pioneered by Joan Robinson (1933). The emphasis is on coordination failure, which is ruled out by New Classical models that assume the economy can be portrayed by a representative agent (or in overlapping generations models, two representative agents, one old and one young). Models in which the labour market does not clear (so that there is an excess supply of labour, with workers who would be willing to work at a lower wage and firms that would hire them at that lower wage) raise the question of why some mutually beneficial trades are not made (see De Vroey 2004 on the long history of attempts by economists to grapple with the elusive concept of involuntary unemployment). Recently, this question has been answered by reformulating the problem in terms of the game-theoretic concepts of strategic complementarity and Social Dilemmas, the *n*-player analogue of Prisoner's Dilemma (Russell Cooper 1998; B. Curtis Eaton 2004). This important advance in understanding has taken the form of a fruitful synthesis with concepts from game theory, allowing for formalization of the long-held informal insight that if all firms increased their hiring, workers might increase their spending in a way that justified the expansion of employment, but that there is no incentive for any one firm to act alone in this manner.

Keynes (1936, Chapter 2) suggested that money wages could be sticky downwards without any irrationality (or in Fisher's phrase, money illusion) on the part of the workers, because workers may quite rationally care about relative wages, which are altered when one group of workers accepts a wage cut. John Taylor's analysis of nominal wage stickiness due to overlapping contracts formalizes that idea, although there remains room for explanations of why wage contracts are made in nominal terms or why different groups negotiate at different times. In the Depression of the 1930s, Gardiner Means attributed nominal rigidities to the 'administered prices' of large corporations. It has recently been questioned whether those prices were as rigid as they appeared, leading to the discovery that Oskar Morgenstern (1931) had already pointed out that price cuts in recession often took the form of offering discounts without changing posted prices (Dimand 2000). Truman Bewley (2000) and Alan Blinder et al. (1998) have taken the daringly unconventional step (for economists) of asking corporate and union executives why they don't cut wages and prices in recessions, shedding light on the relative wage hypothesis of Keynes (1936, Chapter 2).

Another recurring issue is the cyclical pattern of real wages. As the related question of whether real and money wages move in the same direction (money wages being pro-cyclical) this attracted much attention in the wake of Keynes's *General Theory* (Dimand 2002, vol. VIII, reprints three articles on the subject by Lorie Tarshis, two by each of John Dunlop and Richard Ruggles, and one by Keynes, all from 1938–1941). The rigid money-wage version of Keynesian economics implies a counter-cyclical real wage, as does Lucas's monetary misperceptions version of New Classical economics, while real business cycle theory (in which output and employment rise when a positive shock to labour productivity shifts both aggregate supply and labour demand schedules to the right) implies a pro-cyclical real wage. The debate of 1938–1941 continues to recur, with more advanced statistical techniques applied to the same questions, but with inconclusive results (Abraham and Haltiwanger 1995).

RECURRING PATTERNS

Certain issues keep recurring in debates in macroeconomics: Are fluctuations the result of monetary disturbances or real productivity shocks? Is unemployment to be analysed as the malfunctioning of the labour market (due to trade unions or unemployment benefits) or as a macroeconomic phenomenon? Are real wages pro-cyclical or counter-cyclical? Can government counteract instability caused by volatile private investment driven by the difficulty of predicting future profitability, or government itself the source of instability? Can government act freely to stabilize the economy, or are policy-makers endogenous (see Kalecki 1943 and the entries on political business cycles and electoral business cycles in Glasner 1997)? How closely are theory and measurement related, how should they affect each other, and can economists observe things their theories have not told them to expect? Are the consistent microeconomic foundations of representative agent models (or in earlier literature the Marshallian representative firm) worth the cost of ruling out heterogeneity, cooperation problems, and even trade? How sticky are prices and nominal wages, and can this stickiness be explained as the result of rational behaviour? On each of these topics macroeconomists still theorize, measure, test, and argue, and in doing so, unconsciously or not, they 'stand on the shoulders of giants' who discussed these questions before. Typically, advances take the form of discovering how to formalize a concept with a long history, such as increasing returns to scale or strategic complementarity, in a way that permits a fruitful synthesis of two or more concepts long present in the literature. There are refinements and clarifications, as when Fisher (1930, p. 216) gave the first clear and correct statement of the marginal opportunity cost of holding money. Much more rarely, an entirely new and important concept is introduced, most notably Keynes's idea that macroeconomics is a theory of the determination of output as a whole by the intersection of aggregate supply and aggregate demand, by analogy to the microeconomic analysis of the intersection of supply and demand curves for particular goods (see Skidelsky 2009, the dust jacket of which promises to explain 'Why, Sixty Years After His Death, John Maynard Keynes is the Most Important Economic Thinker for America', and also Bateman, et al. 2010 and Dimand et al. 2010). *The Economist* (2009, 'Irving Fisher: Out of Keynes's Shadow') announces that 'Today's crisis has given new relevance to the ideas of another great economist of the Depression era': Irving Fisher's 1933 theory, developed further by Minsky (1982), that macroeconomic stability is affected by the existence of inside debt denominated in nominal terms, with price deflation redistributing wealth between borrowers and lenders and increasing the risk of bankruptcy, and hence risk premia on loans (a debt-deflation process also sketched by Keynes in his 1931 Harris Foundation lectures in Chicago and a paragraph in Keynes 1936, see Dimand 2005). The post-2007 financial crisis has also redirected attention to Austrian business cycle theory (*The Economist* 2010, 'Taking von Mises to Pieces') and, reaching much further back, to 'How Adam Smith Would Fix the Financial Crisis' (Bholat 2009; Mussa 2009).

Another pattern is the postwar internationalization (or Americanization) of macroeconomics, like the rest of economics. There is no longer a distinct Stockholm school of Wicksell's followers, and although the Austrian school of trade cycle theory, founded by Mises and Hayek among the followers of Menger's subjective value theory and Boehm-Bawerk's capital theory, still survives as a critical approach marginal to mainstream economics, it no longer has any particular ties to Vienna, Austria or LSE (see entries in Glasner 1997 and Snowdon and Vane 2002 on these schools and their leading figures). The adoption of a common language and a common set of journals and conferences has improved communication from earlier periods in which Robertson (1915) did not know of Schumpeter (1912), Fisher did not know the writings of Walras, Pareto, and Edgeworth until he had almost finished the dissertation in which he independently invented general equilibrium analysis (so that Samuelson has modestly called it the greatest dissertation in economics but Robert Dorfman argued that it should have been rejected as unoriginal), and such concepts as the accelerator, the multiplier, the Phillips curve, and the real balance effect were independently invented several times (see Hawtrey, Giblin, Kahn, Warming, Meade, and Clark on the multiplier; Carver, Bickerdike, and Aftalion on the accelerator, all in Dimand 2002, vols. II and III and Fisher 1926 on the Phillips curve, which was also estimated by Tinbergen in 1937). But there has also been a cost: diminished knowledge of economics in other languages now accompanies diminished knowledge of the past of economics. It is now largely forgotten that *Econometrica*, founded 1933, initially developed alongside the *Archiv für mathematische Wirtschafts- und Sozialforschung*, founded in 1935, but the latter did not survive the war (see Tinbergen 1937). Thus Baumol and Tobin (1989) found themselves acknowledging that Maurice Allais (1947) had already published the square root rule for the inventory approach to the transactions demand for money (Francis Y. Edgeworth had derived such a square root rule in 1888 for the demand for bank reserves), Malinvaud (1987) has drawn attention to the publication of the overlapping generations model of money in that same appendix of Allais (1947), 11 years before Samuelson, and the 'Golden Rules of Economic Growth' discovered by Edmund Phelps and others in the 1960s are also to be found in Allais (1947). No doubt the rest of that lengthy book will become known as it is independently reinvented piece by piece, but until then, like Bachelier's extensive post-1900 writings on mathematical finance and despite Allais's 1988 Nobel Prize (widely believed to be just for the Allais paradox in choice theory), the rest of the book remains inaccessible to the mainstream of the discipline and is therefore presumed to be inconsequential (just as we know Roy's Identity but cannot identify René Roy).

Along with becoming more international, macroeconomics in the postwar era has steadily become more mathematical. This has often, but perhaps not always, allowed for greater clarity in stating theories, and has also allowed the recasting of concepts in ways suitable for formal modelling, synthesis with other theoretical concepts, and empirical application and testing. The resulting differences in notation and in formality of presentation have also helped to obscure the close relationship between current controversies, questions, and analyses and those of previous generations of economists, resulting in the temporary (or sometimes perhaps permanent) loss of insights and perspectives and on occasion in the laborious reinvention of the wheel in new notation.

NOTE

1. I am grateful for helpful comments on earlier versions of this chapter at an international conference on the history of macroeconomics at Louvain-la-Neuve and at the 'Keynes at 125' mini-conference at the Canadian Economics Association annual meeting in Vancouver in 2008.

BIBLIOGRAPHY

Abraham, K. G. and J. C. Haltiwanger (1995), 'Real wages and the business Cycle', *Journal of Economic Literature*, **33**(3) (September), 1215–64.

Aftalion, A. (1913), *Les crises périodiques de surproduction*, 2 vols, Paris: M. Pivière.

Aghion, P. and P. Howitt (1998), *Endogenous Growth Theory*, Cambridge, MA: MIT Press.

Allais, M. (1947), *Économie et intérêt*, 2 vols, Paris: Imprimerie Nationale.

Bachelier, L. (1900), *Théorie de la spéculation*, Paris: Gauthier-Villars; reprinted in P. Cootner (ed.) with a translation by A. J. Bonness, *The Random Character of Stock Market Prices*, Cambridge, MA: MIT Press.

Backhouse, R. (1995), *Interpreting Macroeconomics: Explorations in the History of Macroeconomic Thought*, London: Routledge.

Barnett, P. (1941), 'Business-cycle theory in the United States, 1860–1900', *Journal of Business of the University of Chicago*, **14** (supplement), 1–124.

Barro, R. (1984), *Macroeconomics*, Cambridge, MA: MIT Press.

Bateman, B., T. Hirai, and M. C. Marcuzzo (eds) (2010), *The Return to Keynes,* Cambridge, MA: Harvard University Press.

Baumol, W. J. and J. Tobin (1989), 'The optimal cash balance proposition: Maurice Allais's priority', *Journal of Economic Literature*, **27**(3) (September), 1160–62; reprinted in R. W. Dimand, (ed.), *The Origins of Macroeconomics*, vol. 3.

Beaudry, P. and F. Portier (2004), 'An exploration into Pigou's theory of cycles', *Journal of Monetary Economics*, **51**(6) (September), 1183–216.

Bénassy, J. -P. (2002), *The Macroeconomics of Imperfect Competition and Nonclearing Markets: A Dynamic General Equilibrium Approach*, Cambridge, MA: MIT Press.

Benjamin, D. and L. P. Kochin (1978), 'Unemployment and the dole: evidence from interwar britain', with discussion by Martin Feldstein, in H. Grubel and M. Walker (eds), *Unemployment Insurance*, Vancouver, BC: Fraser Institute.

Benjamin, D. and L. P. Kochin (1979), 'Searching for an explanation of unemployment in interwar Britain', *Journal of Political Economy*, **79**(3) (June), 441–78.

Bergmann, E. von (1895), *Geschichte der Nationalökonomischen Krisentheorien*, Stuttgart: Kohlhammer.

Beveridge, W. H. (1930), *Unemployment: A Problem of Industry, 1909 and 1930*, London: Longmans, Green.

Bewley, T. (2000), *Why Don't Wages Fall During a Depression?*, Cambridge, MA: Harvard University Press.

Bholat, D. (2009), 'How Adam Smith Would Fix the Financial Crisis', *Challenge*, **52**(6) (November–December), 60–78.

Blaug, M. (2001), 'No history of ideas please, we're economists', *Journal of Economic Perspectives*, **15**(1) (Winter), 145–64.

Blinder, A. S., E. R. Canetti, D. E. Lebow, and J. B. Rudd (1998), *Asking About Prices: A New Approach to Understanding Price Stickiness*, New York: Russell Sage Foundation.

Bridel, P. (1989), *Cambridge Monetary Thought: The Development of Saving-Investment Analysis from Marshall to Keynes*, Basingstoke: Macmillan.

Burns, A. F. and W. C. Mitchell (1946), *Measuring Business Cycles*, New York: National Bureau of Economic Research.

Cannan, E. (1932), 'The demand for labour', *Economic Journal*, **42**(167) (September), 357–70; reprinted in R. W. Dimand (ed.), *The Origins of Macroeconomics*, vol. 8.

Casson, M. (1983), *Economics of Unemployment: An Historical Perspective*, Oxford: Martin Robertson.

Clay, H. (1928), 'Unemployment and wage rates', *Economic Journal*, **38**(149) (March), 1–14; reprinted in R. W. Dimand (ed.), *The Origins of Macroeconomics*, vol. 8.

Cohen, A. J. and G. C. Harcourt (2003), 'Retrospectives: whatever happened to the Cambridge capital theory controversies?', *Journal of Economic Perspectives*, **17**(1) (Winter), 197–212.

Cole, H. L. and L. E. Ohanian (1999), 'The Great Depression in the United States from a neoclassical perspective', *Federal Reserve Bank of Minneapolis Quarterly Review*, **23**(1) (Winter), 2–24.

Cooper, R. (1998), *Coordination Games*, Cambridge: Cambridge University Press.

De Long, J. B. (2000), 'The triumph of monetarism?', *Journal of Economic Perspectives*, **14**(1) (Winter), 83–94.

De Vroey, M. (2004), *Involuntary Unemployment: The Elusive Quest for a Theory*, London: Routledge.

Dimand, R. W. (1988), *The Origins of the Keynesian Revolution*, Aldershot, UK and Brookfield, VT, USA: Edward Elgar and Stanford, CA: Stanford University Press.

Dimand, R. W. (1999), 'Minnie Throop England on crises and cycles: a neglected early macroeconomist', *Feminist Economics*, **5**(3) (November), 107–26.

Dimand, R. W. (2000), 'Oskar Morgenstern on apparent price rigidity in the 1930s: a comment on Kovenock and Widdows', *European Journal of Political Economy*, **16**(3) (September), 571–3.

Dimand, R. W. (ed.) (2002), *The Origins of Macroeconomics*, 10 vols, London and New York: Routledge.

Dimand, R. W. (2003), 'Interwar monetary and business cycle theory: macroeconomics before Keynes', in W. J. Samuels, J. E. Biddle, and J. B. Davis (eds), *A Companion to the History of Economic Thought*, Malden, MA: Blackwell, pp. 325–42.

Dimand, R. W. (2005), 'Fisher, Keynes, and the corridor of stability', in R. W. Dimand and J. Geanakoplos (eds), *Celebrating Irving Fisher: The Legacy of a Great Economist*, Malden, MA: Blackwell, pp. 185–200; reprinted from *American Journal of Economics and Sociology*, **64**(1) (January), 185–99.

Dimand, R. W., R. A. Mundell and A. Vercelli (eds) (2010), *Keynes's General Theory After Seventy Years*, London: Palgrave Macmillan, International Economic Association Conference, vol. 147.

Dreze, J. H. (1991), *Underemployment Equilibria: Essays in Theory, Econometrics and Policy*, Cambridge: Cambridge University Press.

Eaton, B. C. (2004), 'Presidential address: the elementary economics of social dilemmas', *Canadian Journal of Economics*, **37**(4) (November), pp. 805–29.

The Economist (2009), 'Briefing: Irving Fisher: out of Keynes's shadow', 14 February, pp. 72–3.

The Economist (2010), 'Buttonwood: taking von Mises to pieces: why is the Austrian explanation for the crisis so little discussed?', 20 November, p. 87.

Elliott, J. E. (1980), 'Marx and Schumpeter on capitalism's creative destruction', *Quarterly Journal of Economics*, **95**(1) (August), 45–68.

Eltis, W. A. (1984), *Classical Theories of Economic Growth*, London: Macmillan.

England, M. T. (1912), 'Fisher's theory of crises: a criticism', *Quarterly Journal of Economics*, **27**(1) (November), 95–106; reprinted in R. W. Dimand (ed.), *The Origins of Macroeconomics*, vol. 8.

England, M. T. (1913), 'Economic crises', *Journal of Political Economy*, **21**(4) (April), 345–54.

Fel'dman, G. A. (1928), 'On the theory of the growth rates of national income I and II', translated in N. Spulber (ed.), *Foundations of Soviet Strategy for Economic Growth*, Bloomington, IN: Indiana University Press, 1964, pp. 174–99 and 304–31; reprinted in R. W. Dimand (ed.), *The Origins of Macroeconomics*, vol. 3.

Fisher, I. (1896), *Appreciation and Interest*, New York: Macmillan for the American Economic Association; reprinted in vol. 1, *The Works of Irving Fisher* (1997).

Fisher, I. (1907), *The Rate of Interest*, New York: Macmillan; reprinted in vol. 3, *The Works of Irving Fisher* (1997).

Fisher, I. with H. G. Brown (1911), *The Purchasing Power of Money*, New York: Macmillan; reprinted in vol. 4, *The Works of Irving Fisher* (1997).

Fisher, I. (1926), 'A statistical relationship between unemployment and price level changes', *International Labour Review*, **13**(6) (June), 785–92; reprinted in vol. 8, *The Works of Irving Fisher* (1997); reprinted as 'Lost and found: I discovered the Phillips curve', *Journal of Political Economy*, **81**(2) (March), 496–502.

Fisher, I. (1930), *The Theory of Interest*, New York: Macmillan; reprinted in vol. 9, *The Works of Irving Fisher* (1997).

Fisher, I. (1933), 'The debt-deflation theory of Great Depressions', *Econometrica*, **1**(4) (October), 337–57; reprinted in vol. 10, *The Works of Irving Fisher* (1997).

Fisher, I. (1935), 'Are booms and depressions transmitted internationally through monetary standards', *Bulletion de l'Institut International de Statistique*, **28**(X), pp. 1–29; reprinted in R. W. Dimand, (2003), 'Irving Fisher on the international transmission of booms and depressions through monetary standards', *Journal of Money, Credit, and Banking*, **35**(1) (February), 49–90.

Fisher, I. (1997), *The Works of Irving Fisher*, edited by W.J. Barber assisted by R.W. Dimand, and K. Foster, consulting editor J. Tobin, London: Pickering & Chatto.

Friedman, M. (1968), 'The role of monetary policy', *American Economic Review*, **58**(1) (March), pp. 1–19.

Friedman, M. and A. J. Schwartz (1963), *A Monetary History of the United States 1867-1960*, Princeton, NJ: Princeton University Press for National Bureau of Economic Research.

Frisch, R. (1933), 'Propagation problems and impulse problems in dynamic economics', *Economic Essays in Honour of Gustav Cassel*, London: G. Allen &

Unwin; reprinted in H. Hagemann (ed.), *Business Cycle Theory: Selected Texts 1860–1939*, vol. 4.

Glasner, D. (ed.) (1997), *Business Cycles and Depressions: An Encyclopedia*, New York: Garland.

Goodhart, C. (1992), 'Dennis Robertson and the real business cycle theory: a centenary lecture', in J. Presley (ed.), *Essays on Robertsonian Economics*, Basingstoke: Macmillan.

Goodhart, C. and J. Presley (1994), 'Real business cycle theory: a restatement of Robertsonian economics?', *Economic Notes Monte dei Paschi di Siena*, **23**(2), pp. 275–91.

Grossman, G. P. and E. Helpman (1991), *Innovation and Growth in the Global Economy*, Cambridge, MA: MIT Press.

Hagemann, H. (ed.) (2001–2002), *Business Cycle Theory: Selected Texts 1860–1939*, London: Pickering & Chatto.

Harcourt, G. C. and P. A. Riach (eds) (1997), *A 'Second Edition' of The General Theory*, London and New York: Routledge.

Hawtrey, R. G. (1913), *Good and Bad Trade*, London: Constable; reprinted with 1962 preface by author, New York: Augustus M. Kelley, 1970.

Hawtrey, R. G. (1932), *The Art of Central Banking*, London: Longmans, Green.

Hayek, F. A. (1931), *Prices and Production*, London: Routledge.

Hendry, D. and M. S. Morgan (eds) (1995), *Foundations of Econometric Analysis*, Cambridge: Cambridge University Press.

Hicks, J. R. (1935), 'A suggestion for simplifying the theory of money', *Economica*, New Series, **2**(5) (February), 1–19; reprinted in R. W. Dimand (ed.), *The Origins of Macroeconomics*, vol. 3.

Hicks, J. R. (1937), 'Mr Keynes and the "Classics": a suggested interpretation', *Econometrica*, **5**(2) (April), 147–59; reprinted in R. W. Dimand (ed.), *The Origins of Macroeconomics*, vol. 3.

Hoover, K. D. (1988), *The New Classical Macroeconomics: A Sceptical Inquiry*, Oxford: Blackwell.

Hoselitz, B. F. (ed.) (1960), *Theories of Economic Growth*, New York: Free Press.

Hume, D. (1752), *Political Discourses*, as reprinted in Eugene Rotwein (ed.), *David Hume:Writings on Economics*, Madison, WI: University of Wisconsin Press, 1955.

Humphrey, T. H. (1986), *Essays on Inflation*, 5th edn., Richmond, VA: Federal Reserve Bank of Richmond.

Hutt, W. H. (1939/1977), *The Theory of Idle Resources*, London: Jonathan Cape; reprinted Indianapolis, IN Liberty Fund.

Jones, E.D. (1900), *Economic Crises*, New York: Macmillan.

Kalecki, M. (1943), 'Political Aspects of Full Employment', *Political Quarterly*, **4**(4) (October), 322–31; reprinted in R. W. Dimand (ed.), *The Origins of Macroeconomics*, vol. 5.

Kehoe, T. J. and E. C. Prescott (eds) (2002), 'Great depressions of the 20th century', *Review of Economic Dynamics*, **5**(special issue) (January), 1–235.

Keynes, J. M. (1923), *A Tract on Monetary Reform*, London: Macmillan.

Keynes, J. M. (1936), *The General Theory of Employment, Interest, and Money*, London: Macmillan.

Koopmans, T. (1947), 'Measurement without theory', *Review of Economic and Statistics*, **29**(3) (August), 161–72.

Krugman, P. (1990), *Rethinking International Trade*, Cambridge, MA: MIT Press.

Laidler, D. (1991a), *The Golden Age of the Quantity Theory*, Princeton, NJ: Princeton University Press.

Laidler, D. (1991b), 'The quantity theory is always and everywhere controversial: why?', *Economic Record*, **67**(4) (December), 289–306.

Laidler, D. (1999), *Fabricating the Keynesian Revolution*, Cambridge: Cambridge University Press.

Laidler, D. (2004), *Macroeconomics in Retrospect*, Cheltenham, UK and Northampton, MA, USA: Edward Elgar.

Leijonhufvud, A. (1981), *Information and Coordination*, New York: Oxford University Press.

Lianos, T. P. (1979), 'Domar's growth model and Marx's reproduction schema', *Journal of Macroeconomics*, **1**(4) (Fall), 405–12.

Malinvaud, E. (1977), *The Theory of Unemployment Reconsidered*, Oxford: Blackwell.

Malinvaud, E. (1987), 'The overlapping generations model in 1947', *Journal of Economic Literature*, **25**(1) (March), 103–5; reprinted in R. W. Dimand (ed.), *The Origins of Macroeconomics*, vol. 3.

Malinvaud, E. (1998–2000), *Macroeconomic Theory*, 3 volumes, Amsterdam: North Holland/Elsevier.

Minsky, H. P. (1982), *Can 'IT' Happen Again? And Other Essays*, Armonk, NY: M. E. Sharpe.

Mitchell, W. C. (1913), *Business Cycles*, Berkeley, CA: University of California Press.

Mitchell, W. C. (1927), *Business Cycles: The Problem and Its Setting*, New York: National Bureau of Economic Research.

Morgenstern, O. (1931), 'Free and fixed prices during the Depression', *Harvard Business Review*, **10**, 62–8.

Mussa, M. (2009), 'Adam Smith and the political economy of a modern financial crisis', *Business Economics*, **44**(1) (January), 3–16.

Patinkin, D. (1965), *Money, Interest, and Prices*, 2nd edn, New York: Harper & Row.

Pigou, A. C. (1927), *Industrial Fluctuations*, London: Macmillan (2nd edn., 1929).

Pigou, A. C. (1933), *Theory of Unemployment*, London: Macmillan.

Prescott, E. C. (1999), 'Some observations on the Great Depression', *Federal Reserve Bank of Minneapolis Quarterly Review*, **23**(1) (Winter), 25–31.

Ramsey, F. P. (1928), 'Mathematical theory of saving', *Economic Journal*, **38**(153) (December), 543–59; reprinted in R. W. Dimand (ed.), *The Origins of Macroeconomics*, vol. 3.

Robertson, D. H. (1915/1948), *A Study of Industrial Fluctuation*, reprinted with a new introduction, London: P. S. King & Son.

Robertson, D. H. (1926), *Banking Policy and the Price Level*, London: P. S. King & Son.

Robinson, J. (1933), *Economics of Imperfect Competition*, London: Macmillan.

Sandilands, R. J. (2000), 'Perspectives on Allyn Young in theories of endogenous growth', *Journal of the History of Economic Thought*, **22**(3) (Fall), 309–28

Sargent, T. (1987), *Dynamic Macroeconomic Theory*, Cambridge, MA: Harvard University Press.

Schumpeter, J. A. (1912/1934), *The Theory of Economic Development*, translated by Redvers Opie, Cambridge, MA: Harvard University Press.

Schumpeter, J. A. (1939), *Business Cycles*, 2 vols, New York: McGraw Hill.

Sims, C. (1980), 'Macroeconomics and reality', *Econometrica*, **48**(1) (January), 1–48.
Sims, C. (1996), 'Macroeconomics and methodology', *Journal of Economic Perspectives*, **10**(1) (Winter), 105–20.
Skidelsky, R. (2009), *Keynes: The Return of the Master*, New York: Public Affairs.
Slutsky, E. (1937), 'The summation of random causes as the source of cyclic processes', *Econometrica*, **5**(2) (April), 105–46; reprinted in H. Hagemann (ed.), *Business Cycle Theory: Selected Texts 1860–1939*, vol. 4.
Smith, V. C. (1936/1990), *The Rationale of Central Banking and the Free Banking Alternative*, Westminster: P. S. King & Son; reprinted with introduction by Leland Yeager, Indianapolis, IN: Liberty Fund.
Snowdon, B. and H. R. Vane (2002), *An Encyclopedia of Macroeconomics*, Cheltenham, UK and Northampton, MA, USA: Edward Elgar.
Tinbergen, J. (1937), 'Einige Grundfagen der matematischen Konjunkturtheorie', *Archiv für matematische Wirtschafts- und Sozialforschung*, **3**, 1–14, 83–97), reprinted in H. Hagemann (ed.), *Business Cycle Theory: Selected Texts 1860–1939*, vol. 7.
Tinbergen, J. (1939/1968), *Statistical Testing of Business Cycle Theories*, 2 vols, Geneva: League of Nations; reprinted in one volume, New York: Agathon Press.
Tobin, J. (1980), *Asset Accumulation and Economic Activity*, Oxford: Blackwell, and Chicago, IL: University of Chicago Press.
Trigg, A. B. (2002), 'Marx's reproduction schema and the multisectoral foundations of the Domar growth model', *History of Economic Ideas*, **10**(2), 97–113.
Wicksell, K. (1898/1936/1965), *Interest and Prices*, translated by. R. F. Kahn with an introduction by Bertil Ohlin, London: Macmillan, 1936; reprinted New York: A. M. Kelley.
Woodford, M. (2003), *Interest and Prices: Foundations of a Theory of Monetary Policy*, Princeton, NJ: Princeton University Press.
Young, A. A. (1928), 'Increasing returns and economic progress', *Economic Journal*, **38**(152) (December), 527–42; reprinted in R. W. Dimand (ed.), *The Origins of Macroeconomics*, vol. 3.

6. Keynes's *General Theory*, the quantity theory of money and monetary policy

Peter Docherty*

INTRODUCTION: REVOLUTION AND CONSENSUS

Thirty-five years after the publication of Keynes's *General Theory*, Harry Johnson examined what appeared at the time to be the end of the 'Keynesian Revolution'. In that paper, Johnson (1971) examined not only the conditions under which Keynes's *General Theory* had transformed thinking in the 1930s and 1940s about the operation and management of the macroeconomy, he also considered the conditions under which that transformation was in the process of being superseded. The 'monetarist counter-revolution', as Johnson called it, was reasserting both the tendency of economic systems to gravitate to full employment and the validity of the quantity theory of money.[1] Johnson (1971, p. 12) predicted, however, that the counter-revolution would fail, and within 20 years Blinder (1988) was describing the resurgence of Keynesian thinking, and Gordon (1990), and Romer (1993), were documenting the structure and achievements of a *New* Keynesian economics. Interestingly, James Tobin (1981) had offered the interim reflection that the counter-revolution would be more successful than Johnson had predicted.

An important dimension of this New Keynesian economics was its implications for the theory and practice of monetary policy. After a twenty-year period in which money and monetary policy were thought to have little or no effect on the real economy, the so-called principle of *money neutrality*, New Keynesian monetary policy saw a very important causal link between monetary conditions and fluctuations in real economic activity (Clarida et al. 1999, p. 1161). It also advocated that this link be exploited in the management of aggregate demand and the level of economic activity and suggested that the appropriate instrument for the implementation of monetary policy was the short term interest rate rather than a monetary aggregate as had been argued by the monetarists (see Taylor 1993, pp. 200, 202; Romer 2000, pp. 149, 155; and Clarida et al. 1999, p. 1687).

This last point aroused considerable interest among Post Keynesian economists. For some time Post Keynesians had argued that the central contributions of Keynes's *General Theory* were best understood if Keynes's assumption of an exogenous money supply was replaced with the assumption of an endogenous one. Kaldor (1970, 1986, p. 24) and Moore (1979, 1988, pp. 87–110, 263–5) argued this in their interpretations of Keynes, in their disputes with monetarists and in their analysis of how the money supply was determined in real financial systems. The corollary of such an approach to money supply determination is, of course, an interest rate set exogenously by the central bank, and the New Keynesian approach to monetary policy appeared to resonate with this aspect of Post Keynesian monetary theory. Dalziel (2002, p. 512), for example, argued that the shift to explicit interest rate setting both in New Keynesian theory and in the practices of many central banks around the world signalled an end to the role the quantity theory had previously played in modern thinking about monetary policy and thus represented a triumph for Keynes.

But this interpretation carries some curious theoretical implications. The first is that it suggests that endogenous money is *not* antithetical to neoclassically founded models as Kaldor and Moore had originally argued (*cf.* Cottrell 1994, p. 583). The kind of interest rate rules suggested by the New Keynesian approach to monetary policy appears to allow a neoclassical economy to be steered to a position of full employment with acceptable inflation even in the presence of an endogenously determined money supply. This reflects an argument advanced for some time by Pivetti (1991, 2001) who cites Wicksell's (1898) famous system with only inside or credit money as an example that neoclassical economics copes well with endogenous money. It is no accident that Woodford's (2003) work exploring the New Keynesian approach was given the same name as Wicksell's (1898) work and heralded as a return to Wicksellian economics.

But other theorists are less comfortable with this interpretation. De Long (2000, p. 85) for example argues that the essential principles of monetarism and the quantity theory have become embedded in the New Keynesian approach to monetary policy and Setterfield (2004, p. 39; 2005, p. 33) argues that new consensus models with endogenous money lack intrinsic stability mechanisms and thus *fail* to adequately handle endogenous money.

In this chapter I explore further the debate about the status of New Keynesian interest rate rules and argue that great care must be exercised when interpreting them in the light of Keynes's *General Theory*. I argue that the essential spirit of interest rate rules sits more comfortably with the quantity theory than with an endogenous conception of money supply determination. In this sense De Long is correct although Dalziel (2002) raises an important point about these rules that must be taken into account. The chapter proceeds in the following manner. The next section considers the structure of Keynes's analysis in *The General Theory*, and his treatment of the quantity theory of money and monetary policy in particular. The following section examines problems of interpretation that have arisen with respect to *The General Theory*. I then look at the place of Keynesian economics in the development of macroeconomic thinking in the years since the publication of *The General Theory*. The section after shows that New Keynesian models with Taylor rules are consistent with the quantity theory of money rather than embodying its rejection, and that one's attitude to Dalziel's position about the triumph of Keynes hinges on the interpretative issues raised earlier in the chapter. The final section summarizes and concludes.

MONETARY POLICY AND THE QUANTITY THEORY IN *THE GENERAL THEORY*[2]

Kaldor (1983, pp. 17–19) and Pasinetti (1974, pp. 36–41) outline the structure of Keynes's analysis in *The General Theory* in terms of a small set of familiar equations. Largely following the latter, equations 6.1 to 6.4 outline the central structure of the system Keynes considers in Chapters 8 to 15 of *The General Theory*:

$$Y = C + I \qquad\qquad 6.1$$

$$C = f(Y) \qquad\qquad 6.2$$

Equation 6.1 represents the *principle of effective demand* and determines the level of output (Y) as the sum of consumption (C) and investment (I) spending. Equation 6.2 then determines consumption spending as a function of aggregate output and thus income. Assuming a linear consumption function with zero intercept, substitution of 6.2 into 6.1 yields 6.3 in terms of the multiplier where c represents the marginal propensity to consume:

$$Y = \frac{1}{1 - c} \cdot \bar{I} \qquad\qquad 6.3$$

$$I = \varphi(E, i) \qquad\qquad 6.4$$

$$i = \psi(L, M) \qquad\qquad 6.5$$

Equation 6.4 determines investment as a function of expectations about what Keynes (1936, p. 135) called the 'prospective yield' of investment (E) and the rate of interest (i). The rate of interest is determined in equation 6.5 by the interaction of liquidity preference (L), or demand for money (ibid., p. 194), and the money supply (M) which Keynes assumes to be determined by the central bank. The rate of interest determined in this manner along with a given set of expectations about the prospective yield of investment determines the level of investment spending, which with a given marginal propensity to consume then determines equilibrium output, income and employment. Keynes summarizes the argument himself as follows:

> There will be an inducement to push the rate of new investment to the point which forces the supply price of each type of capital asset to a figure which, taken in conjunction with the prospective yield, brings the marginal efficiency of capital in general to approximate equality with the rate of interest. That is to say, the physical conditions of supply in the capital goods industries, the state of confidence concerning the prospective yield, the psychological attitude to liquidity and the quantity of money (preferably calculated in terms of wage units) determine, between them, the rate of new investment.
>
> The ratio . . . between an increment of investment and the corresponding increment of aggregate income, both measured in wage units, is given by the investment multiplier. (ibid., pp. 247–8)

Kaldor adds to this, equation 6.6 which determines the price level (P, where $Q=P.Y$) in terms of nominal wage costs (W), labour productivity (dY/dL), and the elasticity of production with respect to demand (η). This last term itself depends on the degree of capacity utilization and competition in industry.

$$P = (1 + \eta) \cdot \frac{dL}{dY} \cdot W \qquad\qquad 6.6$$

Equation 6.6 summarizes the analysis of prices offered by Keynes in Chapter 21 of *The General Theory* where he describes his own theory of the price level in terms of the relationship between aggregate demand and full employment output (or what we would now call the 'output gap'), as well as the money wage. In this chapter, Keynes (ibid., p. 295) argues that employment will rise in the face of increases in aggregate demand if output is below its full employment level. When output is already at this level, such increases will only lead to increases in the price level. He does, however, allow prices to rise gradually as output nears full employment and he points out that prices may rise due to increases in the wage unit and costs of production even when aggregate demand is constant.

Unemployment can emerge in this Keynesian system where the rate of interest becomes lodged at a rate above the rate which would allow all of the available capital and labour to be fully employed, and this particular cause of unemployment plays a significant role in Keynes's analysis. In discussing the psychological and conventional nature of the rate of interest in his liquidity preference theory, Keynes thus argues that:

> ... [the rate of interest] may fluctuate for decades about a level which is chronically too high for full employment. (ibid., p. 204)

The same point is made at the beginning of Chapter 17:

> It seems, then, that the rate of interest on money plays a peculiar part in setting a limit to the level of employment, since it sets a standard to which the marginal efficiency of a capital-asset must attain if it is to be newly produced. (ibid., p. 222)

Thus for Keynes unemployment is a *monetary* problem and arises because of the *monetary* nature of production and capitalism.

There is, however, a problem with the persistence of the unemployment equilibrium caused by too high a rate of interest in Keynes's system. If wages and prices are flexible downwards, the presence of unemployed resources may well cause a deflation of money wages, prices or both. This may reduce the nominal value of current output, and thus incomes, and this would reduce the overall demand for money via its transactions component. With lower money demand and a fixed money supply, interest rates would fall and reduced interest rates would lead to higher investment spending, aggregate demand, output and employment. This process has been called the *Keynes effect* (Cottrell 1994, p. 593) and its possible operation makes it hard to see how high interest rates could represent a *persistent* cause of unemployment in terms of the analysis of *The General Theory* up to the end of Chapter 15. One interpretation of Chapters 17 and 19 of *The General Theory*, therefore, is that Keynes recognized this problem and set out in these chapters a series of forces designed to prevent the operation of the Keynes effect (see Docherty 2005, pp. 92–6). These forces revolve closely around the unique features of money, in particular its zero elasticities of production and substitution, and how these features interact with the behaviour of money wages under certain conditions. While the detail of the analysis Keynes presents in these chapters is complex, it essentially results in the failure of money wages, and thus prices, to fall when there is significant unemployment, in the failure of money demand to fall in similar circumstances, or of falls in the rate of interest to generate significant increases in investment spending because of the way entrepreneurial expectations react to the conditions under which significant unemployment arises.[3]

The intricacies of this analysis aside, this overall framework provides the context within which Keynes's attitude to the quantity theory of money and the conduct of monetary policy may be understood. He deals with the quantity theory in Chapter 21 but anticipates this argument at the end of his treatment of the incentives to liquidity in Chapter 15 where he argues that:

> ... it is a great fault in the quantity theory that it does not distinguish between changes in prices which are a function of changes in output, and those which are a function of changes in the wage-unit. The explanation of this omission is, perhaps, to be found in the assumptions that there is no propensity to hoard and there is always full employment. (Keynes 1936, p. 208)

In Chapter 21, Keynes's attitude to the quantity theory flows from his treatment of prices as determined by costs of production and aggregate demand in relation to full employment output. Thus the proper way to examine the impact of variations in the money supply on prices for Keynes was not directly but via the framework he had outlined previously in *The General Theory*. Variations in money affect interest rates, changes in interest rates affect investment spending, and changes in investment spending affect aggregate demand and output in relation to full employment output. By assuming that any increase in the supply of money led to a proportionate increase in prices, the quantity theory implicitly assumed full employment and ignored the possibility of independent changes in the wage-unit. Keynes thus regarded the quantity theory as a special case of his more *general theory* of value.

With respect to the treatment of monetary policy in *The General Theory*, Keynes saw two potential applications. The first was the problem of persistent unemployment and the second was the variation of unemployment around its longer term trend across the trade cycle. Since Keynes saw persistent unemployment as caused by an interest rate that was too high, an immediate question was whether monetary policy could be used to reduce interest rates and thus stimulate output and employment. But while Keynes recognizes this possibility, he expresses a great deal of scepticism about its effectiveness. This scepticism is first introduced at the end of Chapter 12 on long-term expectation. In this chapter, Keynes examines the nature of expectations regarding the prospective yield on investment spending, noting the ' ... extreme precariousness of the basis of knowledge on which our estimates of the prospective yield have to be made' (ibid., p. 149) and how *convention* about relying on the persistence of the current situation is used to alleviate the uncertainty caused by this precariousness (ibid., p. 152). The problem is, however, that conventional valuations are liable to sudden and violent shifts as the result of being formed by mass psychology (ibid., p. 154) and this problem is exacerbated by the increased separation of corporate ownership and management that the evolution of stock markets and the increased importance of the liquidity furnished by these markets affords (ibid., pp. 156–7). Hence, even though monetary policy might be able to reduce interest rates, changes in expectations may reduce the marginal efficiency of capital to an equal or greater extent leading to no change in investment spending or aggregate demand.

At the end of his treatment in Chapter 13 of the process that determines the rate of interest, Keynes (ibid., p. 172) also suggests that attempts to reduce the rate of interest by increasing the supply of money may increase investor uncertainty and thus the degree of liquidity preference. Thus, even if the quantity of money is increased by the monetary authority, there may be little change in interest rates under certain conditions.

Keynes analyses the impact of changes in the money supply further at the end of Chapter 15 just prior to his criticism of the quantity theory discussed above. Here Keynes considers the entire risk and maturity spectrum of interest rates rather than simply the short-term rate which central banks had tended to confine themselves to affecting directly. Keynes (ibid., pp. 207–8) argues that the ability of the monetary authority to establish a 'given complex of rates of interest for debts of different terms and risks' is limited by four factors: first, the preference of the monetary authority itself for dealing in debts of particular maturities; second, the possibility that liquidity preference could become absolute below some conventional minimum interest rate; third, the costs of intermediation, especially the need for institutional lenders to cover the risks associated with default, which effectively set a minimum for any lending rate; and lastly persistently rising prices which reduce the 'value of money' and shift the MEC outwards may occur at such a pace that the monetary authority cannot raise nominal interest rates quickly enough to counteract the effect on spending[4] (ibid., p. 309).

A role for monetary policy in setting interest rates at a relatively low level in order to promote full employment is thus implied by the analysis of *The General Theory* but Keynes expresses doubts about the effectiveness of such a policy. For this reason he suggests that fiscal policy is likely to play a more effective role in promoting higher levels of employment especially where this involves publically financed investment spending because the calculation of prospective yields by public officials he saw as being less affected by the negative dimensions of conventional short run influences which tend to characterize the decisions of private investors (ibid., p. 164).

Keynes's treatment of monetary policy for stabilization purposes is closely related to the problems he identifies with its use for reducing persistent unemployment. This treatment is found in Chapter 22 of *The General Theory*. He attributes the 'trade cycle' to three causes: fluctuations in the marginal propensity to consume; fluctuations in the 'state of liquidity preference'; and fluctuations in the marginal efficiency of capital (ibid., p. 313). Of greatest importance, in Keynes's view, is the third of these causes precisely because of the 'precarious' nature of the expectations on which the marginal efficiency of capital is built and because of the tendency of expectations to 'sudden and violent changes' (ibid., p. 315). To complicate matters, a fall in the marginal efficiency of capital is often followed by an increase in liquidity preference, and this combination makes it difficult for monetary policy to deal with a slump:

> Later on, a decline in the rate of interest will be of great aid to recovery and, probably, a necessary condition of it. But, for the moment, the collapse in the marginal efficiency of capital may be so complete that no practicable reduction in the rate of interest will be enough. (ibid., p. 316)

Keynes also argues that monetary policy cannot be used to prevent a downturn by responding to 'over-investment' with an increase in interest rates because this would have a generally depressive effect on the whole economy and not simply on the over-investment alone.

Keynes again implies the potential for fiscal policy as a result of this analysis. But such policy would have two functions. The first would attempt to redistribute income so as to deter 'over-investment' and stimulate the marginal propensity to consume without dampening the kind of investment that is likely to have continued beneficial effects for the economy. These may be thought of as counter-cyclical fiscal measures. The second role for fiscal policy involves *on-going* public involvement in the investment process. If a larger proportion of investment is undertaken within the public domain, the proportion of aggregate spending subject to the violent changes associated with the formation of expectations that underpin private investment spending are minimized because, as argued above, public officials will value investment projects on a more stable long-term basis (Keynes 1936, p. 320; *cf*. p. 164).

The objective of Keynes's analysis in *The General Theory* is thus to explain the phenomenon of unemployment and its persistence through time. It clearly stands in contrast to the strictures of the quantity theory of money, at least in Keynes's eyes, but like the quantity theory it is a fundamentally *monetary* analysis, with the rate of interest playing an important role in generating unemployment equilibrium. While this might suggest a logical role for monetary policy in addressing both persistent unemployment and variations in unemployment across the economic cycle, Keynes identifies a number of potential limitations to the use of monetary policy in this respect and suggests a strong role for fiscal measures.

DIFFICULTIES INTERPRETING *THE GENERAL THEORY*

Notorious difficulties have arisen with the process of interpreting the analysis outlined in the previous section (see Eatwell and Milgate 1983). One common and probably the most widespread interpretation has been that *The General Theory* deals with short run imperfections within an otherwise neoclassical system. The failure of the money wage or the rate of interest, for example, to fall in the face of significant unemployment could be thought of as such a short-term imperfection. This interpretation is supported by the assumptions which explicitly underpin the analysis of *The General Theory* such as its given capital stock and given labour force (ibid., p. 245). It is also supported by the marginal analysis Keynes employs throughout the book that links his argument to the standard neoclassical framework. But what works *against* this interpretation are the constant references Keynes makes to the distinctiveness of his analysis, beginning on page 3 of *The General Theory* where the 'classical' theory is described as a *special* case of the more general analysis Keynes sees himself offering in *The General Theory*. Keynes also argues at a number of points throughout the book that the unemployment equilibrium he obtains should be perceived as *persistent* rather than as short-lived (e.g., ibid., p. 204). A different interpretation of Keynes's work then is that it provides the core theoretical structures for an alternative *long run* analysis of capitalism in which equilibrium is characterized by underemployment of resources rather than by full employment (see especially Garegnani 1978, 1979; Milgate 1982; and Kaldor 1983).

This long run interpretation of *The General Theory* does have its problems, chief among them being that the neoclassical framework in which *The General Theory*'s analysis is conducted lends itself very easily to discussions of rigidities and imperfections that fit nicely within the logic of the short run interpretation. Two things, however, must be remembered with respect to this issue. The first is that Keynes may well have chosen to set what he thought of as structural and long run phenomena within the context of a standard neoclassical framework as a way of gaining a more favourable hearing. Milgate (1977) provides textual evidence from Keynes's correspondence with Roy Harrod that substantiates this possibility. The second is that, *whatever Keynes intended,* structuring a long run theory around the core features of *The General Theory* but with appropriate modification to the framework within which those features are located may constitute a reasonable, logically coherent possibility.

The 'neoclassical synthesis' and, as argued below, the 'New Keynesian synthesis' or 'new consensus' essentially constitutes the first, short run interpretation of *The General Theory*. Post Keynesianism has, however, tended to take a different approach. It either adopts the second, long run interpretation of Keynes (Pasinetti 2005) or it abolishes the concept of long run equilibrium altogether and views time as a series of short runs in which unemployment results from liquidity preference as a response to irreducible uncertainty (Davidson 2003–4). The first of these approaches replaces dimensions of Keynes's analysis which make compatibility with neoclassical theory possible so that the failure of money wages to adjust or of interest rates to fall are no longer simply rigidities within an otherwise neoclassical system but *structural features* of an alternative theoretical framework. These include alternative theories of value such as mark-up or Sraffian pricing (see Lavoie 1992, pp. 129–48; and Pasinetti 1977, pp. 71ff), alternative theories of investment spending that omit cost of capital effects rendering investment insensitive to interest rate changes (see Harcourt 1972; and Garegnani 1978, 1979); and the theory of endogenous money which also fixes the rate of interest (see Kaldor 1986, p. 24; and Moore 1988, pp. 255ff).[5]

Whether the features outlined in Chapters 17 and 19 of *The General Theory* are interpreted as short run impediments or as structural features of the long run economic framework, these ambiguities in interpreting *The General Theory* are important for understanding the relationship between Keynes's work and the current approach to monetary policy considered below.

FROM KEYNESIAN ECONOMICS TO NEW KEYNESIAN ECONOMICS

The approach that dominated interpretation of *The General Theory* in the years following its publication was, as suggested in the previous section, the short run, imperfectionist one. The economic system was viewed as constantly tending towards a steadily growing full employment path but was subject to fluctuations around this path due to periodic shocks of various kinds. The primary problem of economic policy was, therefore, that of stabilization, and *The General Theory* provided the conceptual framework within which thinking about the management of this policy was conducted. Baily (1978) provides a detailed discussion of stabilization policy in the three decades or so after the publication of *The General Theory*. He argues that the volatility of national income in the United States was noticeably lower after World War II than before it, largely as a result of stabilization policy guided by the thinking of the 'Keynesian Revolution' (Baily 1978, p. 15).

Baily (ibid., p. 18) argues that stabilization policy initially lacked a clear cut framework and was instead guided by the relatively simple principle of 'leaning against the wind'. It also faced some important constraints. Monetary policy was constrained by attempts to minimize interest obligations on the large government debt that had accrued in the US and the UK from World War II, and fiscal policy was constrained by a general preference for balanced budgets. But economic managers seemed to develop an improved ability to manage the weapons of stabilization policy as time passed with commentators arguing that the more 'activist' approach to stabilization policy of the 1960s generated less volatile GDP growth and unemployment than had been experienced in the 1950s, while also generating more favourable average values for these variables (see Baily 1978, p. 19; Tobin 1981, p. 32).[6] Panels A and B of Figure 6.1, which plot real GDP growth, the unemployment rate and the annual inflation rate for the US economy in the 1950s and 1960s respectively, provide some support for this perspective. The variability of real GDP growth in Panel A is clearly greater than that in Panel B, while the inflation and unemployment rates are also more stable. This is further supported by Table 6.1 although the *average* values for inflation and the unemployment rate in the 1960s were slightly higher than their values in the 1950s.

Despite the analysis of monetary policy in *The General Theory* considered above, Tobin (1980, p. 52) argues that monetary and fiscal policy were simply regarded as substitutes by policy makers during this period. Baily (1978, p. 16) also argues that while the principles of the Keynesian Revolution (effectively the analysis of Chapter 21 of *The General Theory*) allowed policy makers to stabilize output and unemployment, they gave little direction in combining 'low and stable unemployment with price stability'. This essentially reflects the idea underlying the original Phillips curve and its associated trade-off between inflation and unemployment. This can be represented by equation 6.7:

$$\pi_t = (w - p) - \beta \cdot UE_t \qquad 6.7$$

where w represents a basic claim for increased wages, p represents growth in labour productivity, UE_t represents the unemployment rate, and β is a parameter assumed to be strictly positive. Equation 6.7 can be interpreted

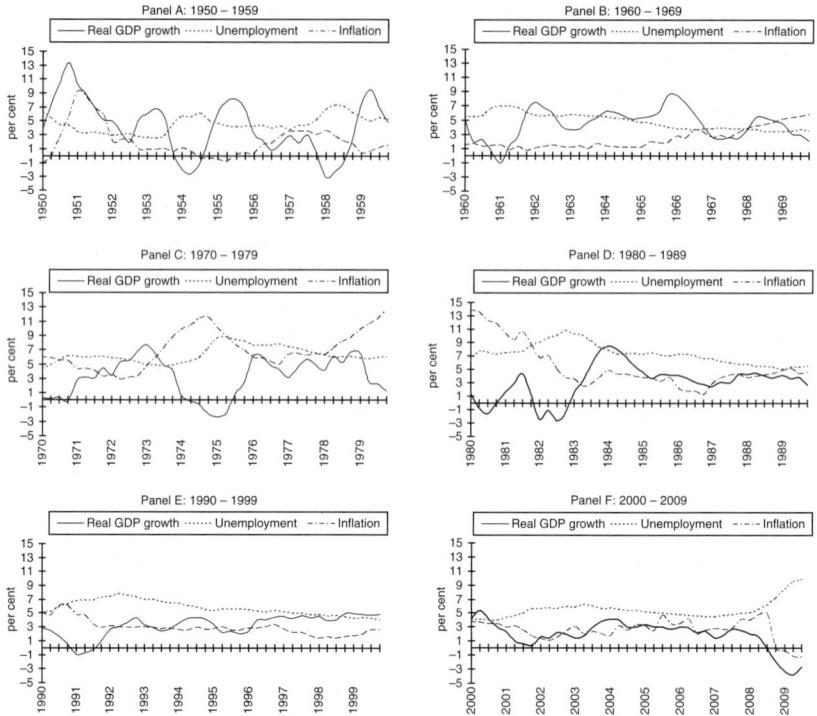

Sources: Federal Reserve Bank of St Louis, FRED Database and US Department of Commerce, Bureau of Economic Analysis, GDPC1 Quarterly Real GDP Series, per cent change in billions of chained 2005 US dollars; US Department of Labor, Bureau of Labor Statistics Current Population Survey unemployment rate, seasonally adjusted; and US Department of Labor, Bureau of Labor Statistics Consumer Price Index for all Urban Consumers, All items.

Figure 6.1   Real annual GDP growth, the unemployment rate and the annual inflation rate for the US economy by decade

as an inflationary process according to which prices are increased to maintain profit margins in response to increased costs (essentially wages) less increases in labour productivity (Tobin 1980, p. 24). Increased wages are driven by workers' basic wage claims less an adjustment for the level of unemployment which undermines the bargaining position of labour and reduces the size of any successful wage claim. Equation 6.7 is thus a dynamic version of equation 6.6 above but also incorporates the insights derived from Phillips (1958).

Tobin (1980, p. 24) also argues that the principles underlying Keynesian stabilization in the 1950s and 1960s formalized the impact of variations in

Table 6.1   Average values and standard deviations for key US macroeconomic variables by decade

Decade	Unemployment Rate		Inflation Rate		Real GDP Growth		Nominal Federal Funds Rate Fund		Real Federal Funds Rate	
	Average	SD	Average	SD	Average	SD	Average	SD	Average	SD
1950s	4.50	1.28	2.06	2.37	4.19	3.91	2.31	0.94	0.83	1.31
1960s	4.77	1.08	2.35	1.48	4.45	2.12	4.07	1.75	1.73	0.72
1970s	6.25	1.14	6.94	2.64	3.26	2.75	7.09	2.58	0.15	1.47
1980s	7.26	1.52	5.34	3.31	3.06	2.67	10.09	3.52	4.75	2.27
1990s	5.76	1.07	2.95	1.11	3.19	1.56	5.15	1.45	2.19	1.24
2000s	5.47	1.35	2.56	1.45	1.95	2.01	3.00	2.01	0.51	1.67

Sources: Federal Reserve Bank of St Louis, FRED Database and US Department of Commerce, Bureau of Economic Analysis, GDPC1 Quarterly Real GDP Series, per cent change in billions of chained 2005 US dollars; Board of Governors, Federal Reserve Board, FEDFUNDS Series; and US Department of Labor, Bureau of Labor Statistics, Consumer Price Index for all Urban Consumers, All Items.

output on unemployment in terms of Okun's Law. This can be expressed in terms of equation 6.8:

$$UE_t = \gamma \cdot (Y^* - Y_t) \qquad 6.8$$

where Y^* represents full employment (or potential) output and γ is a scaling parameter assumed to be strictly positive.

The monetarist counter-revolution challenged this Keynesian 'consensus' in two particular ways. Friedman (1968, p. 8) first argued that workers do not suffer from money illusion so that wage claims will aim to deliver a certain improvement in *real* wages rather than in money wages as implied in the underlying logic of the Phillips curve. Friedman also argued that workers would calculate the real wage in a forward looking way by deducting the expected rate of inflation from money wage growth. The Phillips curve should thus be recast in terms of equation 6.9:

$$\pi_t = \pi_t^e + (w - p) - \beta \cdot UE_t \qquad 6.9$$

Friedman then assumed that inflation expectations were formed adaptively with workers correcting previously held expectations in the light of whether those expectations under or over estimated the realized rate of inflation. This is expressed in equation 6.10:

$$\frac{d\pi_t^e}{dt} = j \cdot [\pi_t - \pi_t^e]$$ 6.10

where π_t is the actual rate of inflation, π_t^e is the expected rate of inflation, and j is a parameter assumed again to be strictly positive.

The second monetarist challenge to the Keynesian orthodoxy was the assertion that markets, including the labour market, operated efficiently and would push the economy towards full employment whenever it was shocked away from this position by random disturbances. Small imperfections may generate frictional and structural unemployment when output is at its potential level, *a natural rate of unemployment* (Friedman 1968, p. 8) but this could *not* be reduced via the use of demand management. If we represent the natural rate of unemployment by UE^*, this hypothesis suggests that Okun's Law as represented in equation 6.8 should be modified slightly as follows:

$$UE_t = UE^* + \gamma \cdot (Y^* - Y_t)$$ 6.11

These two modifications revise the Kaldor-Pasinetti system outlined above. Instead of equations 6.3 to 6.6 and 6.8 representing Kaldor's and Pasinetti's Keynesian system (including unemployment explicitly via Okun's Law), we may combine Kaldor's and Pasinetti's equations 6.3 and 6.4, represent output in terms of a standard IS curve as in 6.12, and represent Kaldor's and Pasinetti's money market in 6.5 in terms of an equation to describe the time path of interest rates responding to money supply-demand imbalances as in 6.13:

$$Y_t = \alpha \overline{A} + \alpha b \cdot \pi_t^e - \alpha b \cdot i_t$$ 6.12

$$\frac{di_t}{dt} = k_1 \cdot \frac{dY_t}{dt} + k_2 \cdot \pi_t - k_2 \cdot \frac{\dot{m}}{m}$$ 6.13

where a represents the standard Keynesian multiplier as in equation 6.3, b represents the interest-sensitivity of investment spending, i_t represents the nominal rate of interest, m represents the nominal money supply, and k_1 and k_2 are demand for money parameters. This gives us a representation of the model envisaged in Friedman in terms of equations 6.9–6.13.

These changes carried with them significant theoretical consequences. On the basis of these changes, Friedman (1968, p. 11) argued that monetary policy could *not*, in the long run, alter the rate of unemployment or real output growth, and that any attempt to increase growth or reduce unemployment via expansionary monetary policy would simply cause inflation without any real effects. He thus reasserted the quantity theory of money with its associated doctrine of money neutrality against the Keynesian orthodoxy of the time. This can be seen by reducing the system of equations 6.9–6.13 to two equations in expected inflation (which must be equal to actual inflation in equilibrium) and unemployment, and solving for their intertemporal equilibrium values. Docherty (2009, p. 499) shows that these values for an identical system to the one described in equations 6.9 to 6.13 are given by:

$$\begin{bmatrix} \pi_t^e \\ UE_t \end{bmatrix} = \begin{bmatrix} \dot{m}/m \\ \dfrac{(w - p)}{\beta} \end{bmatrix} \qquad 6.14$$

and that these equilibrium values are stable provided:

$$k_2 > j \qquad 6.15$$

An increased rate of money supply growth will thus have no effect on unemployment in the revised system and will simply lead to higher inflation. Friedman thus provided *theoretical* grounds on which to argue against a stabilization role for monetary policy (although different to those outlined by Keynes in *The General Theory*) and instead argued that the appropriate role for monetary policy was to restrain money supply growth in order to keep inflation at low and acceptable levels, and to avoid swings in money's growth rate since *short run* fluctuations in output and employment could be caused by money supply fluctuations within his framework (Friedman 1968, pp. 12–14).

The *practical* grounds on which Keynesian demand management fell into disrepute in the years following the publication of Friedman's paper involved the emergence of inflation as a serious economic and social problem in the early 1970s (Johnson 1971, p. 7) followed by stagflation in the mid-1970s, the apparent inconsistency between this phenomenon and the standard Phillips curve analysis of Keynesian theory (Blinder 1988, p. 282), and the seeming inability of Keynesian theory to address these problems. Panel C of Figure 6.1 shows the increase in US inflation that occurred towards the end of the 1960s and into the early 1970s. Monetarism appeared better equipped to deal with the problem of inflation which it saw as serious and for which the recommended policy was simple and easy for non-economists to understand (*cf.* Johnson 1971, p. 7).

Keynesians did not, of course, take the monetarist counter-revolution lying down. Kaldor (1970, 1981, 1985 and 1986), in particular, engaged in a strong anti-monetarist offensive, directing an argument at the heart of the quantity theory and as a by-product, cementing the idea of endogenous money into Post Keynesian monetary theory.[7] For Kaldor (1970), money could not be either in excess or deficient supply for one of two reasons. Either the velocity of circulation would adjust to bring monetary circulation (supply times velocity) into equality with the economy's demand for money, or the monetary authority would adjust supply to meet demand at a given velocity in order to avoid destabilizing fluctuations in interest rates likely to be associated with velocity adjustments. The latter would, however, involve an exogenously determined interest rate and this principle linked Kaldor's anti-monetarist analysis with his previous work on monetary policy. In that work, he advanced an argument similar to that in *The General Theory* where the rate of interest could become structurally fixed above its full employment level causing persistent unemployment (see Kaldor 1939, pp. 57–8; Committee of the Working of the Monetary System 1960, p. 718; *cf.* Docherty 2005, pp. 164–8). In this sense the central bank was responsible for unemployment but the average rate set by the central bank could also be viewed as the outcome of conventional attitudes of market participants and government officials about the appropriate value for this variable.

Keynesians in general, and Kaldor in particular, thus challenged monetarist use of the quantity theory to explain inflation with the idea that the velocity of circulation could be variable. The related concept of shifts in the demand for money function were ultimately of considerable practical importance for the demise of monetarism as the foundation for the conduct of monetary policy (Goodhart 1989, p. 298). The traditional instrument of monetary policy had always been some kind of short-term interest rate, and control of the money supply, or some narrower monetary aggregate, using this instrument relied heavily on the stability of the estimated demand function for the particular aggregate in question. Judd and Scadding (1982) suggest that this condition had been met in a number of countries until the mid-1970s but the onset of higher inflation and higher nominal interest rates led to a number of financial innovations that first increased the velocity of circulation, and later reduced it, so that the demand for a range of monetary aggregates became highly unstable during the 1970s and 1980s. This made monetarist growth targets difficult to achieve using interest rates as the policy instrument, and inflation persisted throughout the 1970s and into the 1980s as panels C and D of Figure 6.1 indicate (see also Mishkin 1997).

The famous instrument switch that occurred during the 1979–1982 period after Paul Volcker took over as Chairman of the Federal Reserve Board represented an attempt to overcome the problem of using interest rates as the instrument for controlling money supply growth. During this period, the Federal Reserve targeted growth in non-borrowed bank reserves in an attempt to control monetary base growth and thus growth in the money supply itself, letting interest rates find their own level with fluctuations in money demand. Money supply growth continued to prove difficult to control but interest rates fluctuated significantly and a serious recession ensued in the US economy in 1982–1983 after the nominal Federal Funds Rate reached 20 per cent and the real Federal Funds Rate reached 10 per cent in 1981 and early 1982. Table 6.1 indicates that the average interest rate, both nominal and real, for the 1980s was higher than for the decades either side due in large measure to this episode. A number of countries thus systematically began to suspend formal money supply growth targets (Goodhart 1989, p. 298) during the mid-1980s as a result of the apparent lack of success of the monetarist doctrine.

Following the suspension of formal monetary targets, there followed in most developed economies a period in which monetary policy was not guided by the same clear principles that had characterized monetarism. Goodhart (1989, pp. 308ff) describes this period of pragmatism for the US and the UK and Macfarlane (1999, pp. 216–17) describes it for Australia. This was essentially a new period of discretion where interest rates were set in relation to inflation, money supply growth, unemployment and exchange rates movements.

At the same time, three theoretical developments were coming together to forge a new direction for monetary policy. Two of these three developments were born during the monetarist ascendancy itself. The first was Poole's (1970) analysis of the conditions under which interest rates constitute the superior monetary policy instrument. Poole showed that even with inflation as the central policy goal, maintaining interest rates at an appropriate level can reduce output volatility around full employment in the presence of stochastic shocks to the demand for money thus keeping inflation closer to its target rate. A corollary of this idea was that changes to the money supply that resulted from shocks to money demand were not necessarily inflationary and could thus be accommodated without the risk of increasing inflation (see De Long 2000, p. 91).

A second development, originally suggested by Kydland and Prescott (1977) but also articulated by Barro and Gordon (1983) and Barro (1986) was the importance of rules rather than discretion for the proper conduct of monetary policy. This perspective extended Friedman's argument for money supply growth to be controlled given long run money neutrality. It suggested an inherent inflationary bias when monetary policy was entrusted to executive government due to the problem of 'time inconsistency'. Even when governments recognize the desirability of restraining money growth to prevent longer run inflation, there is frequently a political incentive to allow faster money supply growth in order to exploit any short-term trade-off with unemployment and improve the chances of re-election. The implication of this idea is that rules need to be separated from the political process and monetary policy needs to be vested in the hands of independent central banks. Thus despite the suspension of formal monetarist policy frameworks in the mid-1980s, theoretical developments concerning monetary policy continued to be founded on quantity theory principles.

The third theoretical innovation of the 1980s was the development of microfoundations for nominal rigidities based on individual optimization behaviour (Gordon 1990). The development of these microfoundations constituted the core of the New Keynesian research agenda (Blinder 1988, pp. 289–92) and provided new theoretical support for money non-neutrality and Keynesian stabilization policies. But this only applied to the short run. Blinder (1988), Romer (1993) and Clarida et al. (1999) all outline the basic features of New Keynesian economics and all include long run neutrality and the short run nature of price stickiness among these features. In the long run, they all see control of the money supply as important for preventing inflation and despite a strong theoretical case for short run stabilization, they all view inflation as the only appropriate long run goal for monetary policy.

Keynesian economics was thus deposed from its dominance as the orthodox macroeconomic framework in the 1970s by the twin forces of a new practical problem to be solved and the emergence of a 'new' body of theory which appeared capable of solving this problem. Monetarism was 'deposed' for quite different reasons. There was no new theory to which central bankers turned as they suspended monetary targeting. As discussed above, monetary policy became essentially pragmatic following this suspension. The reason monetarism failed was essentially a technical one when viewed from *inside* the framework with shocks to velocity essentially disrupting the apparatus available for monetary control. When viewed from *outside* the framework these 'shocks' could be understood as systematic variations in velocity caused by innovations driven in part by attempts to control the volume of money in a financial system always working to ensure that the economy's monetary needs are met. The new theory that eventually did emerge was in many respects Johnson's predicted amalgam of monetarism and Keynesian theory. New Keynesian theory essentially added carefully articulated microfoundations for short run price rigidities to the existing body of monetarist thought and its approach to monetary policy must be understood in this light.

NEW KEYNESIAN INTEREST RATE RULES AND THE QUANTITY THEORY

As discussed above (Introduction), New Keynesian monetary policy revolves around the use of interest rate rules that maintain interest rates at given levels for short periods of time and specify periodic adjustments in response to macroeconomic conditions. These rules are frequently used within an *inflation targeting* framework that aims to keep inflation at some target level or within some target band but allows inflation to drift above this level or band as a result of short run cost shocks (Bernanke and Mishkin 1997). Taylor (1998) argues that this approach to monetary policy, commenced in the United States in the late 1980s, was directly responsible for lower and more stable US inflation as well as greater stability in the path of US GDP. Panels D, E and F of Figure 6.1 indicate these characteristics of US inflation and GDP performance from the second half of the 1980s and the duration of the 1990s and 2000s up to the onset of The Great Recession of 2007–2009. Table 6.1 also indicates lower and more stable values for unemployment and inflation in the 1990s and 2000s as compared to the 1970s and 1980s although not as low as in the 1960s.

The fixed interest rate of the inflation targeting approach implies that the central bank accommodates money demand at the fixed rate. Such an approach thus incorporates endogenous money, and Post Keynesian theorists have concluded either that the Kaldor-Moore approach to monetary theorizing has had some impact on conventional thinking about the conduct of monetary policy (e.g. Dalziel 2002) or that endogenous money is *not* problematic for neoclassical theory (e.g. Pivetti 2001). The first of these perspectives is surprising given the continued emphasis on inflation as a policy goal, the importance of central bank credibility and independence, and the incorporation of rational expectations (all features of the monetarist approach) in the New Keynesian framework (see Bernanke and Mishkin 1997). The second approach is also surprising given the work of Kaldor, Moore, Cottrell (1994), Lavoie (1996) and Rochon (1999) who argue that endogenous money has negative implications for neoclassical economics. This section examines each of these Post Keynesian perspectives in turn.

The first perspective is considered by replacing equation 6.13 in the Friedman (1968) system considered earlier with a version of the interest rate rule originally advocated by Taylor (1993, p. 202):

$$i_t = \bar{r} + \pi_t + \theta_1(\pi_t - \bar{\pi}) - \theta_2(UE_t - \overline{UE}) \qquad 6.16$$

According to 6.16, the central bank sets the nominal interest rate in terms of some base real rate, $\bar{r}$, plus the current inflation rate plus an upwards

adjustment of θ_1 for each percentage point that the inflation rate exceeds
the target inflation rate, $\bar{\pi}$, less an adjustment of θ_2 for each percentage
point that the unemployment rate exceeds the target unemployment rate
$\overline{UE}$.[8] Ideally the base real interest rate used in this equation should be an
estimate of the natural or full employment rate.

The revised Friedman model made up of equations 6.9–6.12 and 6.16
can be reduced to two differential equations, again in expected inflation
and unemployment. Docherty (2009, p. 512) shows that the intertemporal
equilibrium of this system is:

$$
\begin{bmatrix} \pi_t^e \\ UE_t \end{bmatrix} = \begin{bmatrix} \bar{\pi} \\ \dfrac{w-p}{\beta} \end{bmatrix}
$$

6.17

which is stable provided:[9]

$$
\frac{-j\beta\gamma\alpha b\theta_1}{1 + \gamma\alpha b\,[\theta_2 + (1 + \theta_1)\cdot\beta]} < 0
$$

6.18

A model incorporating the interest rate rule thus generates equilibrium
unemployment at the natural rate and equilibrium inflation at the central
bank's target level provided the central bank sets the base real rate of
interest at the natural rate, target unemployment is the full employment
rate, and equal weight is given to the two targets in the policy rule. This
equilibrium is precisely the same as that for the Friedman model with
a money supply growth rate equal to the target inflation rate. But this
similarity is no accident. According to equation 6.16, the real interest rate
should be increased when inflation is above target, other things equal. In
a simple model, the central bank achieves this outcome by reducing the
money supply or its rate of growth. The interest rate is thus the central
bank's policy instrument but market operations which affect the volume
of money constitute the tool (in the sense of Mishkin 2004, p. 415) used to
manipulate this instrument.[10] One way to see this more clearly would be
to add equation 6.16 to the Friedman system as considered above (From
Keynesian Economics) i.e. to equations 6.9 to 6.13 rather than *replacing*
6.13 with the interest rate rule. The resulting model would have two equations determining the interest rate: equation 6.13, representing the role of
the money market; and equation 6.16, representing the policy objective of
the central bank. Assuming the central bank's actions to be effective, the
way to read these equations would be to interpret equation 6.16 as determining the interest rate at any point in time while interpreting equation

6.13 as determining the money supply growth needed to deliver this interest rate given the state of money demand. Money supply growth would thus seem to be endogenous in this specification of the model and we could reflect this endogeneity by rewriting equation 6.13 as follows:

$$\frac{\dot{m}}{m} = \frac{k_1}{k_2} \cdot \frac{dY_t}{dt} + \pi_t - \frac{1}{k_2} \cdot \frac{di_t}{dt} \qquad 6.19$$

Since in equilibrium dY_t/dt and di_t/dt would both equal zero and inflation would be equal to the central bank's target, the rate of monetary growth would be given by:

$$\dot{m}/m = \pi_t = \overline{\pi} \qquad 6.20$$

According to 6.20 the money supply would be equal in long run equilibrium to the target rate of inflation. But care must be taken to interpret the status of money supply growth in this result because while this growth is clearly endogenous in the sense that its value is determined within the system of equations, the right-hand side of equation 6.20 is a *policy target*. It thus tells us the level at which the central bank must set money supply growth to deliver this target. The *reason* that the central bank must set money supply growth to deliver this target is that causality runs from money to inflation and in this *causal* sense, money is, therefore, *exogenous* in the long run in this model.[11]

This perspective calls into question Dalziel's (2002) conclusion that New Keynesian interest rate rules represent an intellectual victory for Keynes. What these interest rate rules do is to guide central bank management of money supply growth that allows them to achieve target inflation as indicated by the quantity theory of money but in a way that overcomes the problem of money demand instability that plagued the conduct of monetary policy in the 1970s and 1980s.

To see how interest rate rules avoid this problem consider two situations: a positive shock to parameter k_1 and a positive shock to inflation itself. In the first of these situations, an increase in k_1 would increase the demand for money in equation 6.19 for the same level of inflation, thus placing upward pressure on interest rates and causing a negative shock to output if the previous rate of monetary growth were to be maintained. But this volatility is avoided if inflation is managed using an interest rate rule. No change to interest rates is dictated by equation 6.16 when k_1 rises, merely an accommodating increase in the money supply by equation 6.19. The rule thus adjusts to short run fluctuations in money demand that pose no inflationary threat and would simply lead to damaging interest rate fluctuations if not accommodated. In the second situation, however, inflation itself is above the target, and an increase in interest rates *is* dictated by equation 6.16. The di_i/dt term in equation 6.19 is now positive indicating that the money supply should be contracted in order to deliver the higher interest rate from the rule, and eventually reduced inflation. In this context, adjustment of the money supply in the standard direction is a requirement for both the identified change in interest rates and the desired reduction in inflation, and money must thus be regarded as exogenous in a causal sense. *Short run endogeneity* is thus sacrificed in favour of adjustments to the money supply in keeping with traditional quantity theory mechanics which render the money supply *exogenous in the long run*.

This interpretation is consistent with the view of new consensus theorists themselves: Romer, for example, argues that the aggregated new consensus model he outlines (and in which the quantity of money is initially *absent*) does not imply that money has no causal role to play in the determination of inflation:

> The important point of this analysis is simply that the increase in the money stock lowers the real interest rate; the only exception is the extreme and unrealistic case when all prices are completely and instantaneously flexible, so that the price level jumps immediately by the same proportion as the money stock. (Romer 2000, pp. 163–4)

His argument implies precisely what was argued earlier in this section that when inflation is above (below) target, the Taylor rule dictates an increase (decrease) in the real rate of interest and this is achieved by a contraction (expansion) of the money stock. And the only case where this does not operate is where quantity theory causation short-circuits the interest rate mechanism and money stock variations impact prices *directly*. Romer does go on to argue that he is not really interested in the quantity of money and that one of the attractive features of the aggregate version of his new consensus model is that it omits direct reference to it, leaving it to operate behind the scenes. And perhaps comments of this type have created the impression that the money stock has no causal importance. But the above quotation indicates the misleading nature of this impression. Taylor also argues that Taylor rules are closely related to the quantity theory of money:

> However, I want to focus on the short-term interest rate side of monetary policy rather than on the money stock side. Hence, I need a different equation. Instead of the quantity equation I use an equation – called a monetary policy rule – in which the short-term interest rate is a function of the inflation rate and real GDP. The policy rule is, of course, quite different from the quantity equation

of money, but it is closely connected to the quantity equation. In fact, it can be easily derived from the quantity equation. (Taylor 1999, p. 322)

He then goes on to explain this derivation and to obtain his famous rule using $MV=PY$ as a starting point.

It is thus difficult to agree with Dalziel (2002) that New Keynesian monetary policy represents a victory for Keynes in anything except the short run. As shown above (Monetary Policy in *The General Theory*) Keynes was antithetical to the quantity theory of money except as operating at full employment. But he was also of the view that unemployment could be a persistent feature of developed economic systems. Thus the problems of interpretation discussed above (Difficulties Interpreting *The General Theory*) play a very important role in understanding whether the current approach to monetary policy represents an intellectual victory for Keynes. Only if the short period interpretation of Keynes is adopted would this be the case. If Keynesian analysis is thought to characterize the long run in any sense, New Keynesian economics does not represent such a victory and Post Keynesians have more work to do.

The second perspective considered at the beginning of this section that endogenous money is not problematic for neoclassical theory is also partly addressed by the above analysis. In the Friedman model considered above, the price level is determined by the quantity of money. If the money supply is rendered endogenous, the price level becomes indeterminate.[12] This is one sense in which endogenous money is inconsistent with neoclassical theory. A second sense relates to the full employment equilibrium to which neoclassical systems gravitate in the long run. The mechanism which ensures this gravitation entails the rate of interest adjusting to the natural or full employment rate. But the successful operation of this mechanism uses a fixed and exogenous money supply as a fulcrum against which to lever the interest rate into its full employment position. If the money supply is endogenous, no fulcrum is available and the mechanism fails to operate. Thus exogenous money is crucial to neoclassical systems and in the long run, the New Keynesian model has determinate prices and full employment precisely because the money supply is *exogenously* controlled by the central bank.

The argument that endogenous money is not a problem for neoclassical theory is sometimes supported with reference to Wicksell (1898). This work is argued to contain an endogenous money supply (Wicksell's 'pure credit' model) but nevertheless successfully allows the economy to gravitate to full employment (see Pivetti 2001). This argument is, however, based on a misunderstanding of Wicksell's analysis since the price level and the rate of inflation are also indeterminate in Wicksell's pure credit model.

Docherty (1995) argues that this model was used by Wicksell simply as a pedagogical device to show the importance of the interest rate for a proper understanding of the quantity theory in a world where banks are central to the money creation process and that Wicksell explicitly recognizes price level indeterminacy in this case. Wicksell reintroduces an *exogenous* money base into the model to render the price level determinate and the model stable at full employment. Wicksellian monetary economics is thus simply a sophisticated version of the quantity theory and it is completely unsurprising, therefore, that a neoclassical model with a Taylor rule, frequently characterized as a return to Wicksellian monetary economics (*cf.* Woodford 2001, p. 232), should be characterized by a long run causal relation running from the quantity of money to the rate of inflation.[13]

All of this analysis calls into question the idea that the New Keynesian approach to monetary policy represents a fundamental change in perspective that reflects the insights of Post Keynesian economics. In the *short run*, the New Keynesian model *does* share important characteristics of the Post Keynesian framework including endogenous money, prices determined by costs of production and market power independently of the quantity of money (*see* Blinder 1988, pp. 289–91; Gordon 1990, p. 1142; and Clarida, Gali and Gertler 1999, p. 1667), and equilibrium characterized by unemployment. Its distinctiveness resides solely in the maximizing behaviour of agents subject to extensive 'real world' constraints. But the outcomes from these New Keynesian models are so similar to those from Post Keynesian models that the force of neoclassical insistence on 'rigorous microfoundations' is severely undermined and amounts to little more than a form of religious conviction.

The long run New Keynesian model, however, is very different. It is characterized by exogenous money, prices determined by the quantity of money, and gravitation of the macroeconomy to full employment. Keynes has thus triumphed in macroeconomics only if the short run, imperfectionist interpretation of *The General Theory* is adopted. If the long run view is taken, the opposite conclusion is inescapable.

CONCLUSION

Johnson's (1971, p. 12) prediction that the monetarist counter-revolution would fail to unravel the impact of Keynes's *General Theory* appears on initial inspection to have been accurate. Since that prediction, monetary targeting has been abandoned and a New Keynesian economics has emerged that is characterized by cost-related prices, unemployment equilibria, money non-neutrality, and interest rate rules that render the money supply endogenous. Since all of these features are shared with Post Keynesian interpretations of *The General Theory* and to some extent provide a rationale for similar policy recommendations as those advocated by Post Keynesians, Dalziel's (2002) argument concerning the victory of Keynes also appears to be vindicated.

But enthusiasm for this 'victory' needs to be tempered for two reasons. The first is that the neoclassical foundations of New Keynesian models incorporate a different causality structure to that in Post Keynesian models, and this implies a different transmission mechanism for policy actions. Post Keynesians may thus be wary of using monetary policy as a counter cyclical policy tool because of its impact on income distribution despite the similar implications monetary policy may have for demand management in Post Keynesian models compared to those in New Keynesian models. But secondly, and more importantly, the features Post Keynesian models share with New Keynesian models are *long run* features in the former but only short run features in the latter. This suggests that the long run policy prescriptions of the two approaches are likely to be very different.

In its long run analysis, New Keynesian economics continues to embody essential monetarist and quantity theory principles, viewing the macroeconomy as fluctuating around a full employment equilibrium, regarding inflation as the only appropriate long run goal for monetary policy and fully incorporating rational expectations and money neutrality in its conception of the economy's behaviour. In this respect we must disagree with Dalziel's (2002) view that Keynes has triumphed and agree instead with Delong (2000) or Tobin's (1980, p. 41) assessment that:

> The synthesis will not be, to the extent that Johnson predicted, the disappearance of monetarism into an eclectic neoclassical neo-Keynesian mainstream. The ideas of the second counter-revolution are too distinctive and too powerful to be lost in the shuffle. They are bound to shape whatever orthodoxy emerges.

There continues to be, therefore, a considerable Post Keynesian research agenda on macroeconomic policy in general and for monetary policy in particular, both on short run and long run issues. Analysing, for example, why inflation, unemployment and GDP growth have been more stable in the period when interest rate rules have been used compared to the 1970s and 1980s would cast considerable light on the operation of monetary policy. This needs to be done, however, using models such as those in Kriesler and Lavoie (2007) and Setterfield (2009) rather than the plethora of New Keynesian models generated over the last 30 years and reported in Clarida, Gali and Gertler et al. (1999). But work is also required on the development and testing of long run models which demonstrate the possibility of long term unemployment equilibria and the potential role for demand management policies including monetary policy, in reducing this kind of unemployment. When Post Keynesian economists convince central banks of the long run implications of *The General Theory*, the demise of the quantity theory and the victory of Keynes's ideas may be heralded more genuinely.

NOTES

*   Thanks to Peter Flaschel, the late Warren Hogan, Marc Lavoie, Gordon Menzies, Louis-Philippe Rochon, Dena Sadeghian and Mario Seccareccia for discussion and comments.

1.   Leeson (2000) offers a more recent and detailed examination of the monetarist counter-revolution.

2.   In Docherty (2011), I examine Keynes's treatment of monetary policy and the quantity theory in connection with his analysis of economic crisis in the *General Theory*. This section expands on that analysis.

3.   I have argued in Docherty (2005, pp. 98–104) that there are questions about the long run, normal nature of the explanation Keynes offers in Chapters 17 and 19 for the persistence of the rate of interest above the full employment rate.

4.   This is the famous reference to Walter Bagehot's quotation of the English saying 'John Bull can stand many things, but he cannot stand 2 per cent' (Keynes 1936, p. 309, footnote 1).

5.   Interestingly, Keynes appears to have presaged both the problems raised for interest-sensitive investment demand in the capital debates of the 1960s and the possibility of endogenous money. Milgate (1977) has shown from drafts of *The General Theory* that Keynes was aware of logical problems with the concept of aggregate capital and its dependence on distributive variables in neoclassical theory but omitted discussion of these problems in the final version of *The General Theory*. Rochon (1997) has shown that Keynes's concept of a revolving fund in the post-*General Theory* 'finance debates' essentially performs the function of endogenous money.

6.   See Romer and Romer (2002) for a more favourable interpretation of the performance of monetary policy in the 1950s.

7.   The idea of endogenous money had, of course, been around for some time, see Lavoie (1984) for a discussion of the history of the concept of endogenous money in Keynesian thinking and Green (1992) for an excellent account of endogenous money in Classical economic theory.

8.   Taylor (1993) uses GDP rather than unemployment and lagged inflation and GDP rather than current values for these variables in his original exposition.

9.   Woodford (2001, pp. 232–3) similarly demonstrates this stability for a model with stochastic innovations to spending and the equilibrium real interest rate.

10.   Bindseil (2004, p. 89) claims that central banks are capable of moving interest rates *without* the adjustment of financial quantities or the need for *any* securities trading. Guthrie and Wright (2000, p. 490) and the Reserve Bank of Australia (2003, p. 2) advance similar arguments but based on a weaker argument that incorporates the presence of a market *expectation* that central banks will trade in securities if necessary. This corresponds to the absence of what Leeper and Gordon (1992) call the 'liquidity effect' of monetary policy actions and for which they found no evidence in the US. However, other empirical studies including Christiano et al. (1996), Hamilton (1997), Bernanke and Mihov (1998) and Carpenter and Demiralp (2008) have found evidence *for* such effects.

11. Setterfield (2005, p. 33) argues that the new consensus model he outlines is *unstable* when the money supply is explicitly introduced because of the absence of a Pigou effect caused by the endogenous nature of money associated with the Taylor rule. But this outcome is the result of the way he introduces the money supply. Rather than constructing an equation to represent the money market as in the present approach and to show how the central bank must act in this market to implement its policy, he generates an additional equation from the equation of exchange that links output directly to the money supply and allows the money supply to be endogenous in this expression. Causation in his model thus runs from interest rates to expenditure to output and then to prices and the money supply simultaneously. But there is no equation in his model constraining the relationship between the money supply and interest rates that resembles a money market. Such a model is indeed characterized by an absence of the Pigou effect and consequent instability but it overlooks the issue of how the central bank implements interest rate changes and the role of the money market in this process.
12. See Docherty (2009, pp. 500–6) for a proof of this result in a Friedman-type model. Sargent and Wallace (1975) demonstrated this some time ago for a monetarist model with rational expectations and flexible prices, and McCallum (1986) also considers the issue.
13. Rogers (1989, p. 23) shares this view: 'Wicksell's monetary theory must be understood as an attempt to extend the application of the quantity theory of money to an economy which has moved beyond the use of metallic money to the use of credit and loans . . .'.

BIBLIOGRAPHY

Baily, M. (1978), 'Stabilization policy and private economic behavior', *Brookings Papers on Economic Activity*, (1), 11–59.

Barro, R. (1986), 'Recent developments in the theory of rules versus discretion', *Economic Journal*, **96** (supplement), 23–37.

Barro, R. and D. Gordon (1983), 'Rules, discretion and reputation in a model of monetary policy', *Journal of Monetary Economics*, **12**(1), 101–22.

Bernanke, B. and F. Mishkin (1997), 'Inflation targeting: a new framework for monetary policy', *Journal of Economic Perspectives*, **11**(2) (Spring), 97–116.

Bernanke, B. and I. Mihov (1998), 'The liquidity effect and long run neutrality', *Carnegie-Rochester Conference Series on Public Policy*, **49**(1), 149–94.

Bindseil, U. (2004), *Monetary Policy Implementation: Theory-Past-Present*, Oxford: Oxford University Press.

Blinder, A. (1988), 'The fall and rise of Keynesian economics', *Economic Record*, **64**(4) (December), 278–94.

Carpenter, S. and S. Demiralp (2008), 'The liquidity effect in the federal funds market: evidence at a monthly frequency', *Journal of Money, Credit and Banking*, **40**(1) (February), 1–24.

Christiano, L., M. Eichenbaum and C. Evans (1996), 'The effects of monetary policy shocks: evidence from the flow of funds', *Review of Economics and Statistics*, **78**(1) (February), 16–34.

Clarida, R., J. Gali and M. Gertler (1999), 'The science of monetary policy: a New Keynesian perspective', *Journal of Economic Literature*, **37**(4) (December), 1661–707.

Committee of the Working of the Monetary System (1960), *Minutes of Evidence*, London: Her Majesty's Stationery Service.

Cottrell, A. (1994), 'Post-Keynesian monetary economics', *Cambridge Journal of Economics*, **18**(6) (December), 587–605.

Dalziel, P. (2002), 'The triumph of Keynes: what now for monetary policy research?', *Journal of Post Keynesian Economics*, **24**(4) (Summer), 511–27.

Davidson, P. (2003–4), 'Setting the record straight on *A History of Post Keynesian Economics*', *Journal of Post Keynesian Economics*, **26**(2), 245–72.

Davidson, P. (2009), 'Alternative explanations of the operation of a capitalist economy', *Challenge*, (November–December), 5–28.

De Long, J. (2000), 'The triumph of monetarism?', *Journal of Economic Perspectives*, **14**(1) (December), 83–94.

Docherty, P. (1995), 'Endogeneity in Wicksell's monetary theory', *History of Economics Review*, **23**, 1–22.

Docherty, P. (2005), *Money and Employment: A Study of the Theoretical Implications of Endogenous Money*, Cheltenham, UK and Northampton, MA, USA: Edward Elgar.

Docherty, P. (2009), 'Re-examining the implications of the new consensus: endogenous money and Taylor rules in a simple neoclassical macro model', *Metroeconomica*, **64**(3) (July), 495–524.

Docherty, P. (2011), 'Keynes's analysis of economic crises and monetary policy in *The General Theory*: its relevance after 75 years', *Review of Political Economy*, **23**(4), 521–35.

Eatwell, J. (1983), 'Theories of value output and employment', in J. Eatwell and M. Milgate (eds), *Keynes's Economics and the Theory of Value and Distribution*, London: Duckworth, pp. 93–128.

Eatwell, J. and M. Milgate (1983), 'Introduction' in J. Eatwell and M. Milgate (eds), *Keynes's Economics and the Theory of Value and Distribution*, London: Duckworth, pp. 1–17.

Friedman, M. (1968), 'The role of monetary policy', *American Economic Review*, **58**(1) (March), 1–17.

Garegnani, P. (1978), 'Notes on consumption, investment and effective demand I', *Cambridge Journal of Economics*, **2**(4) (December), 335–53.

Garegnani, P. (1979), 'Notes on consumption, investment and effective demand II', *Cambridge Journal of Economics*, **3**(1) (March), 63–82.

Goodhart, C. (1989), 'The conduct of monetary policy', *Economic Journal*, **99**(396) (June), 293–346.

Gordon, R. (1990), 'What is New Keynesian economics?', *Journal of Economic Literature*, **28**(3) (September), 1115–71.

Green, R. (1992), *Classical Theories of Money, Output and Inflation: A Study in Historical Economics*, New York: St Martin's Press.

Guthrie, G. and J. Wright (2000), 'Open mouth operations', *Journal of Monetary Economics*, **46**(2) (October), 489–516.

Hamilton, J. (1997), 'Measuring the liquidity effect', *American Economic Review*, **87**(1) (March), 80–97.

Harcourt, G. C. (1972), *Some Cambridge Controversies in the Theory of Capital*, Cambridge: Cambridge University Press.

Johnson, H. G. (1971), 'The Keynesian revolution and the monetarist counter-revolution', *American Economic Review*, **61**(2) (May), 1–14.

Judd, J. and J. Scadding (1982), 'The search for a stable money demand function: a survey of the post-1973 literature', *Journal of Economic Literature*, **20**(3) (September), 993–1023.

Kaldor, N. (1939), 'Speculation and economic stability', *Review of Economic Studies*, **7**, 1–27, reprinted in Kaldor, N. (1980), *Collected Economic Essays:*

Essays on Economic Growth and Stability, New York: Holmes & Meier, 2nd edn, pp. 17–58.

Kaldor, N. (1970), 'The new monetarism', *Lloyds Bank Review*, **97**, 1–17.

Kaldor, N. (1981), 'Origins of the new monetarism', in N. Kaldor (1989), *Collected Economic Essays: Further Essays on Economic Growth*, edited by F. Targetti and A. P. Thirwall, London: Duckworth, pp. 160–77.

Kaldor, N. (1983), 'Keynesian economics after fifty years', in D. Worswick and J. Trevithick (eds), *Keynes and the Modern World*, Cambridge: Cambridge University Press, pp. 1–28.

Kaldor, N. (1985), 'How monetarism failed', in N. Kaldor (1989), *Collected Economic Essays: Further Essays on Economic Growth*, edited by F. Targetti and A. P. Thirwall, London: Duckworth, pp. 178–97.

Kaldor, N. (1986), *The Scourge of Monetarism*, 2nd edn, Oxford: Oxford University Press.

Keynes, J. M. (1936), *The General Theory of Employment, Interest, and Money*, London: Macmillan, published in 2007 on behalf of the Royal Economic Society.

Kriesler, P. and M. Lavoie (2007), 'The new consensus on monetary policy and its post-Keynesian critique', *Review of Political Economy*, **19**(3) (July), 387–404.

Krugman, P. (2000), *The Return of Depression Economics*, London: Penguin.

Kydland, F. and E. Prescott (1977), 'Rules rather than discretion: the inconsistency of optimal plans', *Journal of Political Economy*, **85**(3) (June), 473–92.

Lavoie, M. (1984), 'The endogenous flow of credit and the post Keynesian theory of money', *Journal of Economic Issues*, **18**(3) (September), 771–97.

Lavoie, M. (1992), *Foundations of Post Keynesian Economic Analysis*, Aldershot, UK and Brookfield, VT, USA: Edward Elgar.

Lavoie, M. (1996), 'Horizontalism, structuralism, liquidity preference and the principle of increasing risk', *Scottish Journal of Political Economy*, **43**(3) (August), 275–300.

Lavoie, M. (2004), 'The new consensus on monetary policy seen from a post-Keynesian perspective', in M. Lavoie and M. Seccareccia (eds), *Central Banking in the Modern World*, Cheltenham, UK and Northampton, MA, USA: Edward Elgar, pp. 15–34.

Leeper, E. and D. Gordon (1992), 'In search of the liquidity effect', *Journal of Monetary Economics*, **29**(3) (June), 341–69.

Leeson, R. (2000), *The Eclipse of Keynesianism: The Political Economy of the Chicago Counter-Revolution*, New York: Palgrave Macmillan.

Macfarlane, I. (1999), 'Australian monetary policy in the last quarter of the twentieth century', *Economic Record*, **75**, 213–24.

McCallum, B. (1986), 'Some issues concerning interest rate pegging, price level determinacy, and the real bills doctrine', *Journal of Monetary Economics*, **17**(1) (January), 135–60.

Milgate, M. (1977), 'Keynes on the "Classical" Theory of Interest', *Cambridge Journal of Economics*, **1**(3) (September), 307–15.

Milgate, M. (1982), *Capital and Employment: A Study of Keynes's Economics*, London: Academic Press.

Mishkin, F. (1997), 'Strategies for controlling inflation', in P. Lowe (ed.), *Monetary Policy and Inflation Targeting, Proceedings of a Conference*, Sydney: Reserve Bank of Australia, pp. 7–38.

Mishkin, F. (2004), *The Economics of Money, Banking and Financial Markets*, 7th edn, New York: Pearson-Addison Wesley.

Moore, B. (1979), 'The endogenous money stock', *Journal of Post Keynesian Economics*, **2**(1) (Autumn), 49–70.

Moore, B. (1988), *Horizontalists and Verticalists: The Macroeconomics of Credit Money*, Cambridge: Cambridge University Press.

Pasinetti, L. (1974), *Income Distribution and Growth*, Cambridge: Cambridge University Press.

Pasinetti, L. (1977), *Lectures on the Theory of Production*, London: Macmillan.

Pasinetti, L. (2005), 'The Cambridge School of Keynesian Economics', *Cambridge Journal of Economics*, **29**(6) (November), 837–48.

Phillips, A. (1958), 'The relation between unemployment and the rate of change of money wage rates in the United Kingdom 1861–1957', *Economica*, **25**(100) (November), 283–99.

Pivetti, M. (1991), *An Essay on Money and Distribution*, New York: St Martin's Press.

Pivetti, M. (2001), 'Money endogeneity and money non-neutrality: a Sraffian perspective', in L. P. Rochon and M. Vernengo (eds), *Credit, Interest Rates and the Open Economy*, Cheltenham, UK and Northampton, MA, USA: Edward Elgar, pp. 104–19.

Poole, W. (1970), 'Optimal choice of monetary policy instruments in a simple stochastic macro model', *Quarterly Journal of Economics*, **84**(2) (May), 197–216.

Reserve Bank of Australia (2003), 'The Reserve Bank's open market operations', *Reserve Bank of Australia Bulletin*, June, pp. 1–7.

Rochon, L. (1997), 'Keynes' finance motive: a reassessment. Credit, liquidity preference and the rate of interest', *Review of Political Economy*, **9**(3) 277–93.

Rochon, L. (1999), *Credit, Money and Production: An Alternative Post Keynesian Approach*, Cheltenham, UK and Northampton, MA, USA: Edward Elgar.

Rogers, C. (1989), *Money, Interest and Capital: A Study in the Foundations of Monetary Theory*, Cambridge: Cambridge University Press.

Romer, D. (1993), 'The New Keynesian synthesis', *Journal of Economic Perspectives*, **7**(1) (Winter), 5–22.

Romer, D. (2000), 'Keynesian macroeconomics without the LM curve', *Journal of Economic Perspectives*, **14**(2) (Spring), 149–69.

Romer, C. and D. Romer (2003), 'A rehabilitation of monetary policy in the 1950s', *American Economic Review*, **92**(2), 121–7.

Sargent, T. and N. Wallace (1975), 'Rational expectations, the optimal monetary instrument and the optimal money supply rule', *Journal of Political Economy*, **83**(2) (April), 241–54.

Setterfield, M. (2004), 'Central banking, stability and macroeconomic outcomes: a comparison of new consensus and post Keynesian monetary macroeconomics', in M. Lavoie and M. Seccareccia (eds), *Central Banking in the Modern World*, Cheltenham, UK and Northampton, MA, USA: Edward Elgar, pp. 35–56.

Setterfield, M. (2005), 'Central Bank behaviour and the stability of macroeconomic equilibrium: a critical examination of the "new consensus"', in P. Arestis, M. Badeley, and J. McCombie (eds), *The New Monetary Policy: Implications and Relevance*, Cheltenham, UK and Northampton, MA, USA: Edward Elgar, pp. 23–49.

Setterfield, M. (2009), 'Macroeconomics without the LM curve: an alternative view', *Cambridge Journal of Economics*, **33**(2) (March), 273–93.

Taylor, J. (1993), 'Discretion versus policy rules in practice', *Carnegie-Rochester Conference Series on Public Policy*, **39**(1), 195–214.

Taylor, J. (1998), 'Monetary policy and the long boom', *Federal Reserve Bank of St. Louis Review*, **80**(6), (November/December), 3–11.

Taylor, J. (1999), 'A historical analysis of monetary policy rules', J. Taylor (ed.), *Monetary Policy Rules*, Chicago, IL: National Bureau of Economic Research, pp. 319–44.

Tobin, J. (1980), 'Stabilization policy after ten years', *Brookings Papers on Economic Activity*, **1**, 19–71.

Tobin, J. (1981), 'The monetarist counter-revolution today – an appraisal', *Economic Journal*, **91**(361) (March), 29–42.

Wicksell, K. (1898), *Interest and Prices: A Study of the Causes Regulating the Value of Money*, translated by R. F. Kahn (1936), reprinted in 1965, New York: Augustus M. Kelley.

Woodford, M. (2001), 'The Taylor rule and optimal monetary policy', *American Economic Review*, **91**(2) (May), 232–7.

Woodford, M. (2003), *Interest & Prices: Foundations of a Theory of Monetary Policy*, Princeton, NJ: Princeton University Press.

7. *The General Theory of Employment, Interest, and Money* after 75 years: the importance of being in the right place at the right time

Matthew N. Luzzetti and Lee E. Ohanian

INTRODUCTION

There is no doubt that Keynes's *The General Theory of Employment, Interest, and Money* significantly influenced the economics profession and economic policymakers. 'Google Scholar' at the time of writing showed 14 585 citations to *The General Theory*. To put this in perspective, Robert Lucas's famous 1972 paper 'Expectations and the Neutrality of Money', and Finn Kydland and Edward Prescott's famous 1982 paper 'Time to Build and Aggregate Fluctuations', both of which helped supplant *The General Theory* as the dominant macroeconomics paradigm, and both of which were cited by the Nobel committee when these economists won Nobel Prizes in 1995 and 2004, respectively, had combined citations that account for less than half of the number of *The General Theory*'s citations. And *The General Theory*'s citation count doesn't fully reflect the fact that the Keynesian revolution was perceived by many economists between the late 1930s and 1970, including Nobel Laureates Laurence Klein, Paul Samuelson, Robert Solow and James Tobin, as the only game in town for analysing business cycle fluctuations and for developing government policies to stabilize the economy. For much of this period, Milton Friedman's path breaking work on the quantity theory of money and the associated tenets of monetarism took a backseat to *The General Theory*. Perhaps the best one-liner that represents the influence of Keynes, at least in policymaking circles, was President Richard Nixon's statement 'I am now a Keynesian in economics' after he eliminated the United States' remaining ties to gold in 1971 (Pearlstein 2008).

This chapter discusses *The General Theory* from the *perspective of neoclassical macroeconomics*, which is the macroeconomics that in many quarters replaced *The General Theory* over the last 40 years. We focus our analysis on understanding the impact of *The General Theory* on economic theory and on policymaking, why beginning in the 1970s research economists largely abandoned *The General Theory*, and why some ideas from *The General Theory* continue to have significant impact, particularly among economic policymakers.

The General Theory was published during the Great Depression, one of the most devastating international economic crises, and one in which *The General Theory* offered hope for understanding what otherwise seemed inexplicable, and that also offered a promise for economic policies that could restore prosperity. Our view is that *The General Theory* had such significant and long-lasting impact because Keynes was in the right place at the right time, involving two key elements. For at least some time, the evolution of macroeconomic variables seemed to conform to the predictions of the theory, as wartime spending, at least in the United States, coincided with a wartime economic boom, lending credence to the view that increasing government spending fosters higher employment and output. And the relative economic stability of the 1950s and 1960s convinced many economists that the tenets of *The General Theory* were responsible for curing depression and providing an economic management blueprint for governments. The second element is that fundamental econometric breakthroughs occurred just after publication of *The General Theory*, and these econometric developments provided a methodological basis to advance the ideas in *The General Theory* and provide a quantitative framework for analysing macroeconomic problems.

But the same broad features that gave *The General Theory* such prominence in theory and policymaking for so many years – methodological developments that made it feasible to build and quantify economic models and the empirical features of the macroeconomies – were ultimately the reasons why *The General Theory* was replaced as the dominant macroeconomic paradigm. In particular, the evolution of Muth's approach of rational expectations (Muth 1961), combined with the integration of dynamic general equilibrium theory with recursive methods, made it feasible to develop formally specified dynamic macroeconomies with deeper theoretical foundations than was present in *The General Theory*. And the recognition that supply-side factors were important for fluctuations, together with the breakdown of the Phillips curve, also contributed to the end of the Keynesian Revolution, at least among research economists.

The chapter is organized as follows. In the next section we summarize the elements of *The General Theory* that we choose to discuss. Next, we discuss why *The General Theory* had such a long-lasting impact on economic theory and policymaking. Then we detail the reasons for the decline of *The General Theory* among research economists. We then briefly discuss theoretical innovations in equilibrium macroeconomics that helped supplant *The General Theory* as the primary macroeconomics paradigm. And finally we present some of our conclusions.

SOME DEFINING FEATURES OF *THE GENERAL THEORY*

Keynes certainly intended *The General Theory* to be just that – an overall framework for understanding the macroeconomy, not just an analysis of business cycle fluctuations. As in his essay, 'Economic Possibilities for Our Grandchildren', Keynes opined about what the world might look like in the future. Some of his long-run assessments are of considerable interest in their own right, including Keynes's view that society might become sated with consumption of physical goods, which could lead to solving the problem of scarcity, and the idea that society could run out of profitable investment opportunities. The idea of satiation was discussed in Ohanian (2008), while the notion that there was a finite number of profitable investments sheds light on Keynes's views about the social creation of new ideas, and their importance for growth. That is, either society would run out of ideas, which is an issue that has been explored recently by Chad Jones (2002), or alternatively, that ideas are not that relevant for future growth. And while these and other long-run visions of Keynes are fascinating, both for understanding Keynes and understanding his social views, we focus on some of the most well-known components of *The General Theory*, those which are commonly cited as important passages and which have specific impact.

These include the broad view that economic fluctuations are largely demand-driven, that some of that change in demand is not due to fundamentals, but rather 'animal spirits' that impact expectations about future profitability, and that in turn impact capital investment, that expanding government demand is useful for stabilizing an economy and in particular helping to restore employment loss from a recession, that wages are countercyclical, that there is a tradeoff between inflation and measures of labour utilization, such as unemployment, that consumption, which represents roughly two-thirds of output, is largely determined by concurrent income, which leads to a multiplier related to government spending. Other economists have advanced all of these ideas along many dimensions during the heyday of the Keynesian revolution.

THE IMPACT OF THE GENERAL THEORY ON ECONOMIC THEORY AND POLICY MAKING

The General Theory had a major impact on economic thinking among economists and policymakers for a long time, and in some circles, still remains influential today. The substantial and long-running influence of *The General Theory* is due in our view to a 'perfect storm' of timing of events that surrounded *The General Theory* and turned it into a paradigm shifter that dominated macroeconomics until the 1970s. Specifically, *The General Theory* was written during the Great Depression, a catastrophic episode in which the economic theory of that time seemed to be of little use, and in which there was demand for new ideas that could aid in restoring prosperity. And there are two developments around the time of *The General Theory* that advanced its prominence substantially. One is that the theory seemed to be consistent with the subsequent evolution of economic time series, at least for a while. A second fundamental component is that the major developments in econometric identification and estimation of simultaneous equations models made possible the large-scale econometric models which featured a number of ideas from *The General Theory*.

The General Theory was published in 1936, and seems to have been written in 1935, but it is likely that Keynes was presenting these ideas before this, which is to say that *The General Theory* had its genesis during the Great Depression. This is very important, because the Depression was not only the most broad-based international crisis, involving most of Europe and other advanced countries, but it was also the deepest and most persistent crisis in many of those countries, including the US, Canada, France, and Germany.

The persistence and depth of the Depression seemed to defy explanations based on the equilibrium reasoning of the standard theory of that time, which held that price adjustments would bring supply and demand into balance. But the market-clearing implications of standard equilibrium theory seemed to have little to say about the very high and persistent unemployment that characterized the UK throughout the 1920s and much of the 1930s, and for the US for the entire decade of the 1930s.

And while there is debate over how to measure unemployment in the US during this period, reflecting whether or not to count individuals on government work relief programmes, employment statistics clearly indicate more than a decade of labour market weakness in the US. Cole and Ohanian (1999) report that per-capita hours worked, including those who worked government jobs, had recovered very little by 1939 as compared to the trough levels of 1933. Specifically, total hours worked per adult fell by about 27 per cent between 1929 and 1933, and remained about 22 per cent below its 1929 level in 1939, a decade after the Depression began in the US.

Keynes jumped on the tension of using standard equilibrium reasoning to analyse a prolonged depression in *The General Theory* by reviewing Pigou's analysis of the labour market. Pigou's model, which was presented in *The Theory of Unemployment* (1933), develops a fairly representative model of the labour market by today's standards. The model features a standard labour-leisure tradeoff that is now embedded in the familiar intratemporal first order condition that appears in many models in which a household equates the marginal rate of substitution between consumption and leisure to the marginal product of labour. But as Depressions stretched out for decades across both the UK (whose Depression began after World War I), and the US, it became increasingly difficult to reconcile the chronically persistent high rates of unemployment with a theory that posited wage adjustments in response to variations in nominal prices that ultimately reduced unemployment by equilibrating labour supply and labour demand. Moreover, the persistence of high unemployment that coincided in some countries with rising – not falling – real wages, seemed to be well outside the bounds of equilibrium theory. *The General Theory* was written partly in response to this tension about economic depression and equilibrium theory. Keynes wrote:

> This (specification of Pigou's model) amounts, of course, to assuming that there is no involuntary unemployment in the strict sense, i.e. that all labour available at the existing real wage is in fact employed. (Keynes 1936, p. 274)

Pigou's view was that wage adjustments would bring the supply of labour and demand for labour into balance, just as was the case for any commodity in which competitive market mechanisms were working well. This is where Keynes declared victory, and in which there was not much of a rejoinder. How could Pigou's equilibrium model, or any equilibrium reasoning that was founded on the view that prices would adjust to bring supply and demand together, shed light on such deep and prolonged depressions?

Specifically, it seemed implausible that individuals were unwilling to work at observed wages. And the fact that real wages were rising in some countries during the Depression, including the US, made equilibrium reasoning seem even more off base. The impact of *The General Theory* was partly due to the view that it provided a description of how depression could be so deep and last so long, reflecting the idea that negative expectations – animal spirits – reduced demand, which in turn reduced output and employment. Perhaps even more seductive, Keynes offered policy prescriptions for combating depression that not only promised recovery, but also in some sense seemed too good to be true. *The General Theory* argued that depression was the result of insufficient spending, and that employment and output could be restored by increasing government demand for goods and services. In this sense, higher expenditures could make *everyone* better off. Fiscal policy seemed to offer a free lunch when households or businesses were not spending 'enough'.

In the absence of any other economic theorizing that could provide a framework for analysing the Great Depression, Keynesian economics ultimately became the only game in town. Moreover, following the publication of *The General Theory*, US macroeconomic time series seemed consistent with the predictions of *The General Theory*. Specifically, World War II seemed to provide a major empirical victory for *The General Theory*. A central component of the Keynesian model is that deficient nominal demand is the key factor behind recession and depression, and that expanding demand from government increases employment and output. As government spending soared in the 1940s, rising from about 16 per cent of GDP in 1939 to 48 per cent of GDP in 1944, employment, which had been depressed for more than a decade, jumped sharply, with the unemployment rate falling from 17.2 per cent in 1939 to 1.2 per cent in 1944 (Margo 1993, p. 43).

The presumption that higher government wartime spending expanded aggregate demand, and brought the US economy out of the Depression, set the stage for increasing economists' confidence in the Keynesian model. And data from the 1950s and 1960s further solidified the apparent empirical support for the Keynesian model. The 1950s was stable and the 1960s boomed. The decade-long depression of the 1930s never returned, and even recessions, when they came, were relatively mild.

There was growing consensus that economic stability, featuring low and stable unemployment, reflected the expansion of government economic management consisting of activist monetary and fiscal policy. The 1960s were the heyday of the Keynesian Revolution, which seemed well summarized by Walter Heller, a University of Minnesota economist and adviser to President Kennedy, who coined the term 'fine tuning' to mean the discretionary use of fiscal and monetary policy to keep the economy as close as possible to its 'full employment' level. And many economists believed that the principles of *The General Theory* had conquered the business cycle, as unemployment fluctuated within very narrow bands. Between 1966 and 1969, unemployment ranged between 3.4 per cent and 4 per cent.

But perhaps the most fundamental component that fostered the longevity of *The General Theory* was the breakthroughs in econometric methods that started in the 1940s, shortly after the publication of *The General Theory*. These methodological developments were key in advancing the *qualitative* ideas in *The General Theory* into *quantitative* propositions. More specifically, whether a macroeconomic paradigm achieves long-run influence ultimately lies in how it can be transformed from abstract ideas to concrete quantitative applications. Kydland and Prescott's (1982) real business cycle model had so much influence because it came with a ready-made quantitative framework, featuring a method for approximating recursive equilibria, choosing parameter values, and comparing model economy simulated time series to actual national income and product account data. For *The General Theory*, the econometric developments of the 1940s and 1950s provided a quantitative framework for showcasing Keynes's ideas and for developing a full-fledged quantitative Keynesian toolkit.

Much of *The General Theory*'s impact was based on method, perhaps as much from this quarter as from ideas, despite the fact that there is virtually nothing in the way of methodology in the book. Beginning in the early 1940s, the foundations for modern econometric analyses of simultaneous equations models began to develop, including Trygve Haavelmo's 1944 paper which integrated more formally probability theory with econometric methods, with a focus on simultaneous equations that later earned Haavelmo a Nobel Prize. Just a few years later, the Cowles Commission published important monographs in econometric theory that would become true classics, including *Studies in Econometric Method* edited by William C. Hood and Tjalling Koopmans (1953). This volume included major pieces such as Herb Simon's 'Causal Ordering and Identifiability', which still has considerable impact today, as it relates to the causal ordering that identify many systems in the VAR literature, and 'The Estimation of Simultaneous Linear Economic Relationships' by Tjalling Koopmans and William Hood. A second volume edited by Koopmans in 1950, *Statistical Inference in Dynamic Economic Models*, contained classics on identification by Wald, Hurwicz, and Haavelmo, estimation, by Wald, T.W. Anderson, Koopmans and Hurwicz and precursors to issues about trends, including Hurwicz's small sample bias, and what is structural, including a classic by Koopmans.

These pathbreaking advances were central for the continuation of the Keynesian revolution and the impact of *The General Theory*, as they explicitly made it possible to take the ideas from *The General Theory* and make them concretely quantifiable. These econometric developments formed the basis of the main toolkit used in analysing business cycles in the 1950s and particularly the 1960s. The large-scale econometric models, developed in concert with the Federal Reserve Board, MIT, with Nobel Laureate Franco Modigliani, and Penn, with Albert Ando, as well as the Wharton model under the direction of Nobel Laureate Laurence Klein, were impressive technical feats, as these models ultimately would include hundreds of equations, with each equation summarizing demand or supply behaviour in some part of the economy. These models were used widely within policymaking circles and formed the basis of dozens of Ph.D. dissertations at top economics departments in the 1960s. Chances are, if you ask a macroeconomist who received their Ph.D. in the 1960s about their dissertation topic, they will likely say, 'I worked on the 'x' equation in the MPLS model'.

The breadth of impact that these models had cannot be overstated. Ed Prescott, an Assistant Professor at the University of Pennsylvania, and his Ph.D. student, Thomas Cooley, wrote papers on varying parameter regression (Cooley and Prescott 1973; Cooley and Prescott 1976) to try to formalize the ad-hoc practice of add-factoring in these models, in which practitioners would subjectively adjust estimated equations, often by changing the constant term of the equation, depending on whether the forecast from that equation seemed implausibly high or low. These contributions by Cooley and Prescott are hard to fathom today, given both scholars' current views towards Keynesian macroeconometrics. The contributions by Cooley and Prescott are an important example of the interplay between the development of economic ideas and the associated quantitative applications of those ideas.

The large-scale models had the biggest impact among policymakers, and not surprisingly so. Time series during the 1960s seemed to be consistent with the predictions of the Keynesian model, there was a sense that fine tuning or, more broadly, aggregate demand management, had conquered the business cycle, and the models were at the stage where they could easily be used to make unconditional forecasts as well as the more challenging task of conditional forecasting, in which policymakers would make forecasts under various 'what if' assumptions, such as how much would the unemployment rate change if tax rates, or other policy variables, were changed? Quantitative analyses at virtually all central banks in advanced countries were largely based on large-scale, Keynesian, econometric models. Throughout the 1960s, the legacy of *The General Theory* was vibrant in and out of policy circles, as the economy continued to grow with remarkable stability. And for many observers, this stable prosperity was due in considerable part to the tenets of the Keynesian model.

To gain a better idea of how much the Keynesian model changed aggregate economics, note that it was almost radical in its departure from standard, classical economic thinking, which was founded on incentives, opportunity costs, and marginal choices. In the entire *General Theory*, we found only seven references to the word 'incentive(s)', no references to the phrase 'opportunity cost' and few references to 'marginal productivity' outside of his discussion of classical economics.

THE DECLINE OF THE KEYNESIAN MODEL

By the early 1970s, macroeconomic time series in the US and other economies began to evolve in patterns that were difficult to reconcile with the Keynesian model. And much like the criticism Keynes levelled at equilibrium theory for failing to provide a framework to make sense of chronically high unemployment in the 1920s and 1930s, the 1970s began as a decade in which empirical criticisms were advanced against Keynesian models. These critiques included the forecasting performance of the large-scale, Keynesian econometric models, the increasing recognition that supply-side factors were central for understanding fluctuations, that Phillips curve relationships shifted in ways that were inconsistent with the Keynesian model, and critiques regarding the theoretical foundations of the Keynesian model.

The first significant empirical criticism came from Charles Nelson's (1972) influential paper that showed that low-order integrated autoregressive-moving average (ARIMA) models produced lower mean square error forecasts than the large-scale, Keynesian econometric models. This was particularly important, because ARIMA models do nothing more than generate forecasts from historical serial correlation patterns. This meant that a purely atheoretic model which did nothing more than exploit historical patterns captured in autocovariances was more accurate than the very detailed Keynesian models that were the industry standard. Nelson's work, and subsequent work on relative forecasting performance by others, including the pseudo-Bayesian VARs developed by Robert Litterman (1986), led to considerably less reliance on Keynesian models for unconditional forecasting.

Additional empirical challenges with the Keynesian model began to emerge. These included the fact that empirical relationships were changing in ways that were at variance with the Keynesian model. Perhaps nowhere was the breakdown in relationships more evident than in the Phillips curve. Figures 7.1 and 7.2, which are drawn from Atkeson and Ohanian (2001), demonstrate the significant changes in the relationship between unemployment and inflation that have occurred over time. Figure 7.1 shows monthly observations on CPI inflation and the unemployment rate between 1959 and 1969, the heyday of the Keynesian model. This relationship, which is the focus of Samuelson and Solow's (1960) famous discussion of the Phillips curve, shows a clear negative relationship between these variables, with a correlation of around −0.6. This pattern was interpreted by some economists that unemployment could be permanently kept at low levels provided that there was at least some inflation. But this pattern changes substantially after the 1960s.

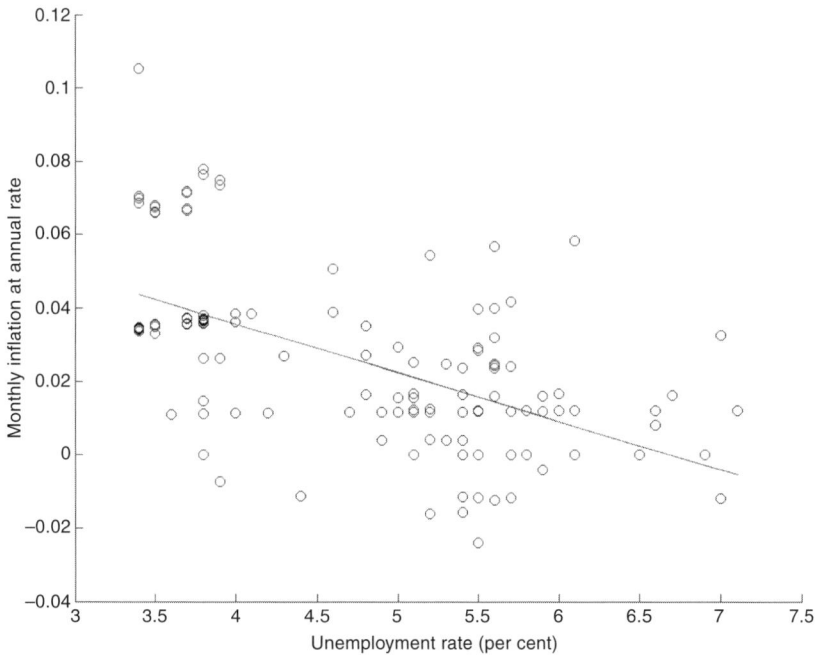

Figure 7.1   CPI inflation versus unemployment rate (1959–1969)

Figure 7.2 shows no relationship whatsoever between these variables between 1970 and 1999, as the regression line has a slope very close to zero. Some economists tried to salvage the Phillips curve by adopting a modification, based on the idea of a non-accelerating rate of inflation level of unemployment, or NAIRU. This suggested a relationship between the change in the inflation rate and the unemployment rate. But as Figures 7.3 and 7.4 show, there is no systematic relationship between these variables either. Lucas and Sargent (1979) jumped on this empirical failure of the Keynesian labour market, much as Keynes had jumped on the apparent empirical failure of the Pigouvian labour market in the 1930s.

Additional evidence that challenged the Keynesian foundation of the dominance of the demand side of the economy is the empirical relationship between nominal prices and real output and real wages and real output over the cycle. An important prediction of some classes of the Keynesian model, and one which was taken up more broadly in other theories, including those of Lucas (1972), is the procyclical behaviour of prices. Figures 7.5 and 7.6, which draw in part from Cooley and Ohanian (1991), show the relationship between detrended real GNP and the GNP deflator between 1930 and 2010.

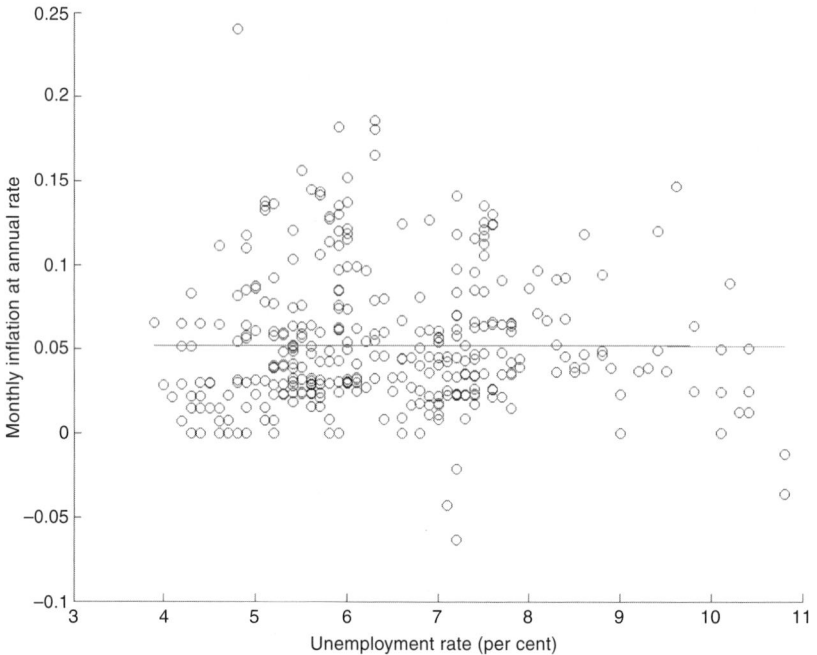

Figure 7.2   CPI inflation versus unemployment rate (1970–1999)

Note that prices are indeed procyclical in the 1930s, which is consistent with *The General Theory*, and they continue to be procyclical through World War II, as the correlation between detrended output and prices is about 0.57 between 1930 and 1947. But after World War II, prices are countercyclical, with a correlation of −0.24 between 1948 and 1999, and −0.528 between 1970 and 2010. Note that changing the measure of prices to inflation does not change this very much, since the relationship is 0.18 between 1970 and 2010.

Figure 7.7 depicts the real wage, measured by real employee compensation, and real GNP net of a Hodrick-Prescott trend between 1948 and 2010. These data clearly show a positive relationship, which indicates that when the economy is in expansion (above trend), so are wages, and when the economy is in recession (below trend), real wages are also below their trend level. This stands in sharp contrast to Keynes's view regarding countercyclical real wages. It is interesting that the implied Keynesian pattern of the cyclicality of real wages was addressed early on by Tarshis (1939) and Dunlop (1938) who studied the cyclicality of real wages. Using annual wage data from the UK from 1860 to 1937 and monthly wage data from the US from 1932 to 1938, Dunlop and Tarshis found nominal and real

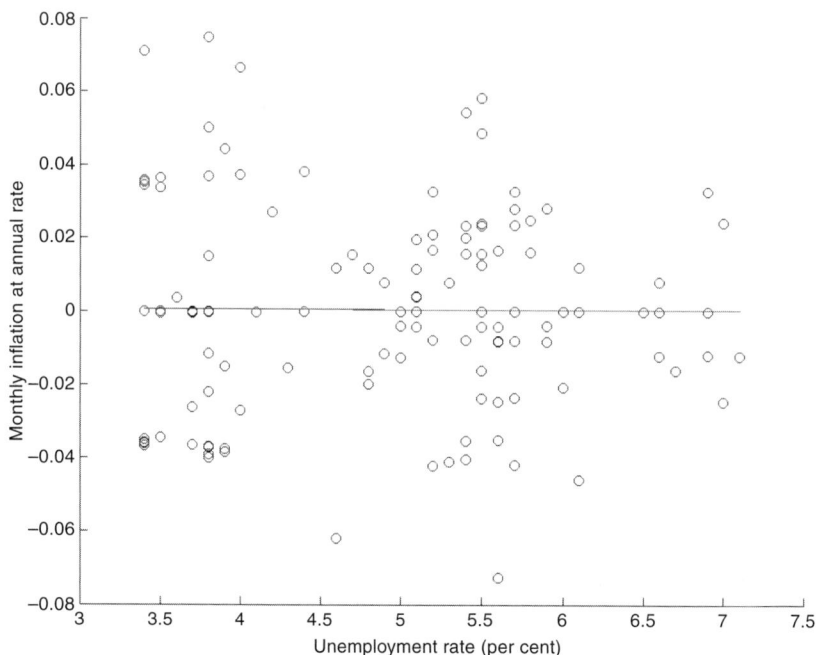

Figure 7.3   CPI inflation difference versus unemployment rate (1959–1969)

wages to be positively correlated over this period. In addition, Tarshis uncovered a negative relationship between real wages and hours worked in the US during the 1930s.

While the Tarshis findings appear to be consistent with the Keynesian model, recent research paints a very different picture of this period. Specifically, Ohanian (2009) and Cole and Ohanian (2004) present theory and evidence that government cartelization policies were responsible for raising real wages and depressing the economy. Ironically, this cartelization view indicates that the depth and persistence of the US Great Depression were because of activist government policies that tried to raise demand, and not because government stood on the sidelines.

The facts that prices are typically countercyclical, and that real wages are typically procyclical, suggests that a substantial fraction of fluctuations may arise from the supply side of the economy, which Keynes largely ignored in *The General Theory*. To address the importance of one supply-side component, Figure 7.8 shows detrended real GDP and detrended total factor productivity (TFP). The graph shows that TFP is clearly procyclical, as TFP is above trend when the economy is above trend, and similarly TFP is below

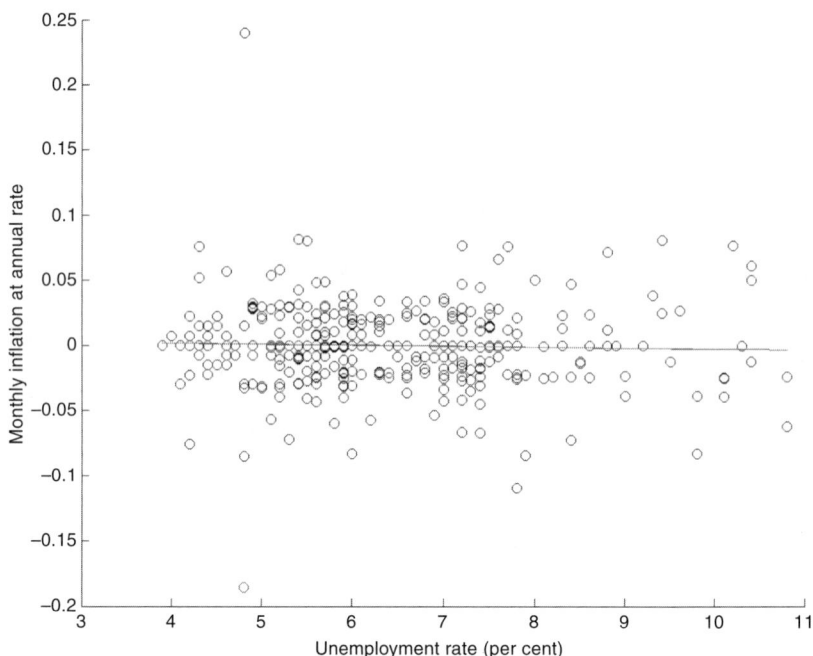

Figure 7.4   CPI inflation difference versus unemployment rate (1970–1999)

trend during recessions, with a correlation of 0.73 between these two series. Of course, the fact that TFP historically is procyclical and relatively volatile is what led Kydland and Prescott and the large body of research that followed to develop the real business cycle programme, in which fluctuations arise from a source not considered in *The General Theory*.

Taken together, this evidence indicates that supply-side factors are quantitatively and systematically important determinants of business cycles. The growing recognition of the importance of supply-side factors, which increased considerably in the 1980s and 1990s, reduced interest in the Keynesian model, as it is largely silent about the supply side of the economy.

Economists also have critically examined detailed elements of *The General Theory* regarding the foundations of consumption and investment. *The General Theory* posited that consumption depended significantly on current income. Many developments of the Keynesian model simplified the Keynesian consumption function to just this single argument:

$$C = C(Y).$$

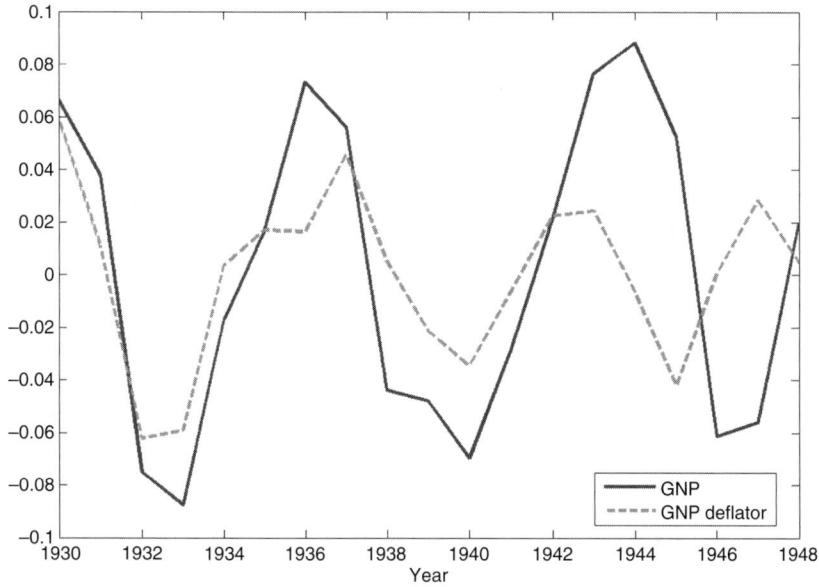

Figure 7.5   Deviations from trend: GNP deflator and output (1930–1947)

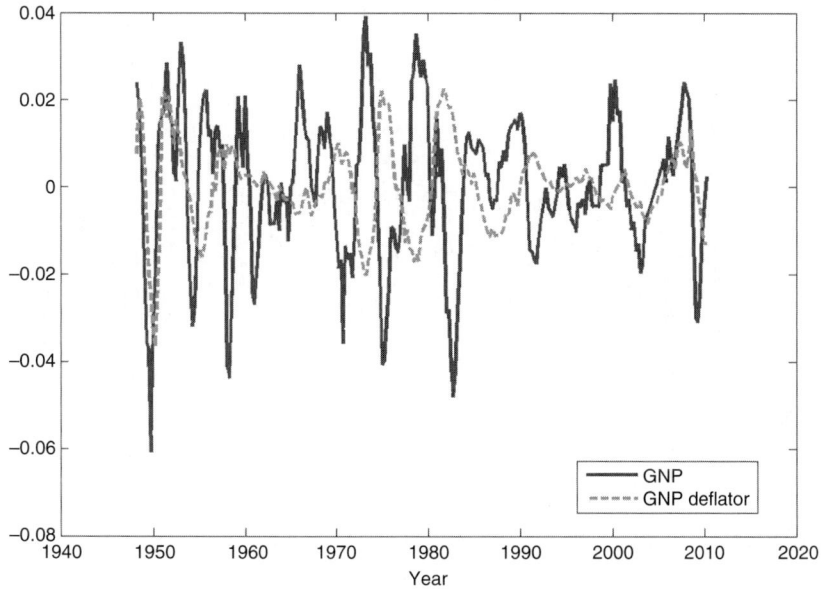

Figure 7.6   Deviations from trend: GNP deflator and output (1948–2010)

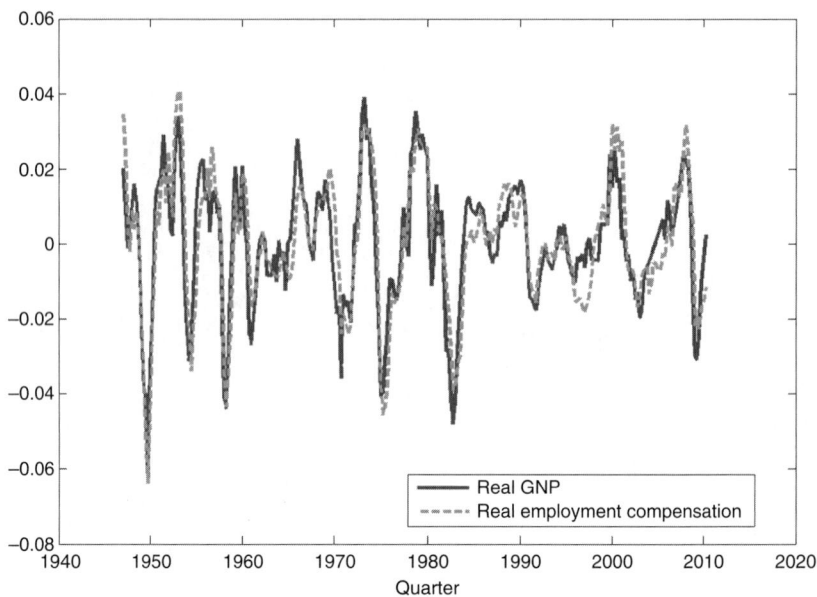

Figure 7.7   US real GNP and real employee comp: deviations from trend

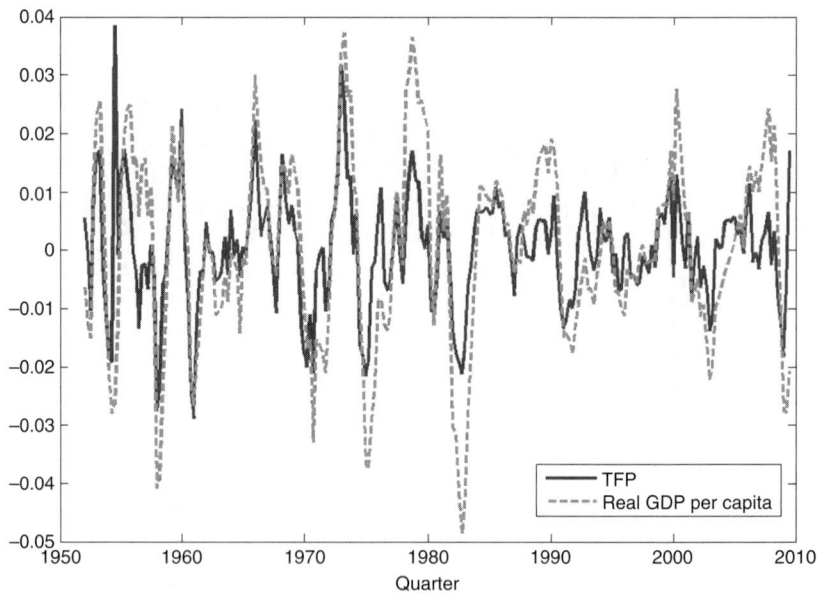

Figure 7.8   TFP and RGDP per capita: deviations from trend

Friedman's permanent income theory (1957), however, provided a very different view about the determinants of consumption. Friedman's model connects closely to modern models of consumption, which stress the importance of intertemporal elements, the smoothing of temporary fluctuations, and the importance of wealth in determining consumption. Friedman argued that consumption was largely determined by permanent income, or wealth. Friedman's theory attracted considerable attention, as it shed light on what appeared to be an anomaly from the perspective of the Keynesian model. Specifically, the marginal propensity to consume was around one in the cross-section, but was significantly less than one in time series observations. Friedman's permanent income theory is consistent with both of these relationships, as cross-sectional data tends to capture long-run features, while relatively high frequency time series captures short-run features. In time series observations, transitory income, which according to Friedman had little impact on consumption, is operative, and thus the regression coefficient in the time series will be biased downwards, which follows from the standard errors-in-variables problem in econometrics. In the cross-section, however, transitory income becomes irrelevant and the marginal propensity to consume is significantly higher.

In terms of investment, Keynes spoke about the importance of animal spirits impacting the quantity of investment in physical capital. Many readers of *The General Theory* interpret this as the notion that expectations can change suddenly and significantly, which then leads to large changes in the quantity of physical investment. As Keynes wrote:

> Most, probably, of our decisions to do something positive, the full consequences of which will be drawn out over many days to come, can only be taken as the result of animal spirits – a spontaneous urge to action rather than inaction, and not as the outcome of a weighted average of quantitative benefits multiplied by quantitative probabilities. (Keynes 1936, p. 162)

But is investment impacted in a quantitatively substantial way by large and sudden changes in expectations about the future? To address this question, we use historical data from the United States to construct Euler equation residuals under the assumption of perfect foresight. This provides a useful test of Keynes's animal spirits view, as the perfect foresight assumption means that investment takes place in a deterministic environment in which those investing correctly see the entire future path of the economy. This extreme assumption regarding expectations is very different from the Keynesian view, in which expectations change suddenly and dramatically over time. Under the Keynesian view, the Euler equation errors should be very large and volatile, representing these large changes in expectations. Moreover, depressions should be periods with very large

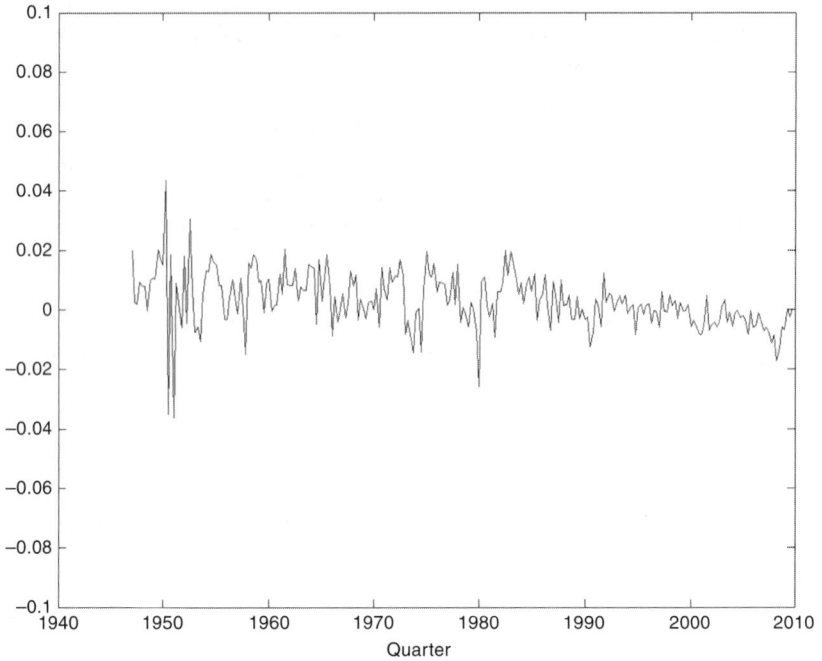

Figure 7.9   Euler equation deviations

negative residuals, as this case represents negative expectations about future returns to capital.

To conduct this analysis, we use a standard model economy with separable utility between consumption and leisure, log preferences over consumption, and in which there is a Cobb-Douglas production technology. The Euler equation is:

$$\frac{\gamma c_{t+1}}{c_t} = \beta(r_{t+1} + 1 - \delta)$$

which yields the Euler equation residual:

$$\varepsilon_{t+1} \equiv \frac{\gamma c_{t+1}}{c_t} - \beta(r_{t+1} + 1 - \delta)$$

We first consider the post-World War II evidence. In contrast to the Keynesian view of large swings in expectations of investors, the Euler equation errors are small and appear to be uncorrelated. Figure 7.9 shows

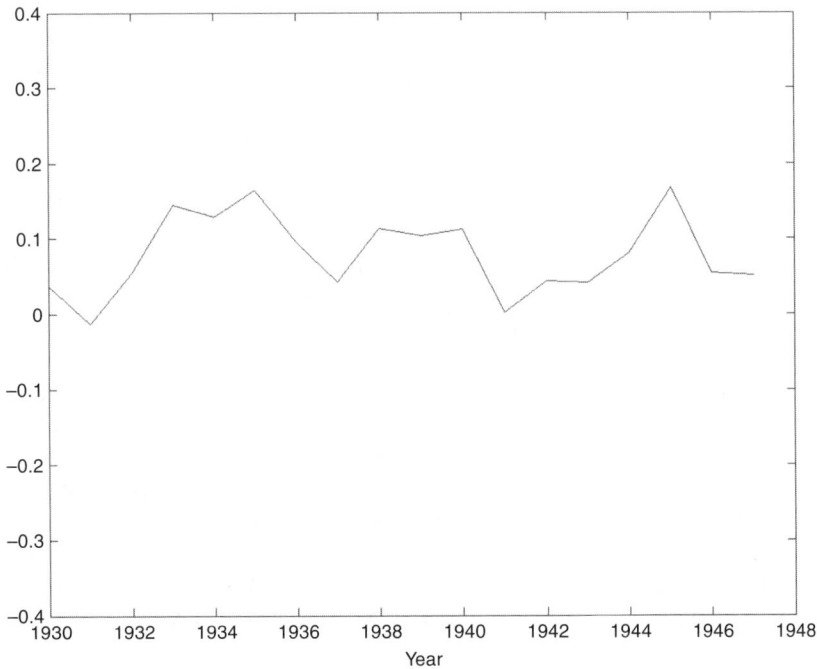

Figure 7.10   Euler equation deviations

quarterly Euler equation residuals from 1947 to 2010. While Keynes provides no benchmark for understanding how big these changes should be, it seems difficult to interpret these changes as having quantitatively important effects. Of course, postwar fluctuations are small – but what about those during the Depression?

Figure 7.10 shows the Euler residuals for the Depression. The residuals are larger, but they are of the wrong sign. Specifically, *The General Theory* implies these residuals should be negative, indicating that investors expected low returns relative to the intertemporal marginal rate of substitution. Instead, the residuals are positive, suggesting that investors were optimistic in expecting higher returns than those that materialized.

EQUILIBRIUM MACROECONOMICS

The Keynesian paradigm dominated macroeconomics, particularly in policy circles, for more than 40 years. And despite the shortcomings of the Keynesian model noted above, there has been considerable effort involved at resuscitating the paradigm (see Gordon 2009). But the Keynesian model as presented in the large econometric models, with hundreds of equations that were not microfounded, was not well suited for the theoretical developments occurring in the 1960s and 1970s in economic theory. Muth (1961) and subsequent research developed the theory of modelling expectations in dynamic settings. Lucas and Prescott (1974) and Mehra and Prescott (1980) showed how to integrate infinite dimensional economies with recursive methods to make it feasible to quantitatively assess fully microfounded dynamic stochastic equilibrium economies. And this all came together in 1982 with Kydland and Prescott's 'Time to build and aggregate fluctuations', which was about as far from the Keynesian world as you can get.

Kydland and Prescott's analysis was one in which fluctuations were entirely from the supply side of the economy; there was no mention of monetary or fiscal policy, or unemployment, and in which the welfare theorems held, such that equilibrium allocations were Pareto optimal. The many innovations in Kydland and Prescott, including an algorithm to approximate the equilibrium, a procedure for choosing parameter values, and a procedure for comparing the model to the data, led to a paradigm shift. This work motivated a number of extensions of the Kydland-Prescott framework, including the incorporation of imperfectly flexible prices and wages such that the model could more closely feature Keynesian ideas (see Chari et al. (2000)). Much macroeconomic research today takes as a foundation the Kydland-Prescott model, even if the features of the model differ considerably from Kydland and Prescott.

Moreover, equilibrium macroeconomics has also addressed questions that previously were considered beyond its grasp. Specifically, equilibrium macroeconomic frameworks are now being used to analyse issues that largely led to the abandonment of equilibrium theory in favour of *The General Theory*, including major economic disruptions such as the Great Depression or World War II. And equilibrium models are generating very different answers for understanding these episodes than *The General Theory*.

In addition to the work on the severity and persistence of the Great Depression cited above (see Ohanian (2009) and Cole and Ohanian (2004)), more recent work has considered the economic boom that occurred during World War II. McGrattan and Ohanian (2010) study how various factors, including higher government spending, impacted the US economy during World War II in a purely neoclassical model. They find that higher government spending did spur economic growth, but not through the channels emphasized in *The General Theory*. Rather, the enormous resource drain of government spending – which exceeded 50 per cent of trend output at the peak of the war – led to higher employment and output through large wealth effects. Specifically, the size and persistence of the war reduced the present value of resources available to households for consumption and investment, which then led to increased employment under the assumption that leisure is a normal good. Thus, higher government spending also expands employment and output in the neoclassical model, but the welfare consequences of this spending differ remarkably from that in *The General Theory*. Specifically, higher wartime spending – which contributes relatively little to private consumption or investment – reduces welfare, whereas raising aggregate demand in the Keynesian model when the economy is below trend employment improves welfare.

CONCLUSION

There is no doubt that *The General Theory* was one of the major economic events of the twentieth century, reflecting the genesis of *The General Theory* during the Depression, the subsequent evolution of macroeconomic time series that seemed to support the predictions of *The General Theory*, and econometric breakthroughs that made the ideas in *The General Theory* quantitatively operational. From the perspective of these two latter events, Keynes was in the right place at the right time. However, this should not detract from the fact that Keynes produced a framework that provided economists and policymakers with a remarkably different way of assessing and fighting depression, which was in itself a major achievement. From this standpoint, the impact of *The General Theory*, which dispensed with equilibrium aggregate economics, was at least as important as the impact of Kydland and Prescott (1982), which at some level dispensed with Keynesian economics.

But some ideas from 1936 persist, at least in policymaking circles. In fact, some of the forecasting models utilized by the Federal Reserve are in many ways similar to the Keynesian models of the 1960s (Brayton et al. 1997). The notion of an inflation-unemployment tradeoff and aggregate demand management to stabilize the economy remains at central banks, and the Keynesian vision provides a well-established framework for carrying this vision on within the context of policies that tie central bank behaviour to the joint mandate of promoting both low unemployment and price stability.

Because of this joint mandate, it is politically unimaginable that a central bank could ever respond to a crisis by indicating either that there was little they could do to increase output, or that attempts to do so might make matters worse. *The General Theory* will continue to have a large audience among policymakers as long as governments are pressed to boost nominal spending during periods of crisis, whether or not those efforts are effective.

BIBLIOGRAPHY

Anderson, T. Jr. (1950), 'Estimation of the parameters of a single equation by the limited-information maximum-likelihood method', in T. Koopmans (ed.), *Statistical Inference in Dynamic Economic Models*, New York: Wiley and Sons, Inc., pp. 311–22.

Atkeson, A. and L. Ohanian (2001), 'Are Phillips curves useful for forecasting inflation?', *Quarterly Review*, Federal Reserve Bank of Minneapolis, **25**(1) (Winter), 2–11.

Brayton, A., A. Levin, R. Tryon, and J. Williams (1997), 'The evolution of macro models at the Federal Reserve Board', unpublished paper.

Chari, V. V., P. Kehoe, and E. McGrattan (2000), 'Sticky price models of the business cycle: can the contract multiplier solve the persistence problem?', *Econometrica*, **68**(5) (September), 1151–80.

Cole, H. and L. Ohanian (1999), 'The Great Depression in the United States from a neoclassical perspective', *Quarterly Review*, Federal Reserve Bank of Minneapolis, **23**(1) (Winter), 2–24.

Cole, H. and L. Ohanian (2004), 'New Deal policies and the persistence of the Great Depression: a general equilibrium analysis', *Journal of Political Economy*, **112**(4) (August), 779–816.

Cooley, T. and L. Ohanian (1991), 'The cyclical behavior of prices', *Journal of Monetary Economics*, **28**(1) (August), 25–60.

Cooley, T. and E. Prescott (1973), 'Systematic (non-random) variation models: varying parameter regression: a theory and some applications', in *Annals of Economic and Social Measurement*, National Bureau of Economic Research, **2**(4), 462–72.

Cooley, T. and E. Prescott (1976), 'Estimation in the presence of stochastic parameter variation', *Econometrica*, **44**(1) (January), 167–84.

Dunlop, J. (1938), 'The movement of real and money wage rates', *Economic Journal*, **48**(191), 413–34.

Friedman, M. (1957), *A Theory of the Consumption Function*, Princeton, NJ: Princeton University Press.

Gordon, R. (2009), 'Is modern macro or 1978-era macro more relevant to the understanding of the current economic crisis?', unpublished paper.

Haavelmo, T. (1944), 'The probability approach in econometrics', *Econometrica*, **12**(supplement) (July), iii–vi, 1–118.

Haavelmo, T. (1950), 'Remarks on Frisch's confluence analysis and its use in econometrics', in T. Koopmans (ed.), *Statistical Inference in Dynamic Economic Models*, New York: Wiley and Sons, pp. 258–65.

Hood, W. and T. Koopmans (1953), 'The estimation of simultaneous linear economic relationships', in W. Hood and T. Koopmans (eds), *Studies in Econometric Method*, New York: Wiley and Sons, pp. 112–99.

Hurwicz, L. (1950a), 'Generalization of the concept of identification', in T. Koopmans (ed.), *Statistical Inference in Dynamic Economic Models*, New York: Wiley and Sons, pp. 245–57.

Hurwicz, L. (1950b), 'Prediction and least squares', in T. Koopmans (ed.), *Statistical Inference in Dynamic Economic Models*, New York: Wiley and Sons, pp. 266–300.

Hurwicz, L. (1950c), 'Least-squares bias in time series', in T. Koopmans (ed.), *Statistical Inference in Dynamic Economic Models*, New York: Wiley and Sons, pp. 365–83.

Jones, C. (2002), 'Sources of US economic growth in a world of ideas', *American Economic Review*, **92**(1) (March), 220–39.

Keynes, J. (1936), *The General Theory of Employment, Interest, and Money*, New York: Harcourt, Brace & World.

Keynes, J. (1963), 'Economic possibilities for our grandchildren', reprinted in *Essays in Persuasion*, New York: W. W. Norton, pp 358–73.

Koopmans, T. (1950a), 'The equivalence of maximum-likelihood and least-squares estimates of regression coefficients', in T. Koopmans (ed.), *Statistical Inference in Dynamic Economic Models*, New York: Wiley and Sons, pp. 301–4.

Koopmans, T. (1950b), 'When is an equation system complete for statistical purposes?', in T. Koopmans (ed.), *Statistical Inference in Dynamic Economic Models*, New York: Wiley and Sons, pp. 393–409.

Kydland, F. and E. Prescott (1982), 'Time to build and aggregate fluctuations', *Econometrica*, **50**(6) (November), 1345–70.

Litterman, R. (1986), 'Forecasting with Bayesian vector autoregressions – five years of experience', *Journal of Business and Economic Statistics*, **4**(1) (January), 25–38.

Lucas, R. Jr. (1972), 'Expectations and the neutrality of money', *Journal of Economic Theory*, **4**(2) (April), 103–24.

Lucas, R. Jr. and E. Prescott (1974), 'Equilibrium search and unemployment', *Journal of Economic Theory*, **7**(2) (February), 188–209.

Lucas, R. Jr. and T. Sargent (1979), 'After Keynesian macroeconomics', *Quarterly Review*, Federal Reserve Bank of Minneapolis, **3**(2) (Spring).

Margo, R. (1993), 'Employment and unemployment in the 1930s', *Journal of Economic Perspectives*, **7**(2) (Spring), 41–59.

McGrattan, E. and L. Ohanian (2010) 'Does neoclassical theory account for the effects of big fiscal shocks? Evidence from World War II', *International Economic Review*.

Mehra, R. and E. Prescott (1980), 'Recursive competitive equilibrium: the case of homogeneous households', *Econometrica*, **48**(6) (September), 1365–79.

Muth, J. (1961), 'Rational expectations and the theory of price movements', *Econometrica*, **29**(3) July, 315–35.

Nelson, C. (1972), 'The prediction performance of the FRB-MIT-PENN model of the US economy', *American Economic Review*, **62**(5) (December), 902–17.

Ohanian, L. (2008), 'Back to the future with Keynes', in L. Pecchi and G. Piga (eds), *Revisiting Keynes*, Cambridge, MA: MIT Press, pp. 105–16.

Ohanian, L. (2009), 'What – or who – started the Great Depression?', *Journal of Economic Theory*, **144**(6) (November), 2310–35.

Pearlstein, S. (2008). 'Keynes on Steroids', *Washington Post*, 26 November 2008.

Pigou, A. (1933), *The Theory of Unemployment*, London: Macmillan.

Samuelson, P. and Solow, R. (1960), 'Analytical aspects of anti-inflation policy', *American Economic Review*, **50**(2) (May), 177–94.

Simon, H. (1953), 'Causal ordering and identifiability', in W. Hood and T.

Koopmans (eds), *Studies in Econometric Method*, New York: Wiley and Sons, pp. 49–74.

Tarshis, L. (1939), 'Changes in real and money wages', *Economic Journal*, **49**(193), 150–4.

Wald, A. (1950a), 'Note on the identification of economic relations', in T. Koopmans (ed.), *Statistical Inference in Dynamic Economic Models*, New York: Wiley and Sons, pp. 238–44.

Wald, A. (1950b), 'Remarks on the estimation of unknown parameters in incomplete systems of equations', in T. Koopmans (ed.), *Statistical Inference in Dynamic Economic Models*, New York: Wiley and Sons, pp. 305–10.

8. The impact of *The General Theory* on economic theory and the development of public policies: a nested vision of Keynes's ideas with the classical vision through a panoramic view of his works

Lall Ramrattan and Michael Szenberg

INTRODUCTION

The evolution of Keynes's economic theories matured into the milestone Keynesian framework of *The General Theory of Employment, Interest, and Money* (Keynes 1936). Prior to this, Keynes's first milestone came in his defence of the gold exchange standard in *Indian Currency and Finance* (Keynes, *Collected Writings* (CW), vol. 1), and the last milestone of Keynes's brilliant career tackled his arguments for the Bretton Woods system in 1944. Between these two milestones lay his panoramic views that credit him with the development of macroeconomics.

Keynes's views from the *Indian Currency* dealing with the gold exchange standard, his *Tract on Monetary Reform* (Keynes, CW, vol. IV) dealing with price stability, his two volume work *A Treatise on Money* (Keynes, CW, vols. V and VI) establishing disparities between investments and savings, and *The General Theory* suggesting a remedy for the Great Depression could be termed the Das Keynes problem. Many see the last work in a rivalry sense that Keynes broke from the classic school, but in the visionary sense Keynes continued to support Smith's vision of capitalism. The established view is to consider his three works as an

> . . . inter-war trilogy that marks the development of John Maynard Keynes's monetary thought from the quantity-theory tradition that he had inherited from his teachers at Cambridge; to his subsequent systematic attempt to dynamise and elaborate upon this theory and its applications; and, finally, to

the revolutionary work with which he changed the face of monetary theory and defined its developmental framework for years to come. (Patinkin 1975, p. 249)

Economists generally are hesitant to consider Keynes as a visionary on par with the likes of Adam Smith. While stalwarts such as Ricardo, Malthus, and Marx predicted the demise of Smith's vision, Keynes had lent support to that vision even during periods of economic crises. In this sense, Keynes's vision is nested within that of Adam Smith's. Placing the models of Smith and Keynes in the same nest allows the successes of capitalism to hatch. They are embedded together for the purpose of tackling spiraling growth and threatening business cycles. The literature that fiercely debates this nesting is whether the two models are a special case of each other, that is, hierarchically nested. A.C. Pigou stated '. . . Keynes' claim that a scheme built on the Marshallian postulates would be embraced as a special case of his own scheme' and that '[the] two schemes are, rather, cousins with common ancestors, both special cases of something more general than either' (Pigou 1950, p. 24).

In this nesting, the Keynesian model has the characteristic of being applicable in times of economic crisis. Its nearness to the Smithian model depends on whether it is called upon. For example, policy rule makers may not believe in the Keynesian system, but would implement it if necessary. This is an example of a distance view of nesting and brings to mind how Ronald Reagan protected Harley Davidson motorcycles from foreign competition and how George W. Bush bailed out financial institutions which were 'too big to fail'.

Smith's vision dealt with the continuous growth of the wealth of a nation, while Keynes's vision dealt with how to sustain that growth in the face of threatening crises. Moreover, Keynes has used different and seemingly contradictory paths in his supporting role, paths so fundamental that different schools have emerged to articulate them and so complex that they survived as irreconcilable paradigms. It appears from his 1937 *The Times* articles (Keynes, CW, vol. XXI) that he considered some of those paths as dummy instruments to be discarded after capitalism is back on the track yet some economists take a diehard point of view of the core statements in Keynes's works, either holding on to their cherished paths or to their anti-Keynesian points of view.

The purpose of this paper is to review Keynes's writings from his early to later economic milestones in order to distill his critical train of economic thought that nested with Smith's vision. No consideration is given to the anomalies, inconsistencies, or even the wrong predictions of his model during the 1970s.

Economics of the *Indian Currency and Finance*

In *Indian Currency* Keynes gave credit to '. . . Ricardo, who pointed out that a currency, is in its most perfect state, when it consists of cheap material, but of an equal value with the gold it professes to represent' (Keynes, CW, vol. I, p. 70). Keynes called this a gold-exchange standard, which establishes a fixed exchange rate between currencies. If 1 ounce of gold = \$20 in the US, and is £5 in the UK, then the exchange rate will be fixed at \$4 = £1. In 1944, Keynes put forward his 'Proposal for an International Clearing Union' at Bretton Woods (Horsefield 1969b, pp. 19–36). The chronicles of the IMF reveal that

> Keynes had no need to borrow ideas; he had long before adumbrated a plan somewhat similar to Harry Dexter White's Stabilization Fund in his *Treatise on Money*, where he had conceived a Supernational Bank which would act as a central bank for central banks. What was needed now was to link such an institution with the control of exchange rates and to clothe it with disciplinary powers. (Horsefield 1969a, p. 16)

Keynes's influence succeeded in making the IMF adopt his policy to declare a currency as 'scarce' if the country did not take action to correct its surplus balance of payments (Keynes, CW, vol. XIV, pp. 401–2, 474).

The *Tract on Monetary Reform*

Keynes's *Tract* appears as the next node following *Indian Currency* in which Keynes developed his macroeconomics thoughts. The issue at this point was 'instability of the standard of value'. Keynes made monetary stability an 'either or' proposition between internal price stability and external foreign exchange rate stability. He expressed his preference for internal over external stability because he believed that the latter will follow once the former is secured. Keynes analysed the question through the equation $n = p(k + rk')$, where n is currency notes, p is the index number of the cost of living, k is people's cash holdings, k' people's cash deposits, and r is bank reserves (Keynes, CW, vol. IV, p. 63). The model predicts that if $(k + rk')$ are constant, then the price level (p) will vary with the quantity of cash (n). The term inflation then relates to increases in cash ($\Delta n > 0$), increases in credit (($\Delta r < 0$), or increases in real balances $[\Delta(k, k') < 0]$. Deflation is defined by reversing the inequality signs. 'The business of stabilizing the price level . . . consists partly in exercising a stabilizing influence over k and k', and, in so far as this fails or is impracticable, in deliberately varying n and r so as to *counterbalance* the movements of k and k'' (Keynes, CW, vol. IV, p. 68, emphasis in original). The goal of these policies is to keep price changes in a normal range, guided by '. . . the state of employment, the volume of production, the effective demand for credit as felt by the banks, the rate of interest on investments of various types, the volume of new issues, the flow of cash into circulation, the statistics of foreign trade and the level of the exchanges' (ibid., pp. 148–9).

The *Tract* was written after the 1922 Genoa, Italy meeting where numerous countries called for the old pre-World War I gold standard based on gold being an international standard for settling debts, and a means of accommodating producers' vested interest in gold (ibid., p. 139). Hawtrey added that vested interest should extend beyond the producers to include the '. . . gold holders and gold creditors. The greatest gold holders are the Central Banks' (Hawtrey 1924, pp. 231–2). By this time, Keynes claimed that '. . . the gold standard was already a barbarous relic. . . .' (Keynes, CW, vol. IV, p. 138). While the UK joined the pre-World War I standard in 1925, it was forced to abandon it in 1931 due to Balance of Payments problems. By 1937 all countries had gotten off the gold-exchange standard. According to Skidelsky, Keynes's '. . . central claim of the *Tract* is that by varying the amount of credit to the business sector, the banking system could even out fluctuations in business activity' (Skidelsky, 1992, p. 153). The claim to have identified a controllable single variable – the supply of credit – capable of determining the level of prices and amount of activity in the economy as a whole is the start of macroeconomics. In summary, '. . . in the modern world of paper currency and bank credit there is no escape from a "managed" currency, whether we wish it or not; convertibility into gold will not alter the fact that the value of gold itself depends on the policy of the central banks' (Keynes, CW, vol. IV, p. 136).

A Treatise on Money

Keynesian theory and policy took a major paradigm leap in his two volumes, *A Treatise on Money*. In the *Treatise* there are more fundamental equations for monetary theory and economic activities, representing 'the most stupendous transfiguration' of the quantity theory but still lacking a marginal utility theory of value basis (Hicks 1982, p. 47). According to another of Keynes's biographers, we '. . . get the best picture of his total contribution to economics in the *Treatise* . . . The fact remains that the future student who wishes to get the full measure of Keynes' importance and influence as an economist will not do so unless he reads the *Treatise*' (Harrod 1951, pp. 403–4). A positive role for savings and investment is established in the *Treatise*, which was later modified in *The General Theory*.

In the *Treatise*, Keynes 'proposed . . . to break away from the traditional method of setting out from the total quantity of money . . . and to start instead . . . with the flow of the community's earnings or money income' by advancing two equations (Keynes, CW, vol. V, pp. 121–3):

$$P = \frac{E}{O} + \frac{I' - S}{R} = \frac{W}{e} + \frac{I' - S}{R} \tag{1}$$

$$\Pi = \frac{W}{e} + \frac{I - S}{O} \tag{2}$$

where E is money income or earnings; O is output of goods; I' is the part of E that is earned by the production of investment goods; S is saving; R is flow of consumption goods and services; W is the rate of earnings per human effort; e is the coefficient of efficiency (output per unit of effort); I is the increment of new investment goods, and Π is the price level of output as a whole.

The essence of the two equations is that the price index matches with the cost of the production index plus the profit index (Patinkin 1982, p. 7). They are novel in one respect that 'the relationship of purchasing power of money . . . and the price level of output as a whole to the quantity and the velocity of circulation is not that direct character which the old-fashioned quantity equations . . . might lead one to suppose' (Keynes, CW, vol. V, pp. 129–32). Because theories of over-investments, under-consumption, and under-savings have predated Keynes's works, less originality may be ascribed to the prediction of the equations, namely, that savings need not equal investment. Keynes claimed that his theory was radically different from the earlier ones, in that it made the crucial emphasis on the *disparity* between investment and saving (Harrod 1951, p. 409; emphasis in original).

Investments and savings can diverge, not only because people would hoard or idle their savings, but because the motives governing them were different enough to cause disproportionate differences. Savings was defined to exclude excess profits that cause producers to increase output, as well as business losses, the differences between actual and expected receipts that cause producers to refrain from wanting to reduce output. By adding excess profits and losses, as defined, back to investment, an accounting equality between savings and investments can then be obtained.

If investment exceeds savings, then upswing and inflation are the likely outcome. Investments create money income to consumers for consumption goods and to producers for producer goods. If the money income from both sources were all spent on consumer goods alone (i.e. none put into savings), then prices will rise because 'more money would be applied in their purchase than had been earned in their production' (ibid., p. 406).

Conversely, if savings exceed investments, then downswings and unemployment are most likely (ibid., p. 404).

The Bank Rate was the major policy instrument for price stability. Keynes elucidated this instrument in the Macmillan Committee before the publication of the *Treatise*.

> High interest rates led to a contraction of credit, the restriction of capital outlay . . . falling off in buying power and a fall in prices . . . wages were very sticky, and severe unemployment and disequilibrium might remain for a long time . . . If we reduced our rates, more capital would be tempted aboard than could be financed by our excess of exports over imports. (ibid., p. 416)

Harrod's quote expresses succinctly Keynes's position. Keynes was also supplementing the Bank Rate policy with Public Works, tariffs on trade, and the liquidity preference concepts.

The General Theory

Keynes generalized his theory towards a solution for macroeconomic crises in *The General Theory* by advancing an economic model in which the factors or *givens* include the existing labour, equipment, the techniques of production, the degree of competition, tastes and habits of consumers, organizational as well as social structures, and the distribution of national income. The *independent variables* within *The General Theory* include the propensity to consume, dC/dY, the marginal efficiency of capital, $I = f(r)$, and the rate of interest, r. The *dependent variables* are the volume of employment and national income (Keynes 1936, p. 245; emphasis added).

The General Theory was a blending of ideas culled from his previous works, integrated with marginal analysis and macroeconomic insights. Keynes said that when the *Treatise* was written he had a sudden realization of '. . . the psychological law that, when income increases, the gap between income and consumption will increase . . . Then appreciably later, came the notion of interest being the measure of liquidity preference . . . And last of all, . . . the proper definition of the marginal efficiency of capital linked up one thing with another' (ibid., p. 15). Here is where the macroeconomic and marginal elements being introduced into consumption, liquidity preference, and the marginal efficiency of capital can be seen. Keynes then propounded the purpose of this theory as follows: '. . . my doctrine of full employment is what the whole of my book is about! Everything else is a side issue to that. If you do not understand my doctrine of full employment, it is perfectly hopeless for you to attempt to explain the book to anyone' (Keynes, CW, vol. XIV, p. 24).

Liquidity preference was also built on ideas from the *Treatise*. Keynes reflected on what he called 'the state of bearishness' in the *Treatise*, but differentiated it from the concept of liquidity preference (Keynes 1936, p. 173). Recognizing that it is a difficult idea, Keynes compared it to the 'propensity to hoard':

> The concept of Hoarding may be regarded as a first approximation to the concept of *Liquidity-preference*. Indeed if we were to substitute 'propensity to hoard' for 'hoarding', it would come to substantially the same thing. But if we mean by 'hoarding' an actual increase in cash-holding, it is an incomplete idea – and seriously misleading if it causes us to think of 'hoarding' and 'not-hoarding' as simple alternatives. (ibid., p. 174)

In *The General Theory*, the role of investment and savings evolved from the potential crises at hand. If consumers are not spending all of their income, '. . . there must be an amount of current investment sufficient to absorb the excess of total output over what the community chooses to consume when employment is at the given level' (ibid., p. 27). If that investment is not forthcoming, employers will not get enough revenues to induce them to maintain that level of employment. The inducement to invest will depend on the state of the marginal efficiency of capital and the rate of interest (ibid., pp. 27–8). Milton Friedman distilled this argument as follows: 'The great contraction . . . was the result of a collapse of demand for invest-ment which in turn reflected a collapse of productive opportunities to use capital. Thus the engine and the motor of the great contraction was a collapse of investment transformed into a collapse of income by the mul-tiplier process' (Friedman 1970, p. 13). Paul Samuelson remarked that 'In the early 1930s, when banks were failing, firms were going bankrupt, and mortgages were in delinquency on a macro scale, it was sensible to worry about liquidity traps, vicious cycles of wage cuts and debt deflation, and inelastic marginal efficiency schedules' (Samuelson 1986, p. 292). Again, '. . . [by] 1938, short-term interest rates had been forced so low that the liquidity-preference function of Keynes seemed required by the facts of the day' (ibid., p. 290).

The supporting role of Keynes to Smith's vision was echoed clearly in Keynes's *The Times* articles. Keynes declared that '. . . it is more important to avoid a descent into another slump than to stimulate . . . a still greater activity than we have' (Keynes, CW, vol. XXI, p. 384). These articles focused on policies in distressed areas where a 'rightly distributed demand' is preferred to 'a greater aggregate demand' (ibid., p. 385), and on the necessity of planning so as '. . . to preserve as much stability of aggregate investment as we can manage at the right and appropriate level' (ibid., p. 387).

In another article in *The Times* (11 March 1937), Keynes further expanded his model for normal times, foreshadowing the more modern models of inflation. For Keynes, inflation is not 'merely that prices and wages are rising . . . It is when increased demand is no longer capable of materially rising output and employment and mainly spends itself in rising prices that it is properly called inflation' (ibid., p. 405). That was a remarkable statement, leading Hutchinson, a renowned economic methodologist, to declare that 'Keynes can be said to have suggested a similar concept to that now called – following Professor Milton Friedman – a "natural rate" of unemployment' (Hutchison 1977, p. 14).

By embedding his critical theory with a syntactical shift, Keynes had set the stage for his nested vision of Adam Smith. Aggregate demand begins a transformation towards 'rightly distributed demand'. Price stability from the *Tract*, which involved '. . . the state of employment, the volume of production, the effective demand for credit as felt by the banks, the rate of interest on investments of various types, the volume of new issues, the flow of cash into circulation, the statistics of foreign trade and the level of the exchanges' (Keynes, CW, vol. IV, pp. 148–9), were transformed into preserving '. . . as much stability of aggregate investment as we can manage at the right and appropriate level' (Keynes, CW, vol. XXI, p. 387). The nesting of a stability element for investment to Smith's vision was necessary: 'There is no reason to suppose that there is "an invisible hand", an automatic control in the economic system which ensures of itself that the amount of active investment shall be continuously of the right proportion' (ibid., pp. 386–7). These messages were supposed to work in concert with the following three propositions that kicked in during times of crises:

Proposition I: *The invisible hand or market forces cannot cope with involuntary unemployment.*

Keynes realized that '. . . the population generally is seldom doing as much work as it would like to do on the basis of current wage' (Keynes 1936, p. 7). Pissarides, a modern innovator of unemployment models, expanded on this proposition as follows: 'A person is said to be involuntarily unemployed if he sees people just like himself holding jobs that he would like to have, but which he is not offered' (Pissarides 1989, p. 2). Keynes presented it in a familiar way in that '. . . more labour than is at present employed is usually available at the existing money-wage, even though the price of wage-goods is rising and, consequently, the real wage falling' (Keynes 1936, p. 10). This introduced two Keynesian Neoclassical postulates: that 'The wage is equal to the marginal product of labor' and that workers balance the utility of wages with the disutility of work.

To state that unemployment is involuntary implies that some form of fiscal policy help may be necessary. Keynes wanted to emphasize that involuntary unemployment should induce the government and nonprofit organizations to come to the rescue, thereby relieving the individual of the necessity of job searching, retraining, self-employment, or to lower his/her aspiration. The New Deal in the 1930s was a major example of a fiscal stimulus to relieve unemployment. The Employment Act of 1946 had permanently shifted responsibility to the Federal government to maintain opportunities for full employment, production, and stable purchasing power for its currency (Okun 1970, p. 37).

Keynes extended his concept of stability beyond slump conditions. To attain stability, policy makers should '. . . preserve as much stability of aggregate investment . . . at the right and appropriate level'. Stability also means to provide enough liquidity to the system, for '. . . a shortage of cash has nearly always played a significant part in turning the boom into a slump' (Keynes, CW, vol. XXI, p. 388). A Keynesian Proposition for stability would therefore be:

Proposition II: *Consumption (and not savings as the classical good economists thought) will through a multiplier process expand output and employment.*

In the Keynesian model,

> Savings and investment are determinates of the system, not determinants. They are twin results of the system's determinants, namely the propensity to consume, the schedule of the marginal efficiency of capital and the rate of interest . . . Saving, in fact is a mere residual. The decision to consume and the decision to invest between them determine incomes . . . The traditional analysis has been aware that saving depends on income but it has overlooked the fact that income depends on investment, in such fashion that, when investment changes, income must necessarily change in just that degree which is necessary to make the change in saving equal to the change in investment. (Keynes 1936, pp. 64, 183–4)

One interpretation of all this is that

> a rise in the disposition to save meant a decline of consumption, and the latter a reduction of investment (dependent on consumption) and a fall in employment and hence a reduction of income, and since savings depends on income, a decline of savings; and therefore, savings equal investment; but only through a process by which the original additional savings become abortive. (Harris 1955, pp. 110–71)

Symbolically, Savings plus Investment can be written as $S = f(Y)$; $Y = f(I)$ or that $S = f[Y(I)]$. Then $\Delta I \rightarrow \Delta Y \rightarrow \Delta S$ such that $\Delta S = \Delta I$.

Keynes found consistency with D. H. Robertson's definition, namely, $Y_t = C_{t-1} + I_{t-1}$. Then, $S_t = I_{t-1} + (C_{t-1} - C_t)$ (Keynes, 1936, p. 78). The essence of these derivations is twofold as expressed by Keynes: 1. 'The investment market can become congested through the shortage of cash. It can never become congested through the shortage of saving' (Keynes, 1937b, p. 669); and 2. 'Saving has no special efficacy as compared with consumption, in releasing cash and restoring liquidity' (Keynes 1938, p. 321).

Proposition III: *The interest rate is not determined in the capital market as the classical economists supposed.*

The rate of interest is determined in stages. The first stage is through the propensity to consume which divides an individual's income into how much one will consume now versus how much will be consumed in the future. The second stage is through the liquidity preference schedule. From the first stage, a person must determine in what form to hold future consumption. This will be determined by his liquidity preference.

> It should be obvious that the rate of interest cannot be a return to savings or waiting as such. For if a man hoards his savings in cash, he earns no interest, though he saves just as much as before. On the contrary, the mere definition of the rate of interest tells us in so many words that the rate of interest is the reward for parting with liquidity for a specified period. (Keynes 1936, pp.166–7)

Interpreters of Keynes, John Richard Hicks, Alvin Harvey Hansen, and Abba Lerner were not content to make $M = L(r)$, where M is the quantity of money, and r is the rate of interest (ibid., p. 168). As Hansen put it, '. . . there is a liquidity preference curve for each income level. Until we know the income level, we cannot know what the rate of interest is' (Hansen 1953, p. 148). Lerner has shown how the marginal efficiency, consumption, and liquidity preference schedule combine with the money supply to determine the rate of interest (Lerner 1961, p. 265). Hicks would revive the Keynesian version of the liquidity preference schedule to include income, giving Keynes '. . . a big step back to Marshallian orthodoxy, and his theory becomes hard to distinguish from the revised and qualified Marshallian theories (Hicks 1982, p. 108).

As a precursor, Hawtrey also focused on the interest rate policy, preferring the short-term rate over Keynes's preference for the long-term rate. Keynes cautioned that

> a low enough long-term rate of interest cannot be achieved if we allow it to be believed that better terms will be obtainable from time to time by those who keep their resources liquid. The long-term rate of interest must be

kept *continuously* as near as possible to what we believe to be the long-term optimum. It is not suitable to be used as a short-period weapon. (Keynes, CW, vol. XXI, p. 389; italics in original)

Keynes gave the rate of interest a central role in his liquidity preference model. Keynes, in finding that the long-term rate could not be controlled well, later switched to fiscal policies. He took on broader 'financial policies – unemployment and the choice of an exchange rate and a standard for sterling' (Moggridge 1992, p. 414). As mentioned previously, Keynes preferred domestic policies, such as price stability, over international matters, such as exchange rate stability (Skidelsky 1992, p. 20). Keynes perceived that the value of the British currency was higher than that of the US Dollar and did not want to peg it to gold. In short he was 'unshackling money from gold' (ibid., p. 154).

Concerns of interest rates are at the heart of Keynes's liquidity preference concept. Central to this concept is the idea that given a choice of holding many different assets for transactions, speculative or precautionary purposes, a person may not see an advantage in holding other assets in preference to money. According to Keynes, '. . . an individual's Liquidity-preference is given by a schedule of the amounts of his resources, valued in terms of money or of wage-units, which he will wish to retain in the form of money in different sets of circumstances' (Keynes 1936, p. 166).

FIRST IMPACT OF KEYNES' *GENERAL THEORY* MODEL AND PROPOSITIONS

The early interpreters of Keynes, dubbed the hydraulic-Keynesians by Coddington (1983), include John Hicks (1937) and Franco Modigliani (1944), who both considered special cases such as investment inelasticity, liquidity trap, and wage rigidity as causes of unemployment (Dow 1985, pp. 58–61). Later interpreters included the reconstituted reductionists such as Robert Clower who thought that the Keynesian model did not clearly identify the fatal flaw of orthodox models in explaining effective demand and unemployment (Clower 1988, p. 81). The reductionists claimed that these Keynesian failures led to further failure by the interpreters of his arguments. Part of the research programme of the interpreters was to reconcile the Keynesian vision with the orthodox system – what Joan Robinson called 'bastard Keynesianism'.

Post Keynesians, such as Luigi Pasinetti, questioned whether a break with Keynes from the Classics had occurred, pointing to reconciliations that were going on '. . . between the group of young economists who had been working with Keynes . . . and those economists who, after publication, tried to reconcile the *General Theory* with traditional thinking' (Pasinetti 1999, p. 3). Pasinetti concluded that a Keynesian revolution 'might as yet remain unaccomplished. When that drastic change arrives, however, it needs to be as significant as Arrow-Debreu's theory was to the Walrasian model' (ibid., p. 13).

Clower and later Axel Leijonhufvud (1968, 1976) presented a choice theoretical reductionist model, in an effort to reconcile the state of equilibrium disagreement between Keynesians and orthodox economists (Coddington 1983, p. 108). The focus according to Leijonhufvud was on '. . . a distinction between what Keynes originally meant and what has become known as "Keynesian economics". . . . where the choice theoretical reductionist model develops objective functions, constraints and interdependence in the framework (Pasinetti 1999, p. 4). Clower's and Leijonhufvud's views can be seen as reconstituted reductionists in the sense that they are not concerned with states of equilibrium but with the schematization of trading at disequilibrium prices in choice theory and the speed with which such prices adjust, which turned out to be slower than in a Walrasian process.

For the purpose of reconstruction, Leijonhufvud speculated that what took place between the publication of *Tract* and *Treatise* was more relevant than what took place between the publication of *Treatise* and *The General Theory* (Leijonhufvud 1968, p. 22). As far as equilibrium is concerned, Keynes thought that the theory of employment as determined from the theory of demand and supply was abandoned in the classical system after it had been contested and debated for a quarter of a century (Keynes 1936, p. 15). Alfred Marshall had superimposed marginal and substitution principles onto Ricardian economics (ibid., p. 29), but was inattentive to the importance of the production and distribution theories of output. Keynes wanted to correct those flawed interpretations of the Classics. That was also the route that Clower and Leijonhufvud followed with their choice theoretical logic in their reductionist model.

First Generation Keynesian Model of the Interpreters/Reconcilers John Hicks and later Alvin Hansen applied the first interpretation of Keynes with the classical and the neoclassical school by building a Keynesian model utilizing liquidity preference $M = L(r, Y)$, investment $I = I(r, Y)$, savings $S = S(r, Y)$, and saving-investment equilibrium $S = I$, where M is money, I is investment, S is savings, Y is income, and r is the rate of interest. In a letter dated 31 March 1937, Keynes related to Hicks that his pioneered model assumes that an '. . . increase in the quantity of money is capable of increasing employment. A strictly brought-up classical economist would not, I should say, admit that' (Keynes, CW, vol. XIV, p. 79). One strand of the money employment relations is that when the money wage rate is fixed, prices will also be fixed, and changes in the quantity of money will affect employment and output (Lowe 1965, p. 229). Building on Hicks's framework, Modigliani offered a nine-equation Keynesian model that sparked off the first Federal Reserve Board-Penn macro-econometric model in the United States. The fifth equation is pivotal for the determination of output and price, which are affected by the control of money and by the upward pressure on wages.

The interpreters of the Hicksian view had the natural inclination to incorporate classical concepts such as Say's Law, Walras' Law, and the Homogeneity Postulate into Hicks's model. But Keynes stood firm on the aggregate basis, thus leaving room for Post Keynesians and reconstructionists to expand and articulate his school of thought. A dominant line of thinking was to let consumption lead to production and employment. As Hyman Philip Minsky puts it '. . . to Keynes, consumption, for the purpose of employment theory, was a part of aggregate effective demand' (Minsky 1975, p. 25). Aggregate effective demand, when introduced into the inverse of the aggregate-supply function, generated the demand for labour. Thus consumption to Keynes always involved current production. In Keynes's words, '. . . the actual level of output and employment depends not on the capacity to produce or on the pre-existing level of income, but on the current decisions to produce, which depends, in turn, on current decisions to invest and on present expectations of current and prospective consumption' (Keynes 1936, p. 32).

The General Theory holds that 'the pure theory of what determines the actual employment of the available resources has seldom been examined in great detail'. Metaphorically, Keynes explained that '. . . if money is the drink which stimulates the system to activity . . . there may be several slips between the cup and the lip' (ibid., p. 171). These 'slips' are grounded in the ideas that when the money supply increases, the interest rate will fall. This occurs because '. . . more money would flow into investment channels and raise prices of securities and investment goods, which is the same thing as reducing interest rates' (Harris 1955, p. 55). But Keynes maintained that the interest rate may not fall because the public may increase its liquidity preference faster than the increase in the money supply. Alongside the liquidity preference problem is the issue of when the interest rate falls, the investment demand schedule may fall faster than an expected fall in the rate of interest, creating an inelasticity situation. Finally, with the fall in the interest rate, investment may not have the expected increase on employment if the Marginal Propensity to Consume (MPC) is falling (Keynes 1936, p. 171).

NEOCLASSICAL SYNTHESIS

The impact of Hicks's, Hansen's and Modigliani's views were codified into the neoclassical synthesis, which according to Hicks, began to emerge from the works of Paul Samuelson, Kenneth Arrow, Milton Friedman, and Don Patinkin. These authors, according to Hicks, '. . . regarded (his *Value and Capital*) as the beginning of their "neo-classical synthesis"' (Hicks 1983, p. 361). Following Pigou's attack on *The General Theory*, a number of economists developed the wealth effect argument to counter Keynes, creating a niche for the neoclassical synthesis to hold that '. . . if such wealth effects were properly integrated in the analysis, full price flexibility . . . was bound to remove all excess demands and supplies' (Grandmont 1983, p. 1). Basically, the Pigou effect has the ability to restore full employment in a Keynesian setting because as wages and prices fall, real wealth will appreciate, prompting wealth holders to save less. This will lead to a lowering of the savings schedule to correspond with a lowering of investment in the classical capital market at full employment – an effect that restores confidence in the orthodox equilibrium system, but triggers the special cases of Keynes's hydraulic system.

Basically, the neoclassical synthesis used microanalysis on '. . . a managed economy which through skillful use of fiscal and monetary policy, channeled the Keynesian forces of effective demand into behaving like a neoclassical model' (Samuelson 1966, vol. 2, p. 1544). The Neoclassical prediction transcends what Samuelson called a Keynesian 'depression version' where cheaper credit is an inoperable policy in the face of the special cases. Among the predictions of the neoclassical synthesis are expansionary monetary policy and austere fiscal policy mixes that bring about the deepening of capital, causing the economy to grow (ibid.). As Arrow put it, the neoclassical synthesis '. . . held that achievement of full employment requires Keynesian intervention but that neoclassical theory is valid when full employment is reached' (Arrow 1967, p. 735).

> Let $W(g)$ be the Walrasian system, and $K(g)$ be the 'true' system, where g is a parameter representing government action (fiscal or monetary). The Samuelson-Keynes view of the world is that full employment is a valid proposition in $K(g)$ only for special values of g, whereas full employment holds in $W(g)$ for all g. The neoclassical synthesis was an important extension of Keynes' model, particularly in the 1950s when models of capital accumulation and technical change developed, where the need arose to fit them into the Keynesian model. (Samuelson 1966, vol. 2, pp. 1543–4)

These Keynesian propositions were considered too abstract at that time.

They were constructed on the basis of a consumption function, an investment function, a liquidity preference function, and some other simple concepts. But an apparatus of such elementary concepts reveals itself entirely insufficient for the complex and differentiated problems one is facing if one attempts to formulate an adequate economic policy applying to post-war society. This implies harmonization of many antagonistic interests, consideration of many sectors of production, many social categories, etc. (Frisch 1966, p. 2).

The eminent Post Keynesian, Paul Davidson, has a partiality for authenticity, opposing Samuelson for triangulating between 'gross substitution' (where any interest bearing capital can substitute for money), 'money neutrality' (where money is neutral on its effect of output), and an 'ergodic hypothesis' (Davidson 2007, pp. 214–15). 'In an ergodic system where the future can be reliably predicted . . . where the gross substitution axiom underlies all demand curves, then as long as prices are flexible, money must be neutral, and the system automatically adjusts to full employment equilibrium' (ibid., p. 215).

The crisis of the mid-1970s challenged the neoclassical synthesis (Blanchard and Fischer 1989, pp. 26–7). The New Classical School emerged at this time, and a New Keynesians model was being developed side-by-side in the mid-1980s. The New Keynesian theory was '. . . developed to replace Samuelson's Keynesians. Just as Friedman's Monetarism had conquered Samuelson's brand of Keynesianism, New Classical theory easily made a mockery of the New Keynesians approach' (Davidson 2007, pp. 208–9). Friedman wrote that '. . . the basic source of the [Keynesian] revolution and the reaction against the quantity theory of money was a historical event, namely the great contraction or depression' (Friedman 1970, p. 11). In the United Kingdom the contraction started in 1925 when Britain went back on gold at the pre-war parity and ended in 1931 when Britain went off gold. In the United States, the contraction started in 1929 and ended when the United States went off gold in early 1933. In both countries, economic conditions were depressed for years after the contraction itself had ended and an expansion had begun. Keynes's point of view about Fisher's Quantity Theory of Money is that velocity of circulation of money would adapt so as to avoid equi-proportional changes in the money supply and prices, thereby shifting the focus from the quantity of money to autonomous spending, mainly business and government expenditures, which are independent of income (ibid., pp. 12–13).

SECOND GENERATION IMPACTS

Like the neoclassical synthesis, the newer theories also ran into dead ends. Rational expectations, random walk of GDP, real business cycle theory, and new Keynesian models were questioned in a leading textbook in that 'empirical support for these challenging ideas has not been as full and convincing as had been hoped by their proponents' (Dornbusch et al. 2008, p. 550). 'What's more, the ideas in part contradict each other . . . Even so the impact of these concepts on both research and policy has been revolutionary.' According to Arrow, the New Classical School differs from the neoclassical synthesis one in that its practitioners wanted to reconcile Keynesian macroeconomics with the rational behaviour of individuals and use a 'complete' rather than an 'incomplete' General Equilibrium model (Arrow 1991, p. 22). According to Samuelson,

> the new classical economics of rational expectations is a return with a vengeance to the pre-Keynesian verities . . . The 'new classical economics' of Robert Lucas, Tom Sargent, Robert Barro and others is truly a counterrevolution and the same cannot be said of 'monetarism'. If I can believe in Lucas' market clearing, then I can no longer believe in the behavior equations and relations of *the General Theory*. (Samuelson 1986, vol. 5, pp. 291–2)

The new classical school thought that '. . . it would be unsatisfactory to "explain" [real-world business fluctuations] by easily correctable market failures . . . fluctuations had to reflect real or monetary disturbance, whose dynamic economic effects depended on cost of obtaining information, cost of adjustment, and so on' (Barro 1989, p. 1). This school can be restricted to the beliefs of the rational expectation school of thought, where the idea of expectation is linked to forecasts generated by true models of the economy. The principles of this school can be further restricted to the real business cycle school that deals with Walrasian General Equilibrium models that emphasize computation (Mankiw and Romer 1991, p. 1).

According to George Akerlof, the neoclassical school has at least six shortcomings – no involuntary unemployment, ineffectiveness of monetary policy, no acceleration of deflation theory, the assumption of optimal savings behaviour, no explanation of stock price volatility, and the persistence of a self-destructive underclass (Akerlof 2005, pp. 473–4). According to Frank Hahn and Robert Solow, the new classical macroeconomists are '. . . claiming much more than could be deduced from fundamental neoclassical principles' (Hahn and Solow 1995, p. 7).

In response to the New Classical School, the New Keynesian School was formed. 'There are numerous different strands to New Keynesian Economics, taken in its broadest possible sense. One major element is the study of imperfect information and incomplete markets . . . They also espoused efficiency wage theories, capital market imperfections, credit rationing and a revised view of the role of monetary policy (Greenwald and Stiglitz 1987, pp. 120, 123).

The New Keynesian School took issue with the New Classical School by pointing out that wages may not adjust to allow full employment. For instance, firms do not just adjust their wage rates altogether on a certain day in the year but adjust their wage rates at various and numerous times during the year. They also point out that government intervention can aid the market by increasing employment and increasing effective demand.

EXPECTATIONS

Expectations cut through all the schools discussed above. In his *Tract* Keynes explained that expectations of an increase in price will create demand for cash and bank deposits, thereby increasing the velocity of circulation of money, prompting inflationary pressures. In his *Treatise* the expected prices of stock and bonds affect the rate of interest, which in turn can create inflation or deflation in an economy. In *The General Theory*, Keynes gave a major role to the '. . . expectation of future yield from capital assets'. He likened speculation to 'bubbles on a steady stream of enterprise' (Keynes 1936, p. 247). In that state, they can do no harm, unless the enterprise becomes the bubbles on a whirlpool of speculation (ibid., p. 159). The unpredictable state of expectations of changes in wages and money on employment had led Keynes to focus on State intervention to provide investment instead, even if people are employed only 'to dig holes in the ground' (ibid., p. 220).

An immediate impact of Keynes's expectation theory was the development of John Hicks's short term model (1 Day or 1 Week) to develop his elasticity of expectation hypothesis. Arrow and Debreu's model of competitive equilibrium found that current and expected prices will jointly clear supply and demand equations in present and future markets. Jean-Michel Grandmont (1983) formulated an intertemporal model that extended the Arrow-Debreu model for sequences of time periods. G. L. S. Shackle developed non-probabilistic statements about the next period outputs, whereby the probability of impossible, possible and, surprising are achieved at specified high or low levels (Ramrattan and Szenberg, 2007a, pp. 47–50).

Keynes spoke of stationary vs. shifting equilibrium, where shifting equilibrium is '. . . the theory of a system in which changing views about the future are capable of influencing the present situation' (Keynes 1936, p. 293). This gave way to the adaptive model whereby individuals adopt an error correcting device because they do not know the environment they face, putting them in a disequilibrium situation based on incorrect expectations (Frydman and Phelps 1986, p. 3). In the 1960s, Franco Modigliani began to use an adaptive expectation model in his Keynesian-based Federal Reserve Bank Board econometric model. The model, however, did not predict the double-digit inflation of the 1970s.

Robert Lucas and Thomas Sargent also worked on a Rational Expectation model to explain the inflation crisis of the 1970s (Lucas and Sargent 1981, pp. 295–301).

> Their model nested Keynesian ideas within some structural parameters, whereby an ith individual at time t will form expectation about price, p_{it}, based on all the information available, Ω_{it}, before making a forecast. Lucas and Sargent assumed $y_{it} = \lambda_i E(y_{it}|\Omega_{it}) + \omega_{it}$, where y is long term expectation, t is time approximately three months, ω_{it} is the atmosphere of mass psychology, and Ω_{it} is the state of the news. Investors, i, calculate the average expectation, E, (such as in a beauty contest where competitors must pick out the prettiest face among photographs that are published in a newspaper) where the expected Keynesian outcome is realized when λ_i is set equal to the inverse of the number of beliefs, say $1/N$ and where ω_{it} is zero. (Pesaran 1987, p. 277)

Keynesian expectation has also found its way into gaming theory as well. Debreu found that a Cournot-Nash type of game has solutions in terms of a fixed-point solution of a correspondence (Debreu 1982, p. 700). It treats expectation in the exogenous sense, and rationality has to do with each player choosing strategies to maximize expected payoff. Aumann and Dreze (2008) have shown how expectation solutions in some games are possible, using common knowledge rationality and common prior assumptions. Sources of common knowledge include public events, rules of a game, and contracts (Geanakoplos 1992, p. 54). Common prior assumptions state that '. . . differences in probability estimates of distinct individuals should be explained by differences in information and experience' (Aumann 2000, p. 603). Others have used a more straightforward approach. For example,

> . . . if there are two goods, x, y, and three individuals, a Cobb-Douglas utility function can be written as: $u = x^{\alpha^i(t)} y^{(1-\alpha)^i(t)}$, where i is an individual, and t is time. Here, the expectations are built into the exponential coefficient. For instance, by setting $\alpha^1(t) = at^1 + bt^2 + \gamma c^3 + d$, $a^2(t) = at^2 + bt^3 + ct^1 + d$, and $a^3(t) = at^3 + bt^1 + ct^2 + d$ the individuals can observe their state space, t^i, and prices, p. (Heifetz and Polemarchakis 1998, p. 172)

Hahn stated that Keynesian expectations,

> . . . in the sense of probability distribution over states of nature, are included in the notion of preferences . . . We must adjoin at least expectations concerning future terms at which trade can take place. These will be conditional expectations . . . One non-Keynesian proposal is to take the expected price to be

conditioned by the state of nature and so independent of observed prices . . . a more or less uncertain future casts a shadow over the present, and not only are we closer to Keynes but, more importantly to reality. (Hahn 1985, p. 34)

Keynesian expectations in the decision making areas were pursued by Leonard Savage (1972) and D.G. Champernowne (1969). Their points are covered in Ramrattan and Szenberg (2008). Roy Radner (1968) was the first to extend such thinking to the Arrow-Debreu model. Radner proposed that excess demand functions, Z, are affected not only by a $p \in \Pi$, but by the states of nature, $s \in S$, yielding a Full Revealing Rational Expectation Equilibrium (FRREE). The FRREE assumption is codified if a one-to-one mapping can be found between the price function, where an allocation, f_s for each $s \in S$, such that $f_s(a)$ maximize the agent, a, state dependent utility function, $E[u_a(x)|s]$ subject to its budget constraint $px \leq pe(a)$. Coupling Walrasian General Equilibrium into Keynesian thought, Hahn found that '. . . Keynes . . . was not at all averse to the idea of rational expectations equilibria – he called them bootstrap equilibria' (Hahn 1985, p. 229).

OTHER KEYNESIAN IMPACTS

Keynes's concerns with unemployment in the 1920s and 1930s made him back away from free trade, which he had earlier supported. When the British government went off the gold standard in 1931, Keynes abandoned his protectionist effort and opted for monetary policy for internal balance (Hahn 1985, pp. 197–8). To Keynes, tariffs could '. . . expand total employment when all Labor was not fully utilized.' Meltzer noted that Keynes '. . . recognized also that each country operating alone must sacrifice either internal or external stability unless some country adopts a credible rule for achieving price stability' (Meltzer 1986, p. 66). Mainly, the Keynesian prescription was for output to adjust. In James Tobin's words, '. . . Keynes' theory added, in the international context as in the analysis of closed economies, adjustments due to variations of output and effective demand' (Tobin 1986, p. 38).

Keynes's ideas on aggregate demand led to development of the Harrod-Domar dual-economy, demand complementarily, balanced growth, and big-push theories in the 1950s. Through the work of Solow, modern endogenous growth models emphasize human capital, education, and health variables in developing areas. As Joan Robinson wrote: 'In the industrial countries there is unemployment and underutilization of plant, and, in particular, extreme overcapacity for the production of steel' (Robinson

1984, p. 204). So unemployment and low profits prevail in the industrial world for lack of demand. There is the Third World which is supposed to be developing: development needs investment and investment needs steel. Here is an enormous real demand and an enormous real oversupply. The underlying parameters for growth in those developmental models are investment and productivity, i.e., how much you invest and how much you get out of it (Bhagwati 1998, p. 402). Davidson, for instance, concluded that '. . . as we entered the 21st century, only the Post Keynesians remain to carry-on in Keynes's analytical footsteps and develop Keynes's theory and policy prescriptions for the 21st century real world of economic globalization' (Davidson 2007, p. 209).

CONCLUSIONS

We have presented Keynes's ideas as they were developed in his major works, reacting to the topical problems of the day. A forward view of his works reveals a buildup of theoretical ideas from the external economy to internal policies culminating in saving and investment theory. This eventually led to the full blown model in *The General Theory*, where his ideas became layered with marginal and macro analysis to address the economics of crises.

John Hicks wrote that the survival of

> . . . classical economics into the post-Keynesian epoch is not the same thing as the survivals of outmoded scientific theories . . . It survives because we have found that we have to attend, sometimes at least, to some of the things which Keynes left out. . . . there can be no doubt at all that Keynes wrote as he did because of the times in which he was living. (Hicks 1981, pp. 233, 234)

Pasinetti's idea that Keynes did not break with the classics is in line with our thinking. Clower's and Leijonhufvud's views of speeding up price adjustment were established to reconcile Keynes with the classics. They were precursors towards constructing a nested vision of Keynes. That the sequencing of Keynes's work is relevant is underscored by Leijonhufvud who held that what took place between the *Tract* and *Treatise* was more relevant than what took place between the *Treatise* and *The General Theory* (Leijonhufvud 1968, p. 22).

Without the nested interpretation, the classical theory would be incomplete. Keynes himself intended that his nesting would generalize the classical system to all real economic problems. 'I shall argue that the postulates of the classical theory are applicable to a special case only and not to the general case, the situation which it assumes being a limiting point of the possible positions of equilibrium' (Keynes 1936, p. 3). Keynes's statement represents a hierarchical nesting view, allowing for Adam Smith's ideas to complement his theory in order to preserve capitalism.

BIBLIOGRAPHY

Akerlof, G. (2005), *Explorations in Pragmatic Economics: Selected Papers of George A. Akerlof*, Oxford: Oxford University Press.

Arrow, K. (1967), 'Samuelson collected', *The Journal of Political Economy*, **75**(5) (October), 730–7.

Arrow, K. (ed.) (1991), *Issues in Contemporary Economics: Vol. 1. Markets and Welfare*, New York: New York University Press.

Aumann, R. (2000), *Collected Papers*, Cambridge, MA: The MIT Press.

Aumann, R. and J. Dreze (2008), 'Rational expectations in games', *American Economic Review*, **98**(1) (March), 72–86.

Barro, R. (1989), *Modern Business Cycle Theory*, Cambridge, MA: Harvard University Press.

Bhagwati, J. (1998), *A Stream of Windows: Unsettling Reflections on Trade, Immigration, and Democracy*, Cambridge, MA: The MIT Press.

Blanchard, O. and S. Fischer (1989), *Lectures on Macroeconomics*, Cambridge, MA: The MIT Press.

Champernowne, D. (1969), *Uncertainty and Estimation in Economics*, San Francisco, CA: Holden Day.

Clower, R. (1988), 'Keynes and the classics revisited', in O. Hamouda and J. Smithin (eds), *Keynes and Public Policy after Fifty Years: Vol. I: Economics and Policy*, New York: New York University Press.

Coddington, A. (1983), *Keynesian Economics: The Search for First Principles*, London: George Allen & Unwin.

Davidson, P. (2007), 'Samuelson and the Keynes/Post Keynesian resolution', in P. Davidson (ed.), *The Collected Writings of Paul Davidson, vol. 4, Interpreting Keynes for the 21st Century*, London, Palgrave-Macmillan, pp. 208–26.

Debreu, G. (1982), 'Existence of competitive equilibrium', in K. Arrow and M. Itriligator (eds), *Handbook of Mathematical Economics*, Amsterdam: Elsevier Science, pp. 677–743.

Dornbusch, R., S. Fischer and R. Startz (2008), *Macroeconomics*, 10th edn, New York: McGraw-Hill and Irwin.

Dow, S. (1985), *Macroeconomics Thought: A Methodological Approach*, Oxford: Basil Blackwell.

Friedman, M. (1970), *The Counter-Revolution in Monetary Theory: First Wincott Memorial Lecture delivered at the Senate House, University of London*, London: The Institute of Economic Affairs.

Frisch, R. (1966), *Maxima and Minima: Theory and Economic Applications*, New York: Rand McNally & Company.

Frydman, R. and E. Phelps (1986), *Individual Forecasting and Aggregate Outcomes: Rational Expectation Examined*, Cambridge: Cambridge University Press.

Geanakoplos, J. (1992), 'Common knowledge', *The Journal of Economic Perspectives*, **6**(4) (Autumn), 53–82.

Grandmont, J. (1983), *Money and Value: A Reconsideration of Classical and Neoclassical Monetary Theories*, Cambridge: Cambridge University Press.

Greenwald, B. and J. Stiglitz (1987), 'Keynesian, new Keynesian and new classical economics', *Oxford Economic Papers*, **39**(1) (March), 119–33.

Hahn, F. (1985), *Money, Growth and Stability*, Oxford: Basil Blackwell.

Hahn, F. and R. Solow (1995), *A Critical Essay on Modern Macroeconomic Theory*, Cambridge, MA: The MIT Press.

Hansen, A. (1953), *A Guide to Keynes*, New York: McGraw-Hill.

Harris, S. (1955), *John Maynard Keynes: Economist and Policy Maker*, New York: Charles Scribner's Sons.

Harrod, R. (1951), *The Life of John Maynard Keynes*, London: Macmillan, St Martin's Press.

Hawtrey, R. (1924), 'A Tract on Monetary Reform book review', *Economic Journal*, **34**(134) (June), 227–35.

Heifetz, A. and H. Polemarchakis (1998), 'Partial revelation with rational expectations', *Journal of Economic Theory*, **80**(1) (May), 171–81.

Hicks, J. (1937), 'Mr Keynes and the classics: a suggested interpretation', *Econometrica*, **5**(2) (April), 147–59.

Hicks, J. (1981), 'The scope and status of welfare economics', in J. Hicks (ed.), *Collected Essays on Economic Theory: Wealth and Welfare*, vol. 1, Cambridge, MA: Harvard University Press, pp. 218–39.

Hicks, J. (1982), *Collected Essays on Economic Theory: Money, Interest and Wages*, Cambridge, MA: Harvard University Press.

Hicks, J. (1983), *Collected Essays on Economic Theory: Classics and Moderns*, Cambridge, MA: Harvard University Press.

Horsefield, J. (1969a), *The International Monetary Fund 1945–1965, Vol. I: Chronicles*, Washington, DC: International Monetary Fund.

Horsefield, J. (1969b), *The International Monetary Fund 1945–1965, Vol. III: Documents*, Washington, DC: International Monetary Fund.

Hutchison, T. (1977), *Keynes versus the Keynesians: Keynes Rediscovered*, London: The Institute of Economic Affairs.

Keynes, J. M. (1936), *The General Theory of Employment, Interest, and Money*, London: Macmillan.

Keynes, J. M. (1937a), 'The general theory of employment', *Quarterly Journal of Economics*, **51**(2) (February), 209–23.

Keynes, J. M. (1937b), 'The "ex-ante" theory of the rate of interest', *The Economic Journal*, **47**(188) (December), 663–9.

Keynes, J. (1938), 'Mr. Keynes and 'finance': comment', *Economic Journal*, **48**(190) (June), 318–22.

Keynes, J. M. (1971–1989), *The Collected Writings of John Maynard Keynes*, London: Macmillan/Cambridge University press for the Royal Economic Society.

Vol. I: *Indian Currency and Finance*

Vol. IV: *A Tract on Monetary Reform*

Vol. V: *A Treatise on Money*, Vol. 1. *The Pure Theory of Money*

Vol. VI: *A Treatise on Money*, Vol. 2. *The Applied Theory of Money*

Vol. XIV: *The General Theory and After, part 2: Defence and Development*

Vol. XXI: *Activities 1931–1939: World Crisis and Politics in Britain and America*

Leijonhufvud, A. (1968), *On Keynesian Economics and the Economics of Keynes*, New York: Oxford University Press.

Leijonhufvud, A. (1976), 'Schools, "revolutions" and research programmes', in S. Latsis (ed.), *Method and Appraisal in Economics*, Cambridge: Cambridge University Press, pp. 65–108.

Lerner, A. (1961), *Everybody's Business: A Re-examination of Current Assumptions in Economics and Public Policy*, New York: Harper and Row.

Lowe, A. (1965), *On Economic Knowledge*, New York: Harper & Row.

Lucas, R. and T. Sargent (1981), 'After Keynesian macroeconomics', in R. Lucas and T. Sargent (eds), *Rational Expectations and Econometric Practice*, Minneapolis, MN: The University of Minnesota Press, pp. 295–319.

Mankiw, G. and D. Romer (eds) (1991), *New Keynesian Economics: Vol. I: Imperfect Competition and Sticky Prices*, Cambridge, MA: The MIT Press.

Meltzer, A. (1986), 'On monetary stability and monetary reform', in Y. Suzuki and M. Okabe (eds), *Toward a World of Economic Stability*, Tokyo: University of Tokyo Press, pp. 51–73.

Minsky, H. (1975), *John Maynard Keynes*, New York: McGraw Hill.

Modigliani, F. (1944), 'Liquidity preference and the theory of interest and money', *Econometrica*, **12**(1) (January), 45–88.

Moggridge, D. (1992), *Maynard Keynes: An Economist's Biography*, London: Routledge.

Okun, A. (1970), *The Political Economy of Prosperity*, New York: W. W. Norton & Company.

Pasinetti, L. (1999), 'J. M. Keynes' "revolution" – the major event of twentieth-century economics?', in L. Pasinetti and B. Schefold (eds), *The Impact of Keynes on Economics in the 20th Century*, Cheltenham, UK and Northampton, MA, USA: Edward Elgar, pp. 3–15.

Patinkin, D. (1975), 'The collected writings of John Maynard Keynes: from the Tract to the General', *Economic Journal*, **85**(338) (June), 249–71.

Patinkin, D. (1982), *Anticipations of the General Theory? And Other Essays on Keynes*, Chicago, IL: The University of Chicago Press.

Pesaran, M. H. (1987), *The Limits to Rational Expectations*, Oxford: Basil Blackwell.

Pigou, A. (1950), *Keynes's 'General Theory': A Retrospective View*, Fairfield, NJ: Augustus M. Kelley.

Pissarides, C. (1989), 'Unemployment and macroeconomics', *Economica*, **56**(221) (February), 1–14.

Radner, R. (1968), 'Competitive equilibrium under uncertainty', *Econometrica*, **36**(1) (January), 31–58.

Ramrattan, L. and M. Szenberg (2007a), 'Expectations', in *International Encyclopedia of the Social Science*, 2nd edn, pp. 47–50.

Ramrattan, L. and M. Szenberg (2007b), 'John R. Hicks: 1904–1989', in *International Encyclopedia of the Social Science*, 2nd edn, pp. 471–2.

Ramrattan, L. and M. Szenberg (2008), 'Memorializing Milton Friedman: a review of his major works, 1912–2006', *The American Economist*, **52**(1) (Spring), 22–38.

Robinson, J. (1984), 'Discussion', in R. Kahn (ed.), *The Making of Keynes' General Theory*, Cambridge University Press, pp. 203–5.

Samuelson, P. (1966), 'A brief survey of post-Keynesian developments', in J. Stiglitz (ed.), *The Collected Scientific Papers of Paul A. Samuelson,* vol. 2, Cambridge, MA: The MIT Press, pp. 1534–50.

Samuelson, P. (1986), 'What would Keynes have thought of rational expectations:

comment', in K. Crowley (ed.), *The Collected Scientific Papers of Paul A. Samuelson*, vol. 5, Cambridge, MA: The MIT Press, pp. 291–6.

Savage, L. (1972), *The Foundation of Statistics*, New York: Dover Publications.

Skidelsky, R. (1992), *John Maynard Keynes: The Economist as Saviour, 1920–1937*, London: The Penguin Press.

Tobin, J. (1986), 'Are there reliable adjustment mechanisms?', in Y. Suzuki and M. Okabe (eds), *Toward a World of Economic Stability*, Tokyo: University of Tokyo Press, pp. 37–50.

PART III

The General Theory and Friedman, Kaldor, Marx and Sraffa

9. 'The right kind of an economist': Friedman's view of Keynes

Roger E. Backhouse and Bradley W. Bateman

INTRODUCTION

Robert Skidelsky (2009, p. 105), in his recent book on Keynes, no doubt speaks for many when he posits a chasm between the ideas of John Maynard Keynes and Milton Friedman.[1] Friedman, 'the high priest of the classical counter-attack' was a representative of the tradition against which Keynes was rebelling who disagreed with Keynes on policy, economic theory, the interpretation of economic history and on methodology. Friedman's attack on demand management policies was based on theoretical differences from Keynes: he defined full employment as the point at which the rate of inflation would be stable, something Keynes did not do, and he modelled economic agents as taking logical, rational decisions that were forward looking, paving the way for the more radical critiques of Keynesianism that came from his younger colleagues, notably Robert Lucas. His vision was of an economy that was inherently stable, the Great Depression not being a symptom of the instability of capitalism (Keynes's diagnosis) but the result of bad monetary policy. Friedman proposed a 'monetary-disequilibrium' theory of the Great Depression, a type of theory from which Keynes had moved away. Methodologically, Skidelsky (2009, p. 81) argues, Friedman's difference from Keynes involved the use of a mechanical schema, in which economic agents were modelled almost as billiard balls, bouncing mechanically from one equilibrium to another. Keynesian economics involved the denial of much of this, for Keynes denied that agents could take rational decisions in the face of uncertainty, arguing that economics could not be based on mechanical models of equilibrium, but had to be a moral science, taking account of the variety of human motives.

There is, of course, much in this view that is correct. Friedman was a long-standing critic of stabilization policy, who shared responsibility for the change in attitudes towards macroeconomic policy making which took place after 1979. His support of free markets was something that

Keynes would not have endorsed, at least not as regards stabilization policy, though he was perhaps not as far from Friedman as is sometimes claimed (Keynes could, after all, claim to be in 'deeply moved agreement' with much of Friedrich Hayek's *The Road to Serfdom* (1944)). This difference was, no doubt, the result of their different backgrounds: Keynes the product of the British ruling class (on which Skidelsky (1983; 2003) has done so much to enlighten us), Friedman the product of a less privileged background (Friedman and Friedman 1998; Cherrier 2011). Economics, for Friedman, was always an empirical, positive science, not a moral science. Friedman had greater confidence in the power of the market to regulate the economy than Keynes ever had. These differences were deep-seated and profound.

Yet there were similarities. Friedman himself has claimed, on several occasions, that Keynes's *The General Theory* (*Collected Writings* (CW), Vol. VII) was a 'great book' and he has endorsed Keynes's approach to economic theory.

> I think his influence on economic theory is, on the whole, a very good one, not because the theory he proposed was right, but he taught us all to look at the problems through different lenses, developed a terminology that has turned out to be very useful to people like myself who never have accepted the basic elements of his theory. And he was the right kind of an economist as an economic scientist from my point of view (Friedman, in Blaug 1990, p. 89).

In a later interview, he elaborated on this view, this time referring explicitly to *The General Theory*.

> I believe that he was a great economist, one of the great economists of our time and that the *General Theory* is a remarkable intellectual achievement. We had a phenomenon that needed an explanation. How could you have widespread unemployment in the midst of an economy with such large productive capacity? That was a phenomenon in search of an explanation and he produced an explanation for it which, in my opinion, was the right kind of explanation. What you need to do is to have a very simple theory that gets at the fundamentals. No theory is successful if it's extremely complicated and difficult, because most phenomena are driven by a very few central forces. What a good theory does is to simplify; it pulls out the central forces and gets rid of the rest. So Keynes's *General Theory* was the right kind of theory. (Friedman, in Snowdon and Vane 2005, p. 202)

Friedman's view may reflect what scholars would consider questionable understandings of Keynes's own views – of the significance Keynes attached to wage stickiness, for instance, or his views on stabilization policy – and thus may be better seen as a response to Keynesianism as it emerged in the 1950s and 1960s than to Keynes himself. However, there is reason for thinking that his endorsement of Keynes as a theorist may represent a genuine similarity in their work. Friedman had no incentive to praise Keynes as a theorist; for he wanted to undermine the basis on which Keynesian policies were built and for that purpose it would have been better for him to question Keynes's credentials as a theorist than to praise them. It would have been easy for him to do so, for had he chosen to criticize Keynes, he would have been joining a crowded field, from committed Keynesians such as Frank Hahn, who contended that though he had brilliant intuitions, Keynes 'did not know how to theorize' (see Blaug 1990) to staunch anti-Keynesians such as Buchanan and Wagner (1977) who argue that Keynes's theorizing is naive. More important, when considering the possible similarities between their works we should note that Friedman's endorsement of Keynes's theory serves to distance Friedman from the new classical theorists who came after, drawing attention to the methodological changes that were brought about by Robert Lucas and his generation. Friedman was in some ways right to claim parallels between his and Keynes's ways of theorizing. The point about adaptive expectations, for example, is that they are backward looking and are not rational (except under very special circumstances); they may not correspond to what Keynes had in mind when he wrote about expectations, but they are a long way from the rational expectations found in more recent macroeconomics. Likewise, Friedman's agents are ones who may make mistakes for long periods of time, not the lightning calculators of the new classical macroeconomics.

The reason for this focus on Friedman is not to defend Friedman. It is that misunderstanding the relationship between Friedman and Keynes causes us to misunderstand Keynes's work and its relationship to modern macroeconomics.[2] To sweep Friedman, Lucas and other opponents of Keynes into a single, homogeneous category, represented essentially by the new classical macroeconomics and real business cycle (RBC) theory, is to present Keynes as standing apart from the whole of modern macroeconomics, not to mention the whole of the macroeconomics that came before *The General Theory*. Keynes becomes, almost by default, the economist who rejected the whole of modern macroeconomics. This is the position taken by some 'fundamentalist' Keynesians such as Paul Davidson (2007, 2009). For these fundamentalists economic theory before and after Keynes is one continuous tradition of 'classical' economics, a mainstream that never absorbed what Keynes said.

[Why] after Keynes's revolutionary analysis, the reader may ask, have mainstream economists resurrected this classical theory as the only valid basis for developing policy prescriptions for the major economic problems of the 21st century? . . . [T]his apparent deification of classical theory was actually not a rising from the dead. The Keynes analysis was never understood by the established leaders and trendsetters of the profession. Instead almost immediately after Keynes published his revolutionary monetary theory it was aborted. (Davidson 2007, p. 173)

In order to recover Keynes and to avoid such 'fundamentalist' inter-pretations of his work, we need to explore the relationship between his ideas and those of his critics in later generations, thereby revealing a Keynes who was more flexible, and more subtle in his theorizing than he is often presented as having been. In preserving a richer, more subtle sense of Keynes's work, we are also able to place him more accurately in his own historical milieu. David Laidler (1999) has shown, without in any way diminishing the scale of Keynes's achievement, that far from being the inventor of modern macroeconomics, that Keynes worked within an emerging tradition of monetary economics that defined the boundaries within which his own work would evolve: that Keynes, rather than over-throwing all that went before, drew extensively on concepts and ideas developed during the 1920s and 1930s to produce the theory that came to be the channel through which those ideas entered economics in the post-Second World War era.

FRIEDMAN: AGAINST THE GRAIN

Milton Friedman is a paradoxical figure. 'The methodology of positive economics' (Friedman 1953) became one of few methodological works that students of economics had to read, yet most of those teachers who recommended it, and most of the students who were exposed to it, used it to justify an approach that differed markedly from Friedman's own way of doing economics. Its message was that theories should not be judged by the realism of their assumptions, a claim that would seem to run counter to Keynes's concern with conceptual clarity as well as his desire to develop theories that related to the world in which we live – recall his remark about Euclidian geometers in a non-Euclidian world (Keynes, CW, vol. VII, p. 16). Yet the message economists took from Friedman – a defence of formal modelling – neither accords with Friedman's practice nor reflects the details of his argument. Consider first some of Friedman's methodo-logical claims.

If one interprets Friedman through the lens of modern economics, it is surprising to find that he recommends immersion in relevant data prior to theorizing. By the canons of inference that underlie conventional econometrics, such an approach is tantamount to data mining, and it runs counter to the falsificationism that many economists would claim to have learned from Friedman's essay. The danger, Friedman contends, is that lack of familiarity with data will result in the construction of silly theories. This is, of course, a position that echoes that taken by Wesley Clair Mitchell and Simon Kuznets, with whom he worked at the National Bureau of Economic Research. Friedman retained a sceptical attitude towards formal econometric methods, even though he acknowledged that he had made extensive use of mathematics and econometrics in his own work. The problem was not that such methods should not be used – clearly they were essential – but that they had been taken too far: 'The computer revolution has, I believe, induced economists to carry reliance on mathematics and econometrics beyond the point of vanishing returns – something that is perhaps inevitable in the first flush of any revolution' (Friedman 1991, p. 36). Economists were devoting more attention to the analysis of data than to the more laborious task of compiling it. This view came out very clearly in his robust response (Friedman and Schwartz 1991) to the critique that David Hendry and Neil Ericsson (1991) mounted against *Monetary Trends in the US and the UK* (Friedman and Schwartz 1982): he brushed aside their criticisms of his statistical methods and chided them for their lack of understanding of how the statistics they were all using had been compiled. His statistical approach had been formed in the 1930s, before the transformation of econometrics brought about at the Cowles Commission in the 1940s, with whom he argued vigorously after his return to Chicago in 1946.

Friedman also adopted what he chose to call a 'Marshallian' approach to economic theory. For this purpose the main feature of his Marshallianism is the use of simple models to analyse a reality that was more complicated. Thus he did not deny that markets might be monopolistically competitive, as Edward Chamberlin and others were arguing, but he argued this predicted nothing that could not be predicted with a judicious use, depending on circumstances, of theories of perfect competition or monopoly. This was, in a sense, the essence of what came to be known as Chicago price theory. A further feature of this preference for simple models was his famous liking for working with models that comprised only one or two equations, in marked contrast to the elaborate models that his Walras-inspired contemporaries were constructing whether in microeconomics or macroeconomics. In his theory of the consumption function, for example, where others were postulating maximization over an *n*-period lifetime, Friedman's theory comprised a two-period model that he could analyse using an indifference curve diagram. Thus, use of a limited menu of simple models meant that many of the phenomena with which he was concerned were not modelled formally, the basic price theory having to be placed in the context of arguments that were expressed either verbally or statistically.

This unorthodox approach came out most clearly in his insistence, frustrating to his Keynesian critics, that the quantity theory was a framework or approach, not a specific doctrine. Thus, for many years, he refused to write down his model. Even the demand function for money, on which he placed so much weight, was not a testable hypothesis so much as an explanation of the factors that were believed to affect the demand for money. When he did specify his model, it turned out to be something close to the IS-LM model, where, though the views against which he was contending were expressed formally (the simple Keynesian theory as involving a fixed price level and the simple quantity theory as involving fixed output), his own theory was expressed informally as involving a loosely specified relationship between changes in prices and output.

> I shall regard the short-run equilibrium as determined by an adjustment process in which the rate of adjustment in a variable is a function of the discrepancy between the measured and the anticipated value of that variable or its rate of change, as well as, perhaps, of other variables or their rates of change. Finally, I shall let at least some anticipated variables be determined by a feedback process from past observed values (Friedman 1970, p. 223).

This is, as Friedman emphasizes, no more than a framework for thinking about the problem: it is not a precise model.[3]

Though his colleagues and students at Chicago testify to his influence, they did not follow him in this heterodox attitude to modelling. From the 1960s and 1970s, under the influence of Gary Becker and Lucas, though Chicago retained a distinctive attitude towards policy, it moved towards more conventional modelling. Whereas Friedman has used maximization as a predictive device, leaving scope for non-rational behaviour in the short run – hence his acceptance of the existence of long and variable lags in the effects of monetary policy – his colleagues at Chicago moved towards a rational choice approach. Though they might be less willing to recognize market failure than their counterparts at MIT, Yale or Stanford, their modelling strategies converged. By the end of the 1970s, though Friedman might be at the peak of his influence as policy adviser, the running in economic theory was being made by a younger generation who did not adopt his methods and whose theories took them in directions that were markedly different from his own. Lucas's policy invariance and neutrality propositions were a far cry from Friedman's conclusions about the powerful effects that monetary policy might exert. There did develop a concern for dynamics, but it was the dynamic stochastic general equilibrium (DSGE) model, as it came to be known, which was methodologically unlike any dynamics contemplated by Friedman.

These methodological differences were reflected in substantive differences over economics, to the extent that Laidler (1990, p. 54) has written of 'the subversion of monetarism by the new classical macroeconomics'. His argument is that Friedman's monetarism rested on two propositions, both established by his empirical work. The first was that the effects of a monetary change were felt first (with a lag of around six months) on output, and only later (after around 18 months or two years) on prices. This was consistent with an eclectic interpretation of the Phillips curve, which stressed both price inflexibility and slow adjustment of expectations. The second was that balance sheet adjustments played an important role in cyclical fluctuations.

> The central element in the transmission mechanism is the concept of cyclical fluctuations as the outcome of balance sheet adjustments, as the effects on flows of adjustments between desired and actual stocks. It is this interconnection of stocks and flows that stretches the effects of shocks out in time, produces a diffusion over different economic categories, and gives rise to cyclical reaction mechanisms. The stocks serve as buffers or shock absorbers of initial changes in rates of flow, by expanding or contracting from their 'normal' or 'natural' or 'desired' state, and then slowly alter other flows as holders try to regain that state. (Friedman and Schwartz 1963b, p. 63; Laidler 1990)

The essence of this process is slow adjustment of portfolios, something that is not compatible with the new classical assumptions about flexible prices and continuous optimization. In contrast with the new classical theory in which monetary shocks are exogenous, whether anticipated or unanticipated, the money supply is partly endogenous: 'Disturbances in the rate of change in the money stock set in train a cyclical adjustment mechanism including a feedback in the rate of change in money itself' (Friedman and Schwartz 1963b, p. 64). The new classical economists achieved theoretical rigour, in the sense of basing their results on more formal micro-foundations, at the price of ignoring the empirical results on which this analysis was based.

Friedman and Schwartz's methods in this work were squarely those of Mitchell's National Bureau, their theory resting on painstaking analysis of the way different variables fluctuated over the cycle. Their conclusions about the cycle meshed closely with their view of the Great Depression, outlined in their extremely influential *A Monetary History of the United States, 1867–1960* (Friedman and Schwartz 1963a), according to which the Depression became so deep because of a catastrophic series of bank failures that resulted in a sharp fall in the money supply.

KEYNES: AGAINST THE GRAIN

When Friedman referred to Keynes's theory, as opposed to his methods, the work he praised most highly was, not surprisingly, *A Tract on Monetary Reform* (Keynes, CW, vol. IV), where Keynes had written of the dangers of inflation and deflation. In this book Keynes had used the framework of the quantity theory to obtain results that were different from those Friedman wanted to achieve: he argued for stabilizing the price level through the use of interest rates, not for controlling the quantity of money, per se. Keynes also focused, as in *The General Theory*, on the short run – this was where he introduced his famous phrase that 'in the long run we are all dead' (ibid., p. 65) and attached great importance to the instability of the demand for money and hence the velocity of circulation. However, despite their differences about the conclusions to draw from it, Keynes's style of reasoning from the quantity theory had much in common with Friedman's. Like Friedman, he used the quantity theory as a framework or an approach to conceptualizing the effects of monetary policy, not as a specific doctrine. His interpretation of the quantity theory, which reflected that of his teacher Alfred Marshall, emphasized the demand for money, not the comparatively mechanical circulation of money found in the writings of, say, Irving Fisher (1911). Keynes's argument rested on many arguments about the dynamic effects of policy changes that were not specified in a formal model.

In *A Treatise on Money* (CW, vols. V and VI) Keynes shifted his attention to saving and investment as the drivers of the business cycle, and towards a more mechanical way of modelling – his so-called 'fundamental equations' – though he still kept within a loose quantity theory framework. He abandoned the quantity theory as his analytical framework in *The General Theory*, but despite Friedman's opposition to Keynes's policy conclusions, this abandonment was not the basis on which he criticized Keynes. Friedman's critique of Keynes's magnum opus was not methodological but substantive: Keynes was wrong in his details and in his conclusions, but not in his methods. When Friedman wrote that Keynes developed many concepts that were very useful to economists who did not accept his policy conclusions and caused them to see the world through different lenses, he was referring to *The General Theory*.

It is also important to note that, despite what might be inferred from much of the subsequent literature, at no point did Keynes reject monetary policy. Indeed, when he summed up his theory in responding to his critics in the *Quarterly Journal of Economics*, he mentioned monetary policy but *not* fiscal policy: 'aggregate output depends on the propensity to hoard, *on the policy of the monetary authority as it affects the quantity of money*, on the state of confidence concerning the prospective yield of capital assets, on the propensity to spend and on the social factors which influence the level of the money wage' (Keynes, CW, vol. XIV, p. 121; emphasis added).

Neither did he recant on his view, expressed most strongly in the *Tract*, that inflation was undesirable. It was simply that in the depression that formed the backdrop to *The General Theory*, inflation was simply not a problem; thus, Keynes did not write about the need for the central bank to control the price level (as he had in the *Tract*), though he did write of the need for price stability. Neither did he write about the need for restoring prices to their former levels, the reason being that he was concerned about stabilizing the level of investment, because low investment could, independently of any price changes, be a cause of high unemployment. This was true irrespective of whether businessmen's expectations were depressed after their experience of a monetary collapse (as had happened in the United States after 1929) or by a combination of factors (in Britain, the return to gold at an over-valued exchange rate combined with the impact of a world depression). However, this emphasis on the need to raise investment to stimulate the level of aggregate demand did not mean he considered monetary policy unimportant: to the contrary, he was emphatic that stimulating investment required low interest rates for otherwise the private sector would not find it attractive to invest. Contrary to popular belief, he did not advocate the use of government deficits as a stabilization policy but focused on the stimulation of private investment.

Keynes's attitude is clearly illustrated when, only five years after *The General Theory*, he made a strong and successful use of the book's basic model to explain to the British public how to prevent the escalation of the war against Hitler from causing inflation. In his pamphlet *How to Pay for the War* (1940), Keynes developed an elegant argument from his basic model of output to explain how taxation could be used during the war to prevent overheating in the economy. He did this while simultaneously arguing that the purchasing power taxed away from consumers during the war could be returned to them after the war the prevent a downturn; thus, the policies he recommended did not mean permanent increases in the tax burden. Though Friedman did not discuss Keynes's work explicitly in his writing on the savings, investment and the inflationary gap (Friedman 1942, 1943), this fell squarely into the same framework as Keynes had used earlier. Unlike some modern commentators, Friedman understood that Keynes's model in *The General Theory* did not guarantee a bias towards either the growth of the state or towards inflation.[4] One could use the model to argue for more or less involvement by the state, for control of inflation as easily as for policies that might lead to inflation. This would be sufficient to explain why Friedman did not have to argue the irrelevancy of Keynes's model in order to obtain the policy outcomes he sought. Criticism of Keynes's theoretical work was not necessary since it did not have to lead to the policies that Keynesians sought.

The significance of Friedman's position on Keynes as a theorist, lies, at least in part, in the fact that many of the points where Friedman parted company with the mainstream of macroeconomic thinking after 1945 were also points where Keynes had pursued a line that had not been followed by his successors. To the uninformed, Keynes's attitude to data might seem poles apart from Friedman's, Keynes perhaps being thought not to share the passion for statistical description that Friedman had picked up at the NBER. But while Keynes had his own approach to data collection, he was just as insistent as Friedman on its importance. Though they might express this differently, with Keynes referring to the role of data in developing one's economic intuitions and Friedman referring to the importance of data to the theory choice, they saw theory as entering the process of economic theorizing at the initial stage, in contrast to the conventional role that it entered only at the end, as a means of testing hypotheses. Keynes was a co-founder of the London and Cambridge Economic Service and was a voracious user of economic data as it existed in his own time. This lifelong interest in the collection and use of basic economic data is reflected, for instance, in the fact that he actively encouraged his younger colleagues James Meade and Richard Stone in their work on the national accounts. Furthermore, although they were responding to work of a very different character, Keynes and Friedman shared a suspicion of econometrics. Keynes's objections to the work of Jan Tinbergen (see Bateman 1990) were not objections to use of data and an empirical approach to economics, but rather expressed skepticism based on technical arguments about the appropriateness of the methods Tinbergen was using and the adequacy of the data to support the type of inferences he wanted to make from his data. Friedman's scepticism about modern econometric methods is shown by the response he and Schwartz made to the critique David Hendry and Neil Ericsson mounted against *Monetary Trends*.

Their shared interest in data and the empirical framing of their work is not the only place where they shared an approach to economics. Friedman chose to describe himself as a Marshallian and there can be no doubt as to Keynes's debt to Marshall who was not only his teacher but also his sponsor at the beginning of his academic career. Though the *Treatise* marked a move away from the Marshallian trade cycle theory of the *Tract*, a move that was taken further in *The General Theory*, his way of theorizing remained thoroughly Marshallian in ways that exhibit clear parallels with Friedman.[5] One of the reasons why subsequent generations of macroeconomists found *The General Theory* so frustrating was that though Keynes articulated something that could legitimately be described as a model, he did not put it all together as a general equilibrium model of the type that swept the profession following the Second World War. Keynes liked to frame his prose in the language of the mathematical function for ease in organizing the elements of his argument and working with them to lay out their influence on each other, he felt that the freedom necessary to thinking through those influences was lost if the functions were understood only as generating fixed numerical coefficients.[6] As a proponent of economics as a 'moral science', he believed that the relationships in a capitalist economy were not reducible to fixed numbers.

The components of what became IS-LM, the first effort to recast Keynes's model from *The General Theory* in what might be seen as a modern general equilibrium model are, indeed, all present in *The General Theory*, but Keynes did not put them together to obtain that model. Keynes had learned from his failure with the *Treatise* that using mathematical models of the economy in a fixed and rigid way kept him from being able to capture the kinds of human behaviours that were at the heart of capitalism's inability to provide stable employment. He understood that he needed to avoid the 'magic formula mentality' of the *Treatise*, which had been so unsuccessful.

CONCLUSIONS

Though they disagreed fundamentally over the role of government in the economy and on the role that intellectuals should play in solving the world's problems, it is easy to see why Friedman considered Keynes to be 'the right kind of an economist'. They agreed in being aware of the dangers of inflation and in attaching great importance to monetary policy. Keynes ultimately moved away from the quantity theory approach, though he did not renounce it explicitly, which is consistent with Friedman's not criticizing him for abandoning it. Despite their disagreement over policy, therefore, there was considerable agreement over how to approach economic theory. Beneath this lay methodological similarities: they used data to inform theorizing; they advocated a Marshallian, step-by-step approach towards economic theorizing; and formal models provided no more than a framework within which economic problems could be discussed. They were both sceptical about the 'scientism' of both formal economic theories and formal econometric methods. They both dissented from what became the dominant trends in economics after 1945. Yet in both cases, they did not interfere to discourage their followers from going in this direction: Keynes encouraged the work of John Hicks and Roy Harrod, whilst Friedman's students included Robert Lucas and Gary Becker. They attached more importance to fundamental ideas (though they differed dramatically on what those ideas were) than to the way in which they were developed.

But how does this affect our understanding of Keynes? Negatively, we can conclude that, though Keynes's methodology differs quite dramatically from the methodology (or perhaps the family of methodologies) that have formed the basis for the mainstream in post-1945 macroeconomics, his informal approach may not get to the heart of what is important about his economics. It may indeed be the case that the view of how expectations are formed in the presence of fundamental uncertainty outlined in Chapter 12 may rule out over-elaborate mathematical modelling (at least given our present state of knowledge) but rejection of such methods is not sufficient. Friedman shared many of Keynes's methodological views but took them in a very different direction. Keynes's willingness to encourage methodologically diverse developments in *The General Theory* (Backhouse and Bateman 2010), and the diversity of the methodological positions by which anti-Keynesian positions have been sustained confirms this view the importance of the book lies not in its methodology but in its substantive arguments about the economy.

Attention is often drawn to Keynes's claim to be making a radical break from the past. *The General Theory* made an analogy with non-Euclidian geometry (presumably with echoes of Einstein) and its dismissal of 'the classical theory'; and in the *Quarterly Journal of Economics* he accused the classical theory of being one of those 'pretty, polite techniques which tries to deal with the present by abstracting from the fact that we know very little about the future' (Keynes, CW, vol. XIV, p. 215). Keynes was hardly modest in his claims. And yet, looking closer, he expresses caution: 'I am more attached to the comparatively simple fundamental ideas which underlie my theory than to the particular forms in which I have embodied them, and I have no desire that the latter should be crystallized at the present stage of the debate' (ibid., p. 111). Those simple ideas, he went on to claim, were that the rate of interest (and hence monetary policy) determined investment, and the multiplier.

In looking for those substantive arguments, it is important to remember that Keynes should be seen as a monetary economist – indeed, a dimension not discussed here is that much of his work involved specifically *international* monetary economics, a dimension that surfaces periodically even in *The General Theory* – not, as it would have been easy to infer during much of the Keynesian era, as the economist who argued that fiscal policy should replace monetary policy as the centre of attention. It seems safe to say that in 2008, Friedman and Keynes would have agreed on the importance of avoiding a collapse in the banking system, and with it the money supply.[7] Keynes reached new conclusions through his imaginative use of concepts and ideas that he and his contemporaries had developed. He reached conclusions that were different from Friedman's because he had a different vision of capitalism that caused him to use the flexibility inherent in his method to develop a theory that addressed the needs of his day, whether those needs were curing unemployment in the 1930s or preventing inflation during the Second World War. His influence (which was greater than that of any other economist of his day) perhaps lies less in some analytical trick or methodological innovation than in having a clear vision of capitalism and a creativity in using theoretical and conceptual tools to articulate policies that were consistent with that vision. Friedman did the same, but starting from a radically different vision he reached very different conclusions.

NOTES

1. The rest of this paragraph draws primarily on Skidelsky (2009, pp. 105–9). Note that, though he emphasizes the difference, he observes (2009, pp. xvi–xvii) that both Keynes and Friedman believed that some unemployment was due to inflexible wages and prices.
2. This concern differentiates the paper from other comparisons of Keynes and Friedman, such as Wood (1980) and Dostaler (1998).
3. Though the point is not pursued here, it is significant that this is a dynamic argument. Backhouse and Laidler (2004) have argued that dynamic arguments were central to monetary economics in the 1930s, the period in which Friedman was trained in Chicago. In attaching importance to dynamic arguments that cannot be captured in a formal, static model, Friedman was following Keynes.
4. For example, James Buchanan and Richard Wagner (1977) argued that Keynes's model of the economy necessarily led to inflation, growth of the state, and ever growing budget deficits.
5. On Keynes as a Marshallian, see Leijonhufvud (2006).
6. See O'Donnell (1997) and Backhouse (2010).
7. It can easily be forgotten that one role of Friedman's policy of a constant growth rate of the money supply was to prevent disastrous collapses of the money supply such as happened in 1929–30.

BIBLIOGRAPHY

Backhouse, R. E. (2010), "An abstruse and mathematical argument": the use of mathematical reasoning in the *General Theory*', in B. W. Bateman, T. Hirai and C. Marcuzzo (eds), *The Return to Keynes: Keynes and Keynesian Policies in the New Millennium*, Cambridge, MA: Harvard University Press, pp. 133–47.

Backhouse, R. E. and D. Laidler (2004), 'What was lost with IS-LM', *History of Political Economy*, **36**(supplement 1), 25–56.

Backhouse, R. E. and B. W. Bateman (2010), 'Whose Keynes?' in R. Dimand, R.

Mundell and A. Vercelli (eds), *Keynes's General Theory: A Reconsideration after Seventy Years*, London: Palgrave Macmillan, pp. 8–27.

Bateman, Bradley W. (1990), 'Keynes, induction and econometrics', *History of Political Economy*, **22**(2) (Summer), 359–79.

Blaug, M. (1990), *John Maynard Keynes: Life, Ideas, Legacy*, London: Macmillan.

Buchanan, J. and R. Wagner (1977), *Democracy in Deficit: The Political Legacy of Lord Keynes*, New York: Academic Press.

Cherrier, B. (2011), 'The suspicious consistency of Milton Friedman's science and politics', in P. Mirowski, T. Stapleford and R. Van Horn (eds), *Building Chicago Economics: New Perspectives on the History of America's Most Powerful Economics Program*, Cambridge: Cambridge University Press.

Davidson, P. (2007), *John Maynard Keynes*, London: Palgrave.

Davidson, P. (2009), *The Keynes Solution: The Path to Global Economic Prosperity*, London: Palgrave.

Dostaler, G. (1998), 'Keynes and Friedman: divergences and convergences', *European Journal of the History of Economic Thought*, **5**(2), 317–47.

Fisher, I. (1911), *The Purchasing Power of Money*, New York: Macmillan.

Friedman, M. (1942), 'The inflationary gap: II. Discussion of the inflationary gap', *American Economic Review*, **32**(2) (June), 314–20.

Friedman, M. (1943), 'The spendings tax as a wartime fiscal measure', *American Economic Review*, **33**(1) (March), 50–62.

Friedman, M. (1953), 'The methodology of positive economics', in M. Friedman (ed.), *Essays in Positive Economics*, Chicago, IL: Chicago University Press, pp. 3–43.

Friedman, M. (1970), 'A theoretical framework for monetary analysis', *Journal of Political Economy*, **78**(2) (March/April), 193–238.

Friedman, M. (1991), 'Old wine in new bottles', *Economic Journal*, **101**(404) (January), 33–40.

Friedman, M. and R. Friedman (1998), *Two Lucky People*, Chicago, IL: University of Chicago Press.

Friedman, M. and A. J. Schwartz (1963a), *A Monetary History of the United States, 1867-1960*, Princeton, NJ: Princeton University Press.

Friedman, M. and A. J. Schwartz (1963b), 'Money and business cycles', *Review of Economics and Statistics*, **45**(1) (February) (supplement), 32–64.

Friedman, M. and Schwartz, A. J. (1982), *Monetary Trends in the United States and the United Kingdom: Their Relations to Income, Prices and Interest Rates, 1867–1975*, Chicago, IL: University of Chicago Press.

Friedman, M. and A. J. Schwartz (1991), 'Alternative approaches to analyzing economic data', *American Economic Review*, **81**(1) (March), 39–49.

Hayek, F. (1944), *The Road to Serfdom*, Chicago, IL: University of Chicago Press.

Hendry, D. F and N. R. Ericsson (1991), 'An econometric analysis of UK money demand in *Monetary Trends in the United States and the United Kingdom* by Milton Friedman and Anna J. Schwartz', *American Economic Review*, **81**(1) (March), 8–38.

Keynes, J. M. (1971–1989), *The Collected Writings of John Maynard Keynes*, London: Macmillan/Cambridge University Press for the Royal Economic Society.
Vol. IV: *A Tract on Monetary Reform*
Vol. V: *A Treatise on Money*
Vol. VI; *A Treatise on Money*

Vol. VII: *The General Theory of Employment, Interest, and Money*

Vol. XIV: *The General Theory and After: Part II Defense and Development*

Laidler, D. (1990), 'The legacy of the monetarist controversy', *Federal Reserve Bank of St Louis Review*, **72**(2) (March), 49–64.

Laidler, D. (1999), *Fabricating the Keynesian Revolution: Studies of the Inter-War Literature on Money, the Cycle, and Unemployment*, Cambridge: Cambridge University Press.

Leijonhufvud, A. (2006), 'Keynes as a Marshallian', in R. E. Backhouse and B. W. Bateman (eds), *The Cambridge Companion to Keynes*, Cambridge: Cambridge University Press.

O'Donnell, R. (1997), 'Keynes and formalism', in G. C. Harcourt and P. A. Riach (eds), *A 'Second Edition' of the General Theory*, London: Routledge, pp. 94–119.

Skidelsky, R. (1983), *John Maynard Keynes, Volume 1: Hopes Betrayed, 1883–1920*, London: Macmillan.

Skidelsky, R. (2003), *John Maynard Keynes, 1883–1946: Economist, Philosopher, Statesman*, London: Macmillan.

Skidelsky, R. (2009), *Keynes: The Return of the Master*, London: Allen Lane.

Snowdon, B. and H. Vane (2005), *Modern Macroeconomics: Its Origins, Development and Current State*, Cheltenham, UK and Northampton, MA, USA: Edward Elgar.

Wood, J. H. (1980), 'Keynes and Friedman in historical perspective', in T. M. Havrilesky and J. T. Boorman (eds), *Current Issues in Monetary Theory and Policy*, Arlington Heights, IL: AHM Publishing Corporation, pp. 49–53.

10. Keynes after Sraffa and Kaldor: effective demand, accumulation and productivity growth

Alcino F. Camara-Neto and Matías Vernengo

INTRODUCTION

One of the most controversial propositions in macroeconomics is that the economy is driven by demand. In *The General Theory*, Keynes clearly argued that the system would fluctuate in the long run around a position considerably below full employment. In other words, he believed that the economy would settle below full employment, and that lack of demand, rather than a supply constraint, was the main cause for underemployment equilibrium. Some orthodox authors would deny that in all circumstances, but the conventional wisdom seems to accept that, whereas the proposition is correct in the short run, it cannot be taken seriously in the long run. In the long run, the supply constraint is inexorable.

It is particularly problematic that the conventional reading of Keynes assumes that unemployment can only result from some type of imperfection, typically some sort of price rigidity be that in the market for goods or in the so-called factor markets. Keynes correctly noted that only by abandoning the presupposition of a natural rate of interest would it be possible to establish his unemployment equilibrium in the long run. Piero Sraffa's critique of the marginalist theory of capital proved an essential piece of the argument against the natural rate of interest.

Yet, even after dealing with the question of unemployment equilibrium in the long run, Keynes's theory of effective demand did not contemplate the process of accumulation. Nicholas Kaldor was the central author extending the principle of effective demand to the long run. Kaldor's models developed from the mid-1960s onwards suggest that the Keynesian proposition is valid, not only the short run, but also in the long run. Most authors suggest that the thrust of the Kaldorian model lies in the super-multiplier (Dixon and Thirlwall 1975, p. 203). This chapter argues that without the so-called Kaldor-Verdoorn's Law (hereafter KVL) it is not possible to fully extend the Keynesian proposition to the long term, and, as a result, the KVL should be seen as central as the supermultiplier in the Kaldorian model. The KVL explains the rate of change of labour productivity, and, as a result, makes endogenous the change in the capacity limit of the economy.

The remainder of the chapter is divided into three sections. The following section discusses in what sense Keynes's principle of effective demand in *The General Theory* may be seen as a short run proposition, and to what extent it is amenable to be extended to the long run. Sraffa's work is shown to be central for an understanding of Keynes's long run theory of unemployment. The subsequent section analyses the relevance of the KVL, together with the supermultiplier, in providing the theoretical foundation for the principle of effective demand in the long run. The last section provides a brief discussion of policy implications of Sraffa's and Kaldor's extensions of Keynes's analysis.

THE CAPITAL CRITIQUE AND THE KEYNESIAN REVOLUTION

The conventional interpretation of the Keynesian Revolution, as it is consolidated in academia and in policy-making circles, implied that fiscal policy, in particular budget deficits, should be used in recessionary periods.[1] The ultimate cause of unemployment was to be seen in some sort of market imperfection, be that a rigidity of the rate of interest (as in the Liquidity Trap case) or the nominal wage.[2]

Careful reading of *The General Theory* should cast serious doubts regarding the conventional interpretation that emphasizes wage rigidities, since in Chapter 2 of his book Keynes tells us that 'the complete results of a change in money-wages are more complex, as we shall see in chapter 19', and those changes in wages are fully considered in that chapter (Keynes 1936, p. 12, n. 1). As a result, Keynes's arguments in Chapter 19 are not based on any type of price rigidity. Also, in Chapter 15 Keynes tells us 'after the rate of interest has fallen to a certain level, liquidity preference may become virtually absolute . . . [b]ut . . . I know of no example of it hitherto' (ibid., p. 207). In other words, a downward rigidity of the rate of interest, while possible in theory, was not in practice the cause of unemployment either. The rigidity or imperfectionist argument that came to be associated to Keynes's name, hence, has no basis in *The General Theory*.

Keynes recognized that 'it is on the effect of a falling wage and price level on the demand for money that those who believe in the self-adjusting quality of the economic system must rest the weight of their argument', in a mechanism that became known as the Keynes effect (ibid., p. 266). According to Keynes '. . . the reduction in the wages-bill . . . will diminish the need for cash for income and business purposes . . . reduce *pro tanto* the schedule of liquidity-preference . . . reduce the rate of interest and thus prove favourable to investment' (ibid., p. 263). Hence, Keynes clearly understood that price and wage flexibility might lead to full employment equilibrium.

Further, Pigou (1943) argued that wealth effects implied that deflation would lead to an expansion of consumption, and also push the economy towards full employment, usually referred to as the Pigou effect (Patinkin 1987). Keynes, however, emphasized that forces that moved the economic system away from full employment countered the self-adjusting forces created by deflation. In particular, a reduction in wages involved redistribution of income from workers to capitalists and would put pressure on 'those entrepreneurs who are heavily indebted . . . with severely adverse effects on investment' (Keynes 1936, pp. 262, 264).[3] It is important to note that Keynes's arguments against the so-called Keynes effect can also be extended to the Pigou effect.

The upshot of Keynes's discussion of the effects of price and wage flexibility in Chapter 19 of *The General Theory* is that there is no guarantee that the system would move towards full employment. Fundamentally, one would have to assume that the positive wealth effects would be systematically larger than the negative effects imposed by the burden of debt. Since there is no reason to believe that this is the only theoretically reasonable assumption, let alone whether that would be empirically relevant, Keynes concludes that:

> [We] oscillate, avoiding the gravest extremes of fluctuation in employment and prices in both directions, round an intermediate position appreciably below full employment and appreciably above the minimum employment a decline below which would endanger life. But we must not conclude that the mean position thus determined by . . . those tendencies which are likely to persist, failing measures expressly designed to correct them, is, therefore, established by laws of necessity. (ibid., p. 254)

In other words, full employment is a mere possibility, but the system has no necessary tendency towards it, and there is no reason to believe that under normal circumstances, and without government intervention, it would be achieved. Several different positions of equilibrium in the long run, determined by the persistent forces of the capitalist system, could be established, and *persistent* unemployment would be the norm.

Uncertainty would make things worse, but even if expectations were always fulfilled there would be no reason to believe that deflationary forces would make the system move towards full employment. Keynes emphasized that '. . . the extreme precariousness of the basis of knowledge in which our estimates of the prospective yield have to be made', implied that the system was unstable; but only under particular circumstances, when '. . . the capital development of the country becomes a by-product of the activities of a casino . . .' would instability be extremely harmful (ibid., p. 159).

In this sense, it is difficult to agree with Minsky's interpretation that Keynesian economics should be seen as the 'economics of permanent disequilibrium' (Minsky 1975, p. 68). In this context it is important to remember the often-quoted passage of *The General Theory* where Keynes tells us that '. . . it is an outstanding characteristic of the economic system in which we live that, whilst it is subject to severe fluctuations in respect of output and employment, it is not violently unstable' (Keynes 1936, p. 249).[4] This indicates that a great degree of steadiness, despite the existence of fundamental uncertainty, results from the existence of conventions and institutional arrangements that allow the system to be relatively stable.

In this sense, it seems clear that in *The General Theory* Keynes was able to show that in the long run the system has a tendency to get stuck at a position of equilibrium that is suboptimal. It also seems clear that the conventional view which assumes that Keynes moved from an interpretation of the system with flexible prices and fixed quantities in the *Treatise* to one of fixed prices and flexible quantities in *The General Theory*, as interpreted by Leijonhufvud (1968), is incompatible with a careful reading of Chapter 19 of the latter book (Amadeo 1989, p. 4).

However, even though *The General Theory*'s unemployment equilibrium is not a short run result in the sense that prices and wages are flexible, it is short run in the sense that the capital stock is fixed. In other words, the long run level of employment is determined for a given level of investment, but the effects of investment on productive capacity are not taken into consideration. Further, Keynes argued that investment was governed by *animal spirits*, '. . . a spontaneous urge to action rather than inaction' (Keynes 1936, p. 161). This implies that investment is seen as exogenous to the system and determined by individual initiative of entrepreneurs.[5]

Yet, in a somewhat contradicting view, Keynes argues that there is no '. . . material difference . . . between [his] schedule of the marginal efficiency of capital . . . and the demand curve for capital contemplated by some of the classical [sic] authors' (ibid., p. 179).[6] This view of investment as inversely related with the rate of interest is problematic for at least three reasons, two related to inconsistencies with the notion of capital implicit in the marginalist theory and one associated to the empirical evidence.

The capital debates, sparked to a great extent by Sraffa's revival of the surplus approach, have shown that reswitching and reverse capital deepening are possible, and, as a result, the marginalist view of an inverse relation between capital intensity and its remuneration is not valid. The point is that when capital is defined, not as a quantity measured in value of an amorphous factor of production, but as a produced means of production, then it is generally not possible to determine a univocal relation between the demand for capital and its price.[7] In that case, there is no guarantee that a reduction of the rate of interest would lead to higher investment and through the multiplier to the full employment level of savings.

It is important to note, in this context, that when confronted with the empirical evidence that there was no inverse relation between the remuneration of labour (real wages) and the quantity of labour demanded, Keynes was fast to get rid of the assumption of decreasing marginal returns.[8] Keynes suggests that Kalecki's assumption of constant returns seems more appropriate (Keynes, CW, vol. XIII, p. 405). Keynes's willingness to part with the marginalist labour demand schedule seems to indicate that, if similar problems were pointed out with respect to the demand schedule for capital, he would most likely feel inclined to abandon it, too.

Also, the critique of the marginalist theory of capital provides a theoretical basis for Keynes's rejection of the concept of a natural rate of interest (Keynes 1936, pp. 242–4). Keynes's acceptance of the notion of the marginal efficiency of capital implies that there is a sufficiently low interest rate that would be associated with an investment that would produce the full employment level of savings. Excluding imperfectionist arguments related to the downward rigidity of the interest rate, or the possibility that a negative interest rate would be required to increase investment to its full employment savings level, it would seem that the acceptance of the marginal efficiency of capital is in contradiction with the notion of a 'highly conventional' rate of interest (ibid., p. 203).[9]

The critique of the marginalist notion of capital shows that there is no logical basis for a real rate of interest determined by the productivity of capital, and shows that the limitations of the so-called loanable theory of interest are deeper than Keynes suspected. In that sense, Sraffa's critique of the neoclassical notion of capital is essential for the position, according to which

> There is no unique long-period position of equilibrium equally valid regardless of the character of the policy of the monetary authority. On the contrary there are a number of such positions corresponding to different policies. (Keynes, CW, vol. XXVII, pp. 54–5)

In other words, the long run equilibrium rate of interest is fundamentally associated to the policy regime controlled by the monetary authority, and that was the main reason for Keynes's advocacy of capital controls and a policy of relative low interest rates to promote the so-called euthanasia of the rentier.

But the fact that the rate of interest has little or no relation with investment does not mean that changes in the interest rate do not have any impact on the level of activity.[10] Pivetti observes that '. . . if money plays an important role in determining income distribution, it will also play an important role in the determination of the level and composition of output' (Pivetti 1985, p. 100). Keynes was perfectly aware of the effects of income distribution on the level of output. Referring to the effects of a fall in real wages Keynes argues that:

> The transfer from wage-earners to other owners of other factors is likely to diminish the propensity to consume. The effect of the transfer from entrepreneurs to rentiers is more open to doubt. But if rentiers represent on the whole the richer section of the community and those whose standard of living is least flexible, then the effect of this [real wage reduction on output] also will be unfavorable. (Keynes 1936, p. 262)

Also, a reduction in interest rates allows increasing private and public debt accumulation at sustainable levels, and, as a result, is provides a strong encouragement for demand expansion.[11] In other words, even though investment is not inversely related to the rate of interest, it is very likely that other components of aggregate demand are. However, in contrast to the marginalist theory of capital that suggests that a natural rate of interest generates the amount of investment that corresponds to full employment savings, the alternative based on Keynes implies that only under certain institutional conditions the rate of interest would be sufficiently low to stimulate aggregate demand and produce full employment.

Finally, if the theoretical reasons for rejecting the inverse relationship between capital intensity and the interest rate were not sufficient, it is relevant to note there is almost no empirical evidence for that proposition. Chirinko argues that '. . . the response of investment to price variables tends to be small and unimportant relative to quantity variables . . .,' that is, interest rates have little effect, and the level of activity is central (Chirinko 1993, p. 1906). Also, Blomström et al. (1996) show that in the correlation between investment and output growth causality seems to run from the former to the latter. This implies that the weight of the evidence favors the accelerator as an explanation of investment behaviour.[12]

It should be noted that the favourable evidence regarding the accelerator, and the absence of any evidence for a negative relation between investment and the interest rate, seems to indicate that the capital critique is empirically relevant. As noted by Petri (2003, p. 27) the inelasticity of investment with respect to the rate of interest not only suggests that res-witching and reverse capital deepening are sufficiently strong as to make the marginalist relation between abundance and remuneration inop-erative. Be that as it may, the lack of responsiveness of investment to the interest rate implies that the former cannot adjust to full employment savings, and that it must be explained exogenously by other variables (e.g. output change). In that sense, it seems reasonable to conclude that the extension of Keynes's theory of effective demand to the long run must involve the incorporation of the acceleration principle.

EXTENDING *THE GENERAL THEORY* TO THE LONG RUN

Nicholas Kaldor's work on growth incorporated the multiplier and the accelerator, and in many respects represents the main extension of the principle of effective demand to the long run (Vernengo and Rochon 2001). However, Kaldor only incorporated the idea of the supermultiplier, which is central in his extension of Keynes's theory, in the second half of the 1960s.

Kaldor's work on growth can be analytically separated into two distinc-tive phases (Targetti 1991). The young Kaldor, so to speak, was interested in distribution, and his models assumed, as a reasonable *stylized fact* of the post-war period, that full employment was the norm.[13] Kaldor's distribu-tion models solved Harrod's knife-edge instability problem, which implied that an actual growth rate beyond the warranted rate of growth (and the natural or full employment growth) would lead to a persistent divergence and ever-higher prices. In the Kaldorian model, an increase of the rate of growth above the level compatible with the full employment of resources would lead to a rise in prices, and a reduction in real wages. Given that the propensity to save out of profits is higher than the propensity to save out of wages, the reduction in real wages would have a negative effect on effective demand, reducing the rate of growth to the level compatible with a stable distribution of income (Kaldor 1955–6, p. 84).

In many respects, it might be argued that the Kaldorian distribution models remained within the confines of Say's Law, since they assumed full employment. However, Kaldor was a pragmatic theorist whose main methodological contribution to the critique of mainstream economics was the idea of *stylized facts*, broad regularities that models should incorporate and/or explain (Toner 1999, p. 120). Thus, by the mid-1960s his concerns had turned to 'the relatively slow rate of economic growth of Britain' (Kaldor 1966, p. 282).

The epistemological break occurred in 1966 with his famous inaugural lecture at the University of Cambridge on the causes of British economic decline (ibid.).[14] The mature Kaldor emphasizes the balance of payments constraint and its effects on labour productivity. The assumption of full employment is completely abandoned. The precise reasons for Kaldor's change of perspective are beyond the scope of this chapter, but one can speculate that the loss of the international reserve position by the pound, and the ensuing problems associated with the balance of payments were central for the development of his demand-led models.[15] Kaldor was mainly concerned that in Britain '. . . the maintenance of full employment might prove incompatible with a continued equilibrium in the balance of payments under a regime of fixed exchange rates' (Kaldor 1971, pp. 497–8).

In this context, an essential element of the Kaldor mark II models is the adoption of the Hicksian supermultiplier.[16] Kaldor (ibid., p. 505) argued that investment was not an exogenous element of demand, following the acceleration principle, and that:

> If we consider the problem in terms of the *growth rates* of demand, and not just in terms of the *levels* of demand, we can no longer treat the level of domestic investment as being autonomously determined; industrial investment will be all the greater the faster the demand for the products of industry is growing and the more fully its existing capacity is utilized (ibid.).

The solution involves the multiplier and the accelerator principles '. . . lumped together, in the notion of a supermultiplier to gauge the true effect of an increase in exogenous demand' (Kaldor 1983, p. 195).[17] The supermultiplier expresses the effect of autonomous spending on the level of output, taking into consideration the fact that productive capacity adjusts to demand.

In the sense that productive capacity is not fixed, the supermultiplier provides an apt extension of Keynes's principle of effective demand to the long run. The supermultiplier implies that the *level* of output, when productive capacity is fully adjusted to demand, is determined by the autonomous components of demand. However, the *rate of growth* of the productive capacity limit remains exogenous to the model. In other words, if the Kaldorian model ended there, productivity would be exogenous, and one would fall on '. . . the usual hypothesis . . . that the growth of productivity is mainly to be explained by the progress of knowledge in science and technology' (Kaldor 1966, p. 290).

The fundamental role of the KVL is to endogenize the rate of growth of labour productivity. The KVL suggests that there is a strong correlation between the growth of labour productivity and the rate of growth of economic activity.[18] It is only with the KVL that the *rate of growth* rather than the *level* of the productive capacity limit is determined by autonomous demand. In that sense, the inflationary barrier, the capacity limit that if exceeded would lead to inflation, is endogenously determined by demand. As autonomous demand expands, the capacity limit moves further away.[19]

This should not be interpreted as suggesting that demand-pull inflation cannot take place. If the rate of growth of demand outpaces the rate of growth of productivity the economy may very well hit the proverbial inflation barrier. In other words, the question of whether there will be a correlation between inflation and unemployment will depend on the size of coefficients, which might vary from period to period. It must be noted, also, that under certain conditions expansionary demand may be perfectly compatible with price stability, and with an inflation barrier that recedes as the economy grows.[20]

Kaldor was interested in the relative decline of the UK and, as a result, measured the Verdoorn's Law in a cross-section of countries.[21] He averaged out the rate of labour productivity and output growth between 1953–1954 and 1963–1964, and that was sufficient to deal with the cyclical fluctuation of both variables. This set the standards for the discussion and analysis of the KVL. However, nothing indicates that the KVL is not operational over time in a given economy. The reason for using a cross-section of countries and averaging out the data over relatively long periods seems to be related to the need of dealing with the trend effects of output on productivity. If one were to measure the KVL in time series one would have to separate cyclical and trend effects. In that case, one must deal with the cyclical properties of labour productivity and output.

It must be emphasized that the KVL when measured over time becomes intertwined with another well-known macroeconomic regularity, namely: Okun's Law. Okun argued that, in the United States, '. . . in the postwar period, on the average, each extra percentage point in the unemployment rate above four per cent has been associated with a three per cent decrement in real GNP' (Okun 1962, p. 99).[22] The relation implies that labour productivity, the ratio of output to employment, is pro-cyclical. This suggests that the proper consideration of both regularities implies that Okun's Law deals with the cyclical characteristics of the relation between demand growth and labour productivity, while KVL is related to the trend or structural elements of the same relationship.

The incorporation of the KVL's effect into the long run supermultiplier model implies that not only employment and accumulation, meaning the level of full capacity output growth, but also the rate of change of the capacity limit, associated with productivity growth, is ultimately determined by demand forces. If the Sraffian critique of capital theory freed the Keynesian model of the notion of a natural rate of interest, and allowed a long run equilibrium with unemployment, the Kaldorian model incorporating the supermultiplier and a theory of productivity growth provided a coherent alternative to the Ramsey-Solow-Lucas-Romer supply constrained approach to growth.

CONCLUDING REMARKS

Keynes believed that markets did not produce socially efficient outcomes, and that persistent unemployment could be a persistent characteristic of the economic system. The formal presentation of that idea was based on the principle of effective demand. Keynes emphasized that the novelty of his analysis, with respect to the marginalist model that preceded *The General Theory*, was that the level of income, rather than the rate of interest equilibrated investment and savings. For that reason he believed that the notion of a natural rate of interest should be abandoned.

The natural rate of interest is ultimately related to the marginalist theory of capital, and the notion of an inverse relation between investment and the rate of interest. For that reason, the understanding of the theoretical and empirical limitations of the neoclassical theory of capital, developed by Sraffa and his followers, is essential for providing support to Keynes's point about the possibility of unemployment equilibrium in the long run. The most successful adaptation of Keynes's ideas to the long run is based on the notion of a supermultiplier. Not only output is demand determined, but also capacity utilization adjusts to demand, according to supermultiplier models.

Yet, in these models the rate of change of the capacity limit is exogenous. Kaldor was instrumental in introducing the notion of Verdoorn's Law into supermultiplier models of economic growth. The central contribution associated to the interaction of demand-led growth models and the KVL is that they suggest that the capacity limit of the economy is endogenous. In a sense, it can be suggested that the KVL provides the demand side explanation for a variable capacity limit. The lack of evidence for a stable natural rate of unemployment (e.g. Fair 2000) suggests that, beyond the theoretical problems raised by the idea of the supply constraint, there is little empirical basis to use it as a guide for policy.

The policy implications of supermultiplier models that incorporate the KVL are pervasive, and they are the basis for the analysis of long-term Keynesian policies. For example, the current fears of fiscal expansionism and increasing budget deficits and public debt as a result of the so-called Great Recession are exaggerated, to say the least, according to this perspective. If excessive demand expansion had negative inflationary implications one would expect that a higher premium would be required for holding Treasury bonds. The fact that this did not take place, or for example in the aftermath of the Great Depression and World War II when the debt-to-GDP ratio in the United States reached the level of approximately 120 per cent, suggests that markets know better than mainstream economists.

In that sense, one might be tempted to believe that expanding demand is painless, and as some critics of long run Keynesian ideas would say, according to Keynesians we live in a world with no contradictions, in which full employment and better income distribution can be easily achieved. That is obviously far from the truth. However, the nature of the constraints faced by governments trying to expand demand is often misjudged. The two fundamental reasons for the inability to expand demand are, in the case of most countries, in particular developing ones, the balance of payments, and the social conflict associated with changes in income distribution.

In the case of developing countries that must import capital and intermediary goods in order to grow, demand cannot be expanded beyond its capacity to export and obtain hard currency without incurring external debt commitments. Even if international financial markets allow for growth beyond the current account limits in the short run, it must be noted that sooner or later exports would have to suffice not only to import the essentials for accumulation, but also to face the increasing demands of the debt burden. For no other reason debt crises are recurrent in developing countries.

Finally, in developed countries like the United States the balance of payments does not impose an overwhelming barrier to the expansion of demand. However, that does not imply that there are no limits to demand expansion. In fact, the recent financial crisis is a good example of the limitations that income distribution imposes on demand expansion. The ultimate causes of the crisis are associated to the significant changes over the last 30 years in income distribution, that have led to wage stagnation and increasing concentration of income and wealth at the top. In order to maintain their level of consumption most families have been forced to increase indebtedness in unsustainable levels, and as a result the American economy has been trapped in cycles of bubble-driven booms with subsequent and increasingly deeper busts.

A more sustainable expansion of demand would require a significant change in income distribution patterns, but those, alas, are not easy to promote without significant political support. Before the economy reaches its supply constraint, several contradictions impede the expansion of demand. Contrary to conventional wisdom, demand management policies are fraught with conflict, and do not imply that we live in the best of all possible worlds.

NOTES

1. It must be noted that Keynes does not directly talk about budget deficits in *The General Theory*, preferring to emphasize what he calls the socialization of investment (Keynes 1936, p. 378). In the discussions regarding budgetary policy during World War II, Keynes (Keynes, *Collected Writings* (CW), vol. XXVII, pp. 405–13), he emphasized the importance of separating the current budget from the capital budget, and the importance of maintaining the former balanced over the cycle, while the latter should be used for the long run objective of full employment.
2. Hicks (1937) and Modigliani (1944) are the key contributions in the ascent of the so-called neoclassical synthesis. In policy circles, there are at least two turning points accepted as marking the rise of Keynesian policies in the United States: first, after Roosevelt's recession of 1937–1938, when fiscal deficits became the central policy tool, and, second, the Kennedy-Johnson tax cut of 1964. By the 1970s, even Nixon would claim to be a Keynesian.
3. The Keynes effect depends on the negative relationship between investment and the rate of interest, and, as a result, is open to the capital debate critique. That is not the case with the Pigou effect. Kalecki (1944), in a direct response to Pigou, showed, similarly to Keynes, that in the case of a price decline the real value of currency and demand deposits increased, but that was offset partially or completely by the increase in the real burden of those that had borrowed from the banks. In other words, in a deflationary situation the burden of debt increased. Irving Fisher (1933) had also pointed out the negative effects of debt-deflation.
4. Interestingly enough, in this respect Minsky's position resembles Patinkin (1956), who insists that the Keynesian idea of unemployment equilibrium is incorrect and it should be correctly termed unemployment disequilibrium. For a discussion of Patinkin's views and his rejection of the neoclassical synthesis emphasis on wage rigidity see Rubin (2002).
5. For a modern interpretation along these lines that emphasizes the role of expectations, confidence and psychological factors in explaining the instability of the economic system see Akerlof and Shiller (2009). It is important to notice that Keynes seems to emphasize conventional rather than psychological forces in the determination of the long run rate of interest (Keynes 1936, p. 203).
6. By classical authors Keynes is, as it is well known, referring fundamentally to marginalist authors. In fact, even though he usually uses the term classical, in the page right before the above-mentioned quote Keynes, refers, more appropriately, to the neoclassical school (Keynes 1936, p. 177).
7. For example, if the price of a certain machine used in the production of a few consumption goods falls, one would expect that substitution effects would lead to increased demand for that machine. Depending on the elasticity of the demand for that machine, however, the income of the producer may fall, and if we assume that the producer demands consumer goods that are intensive in the use of that particular machine, then the fall in the price of the machine may ultimately lead to less demand for that machine. The income effect would be perverse and could more than compensate the substitution effect. The fact that the machine is a produced good used in the production of other goods generates an interdependence that invalidates the generality of the neoclassical views on scarcity and relative price. Davidson (1982, pp. 14–23) argues

that Post Keynesians emphasize income effects over substitution effects. Petri (2003) provides an overview of the Sraffian critique of neoclassical theory.

8. Dunlop (1938) and Tarshis (1939) had shown that real wages were positively correlated with output.

9. Sraffa (1960, p. 32) also suggests that the rate of interest could be determined exogenously to the system by the institutional arrangements of society. For the affinity of Keynes's and Sraffa's conception of the long-term rate of interest see Vernengo (2001, p. 350).

10. It cannot also be suggested that Keynes was primarily concerned with monetary policy and disregarded fiscal policy to a secondary plane (e.g. Tily 2006). Not only was Keynes committed to the so-called socialization of investment, which is clearly connected to some form of government fiscal action regarding investment, which seems to be the driving force behind his war efforts to separate the current from the capital budget, but also he seemed to be on board with Abba Lerner's functional finance (Colander 1984). In a letter to James Meade in April 1943 Keynes says that he '. . . read an interesting article by Lerner on deficit budgeting, in which he shows that, in fact, this does not mean an infinite increase in the national debt, since in course of time the interest on the previous debt takes the place of the new debt which would otherwise be required . . . His argument is impeccable.' This leaves little margin of doubt of where Keynes stood on the validity of functional finance (Keynes, CW, vol. XXVII, p. 320).

11. It is well known that the last three booms and busts of the North American economy have been associated to consumption-based expansions fuelled by private debt accumulation. For a discussion of some of the characteristics of the unsustainable patterns of the American expansion see Pollin (2003).

12. Keynes was not convinced by the accelerator principle, in his correspondence with Harrod, and tended to reject it (Keynes, CW, vol. XIV, pp. 321–50). However, it must be noted that from a theoretical point of view it does not affect the logic of effective demand whether investment is an autonomous or a derived demand. Also, the accelerator is perfectly compatible with the rejection of the marginalist notion of capital, which is central for the rejection of the notion of a natural rate of interest. From that point of view, it seems that it is perfectly compatible with Keynes's own theoretical framework.

13. Targetti (1991, p. 411) suggests that Kaldor's works from 1957 to 1962 should be seen as substantially different from those developed in the late 1960s and the 1970s. The early models also assume free competition, and a one-sector economy, which would be abandoned in later models. The distinction between Kaldor's early and mature work on growth are also discussed in Vernengo and Rochon (2001).

14. In the lecture, Kaldor suggested that labour shortage was the main cause of British sluggish growth, but as noticed by Thirlwall (1987, p. 85) he soon retracted that position arguing that the lack of export dynamism was behind the poor economic performance.

15. Also, one should not dismiss the influences of his teacher at the London School of Economics, Allyn Young, and his preoccupation with increasing returns, and his experience working with Gunnar Myrdal and Petrus Johannes Verdoorn at the Economic Commission for Europe (ECE), where he was introduced to the idea of cumulative causation and Verdoorn's econometric study. See Thirlwall (1987) for a discussion of these intellectual influences.

16. See Hicks (1950, p. 62).

17. For a more recent discussion of the supermultiplier see Bortis (1997) and Serrano (1995).

18. Verdoorn (1949, p. 59) argues that 'in the long run a change in the volume of production, say about 10 per cent, tends to be associated with an average increase in labor productivity of 4.5 per cent'. The Verdoorn coefficient close to 0.5 is also found in Kaldor's estimation of the law. Kaldor (1966, p. 289) reports a 0.484 coefficient.

19. It is interesting to note that at the same time that Kaldor was developing his model with a demand determined capacity limit, mainstream economics was reincorporating the idea of a very rigid supply constraint by incorporating Friedman's (1968) notion of a

natural rate of unemployment, the analogous situation in the labour market would be Wicksell's natural rate of interest that Keynes had dismissed. Most empirical models measure the natural rate of unemployment or the Non-Accelerating Inflation Rate of Unemployment (NAIRU) as dependent on the actual rate of unemployment, and as a result implicitly accept the notion that the demand policies that affect the current level of unemployment will affect the long-term unemployment level associated with stable inflation (e.g. Staiger et al. 2002). However, the theoretical justification for the inward shift of the Phillips Curve is often associated to changes in labour market behaviour, i.e. the increasing use of temporary workers and greater labour market flexibility, which led to reduced labour force bargaining power (Katz 1999). In other words, the capacity limit is still seen as exogenous and dependent on the labour market dynamics.

20. Also, inflation may arise from causes that are orthogonal to demand, for example cost-push pressures. In that sense, there is no reason to believe that there is a simple relation between the level of activity as reflected by unemployment, for example, and inflation. There is, in the Kaldorian extension of the Keynesian model no reason for believing in a stable Phillips curve, or a vertical one, or even a horizontal one. But under different circumstances all of the above may occur even though there is no systematic force shaping the relation between quantities and prices.

21. This is the same procedure utilized by Verdoorn (1949).

22. There is a second definition of Okun's Law that relates unemployment to the gap between actual and potential output (Okun 1962, p. 100). Jeon and Vernengo (2008) provide a simple empirical analysis of Okun and Verdoorn effects in the United States.

BIBLIOGRAPHY

Akerlof, G. A. and R. Shiller (2009), *Animal Spirits*, Princeton, NJ: Princeton University Press.

Amadeo, E. (1989), *Keynes's Principle of Effective Demand*, Aldershot, UK and Brookfield, VT, USA: Edward Elgar.

Blomström, M., R. Lipsey, and M. Zejan (1996), 'Is fixed investment the key to economic growth?', *Quarterly Journal of Economics*, **111**(1) (February), 269–76.

Bortis, H. (1997), *Institutions, Behavior and Economic Theory*, Cambridge: Cambridge University Press.

Chirinko, R. (1993), 'Business fixed investment spending', *Journal of Economic Literature*, **31**(4) (December), 1875–911.

Colander, D. (1984), 'Was Keynes a Keynesian or a Lernerian?', *Journal of Economic Literature*, **22**(4) (December), 1572–5.

Davidson, P. (1982), *International Money and the Real World*, London: Macmillan.

Dixon, R. J. and A. P. Thirlwall (1975), 'A model of regional growth rate differences on Kaldorian line', *Oxford Economics Papers*, **27**(2) (July), 201–14.

Dunlop, J. (1938), 'The movement of real and money wage rates', *Economic Journal*, **48**(191) (September), 413–34.

Fair, R. (2000), 'Testing the NAIRU model for the United States', *The Review of Economics and Statistics*, **82**(1) (February), 64–71.

Fisher, I. (1933), 'The debt-deflation theory of great depressions', *Econometrica*, **1**(4) (October), 337–57.

Friedman, M. (1968), 'The role of monetary policy', *American Economic Review*, **58**(1) (March), 1–17.

Hicks, J. R. (1937), 'Mr Keynes and the "classics": a suggested interpretation', *Econometrica*, **5**(2) (April), 147–59.

Hicks, J. R. (1950), *A Contribution to the Theory of the Trade Cycle*, Oxford: Clarendon Press.

Jeon, Y. and M. Vernengo (2008), 'Puzzles, paradoxes, and regulations: cyclical and structural productivity in the United States (1950–2005)', *Review of Radical Political Economy*, 40(3) (September), 237–43.

Kaldor, N. (1955–6), 'Alternative theories of distribution', *Review of Economic Studies*, **23**(2), 83–100.

Kaldor, N. (1966), 'Causes of the slow growth in the United Kingdom', in F. Targetti and A. P. Thirlwall (eds), *The Essential Kaldor*, London: Duckworth, pp. 282–310.

Kaldor, N. (1970), 'The case for regional policies', in F. Targetti and A. P. Thirlwall (eds), *The Essential Kaldor*, London: Duckworth, pp. 311–26.

Kaldor, N. (1971), 'Conflicts in national economic objectives', in F. Targetti and A. P. Thirlwell (eds), *The Essential Kaldor*, London: Duckworth, pp. 495–515.

Kaldor, N. (1983), 'Keynesian economics after fifty years', in F. Targetti and A. P. Thirlwall (eds), *The Essential Kaldor*, London: Duckworth, pp. 164–98.

Kalecki, M. (1944), 'Prof. Pigou on the classical stationary state: a comment', *Economic Journal*, **54**(213) (April), 131–2.

Katz, L. F., A. B. Krueger, G. Burtless, and W. T. Dickens (1999), 'The high-pressure US labor market of the 1990s', *Brookings Papers on Economic Activity*, **30**(1), 1–87.

Keynes, J. M. (1936), *The General Theory of Employment, Interest, and Money*, London: Macmillan.

Keynes, J. M. (1971–89), *The Collected Writings of John Maynard Keynes*, London: Macmillan/Cambridge University Press for the Royal Economic Society
Vol. XIII: *The General Theory and After*. Part I, *Preparation*
Vol. XIV: *The General Theory and After*. Part II, *Defence and Development*
Vol. XXVII: *Activities 1940–1946: Shaping the Post-War World: Employment and Commodities*

Leijonhufvud, A. (1968), *On Keynesian Economics and the Economics of Keynes*, New York: Oxford University Press.

Minsky, H. P. (1975), *John Maynard Keynes*, New York: Columbia University Press.

Modigliani, F. (1944), 'Liquidity preference and the theory of interest and money', *Econometrica*, **12**(1) (January), 45–88.

Okun, A. M. (1962), 'Potential GNP: its measurement and significance', in *Proceedings of the Business and Economics Statistics Section*, American Statistical Association, pp. 98–104.

Patinkin, D. (1956), *Money, Interest and Prices*, Evanston, IL: Row, Peterson.

Patinkin, D. (1987), 'Real balance effects', in J. Eatwell, M. Milgate, and P. Newman (eds), *The New Palgrave Dictionary of Economics*, London: Macmillan.

Petri, F. (2003), 'A Sraffian critique of general equilibrium theory, and the classical-Keynesian alternative', in F. Petri and F. Hahn (eds), *General Equilibrium: Problems and Prospects*, New York: Routledge, pp. 387–421.

Pigou, A. (1943), 'The classical stationary state', *Economic Journal*, **53**(212) (December), 343–51.

Pivetti, M. (1985), 'On the monetary explanation of distribution', *Political Economy*, **1**, 73–103.

Pollin, R. (2003), *Contours of Descent: US Economic Fractures and the Landscape of Global Austerity*, London: Verso.

Rubin, G. (2002), 'From equilibrium to disequilibrium: the genesis of Don Patinkin's interpretation of the Keynesian theory', *European Journal of History of Economic Thought*, **9**(2), 205–25.

Serrano, F. (1995), 'Long period effective demand and the Sraffian supermultiplier', *Contributions to Political Economy'*, **14**(1) (January), 67–90.

Sraffa, P. (1960), *Production of Commodities by Means of Commodities*, Cambridge: Cambridge University Press.

Staiger, D., J. Stock, and M. Watson (2002), 'Prices, wages and the US NAIRU in the 1990s', in A. Krueger and R. Solow (eds), *The Roaring Nineties*, New York: Russell Sage Foundation, pp. 3-60.

Targetti, F. (1991), 'Change and continuity in Kaldor's thought on growth and distribution', in E. J. Nell and W. Semmler (eds), *Nicholas Kaldor and Mainstream Economics*, New York: St Martin's Press.

Tarshis, L. (1939), 'Changes in real and money wages', *Economic Journal*, **49**(193) (March), 150–54.

Thirlwall, A. P. (1987), *Nicholas Kaldor*, New York: NYU Press.

Tily, G. (2006), 'Keynes's theory of liquidity preference and his debt management and monetary policies', *Cambridge Journal of Economics*, **30**(5) (September), 657–70.

Toner, P. (1999), *Main Currents in Cumulative Causation*, New York: St Martin's Press.

Verdoorn, P. J. (1949), 'Fattori che regolano lo sviluppo della produttività del lavoro', *L'industria*, **1**, 3–10.

Vernengo, M. (2001), 'Sraffa, Keynes and "The Years of High Theory"', *Review of Political Economy*, **13**(3), 343–54.

Vernengo, M. and L. P. Rochon (2001), 'Kaldor and Robinson on money and growth', *European Journal of the History of Economic Thought*, **8**(1), 75–103.

11. *The General Theory*, Marx, Marxism and the Soviet Union

Gilles Dostaler[1]

> When my new theory has been duly assimilated and mixed with politics and feelings and passions, I can't predict what the final upshot will be in its effect on action and affairs. But there will be a great change, and, in particular, the Ricardian foundations of Marxism will be knocked away.
>
> Keynes to George Bernard Shaw, 1 January 1935

> The boys, who cannot grow up to adult human nature, are beating the prophets of the ancient race – Marx, Freud, Einstein – who have been tearing at our social, personal and intellectual roots, tearing them with an objectivity which to the healthy animal seems morbid, depriving everything, as it seems, of the warmth of natural feeling.
>
> Keynes, 'Einstein', *The New Statesman and Nation*, 21 October 1933

INTRODUCTION

There is a huge literature concerning the impact of Keynes's *General Theory* on the evolution of economic theory, as well as on the development of public policy in the capitalist countries in the postwar period. In the following pages, we will examine the relations between *The General Theory* – which Keynes announced would knock away the Ricardian foundations of Marxism – Marx, Marxists and the first country whose government claimed to draw upon Marxism, the Soviet Union. The importance of *The General Theory* was such that it could not leave Marxism indifferent, or unscathed. This, of course, requires that we devote a few words to the complex love-hate relationship between Keynes and Marx. We will begin by recalling the debate between Keynes and George Bernard Shaw over Marx and Stalin, which raises the issue of the 'Ricardian foundations of Marxism'. We will then examine the significance of this expression, and show that therein lays a contradiction, as Marx is considered at the same time a non-classical economist and a precursor of the theory of effective demand. We will see that Keynes explicitly borrows some of Marx's formulation when he elaborates his 'monetary theory of production'. From there, we will turn our attention to the more basic questions of the nature of money, the love of money, and the drive to accumulation, where we will find Keynes, Marx and Freud in the same camp. We will then look at a different, but related subject, the impact of *The General Theory*, first on Marxism in Western countries, and subsequently in the Soviet Union and its satellites. Of course, the view of Marx, as of Keynes, we will discover here is quite different from the one discussed earlier in the chapter. 'Keynesianism' should not be confused with Keynes's thought. As we know, on at least one occasion, Keynes said that he was the only 'non-Keynesian' present. On a few occasions, Marx also distanced himself from Marxism. Finally we will introduce a section on Keynes's attitude towards Russia and the Soviet Union, where his wife was born and raised. We will see that his attitude towards the Soviet Union was as complex and evolutionary as his relationship with Marx.[2]

KEYNES AND MARX'S POLITICAL VISION: SHAW AND STALIN

In *The New Statesman and Nation*, in the autumn of 1934, a controversy centred on Marxism and Stalin opposed Keynes, and his friends H. G. Wells and George Bernard Shaw. On 27 October the periodical (Keynes chaired the Board of Directors) published the text of an interview between Stalin and H. G. Wells. On 10 November, Keynes replied to a comment added by George Bernard Shaw to this interview, writing: 'Shaw and Stalin are still satisfied with Marx's picture of the capitalist world, which had very much verisimilitude in his day but is unrecognisable, with the rapid flux of the modern world, three-quarter of a century later. They look backwards to what capitalism was, not forward to what it is becoming' (Keynes, *Collected Writings* (CW), vol. XXVIII, item 2, pp. 32–3).[3] Furthermore, as he wrote to the Editor on 24 November, 'I suspect that Bernard Shaw's preference for tyrants is mainly due to his being impressed with the difficulties of persuasion. It is easier to persuade a tyrant to adopt one's policy than to persuade the democracy' (Keynes, CW, vol. XXVIII, item 3, p. 36).

According to Keynes, in the era of Marx, power in society was held by capitalists – the leaders of the City and the captains of industry – at the expense of the previous aristocratic and land-owning régime. But now that power was passing from them by 'a peaceful process of evolution' to a class of wage-earners, which was not the proletariat: 'Thus, for one reason or another, Time and the Joint Stock Company and the Civil Service have silently brought the salaried class into power. Not yet

a Proletariat. But a Salariat, assuredly. And it makes a great difference'
(ibid., p. 34). Revolution, adds Keynes, is against personal power, but 'in
England to-day no one has personal power' (ibid.). The party representing
the interest of this Salariat is the Labour Party: 'In this country hence-
forward power will normally reside with the Left. The Labour Party will
always have a majority' (ibid., p. 36). Of course, Keynes was not proven
right, at least for some time. In that same year the Labour Party adopted
a new platform, 'For Socialism and Peace'. Its most radical aspects would
be dropped after the 1935 electoral defeat, and the new 1937 programme
would be known as 'Labour's Immediate Programme'. The latter borrowed several elements from the Keynesian approach. However, it was not
until 1944, with the adoption of a document prepared by Hugh Dalton,
Evan Durbin and Hugh Gaitskell, called 'Full Employment and Fiscal
Policy', that the objective of full employment, and the methods proposed
by Keynes to bring it about would be definitively adopted by the Labour
Party, the day before its first majority victory. It would thus take nearly
ten years for Labour to obtain his first majority, and launch the Keynesian
revolution in Great Britain.

Of Marx's *Capital*, Keynes wrote in 1925, coming back from his honey-
moon in the USSR:

> How can I accept a doctrine which sets up as its bible, above and beyond criti-
> cism, an obsolete economic textbook which I know to be not only scientifically
> erroneous but without interest or application for the modern world? How can I
> adopt a creed which, preferring the mud to the fish, exalts the boorish proletar-
> iat above the bourgeois and the intelligentsia who, with whatever faults, are the
> quality in life and surely carry the seeds of all human advancement? (Keynes,
> CW, vol. IX, item 1, p. 258)

He appreciated Engels more: 'But I've made another shot at old K.M. last
week, reading the Marx–Engels correspondence just published, without
making much progress. I prefer Engels of the two . . . But if you tell me
that they discovered a clue to the economic riddle, still I am beaten – I
can discover nothing but out-of-date controversialising' (letter to George
Bernard Shaw, 1 January 1935, Keynes, CW, vol. XXVIII, item 5, p. 42).
In a letter to Shaw on 2 December 1934, Keynes compared *Das Kapital* to
the *Koran*:

> My feelings about *Das Kapital* are the same as my feelings about the *Koran*. I
> know that it is historically important and I know that many people, not all of
> whom are idiots, find it a sort of Rock of Ages and containing inspiration. Yet
> when I look into it, it is to me inexplicable that it can have this effect . . . How
> could either of these books carry fire and sword round half the world? (Keynes,
> CW, vol. XXVIII, item 4, p. 38)

MARX AS A CLASSICAL ECONOMIST

A new book was needed to describe the functioning and the problems of the new form of capitalism. Keynes first thought that *A Treatise on Money*, published in 1930, would be this book. But as soon as it was published, he felt dissatisfied, writing to his mother on 14 September: 'Artistically, it is a failure – I have changed my mind too often during the course of it to be a proper unity' (Keynes, CW, vol. XIII, item 1, p. 176). In reality, the theory advanced in this massive two-volume book, with its hypothesis of full employment and emphasis on price movements, did not supply the weapons necessary to rationalize the interventionist policies that Keynes advocated, from the middle of the 1920s, within the British Liberal Party. The ink of this book hardly dried, Keynes embarks on the writing of a revised version, which will finally become a new book. His young friends and disciples of the Cambridge 'Circus' would contribute to the elaboration of the ideas of his new book. Keynes, who was not afraid of criticism, would allow himself to be influenced by severe comments from Ralph Hawtrey, Dennis Robertson, and even Friedrich Hayek.

At the time of the debate on Marxism mentioned above, Keynes had started sending chapters of his new book to the printers, using the proofs for his Cambridge lectures, which were now called 'The general theory of employment'. This is the context in which he wrote to his friend George Bernard Shaw on 1 January 1935: 'To understand *my* state of mind, however, you have to know that I believe myself to be writing a book on economic theory which will largely revolutionise – not, I suppose, at once but in the course of the next ten years – the way the world thinks about economic problems.' Virginia Woolf related having lunch with Maynard and Lydia during which Keynes's work was discussed. She described in the 6 January 1935 entry of her diary her friend's 'gigantic boast' as follows: 'M. own letter said that he thinks he has revolutionised economics; in the new book he is writing. "Wait ten years, & let it absorb the politics & the psychology & so on that will accrue to it; & then you'll see – the old Ricardo system will be exposed; & the whole thing set on a new footing." This he wrote in so many words: a gigantic boast; true I daresay' (Woolf 1982, vol. 4, p. 272). As to confirm Virginia Woolf's impression, Keynes ends his letter to Shaw with these provocative words: 'I can't expect you, or anyone else, to believe this at the present stage. But for myself I don't merely hope what I say, in my own mind I'm quite sure' (Keynes, CW, vol. XIII, item 4, pp. 492–3).

The first of three mentions of Marx in *The General Theory* takes place in a note of the very short first chapter: '"The classical economists" was a name invented by Marx to cover Ricardo and James Mill and their *predecessors*, that is to the founders of the theory which culminated in the Ricardian economics' (Keynes, CW, vol. VII, p. 3).[4] Keynes adds that he includes in this group the followers of Ricardo, '(for example) J. S. Mill, Marshall, Edgeworth and Prof. Pigou' (ibid.). Now, this makes for very surprising bedfellows, since we learn in other writings that Keynes includes Marx among the classical economists.

Keynes gives some important clarification in the autobiographical paper read to the Bloomsbury Memoir Club, in 1938. Writing about his 'early beliefs', while he was an active Apostle,[5] he recalls the importance for him and his friends of Moore's *Principia Ethica*, published in 1903. He presents Moore's vision of good, taken from the chapter 'The Ideal', as a religion, that still appears to him, 30 years later, as the right religion, still closer to the truth than the others with which he was then not familiar: 'It was a purer, sweeter air by far than Freud cum Marx. It is still my religion under the surface' (Keynes, CW, vol. X, item 2, p. 442). He also contrasts this view with Jeremy Bentham. An influential thinker, philosopher, jurist, politician and economist, Bentham founded his doctrine on the conviction that individuals rationally calculate pleasure and pain, maximizing their satisfaction according to the principle of psychological hedonism. A friend of Ricardo, James Mill and Malthus, Bentham was an important influence on both classical and neoclassical economics. Importantly, the fundamental intuitions of *Principia Ethica* allowed Keynes and his friends to free themselves of the Benthamite tradition, which he now considered 'the worm which has been gnawing at the insides of modern civilization and is responsible for its present moral decay' (ibid., p. 445).

Bentham's perspective constituted the philosophic foundation for classical economics. Moreover, according to Keynes, by overvaluing economic calculations in human affairs, it worked to the detriment of Moore's ideals. It was, in his view, at the same time the basis of Marxism, which he considered as the *reductio ad absurdum* of Benthamism. Marx, as much as Ricardo, overestimated the importance of the economic factor. This is the meaning of the 'Ricardian foundations of Marxism' that Keynes intended to knock away in his book. Two years before its publication, he wrote that Marxism, like laissez-faire economics, originated in Benthamite utilitarianism. Marx was inspired by Ricardo, whose economic determinism he adopted: 'Indeed, Marxism is a highly plausible inference from the Ricardian economics, that capitalistic individualism cannot possibly work in practice' (Keynes, CW, vol. XIII, item 3, p. 488).[6] In this latter paper, derived from a radio broadcast in which he declared himself a heretic, Keynes claimed that Marxism was a form of orthodoxy. In his reply to Shaw, already quoted, he wrote that, like conservatism, communism 'enormously overestimates the significance of the economic problem. The economic problem is not too difficult to solve. If you leave it to me, I will look after it' (Keynes, CW, vol. XXVIII, item 2, p. 34).[7]

Similar ideas are developed in conferences given at Oxford in 1924 and Berlin in 1926 and published by Hogarth Press that same year as *The End of Laissez-Faire* (Keynes, CW, vol. IX, item 2). *Laissez-faire* and classical liberalism are identified by Keynes in this work with conservatism. A foundation of classical political economy of which Ricardo is the principal representative, *laissez-faire* economics is born out of the combination of two currents of thought: conservative individualism and democratic socialism, or egalitarianism. This apparent oxymoron permitted economists to associate private gain with public good. Individualism and *laissez-faire* thus became, and remain in Keynes's time, the Church of Great Britain.

MARX AS A NON-CLASSICAL ECONOMIST

Thus, the classical citadel, from which Keynes, with difficulty, liberated himself, and which he attacked in *The General Theory*, appears to include Marx and Marxism, though not without some contradiction. In the two other allusions to him in *The General Theory*, Marx is opposed to an important idea of the classical tradition in economics: Say's Law of Markets, according to which aggregate supply creates its own demand. The consequence of this law is the absence of involuntary unemployment. For Ricardo and his disciples, the free play of markets leads automatically to full employment. The classical economists are thus not interested in what determines the level of employment, but by the distribution of this employment. According to Keynes, this vision dominated economics for more than a century. Against this, he set out the new theory of effective demand that is formulated in *The General Theory*, and founded among other ideas on the concept of the propensity to consume. Whenever income increases, demand for consumer goods increases, but not in the same proportion. Very few economists did not accept Say's Law; Marx was among them. While Chapter 2 is devoted to the criticism of the classical theory, Chapter 3 gives a first version of Keynes's theory of effective demand, which 'could only live on furtively, below the surface, in the underworlds of Karl Marx, Silvio Gesell or Major Douglas' (Keynes, CW, vol. VII, p. 32). Of course, this recognition resembles a kiss of Judas, since Keynes put Marx on the same footing as two rather obscure economists.[8] Allergic to Marx's political vision, Keynes has more sympathy for Gesell's view, of which he wrote: 'The purpose of the book [Gesell's *The Natural Economic Order*] as a whole may be described as the establishment of an anti-Marxian socialism, a reaction against *laissez-faire* built on theoretical foundations totally unlike those of Marx in being based on a repudiation instead of an acceptance of the classical hypotheses, and on an unfettering of competition instead of its abolition. I believe the future will learn more from the spirit of Gesell than from that of Marx' (ibid., p. 355).

Marx, however, is a most renowned and articulate critic of Say's Law of markets. It was with Marx that unemployment fully entered economic analysis, and was presented as one of capitalism's main phenomena, illustrating the contradictions of an economic and social transitory system, inevitably destined to disappear. Far from being accidental, unemployment, like the economic crises with which it is linked, is a necessity, a fundamental aspect of capitalism. In *Wage-Labour and Capital*, Marx affirmed that 'the industrial war of the capitalists among themselves . . . has the peculiarity that its battles are won less by recruiting than by discharging the army of labour' (Marx 1848, p. 266). The presence of the term 'army' almost 20 years before the publication of Volume I of *Capital* is noteworthy. The description of unemployment as an 'industrial reserve army', which grows or contracts according to the phases of the business cycle, is one of Marx's most famous metaphors.[9] It encapsulates the idea, already present in mercantilism and found in Keynes and his disciples, of the link between pressures on wages and unemployment. For Marx, the industrial reserve army is essential for maintaining profit rates and thus to the very existence of capitalism. Keynes's young friend and disciple Joan Robinson wrote: 'I see at a glance that Keynes is showing that unemployment is going to be a very tough nut to crack, because it is not just an accident – it has a function. In short, Keynes put into my head the very idea of the reserve army of labour that my supervisor had been so careful to keep out of it' (Robinson 1953, p. 265).

Keynes's main effort in economic theory consisted in trying to demonstrate that the problem of unemployment could be resolved within capitalism by supplying a different explanation, one challenging the neoclassical approach. According to Joan Robinson, Keynes would have arrived at the theory of effective demand sooner if he had started from Marx and not from orthodox theory. For her, Michal Kalecki was lucky to never have been exposed to classical theory and to have known only Marx and Rosa Luxemburg.[10] This is why he arrived more quickly at a similar and in some regards superior theory to that of Keynes:

> Kalecki had one great advantage over Keynes – he had never learned orthodox economics . . . The only economics he had studied was Marx. Keynes could never make head or tail of Marx . . . But starting from Marx would have saved him a lot of trouble. Kahn, at the 'circus' where we discussed the *Treatise* in 1931, explained the problem of saving and investment by imagining a cordon round the capital-good industries and then studying the trade between them

and the consumption-good industries; he was struggling to rediscover Marx's schema. Kalecki began at that point. (Robinson 1964, pp. 95–6)[11]

This did not seem to convince Keynes. When Joan Robinson published *An Essay on Marxian Economics* in 1942, one of the first works sympathetic to Marx written by a member of the academic establishment, Keynes wrote to her on 20 August:

> I found it [your book on Marx] most fascinating . . . This is in spite of the fact that there is something intrinsically boring in an attempt to make sense of what is in fact not sense . . . I am left with the feeling, which I had before on less evidence, that he had a penetrating and original flair but was a very poor thinker indeed, – and his failure to publish the later volumes probably meant that he was not unaware of this himself. (Dostaler 2007, p. 94)

THE MONETARY THEORY OF PRODUCTION

Joan Robinson was wrong when she wrote that 'Keynes could never make head or tail of Marx'. Not only did he read, while preparing *The General Theory*, a book by H. L. McCracken (1933) presenting Marx's theory of value and crises, but we have reasons to believe that he read at least part of *Capital*,[12] and that his opinion of Marx's insights were somewhat different from what he wrote probably as a provocation towards his young friends. To his students, in particular, he was much more positive. Each autumn he gave a series of lectures called 'The Pure Theory of Money', the title of the first volume of the *Treatise*.[13] On 10 October 1932, during the first lecture of the Michaelmas term, he declared to his students: 'Gentlemen, the change in the title of these lectures – from "The pure theory of money" to "The monetary theory of production" – is significant' (L. Tarshis, 'The Keynesian revolution in the 1930s', unpublished manuscript quoted by Skidelsky 1992, p. 460).[14] Such was the title that he then decided to give to what would become *The General Theory of Employment, Interest, and Money*. He also gave this title to a short but important paper published the following year in the *Festschrift* in honour of Arthur Spiethoff (Keynes CW, vol. XIII, item 2).

To his students, he explained the important differences between a pure exchange economy, which is the object of classical economics, and a monetary or entrepreneur economy. In the second, money plays an active role in the economy. Here it is the quantity theory, with its view of the neutrality of money, which is the villain.[15] It is here that Marx enters the scene. Keynes explained that his objective was henceforth to explain the level of production in a monetary economy. This expression does not refer to the customary distinction between a barter and a money economy. In the latter, money is only a means to carry out exchanges. Marx, he recognized, escaped this error by distinguishing between the circulation of commodities and the circulation of capital. He understood well the difference between a real-exchange economy and a monetary economy with his distinction between the formula of commodity circulation C-M-C', and that of capital circulation M-C-M', where M represents money and C commodities. Here is what we read in a draft of Chapter 2 dated from 1933 and entitled 'The distinction between a co-operative economy and an entrepreneur economy':

> The distinction between a co-operative economy and an entrepreneur economy bears some relation to a pregnant observation made by Karl Marx.. . .He pointed out that the nature of production in the actual world is not, as economists seem often to suppose, a case of C-M-C', i.e. of exchanging commodity (or effort) for money in order to obtain another commodity (or effort). That may be the standpoint of the private consumer. But it is not the attitude of *business*, which is a case of M-C-M', i.e. of parting with money for commodity (or effort) in order to obtain more money. (Keynes, CW, vol. XXIX, item 1, p. 81)

Keynes adds in a footnote that Marx explained that the difference between M' and M, the surplus value, is negative in periods of depression and crisis:

> Marx, however, was approaching the intermediate truth when he added that the continuous excess of M' would be inevitably interrupted by a series of crises, gradually increasing in intensity, or entrepreneur bankruptcy and underemployment, during which, presumably, M must be in excess. My own argument, if it is accepted, should at least serve to effect a reconciliation between the followers of Marx and those of Major Douglas, leaving the classical economists still high and dry in the belief that M and M' are always equal. (ibid., p. 82)

Keynes treated this subject in his second lecture of Michaelmas term, on 23 October 1933. Notes by Robert Bryce contain elaborate references to Marx and the difference between the C-M-C' formula and the M-C-M' formula:

> The economist thinks of C-M-C' while the businessman actually is interested in M-C-M'. M' minus M, Keynes thinks, is the source of Marx's surplus value. Marx says that when M' tended to exceed M, the capitalists get so much purchasing power that there is not enough balance or remaining for buying commodities. A crisis than develops, M'-M goes negative and capitalists lose heavily. There is a kernel of truth in Marx's theory. (Rymes 1989, p. 93)

Except in period of crisis, economies tended to inflation in Marx's time. They now tend to be deflationary and thus Keynes believes the tendency is for M' to be generally less than M,[16] and not, as for classical economists, M' = M. This Keynes links explicitly to fluctuations in effective demand. According to Tarshis, 'under capitalism, Marx pointed out production is carried so that money investment in labour and goods will produce more money' (ibid., p. 94). In Fallgatter's notes, we read: 'Therefore, Marx's view is right' (ibid., p. 95).

THE LOVE OF MONEY AS A PATHOLOGY[17]

We can thus see important points where ideas developed by Keynes in *The General Theory* intersect with some of Marx's main theses: the reserve army of labour and involuntary unemployment, schemes of reproduction and effective demand, the rejection of Say's Law and of the quantity theory of money, the characteristics of a monetary production economy as opposed to a real exchange economy. To this, we should add the falling rate of profit, and the decreasing marginal efficiency of capital; the relation between the rate of profit, and the rate of interest. Even the labour theory of value, which Joan Robinson considers as an irrelevant issue (Robinson 1948, p. 110), is viewed by Keynes with sympathy:

> I sympathise, therefore, with the pre-classical doctrine that everything is *produced* by *labour* . . . It is preferable to regard labour, including, of course, the personal services of the entrepreneur and his assistants, as the sole factor of production, operating in a given environment of technique, natural resources, capital equipment and effective demand. This partly explains why we have been able to take the unit of labour as the sole physical unit which we require in our economic system, apart from units of money and of time. (Keynes, CW, vol. VII, p. 214)[18]

The General Theory and *Capital*, as against classical and neoclassical tradition, thus integrate the real and the monetary, even if it is not in the same manner, and, even if Marx, in a certain way, remains closer to the classical tradition than Keynes. But, beyond the relation between the real and the monetary, lies the question of the nature of money, and of the relations of human beings with this mysterious, many-sided, symbolic as well as real, object, relations which plunge into the depths of psychology.

Keynes and Marx had, on a personal level, very different relations with money. Marx was short of it all his life and was constantly helped by his friend, the gentleman revolutionary Friedrich Engels,[19] to whom he wrote, after having finished the manuscript of *A Contribution to the Critique of Political Economy*, on 21 January 1859: 'I don't suppose anyone has ever written about "money" when so short of the stuff. Most *autores* on this

SUBJECT have been on terms of the utmost amity with THE SUBJECT OF THEIR RESEARCHES' (Marx and Engels 1983, p. 250; words in capitals in English in the orginal German text).[20] Keynes was most certainly at peace with the subject of his research. He made a lot of money through speculation and his writings, and left at his death a fortune estimated at about 12 million in today's euros.

Despite their different personal experience, both had the same vision of money, of money making and of the pathological relations of human beings with money. Money is of course a standard of value and a means of exchange. But it is also an object of desire, which is accumulated for its own sake. Aristotle, for whom Keynes as well as Marx had the greatest admiration, coined the term 'chrematistic' to designate the accumulation of money wealth, and thought it was unnatural and dangerous for the stability and future of society. Of the love of money, Keynes said in diverse occasions that it was the moral problem of our time. Coming back from his trip in the USSR in 1925, he wrote that Bolshevism had one virtue: it had displaced the love of money from the central position it occupies in capitalism. In Russia, motivation based on monetary considerations ceased to dictate social action: 'But in the Russia of the future it is intended that the career of money-making, as such, will simply not occur to a respectable young man as a possible opening, any more than the career of a gentleman burglar or acquiring skill in forgery and embezzlement' (Keynes, CW, vol. IX, item 1, p. 260). This constitutes 'a tremendous innovation' (ibid., p. 261) while 'modern capitalism is absolutely irreligious, without internal union, without much public spirit, often, though not always, a mere congeries of possessors and pursuers' (ibid., p. 267).

The love of money is associated with saving and thrift, the postponement of consumption to an indefinite future, abstinence, the refusal of pleasure. Here, economics joins Victorian morality, against which Keynes, and his friends in the Bloomsbury Group struggled, from the outset of the century. Keynes associated Puritanism with the praise of savings. To this is linked, at a theoretical level, the classical vision of interest as a reward for abstinence, which Keynes would replace by the view of interest as the price of renouncing liquidity.

We find analogous ideas in Marx, in the Marxian vision of the accumulating capitalist as 'personified capital . . . Fanatically bent on making value expand itself, he ruthlessly forces the human race to produce for production's sake' (Marx 1867, p. 649). There is, in the capitalist, 'a Faustian conflict between the passion for accumulation, and the desire for enjoyment' (ibid., p. 651).[21] For Marx, as for Keynes, it is the hoarder who is immoral and guilty: neglect of productive as well as recreative arts, accumulation for accumulation, profits for profits, work for work. We must remark here that the relation between savings and investment is different between our two authors. For Keynes, they have to be adjusted as they are the results of the decisions of different categories of agents. For Marx, it is the capitalists who are the real savers, and they must not be confused with Harpagon or Midas, the avaricious:

> Our hoarder is a martyr to exchange-value, a holy ascetic seated at the top of a metal column. He cares for wealth only in its social form, and accordingly he hides it away from society. He wants commodities in a form in which they can always circulate and he therefore withdraws them from circulation. He adores exchange-value and he consequently refrains from exchange. The liquid form of wealth and its petrification, the elixir of life and the philosophers' stone are wildly mixed together like an alchemist's apparitions. His imaginary boundless thirst for enjoyment causes him to renounce all enjoyment. Because he desires to satisfy all social requirements, he scarcely satisfies the most urgent physical wants. While clinging to wealth in its metallic corporeality the hoarder reduces it to a mere chimaera. (Marx 1859, p. 134)

Keynes deprecated men of money, thought them inferior to artists and scientists, hoped and prayed for 'the euthanasia of the rentier' (Keynes, CW, vol. VII, p. 376), and considered the love of money a pathology, one which, nevertheless, constituted capitalism's most powerful motive. In an ideal society, 'The love of money as a possession – as distinguished from the love of money as a means to the enjoyments and realities of life – will be recognized for what it is, a somewhat disgusting morbidity, one of those semi-criminal, semi-pathological propensities which one hands over with a shudder to the specialists in mental disease' (Keynes, CW, vol. IX, item 4, p. 329). Among those specialists in mental disease, Keynes certainly thought of Freud, of whose views on money he was very familiar. Here is what he wrote about a novel by H. G. Wells:

> Unless they have the luck to be scientists or artists, they fall back on the grand substitute motive, the perfect *ersatz*, the anodyne for those who, in fact, want nothing at all – money . . . Clissold and his brother Dickon, the advertising expert, flutter about the world seeking for something to which they can attach their abundant libido. But they have not found it. They would so like to be apostles. But they cannot. They remain business men. (Keynes, CW, vol. IX, item 3, pp. 319–20)

But there is something more profound here, and it is the death instinct. To love money is infantile and can conjure a fear of death in the person who succumbs to it. Capitalism, a system founded on the love of money, has proven itself incapable of confronting the question of death. It can only survive through accumulation, 'so that the thought of ultimate loss which often overtakes pioneers, as experience undoubtedly tells us and them, is put aside as a healthy man puts aside the expectation of death' (Keynes, CW, vol. VII, p. 162). Death is inexorable, but money, which Keynes describes as 'above all, a subtle device for linking the present to the future' (ibid., p. 294), acts as a shield from the inevitable:

> The 'purposive' man is always trying to secure a spurious and delusive immortality for his acts by pushing his interest in them forward into time. He does not love his cat, but his cat's kittens; nor, in truth, the kittens, but only the kittens' kittens, and so on forward for ever to the end of catdom. For him jam is not jam unless it is a case of jam tomorrow and never jam today. Thus by pushing his jam always forward into the future, he strives to secure for his act of boiling it an immortality. (Keynes CW, vol. IX, item 4, p. 330)

Paradoxically, as illustrated by the myth of Midas, this accumulation of money leads to death. Midas obtained from the God that all that he touched transformed itself into gold. Consequently, the food and drinks that he touched were transformed in gold, and he was in danger of dying on his gold pile. In the same manner, the indefinite accumulation of monetary wealth may lead society to its ruin. The desire for liquidity is morbid, an instinct that leads to death. And yet, it is because we fear death that we desire liquidity. We approach death even as we believe to be fighting against it; we drown as we attempt to cross the river of time in a leaking raft.

In spite of all this, money is the motor of capitalism and accumulation is unavoidable. Borrowing this time from Freud's theory of sublimation, Keynes explains how the neurotic quest for money helps to channel aggressive and sadistic instincts:

> Moreover, dangerous human proclivities can be canalised into comparatively harmless channels by the existence of opportunities for money-making and private wealth, which, if they cannot be satisfied in this way, may find their outlet in cruelty, the reckless pursuit of personal power and authority, and other forms of self-aggrandisement. It is better that a man should tyrannise over his bank balance than over his fellow-citizens; and whilst the former is sometimes denounced as being but a means to the latter, sometimes at least it is an alternative. (Keynes, CW, vol. VII, p. 374)

Accumulation is of course at the center of Marx's vision of the development of capitalism. The capitalist hears from the sky: 'Accumulate, accumulate! That is Moses and the prophets' (Marx 1867, p. 652). He has no choice. Competition, which is the way of life capitalism, compels him to accumulate. Accumulation is the source of enrichment, of progress, of technological changes. But at the same time, it leads capitalism to death. The source of progress is at the same time the source of decay: 'Accumulation of wealth at one pole is, therefore, at the same time accumulation of misery, agony of toil, slavery, ignorance, brutality, mental degradation, at the opposite pole, i.e., on the side of the class that produces its own product in the form of capital' (ibid., p. 709). This was clearly seen by Joseph Schumpeter who said that one of the great discoveries of Marx is to have understood that the origin of crisis lies in the process of capitalist development. The overthrow of capitalism and its replacement by socialism is the only path out of this system. The main difference between Marx and Keynes is that the first believed that crisis will inexorably lead to the end of capitalism and its replacement by socialism, as the second believed that capitalism could be reformed. But even here, nuance is required. At the end of his life, Marx wrote about a possible pacific transition to socialism, which led Hollander (2008) to call him the first revisionist. And, on different occasions, Keynes evoked a 'socialism of the future' which is sometimes called social-liberalism or liberal socialism. Notably things were understood differently in Marxist circles, in the Soviet Union for example after the publication of *The General Theory*, as we shall now see.

THE GENERAL THEORY AND MARXISM

The reactions to *The General Theory* among the Western Marxists varied greatly. The most orthodox, in particular those who were members of Communist parties or Trotskyist groups, were mainly hostile, and rejected Keynes's ideas as a desperate attempt to rescue a condemned economic system. For at least some amongst them, the crisis started in 1929 marked the beginning of the end for capitalism.

This hostility of Marxist thinkers was particularly strong in France, where the Communist Party was very powerful in the 1940s and 1950s. While in October 1946, Jean Domarchi, who was not a Marxist, writing in *Les Temps modernes* (the review founded by Jean-Paul Sartre) tried to show the compatibility between Marx's schemes of reproduction, and Keynes's equations of effective demand, *la Nouvelle critique*, edited by the Communist Party, in issues published in 1949 launched a violent assault against Keynes's theory. It was said that Keynesianism was henceforth the official doctrine of the French administration.[22]

The 1970s saw the decline in the influence of the Communist Party and the emergence of new currents of thinking. The schools of thought known as Regulation and Conventions put forward an original synthesis of Marxism, Keynesianism and Institutionalism. Another current, 'Critical Marxism', associated in particular with the series 'Intervention en économie politique' and the Cahiers d'économie politique, proposed a new reading of Marx inspired by Keynes. Gérard Duménil, for his part, in a book examining Marx and Keynes on the economic crisis, argued their views were fundamentally different and opposed (Duménil 1977).

It was in the Anglo-American world that Marxism, much less established, or recognized than in France, or in other Latin countries, particularly Italy, was more receptive to Keynesianism, and where efforts were made to rethink Marx in the light of Keynes's thought. The pioneer here was Paul Sweezy, who was first a disciple of Hayek, in his book *The Theory of Capitalist Development*, published in 1942. The Keynesian-Marxist synthesis that he put forward lead him to call into question fundamental ideas developed by Marx, such as the tendency of the rate of profit to fall, which was replaced by the tendency of the surplus to rise. Sweezy developed his ideas with his co-author Paul Baran in *Monopoly Capital*, published in 1966, and wrote about them extensively in *Monthly Review* which he co-founded. At the same epoch, the German-born economist Paul Mattick, established in the United States and close to a more radical Communist tendency, reiterated the opposition between the two authors in *Marx and Keynes: the Limits of the Mixed Economy*, even though he recognized some similarities between them: 'There is a necessary connection between Marx and Keynes. Marx anticipated Keynes' criticism of the neo-classical theory through his own criticism of classical theory; and both men recognised the capitalist dilemma in a declining rate of capital formation' (Mattick 1969, p. 21). Years before, in 1951, the British economist John Eaton wrote, in his *Marx against Keynes*, that Keynesian economics is 'the vulgar economy of monopoly capitalism in crisis and decay' (Eaton 1951, p. 85).

Kalecki's work linked a theory of effective demand to a classical-Marxian view of distribution, and played a major role in the emergence of what has been called since 1975 a Post-Keynesian school of thought, which, like the Regulation School in France, takes its inspiration from Keynes, Marx and institutionalism.[23] Piero Sraffa worked away from the late 1920s at a major restatement of Ricardo's theory which, finally published in 1960, gave birth to a neo-Ricardian school of thought. Sraffa said (in a private conversation with the author) that his book, *Production of Commodities by Means of Commodities*, could not have been published, if Marx's *Capital* had not been written.[24] Sraffa considered that Marx's and Ricardo's theses were fundamentally identical. This is in accordance with Keynes's view of the relationship between the two authors (as outlined at the beginning of this chapter). But what Keynes and Sraffa conclude from this convergence is radically different. Far from rejecting the Ricardian theory that Keynes wished to replace, Sraffa considers that it complements

Keynes's theory of effective demand, about which he emphasizes some shortcomings.

KEYNES AND THE SOVIET UNION

Until the end of the Second World War, only one country adhered officially to Marxism: the USSR, which emerged after the Bolshevik revolution of 1917 in Russia. It is worth recalling that Keynes's relation to Soviet communism, which claimed to put Marx's project into practice, ran hot and cold, and was not without its ambiguities. At first he applauded the Bolshevik Revolution, about which he wrote to his mother on 30 March 1917: 'I was immensely cheered up and excited by the Russian news. It's the sole result of the war so far worth having'. On 24 December, after the government announced food rationing measures, he wrote to her:

> My Christmas thoughts are that a further prolongation of the war, with the turn things have now taken, probably means the disappearance of the social order we have known hitherto. With some regrets I think I am on the whole not sorry. The abolition of the rich will be rather a comfort and serve them right anyhow. What frightens me is the prospect of *general* impoverishment. In another year's time, we shall have forfeited the claim we had staked out in the New World and in exchange this country will be mortgaged to America.
>
> Well, the only course open to me is to be buoyantly Bolshevik; and as I lie in bed in the morning I reflect with a good deal of satisfaction that, because our rulers are as incompetent as they are mad and wicked, one particular era of a particular kind of civilisation is very nearly over. (Keynes, CW, vol. XVI, item 1, pp. 265–6)

On 23 February 1919, he wrote, again to his mother, that the Russian government had offered him a decoration: 'Being a Bolshevik, however, I thought it more proper to refuse' (Keynes, CW, vol. XVI, item 2, p. 267). At the same time, he angered his Bloomsbury friends by rejoicing at the establishment of a liberal Russian government at Archangel, following advances by Alexander Koltchak's White Russian troops, and armed intervention from the Allies. After Koltchak's defeat, and execution, he recognized this policy as a mistake. In 1921 Keynes proclaimed the failure of the Bolshevik experiment, in which the European working classes had placed so much hope (Keynes, CW, vol. XVII, item 1, pp. 269–70). The following year, after having studied in detail the USSR's economic situation as well as having met and admired the country's Minister of Foreign Affairs, Chicherine, he wrote: 'An extraordinary experiment in socialism is in course of development. I think that there may be solid foundations on which to build a bridge. Revolutions are not kid-glove affairs, particularly in Russia. But a mere disgust and moral indignation, which has not even the curiosity to discover the facts, is never by itself the right reaction to a great historical event' (Keynes, CW, vol. XVII, item 2, p. 420).

As the years went by and Bolshevism was transformed into Stalinism, Keynes became more and more allergic to the USSR, and increasingly placed Stalinism in the same camp as Fascism. In a letter to Martin on 25 July 1937, he reminded the latter that Stalin was destroying the old Communist Party, 24 per cent of whose members had been executed, arrested, exiled or fired. He added: 'Stalin's position will soon be indistinguishable from that of the other dictators, and it would seem to be entirely in character that his foreign policy will be opportunist, and an eventual agreement between him and Germany by no means out of the question, if it should happen to suit him' (Keynes, CW, vol. XXVIII, item 7, p. 72). Keynes was often wrong in his political predictions, but here he displayed remarkable foresight, two years before the German-Soviet Pact. He concluded this letter by stressing the increasing similarity of totalitarian states.

Keynes's hostility to Soviet communism did not prevent him from sympathizing with the young communists he frequented at the Apostles gatherings, and in the Left Book Club, as well as supporting the freedom of speech of the communists' sympathizers. When Harold Laski, a London School of Economics professor, and member of the Labour Party, of which he became President in 1945, was threatened with a demotion and a reduction in salary as a result of comments made in the Soviet Union that were favourable to communism, Keynes was indignant at such a monstrous idea, and vigorously defended a man to whom he was opposed: 'Too many of the younger members of the Left have toyed with Marxist ideas to have a clear conscience in repelling reactionary assaults on freedom. Thus the importance of impressing the minds of the Right and of the Left alike that not the smallest breach should be allowed in the fortifications of liberty' (Keynes, CW, vol. XXVIII, item 1, p. 27). Of the young communist Apostles, of whom it will be later discovered that four were recruited as Soviet spies,[25] Keynes wrote:

There is no one in politics today worth sixpence outside the ranks of liberals except the post-war generation of intellectual Communists under thirty-five. Them, too, I like and respect. Perhaps in their feelings and instincts they are the nearest we now have to the typical nervous non-conformist English gentleman who went to the Crusades, made the Reformation, fought the Great Rebellion, won us our civil and religious liberties and humanized the working class. (Keynes, CW, vol. XXI, item 1, pp. 494–5)

THE SOVIET UNION AND KEYNES

Surprisingly, until the publication of *The General Theory*, the opinion on Keynes in the USSR was rather positive.[26] This was partly due to the mutual esteem between Lenin and Keynes. Keynes estimated that Lenin was very clever writing 'that the best way to destroy capitalism was to debauch the currency' (Keynes, CW, vol. II, p. 148). At the same time, he did not consider Lenin as a dogmatic dictator, but as 'a pragmatic experimenter in economic matters, unafraid of tampering with the fundamental principles of his faith, as demonstrated by the New Economic Policy (NEP)' (Keynes, CW, vol. XVII, item 3, p. 437). Keynes wrote to Lenin in 1922 asking him to prepare an introduction to a series of articles on USSR that he was editing for *The Manchester Guardian Commercial*. Lenin's poor health prevented him from doing so.

This esteem was reciprocal. Lenin was well acquainted with Keynes's works and made a certain number of references to them in important speeches. He was very sympathetic to the recommendations of Keynes in *The Economic Consequences of the Peace*, particularly the proposal to cancel all war debts, and ordered the book to be translated in Russian. Several others of Keynes's works were translated in Russian. Lenin praised his description of the Paris Peace conference and the Versailles Treaty, and in particular his portrait of Woodrow Wilson. More generally, he considered that Keynes offered penetrating analysis of contemporary economic problems. Of course, their political positions were totally different, and Lenin also described Keynes as a bourgeois economist, and a determined opponent to Bolshevism. He probably never read some of the passages quoted in the last section. Lenin died in January 1924, but his prestige remained such that received opinion on Keynes remained positive for some time.

Trotsky had also offered positive comments on Keynes, 'a most prominent English economist' (Turner 1969, p. 15). Trotsky was present when Keynes gave a report on the economic situation in England to the plenum of the National Economic Council of the Supreme Soviet of the National Economy on 14 September 1925. The following year, Keynes published a review of a book by Trotsky on England, a book which attacks the British Labour Party because it believes in socialism without revolution. Keynes is of course opposed to this view: 'Trotsky's book must confirm us in our conviction of the uselessness, the empty-headedness of force at the present stage of human affairs' (Keynes, CW, vol. VIII, item 1, p. 67). But he also said of Trotsky: 'Yet there is a certain style about Trotsky. A personality is visible through the distorting medium. And it is not all platitudes' (ibid., p. 63).

Things changed radically with the rise to power of Stalin, who never spoke directly of Keynes, but probably directed others as to the way to criticize Keynesianism. A first mention of *The General Theory* appeared in 1938, in an article by L. Freiman on 'Unemployment in the capitalist countries'. It was followed by other mentions, in book reviews, stressing in particular the fact that Keynes was favourable to the reduction of wages! A first complete review of *The General Theory* was published shortly after Keynes's death in 1946, signed by I. G. Blyumin, one of the foremost Soviet economists, and an expert on 'bourgeois' economic thought. The book was described as 'the gospel of a new school of bourgeois political economy thought that has written on its banner the transition to a "regulated economy"' (Turner 1969, p. 38), which is impossible under capitalism: 'The Keynesian program to save capitalism has a utopian character. It faces a utopian task – to fight crises and unemployment with the preservation of the bases of the capitalist class' (ibid., p. 41).

A first Russian translation of *The General Theory* was published in 1948. It was preceded by a long and very critical introduction by Blyumin, accompanied by critical editorial notes and there were even some probably intended omissions, for example the passage on Gesell. Articles became more numerous and critical after this date. Keynes's ideas were now presented as reactionary, under the guise of social demagoguery, as the ideology of monopoly capital, and British imperialism. This was of course closely linked to the beginning of the cold war. A first description of Keynes, very positive, was published in a Soviet encyclopaedia in 1936. Here is the revised edition of 1953: 'English vulgar bourgeois economist, ideologist of imperialistic reaction and wars, unmasked by V. I. Lenin in 1920 as an avowed bourgois, a ruthless opponent to bolshevism, which he, as an English philistine, pictures in an ugly, savage and brutal manner' (ibid., p. 13). Not a word on the positive comments of Lenin. This was the tone of the numerous articles and books devoted to Keynes who appeared now as the leader of bourgeois economists and the principal intellectual adversary of communism.

This change was of course closely linked to the growing influence of Keynesianism in the Labour movement in the capitalist countries, particularly in the social-democratic parties and in the Labour Party in England, which would launch the Keynesian revolution after winning the elections of 1945: 'Through the right-wing socialists, Keynesian ideas penetrate the working-class. . .The fight against Keynesianism is one of the most important tasks of the ideological work of Marxist economic theory' (Blyumin quoted by ibid., p. 57). It is necessary to unmask Keynes, and reveal his intent to deceive workers and divert them from the class struggle and the revolution, to denounce the reformism and revisionism now identified with Keynesianism. The attacks against Western socialist movements by Soviet thinkers were most of the time even more brutal than the attacks against the true conservatives. The expression 'Social-fascism' was coined at that time, and Keynesianism was sometime described as serving Fascism, with reference being made to Keynes's preface to the German edition of his book. Manifestly, Soviets were afraid of the spread of Keynes's influence on the left in capitalist countries, and even of the role of his ideas in the prolongation of capitalism's life. Keynesianism was described in the title of an article by A. I. Kochetkov as 'the ideology of the reactionary imperialist bourgeoisie', Keynes being presented as more reactionary than Malthus and Marshall! I. Kuzminov describes him as 'the ideologist of imperialist reaction and war'.

But at the same time, a contradictory movement was going on starting in the 1950s, with economists such as Leonid Kantorovich, V. S. Nemchinov and V. V. Novozhilov,[27] who made important contributions to the development of mathematical and orthodox economic theory, which they did not consider as contradictory with Marxism. Oskar Lange was of course the pioneer in this movement. In a small book published after his return from Chicago to Poland he wrote that we can apply the principles of Keynesianism to the Marxist theories of imperialism. More generally, he considered that Marxism can be strengthened with mathematical and marginalist techniques, and that the attachment to the labour theory of value was an obstacle to be overcome.[28]

With the passage from the cold war to pacific coexistence, after the death of Stalin in 1953, and the rise to power of Khrushchev, when the Twentieth Congress of the Communist Party of the USSR denounced the Stalinist cult of personality, the tone changed in the evaluation of Keynes, passing from vituperation to refutation. Soviet economists recognized that the criticisms of the Stalinist period were inadequate, and now admitted that some planning was possible in capitalist countries and that Keynes provided theoretical bases for the regulation of capitalism. A distinction was now drawn between Keynesianism and the neoliberalism (or conservatism) of thinkers such as Friedrich Hayek and Milton Friedman. And even within the Keynesianism camp, a left-wing current, with authors like Joan Robinson was identified. But this being said, Keynesianism remained linked to revisionism and reformism, and warnings were issued against conflating or attempting to fuse Marxism and Keynesianism. While it was now recognized that war was not the solution to the competition between socialism and capitalism, there could not be peaceful coexistence on the ideological front. In the preface to a

Hungarian translation of *Capital*, Peter Erdös described Keynes as one of the most prominent bourgeois economists of the past half-century, and that his challenge to Say's Law demonstrated courage. But Keynes was mistaken to think that capitalism was the only viable system: the struggle today was between a senile capitalism, and a young and vigorous socialism.

All this changed suddenly in 1989. The Soviet Union's 'young and vigorous socialism' fell with the Berlin wall. Thereafter, only a few countries evoked communism and Marxism, the primary example, of course, being China, but this in a peculiar way, with an economy that is very far from socialist principles. In this respect, the government discourse in China has certain Orwellian or schizophrenic overtones. As for Keynes, with the emergence of neoliberalism in the 1970s, the author and his ideas entered a kind of purgatory. Rather than moving from Marx to Keynes, and from socialism to a 'third way', Russia and its former satellites chose Friedman or Hayek as their heroes. But the earth moved again with the financial and economic turmoil that began in 2008. Keynes has been resurrected and, in some cases, Marx is not too far behind. One thing is certain, Marx's and Keynes's discourses on the pathological love of money, the unrestrained drive to accumulation and the ravages of speculation are more topical than ever, and this is as true for the two former adversaries in the cold war, the Russian Federation and the United States, as it is for people elsewhere in the world.

Of course, Keynes and Marx do not see and do not describe the same capitalism. Paradoxically, it is Keynes's vision which is more pessimistic. For Marx, capitalism is an intrinsically dynamic system, destructive and creative at the same time. The pages of the *Communist Manifesto* appear in some passages as a praise of capitalism and its world-wide expansion. Marx seems sometimes fascinated by this most powerful economic system that the world has experimented. Keynes sees it rather as a decadent system:

> The decadent international but individualistic capitalism, in the hands of which we found ourselves after the War, is not a success. It is not intelligent, it is not beautiful, it is not just, it is not virtuous – and doesn't deliver the goods . . . But when we wonder what to put in place, we are extremely perplexed. (Keynes, CW, vol. XXI, item 1, p. 239)

It can be described as the worst system with the exception of all others. These two visions are not necessarily antagonistic. They are of course different but are two complementary emphases that mutually enrich themselves. They constitute a legacy that we must not squander.

NOTES

1. I am grateful to the following persons who read, commented, and suggested corrections: Robert Armstrong, Carol Benetti, Gilles Bourque, Marielle Cauchy, Duncan Cameron – who corrected my idiosyncratic English – and Robert Nadeau. I am obviously responsible for any faults in the final product. I benefited from the financial support of the Social Sciences and Humanities Research Council of Canada, which I thank.
2. Some of the ideas of this chapter are developed in Dostaler (2007).
3. But let us note that Shaw, who thought that H. G. Wells 'has made a blazing idiot of himself' in this interview with Stalin, replied to Keynes on 30 November: 'I have picked Marx's mistakes to pieces as meticulously as anybody; but I am always very careful to reserve the fact that he was an Epoch Maker' (Keynes, CW, vol. XXVIII, item 4, p. 37).
4. Keynes first mentions this definition of the classical theory as coined by Marx in the first lecture of the autumn (Michaelmas in the Cambridge jargon) term, on 15 October 1934.
5. On the Apostles, a secret society founded in Cambridge in 1820, and on the Bloomsbury Group, see Dostaler (2007), First Interlude.
6. The Marxist economist Maurice Dobb, member of the British Communist party, but also colleague and friend of Keynes, believed that there was more continuity than divergence between Ricardo and Marx. See Dobb (1937).
7. In the preface to his *Essays in Persuasion*, Keynes writes: 'For the western world has already the resources and the technique, if we could create the organisation to use them, capable of reducing the economic problem, which now absorbs our moral and practical energies, to a position of secondary importance' (Keynes, CW, vol. IX, p. xviii).
8. Clifford H. Douglas (1879–1952) was the inspiration behind the populist Social Credit movement, which had some success in Australia, Canada and New Zealand. Of Silvio Gesell (1862–1930), author of *The Natural Economic Order* (1916) and promoter of a 'melting' money, unsuitable for accumulation, Keynes wrote that he was a builder of an 'anti-Marxian socialism' (Keynes, CW, vol. VII, p. 355). This presence of the idea of effective demand is mentioned in the second lecture of Michaelmas term, 15 October 1934, where Keynes adds, according to his students, that 'the assumption that demand and supply prices for aggregate output are always equal . . . also accounts for the ultra-orthodoxy of the Communists, who take the Ricardian argument to show that nothing can be gained from mere interference. . .Bryce noted that Communism is the logical outcome of the classical theory' (Rymes 1989, p. 135).
9. In the upward phase, the positive effects of accumulation on employment prevail over the negative effects of technological change and the contrary happens in the downward phase. It is not a state of equilibrium.
10. In 1932, Michal Kalecki, then an obscure Polish economist, proposed a model containing, in a succinct and formalized manner, the essential elements of *The General Theory*. Keynes's friends were surprised at how quickly Kalecki understood and assimilated Keynes's new arguments when he arrived in Cambridge in 1936!
11. From there on, many commentators stressed the similarities between Marx's schemes of reproduction and Keynes's equations of effective demand. Among the firsts, see Fan-Hung (1939), Alexander (1940) and Tsuru (1942). See also Robinson (1948) and Lecaillon (1950). We must add here that investment, which is a key variable in both systems, does not have the same meaning. For Marx, it is inseparable from the incorporation of new techniques. For Keynes, it is before all an expense and capitalism is threatened by its insufficiency.
12. He most probably had conversations with Sraffa who had a very deep knowledge of Marx, to whom he was much more sympathetic than Keynes. On this see Behrens (1985).
13. Thomas Rymes transcribed and reconstructed these notes as 'notes of a representative student' in Rymes (1989).
14. Laurie Tarshis was a Canadian student who attended Keynes's lectures from 1932 to

1935. He was the author of what is probably the first Keynesian textbook, *Elements of Economics* (1947), eclipsed by Paul Samuelson's *Economics*, published the following year. Tarshis's book was considered by many as leftist and even influenced by communism!

15. In fact, Say's Law of markets and the quantity theory are the two faces of the same medal. Both stand or fall together.
16. But here there is a difference between Bryce's notes and those of Tarshis, for whom Keynes says that M' can be either greater or less than M.
17. Some of the ideas of this part of our chapter are developed at length in Dostaler and Maris (2009). See also for a previous and reduced version in English, Dostaler and Maris (2000).
18. On this, see the debate between Dillard (1984, 1986) and Burkett (1986). For Dillard, the labour theory of value is one of the numerous doctrines shared by Marx and Keynes. Burkett considers that there is a crucial difference between the two, value being a category of distribution for Keynes and a property of commodities for Marx. Obviously, the beginning of the above quotation from Keynes contradicts Burkett's viewpoint. Dillard considers that there is no productivity of capital in Marx; Burkett writes that Keynes endorses the productivity theory. In reality, the marginal efficiency of capital of Keynes must not be confused with the marginal productivity of capital of neoclassical theory. For Mattick (1969, p. 4), Keynes effectuates a 'partial return to the labour theory of value'. On other aspects of the debate on the relation between Marx and Keynes, see Brandis (1985, 1987) and Fichtenbaum and Shahidi (1987). See also some of the papers collected in Deleplace and Maurisson (1985) and Helburn and Bramhall (1986).
19. See Hunt (2009).
20. On Marx's relations with money, see Gardaz (1987).
21. Heilbroner (1984) remarks that the socioanalysis of market relations with Marx is similar to the unconscious in Freud.
22. On the French Marxists' reactions to Keynes, see Lecaillon (1950).
23. On Kalecki and the synthesis of Keynes and Marx, see Howard and King (1992) and Sardoni (1986).
24. See Dostaler (1982).
25. Anthony Blunt, Guy Burgess, Leo Long and Michael Straight. Keynes was close to the first two of them.
26. On the reception of Keynes's ideas in the USSR, the main reference is Turner (1969). See the review article of this book by Letiche (1971).
27. They received the Lenin Prize for their work in economics in 1965. In 1949, Kantorovich was awarded the Stalin Prize in mathematics and in 1975, the Prize of the Bank of Sweden in Memory of Alfred Nobel.
28. I remember the International Economic Association congress held in Budapest in 1974 where one participant from an Eastern country proclaimed: 'We all speak here the same language, the language of modern economics'!

BIBLIOGRAPHY

Alexander, Sidney S. (1940), 'Mr. Keynes and Mr. Marx', *Review of Economic Studies*, **7**(2) (February), 123–35.

Baran, p. and P. Sweezy (1966), *Monopoly Capital*, New York: Monthly Review Press.

Behrens, R. (1985), 'What Keynes knew about Marx', *Studi Economici*, **40**(26), 3–14.

Brandis, Royall (1985), 'Marx and Keynes? Marx or Keynes?', *Journal of Economic Issues*, **19**(3) (September), 643–59.

Brandis, Royall (1987), 'Marx and Keynes? Marx or Keynes? A reply', *Journal of Economic Issues*, **21**(1) (March), 470–3.

Burkett, Paul (1986), 'Dillard on Keynes and Marx: comment', *Journal of Post Keynesian Economics*, **8**(4) (Summer), 623–31.

Deleplace, Ghislain and Patrick Maurisson (eds) (1985), *L'hétérodoxie dans la pensée économique: K. Marx, J. M. Keynes, J. A. Schumpeter*, Paris: Anthropos.

Dillard, Dudley D. (1984), 'Keynes and Marx: a centennial appraisal', *Journal of Post Keynesian Economics*, **6**(3) (Spring), 421–32.

Dillard, Dudley D. (1986), 'Dillard on Keynes and Marx: rejoinder', *Journal of Post Keynesian Economics*, **8**(4) (Summer), 632–7.

Dobb, Maurice H. (1937), *Political Economy and Capitalism: Some Essays in Economic Tradition*, London: Routledge & Kegan Paul.

Dostaler, Gilles (1982), 'Marx et Sraffa', *L'Actualité économique*, **58**(1–2), 95–114.

Dostaler, Gilles (2007), *Keynes and his Battles*, Cheltenham, UK and Northampton, MA, USA: Edward Elgar.

Dostaler, Gilles and B. Maris (2000), 'Dr Freud and Mr Keynes on Money and Capitalism', in John Smithin (ed.), *What is Money?*, London and New York: Routledge, pp. 235–56.

Dostaler, Gilles and B. Maris (2009), *Capitalisme et pulsion de mort*, Paris: Albin Michel.

Duménil, Gérard (1977), *Marx et Keynes face à la crise*, Paris: Économica.

Eaton, John (1951), *Marx against Keynes*, London: Lawrence & Wishart.

Fan-Hung (1939), 'Keynes and Marx on the theory of capital accumulation, money and interest', *Journal of Political Economy*, **47**(1), 28–41.

Fichtenbaum, Rudy and Hushang Shahidi (1987), 'Marx and Keynes? Marx or Keynes? A comment', *Journal of Economic Issues*, **21**(1) (March), 467–70.

Gardaz, M. (1987), *Marx et l'argent*, Paris, Économica.

Heilbroner, Robert (1984), 'Economics and political economy: Marx, Keynes, and Schumpeter', *Journal of Economic Issues*, **18**(3) (September), 681–95.

Helburn, Suzanne W. and David F. Bramhall (eds) (1986), *Marx, Schumpeter and Keynes: A Centenary Celebration of Dissent*, London: M. E. Sharpe.

Hollander, Samuel (2008), *The Economics of Karl Marx: Analysis and Application*, Cambridge: Cambridge University Press.

Howard, Michael and John King (1992), 'Keynes, Marx and political economy', in Bill Gerrard and John Hillard (eds), *The Philosophy and Economics of John Maynard Keynes*, Aldershot, UK and Brookfield, MA, USA: Edward Elgar, pp. 231–45.

Hunt, Tristam (2009), *The Frock-Coated Communist: The Revolutionary Life of Friedrich Engels*, London: Allen Lane.

Keynes, J. M. (1936), *The General Theory of Employment, Interest, and Money*, London: Macmillan

Keynes, J. M. (1937), 'The general theory of employment', *Quarterly Journal of Economics*, **51**(1) (February), 209–23.

Keynes, J. M. (1971–1989), *The Collected Writings of John Maynard Keynes*, London: Macmillan/Cambridge University Press for the Royal Economic Society

Vol. II: *The Economic Consequences of the Peace*

Vol. VII: *The General Theory of Employment, Interest, and Money*

Vol. IX: *Essays in Persuasion*

1. A Short View of Russia, pp. 253–71.

2. The End of Laissez-Faire, pp. 272–94.
3. Clissold, pp. 315–20.
4. Economic Possibilities of Our Grandchildren, pp. 321–32.
Vol. X: *Essays in Biography*
1. Trotsky on England, pp. 63–7.
2. My Early Beliefs, pp. 433–50.
Vol. XIII: *The General Theory and After: Part I, Preparation*
1. Letter to F. A. Keynes dated 14 September 1930, p. 176.
2. A monetary theory of production, pp. 408–11.
3. Poverty in plenty: Is the economic system self-adjusting?, pp. 485–92.
4. Letter to G. B. Shaw dated 7 January 1935, pp. 492–3.
Vol. XIV: *The General Theory and After: Defense and Development*
1. The General Theory of Employment, pp. 109–23.
Vol. XVI: *Activities 1914–1919 The Treaty and Versailles*
1. Letter to Mrs. Keynes dated 24 December 1917, pp. 265–6.
2. Letter to Mrs. Keynes dated 22 February 1918, p. 267.
Vol. XVII: *Activities 1920–1922: Treaty Revision and Reconstruction*
1. Europe's economic outlook, IV: The earnings of labour, pp. 265–71.
2. The financial system of the Bolsheviks, pp. 403–8.
3. Russia, pp. 434–40.
Vol. XXI: *Activities 1931–1939: World Crises and Politics in Britain and America*
1. National self-sufficiency, pp. 233–46.
2. Democracy and efficiency, pp. 491–500.
Vol. XXVIII: *Social, Political and Literary Writings*
1. Professor Laski and the Issue of Freedom, pp. 25–7.
2. Mr. Keynes Replies to Shaw, pp. 30–5.
3. Letter to the Editor, pp. 35–6.
4. Letter from G. B. Shaw dated 30 November 1934, p. 37.
5. Letter to G. B. Shaw dated 2 December 1934, p. 38.
6. Letter to G. B. Shaw dated 7 January 1935, p. 42.
7. Letter to Kingsley Martin dated 25 July 1937, pp. 71–3.
Vol. XXIX: *The General Theory and After: A Supplement*
1. The Distinction between a Co-operative Economy and an Entrepreneur Economy, pp. 76–87.
Lecaillon, Jacques (1950), 'Marx et Keynes devant la pensée économique contemporaine', *Revue économique*, **1**(1), 72–87.
Letiche, John M. (1971), 'Soviet views on Keynes: a review article. Surveying the literature', *Journal of Economic Literature*, **9**(2) (June), 442–58.
Marx, Karl (1848/1977), 'Wage-Labour and Capital', in David McLellan (ed.), *Karl Marx: Selected Readings*, Oxford: Oxford University Press, pp. 248–68.
Marx, Karl (1859/1970), *A Contribution to the Critique of Political Economy*, New York: International Publishers.
Marx, Karl (1867/1909), *Capital: A Critique of Political Economy*, vol. 1, *The Process of Capitalist Production*, Chicago, IL: Charles H. Kerr & Company.
Marx, Karl and Friedrick Engels (1983), *Collected Works*, vol. 40, New York: International Publishers.
Mattick, Paul (1969), *Marx and Keynes: The Limits of the Mixed Economy*, Boston, MA: P. Sargent.
McCracken, Harlan L. (1933), *Value Theory and Business Cycles*, New York: Falcon Press.

Robinson, Joan (1948/1968), 'Marx and Keynes', in D. Horowitz (ed.), *Marx and Modern Economics*, New York: Monthly Review Press, pp. 103–16.

Robinson, Joan (1953/1973), 'Essays 1953 (On re-reading Marx)', in J. Robinson (ed.), *Collected Economic Papers*, vol. 4, Oxford: Basil Blackwell, pp. 247–68.

Robinson, Joan (1964/1965), 'Kalecki and Keynes', in J. Robinson (ed.), *Collected Economic Papers*, vol. 3, Oxford: Basil Blackwell, pp. 92–9.

Rymes, Thomas K. (ed.) (1989), *Keynes's Lectures 1932–35: Notes of a Representative Student*, Ann Arbor, MI: University of Michigan Press.

Sardoni, Claudio (1986), 'Marx and Keynes on effective demand and unemployment', *History of Political Economy*, **18**(3) (Fall), 419–41.

Skidelsky, Robert (1992), *John Maynard Keynes, The Economist as Saviour: 1920–1937*, vol. 2, London: Macmillan.

Sraffa, P. (1960), *Production of Commodities by Means of Commodities*, Cambridge: Cambridge University Press.

Sweezy, P. (1942), *The Theory of Capital Development*, New York: Oxford University Press.

Tsuru, S. (1942), 'On reproduction schemes', in P. M. Sweezy (ed.), *The Theory of Capitalist Development*, New York: Monthly Review, pp. 365–74.

Turner, Carl B. (1969), *An Analysis of Soviet Views on John Maynard Keynes*, Durham, NC: Duke University Press.

Woolf, Virginia (1982), *The Diary of Virginia Woolf*, vol. 4, New York: Harcourt Brace Jovanovich.

PART IV

The General Theory and new interpretations

12. *The General Theory*: seventy-five years later

Omar F. Hamouda

Resurgence of the name of Keynes has never caught more attention among journalists and politicians nor provoked such debate worldwide than since the start of the 2007 financial crisis. While the principles of reigning macro-economics have been put under attack, the profession is slow to provide leadership, based on knowledge of economics, as to how to comprehend this latest caprice of the economy. The discussion has been left, in the eyes of the larger public, to opinions and speculation, largely in blogs, editorial columns and political action committees, in which the proponents either appeal to or are appalled by the name of Keynes, as if his policies are the source of inspiration or the cause of the current economic situation. There is much nonsense in what is attributed to Keynes, whether to his economic theory or his policies. Perhaps given the present circumstances, the time is ripe to assess or reassess *The General Theory of Employment, Interest, and Money* and its legacy.

Why is it that the profession cannot converge to some general compre-hension of what Keynes's general theory is? Despite 75 years of discussing, debating, accepting, and rejecting the would-be paradigm of Keynes, *The General Theory* has simply not been read for its fundamentals on its own terms. It has instead been analysed piecemeal and through the lenses, often opinionated or partisan, of the secondary literature, with an unwarranted focus on so-called errors of Keynes. This has, over the years, created distortions and unfounded myths and moved the discipline away from Keynes's contribution.

In *Money, Investment and Consumption: Keynes's Macroeconomics Rethought* (Hamouda 2009), it is explained how Keynes's theory was stifled from the moment it came into being. The focus of that study was to show that Hayek, Robertson and Hicks derailed Keynes's contribu-tion and that Keynesianism, which ensued in diverse forms, was and still is nothing but a Marshallian neo-classical approach, a theory of which Keynes was very critical in the first place. In this same study it is also hinted without much elaboration that Keynes's pupils, especially Richard

Kahn and Joan Robinson, did not help either in elucidating what the new paradigm was. They themselves were very quickly entangled in Hayek's and Robertson's authoritative, critical opposition and in Hicks's very powerful and pedagogically appealing IS-LM interpretation that instantly became, in the profession, the reference point from which it was thought Keynes must have begun and without which since no stripe of Keynesians or anti-Keynesians can do.

The aim of the present chapter is twofold:

a) To give a brief explanation as to how the early generation of Post Keynesians, while critical, were nonetheless riding on the coattails of the neo-classical economists. They misunderstood Keynes's paradigm shift and, to some extent, misled subsequent generations. Having too quickly dismissed and then ignored *A Treatise on Money* (hereafter *The Treatise*), they deprived themselves of the essential background setting from which Keynes built *The General Theory*. As a consequence, Post Keynesians,[1] more or less unified in their attacks on what they termed Bastard-Keynesianism, were unable as a group to agree on a common understanding of Keynes's contribution in *The General Theory*.
b) To argue that the general theory underlying *The General Theory* cannot be understood without *The Treatise* as its background. The two books are sewn of the same whole cloth.

In the much larger perspective, Keynes's unexplored macroeconomic theory is yet to be dealt with, and as a consequence *The General Theory* even after 75 years is yet to be understood.

FALSE START

Keynes developed a coherent, complete theory, as the blueprint of the market economy, to understand its economic dynamics. Elaborating from *The Treatise* through *The General Theory*, he articulated his two major breakthroughs: one in *value theory*, the other in *monetary theory*. His own *theory of value* was first expressed in the fundamental equations found in *The Treatise* and then blended into the 'wage-unit' in *The General Theory*. His unique *monetary theory* was explicit in both works, but in *The General Theory* it became more focused, to reveal his concept of 'liquidity preference'.

Keynes's theory of value was truly a new alternative, which went completely unnoticed in the profession. It did not depend on labour, as did the Classics's, nor on utility, as does neo-classical theory. It is a hybrid, in which the overall price-level is an index made of two cost components: an average cost of production, and some measure of profit reflecting market fluctuations through discrepancies between saving and investment. Since to the cost side there is the receiving counterpart, Keynes's overall price-level index can also be read as made of two monetary components: an average income paid to those involved in putting effort into production, and an average income or return to those investing liquidity into production. It is this conception of price index, as an alternative to the Fisherian $MV = PT$, that allowed Keynes to expand his approach beyond the Quantity Theory of Money.

In the macroeconomic perspective of *The Treatise*, to develop his theory, Keynes separated (total) profits from total income, thus introducing the income of the community as identical to the cost of production, while leaving the income of the shareholders, traders, and the like as something different. By extension, he thus distinguished the saving out of total income from the saving out of the community income. He made the prices of consumer (or final) goods depend on past and current output, while the prices of investment (or capital or intermediary) goods depend, implicitly in *The Treatise* and explicitly in *The General Theory*, on the investors' perspective of future earnings. He thus made the prices of investment goods independent of the prices of consumer goods. His defining Income, Profits, Saving, and Investment differently from their ordinary meanings created such semantic difficulty that none of Keynes's contemporaries had enough patience or willingness to invest in thinking in his terms and hence within his new paradigm, let alone in accepting them. Along with the myth of inarticulateness that commentators and critics developed about his semantics, Keynes's many attempts to clarify his terminology and methodology were interpreted as changes of mind. His interpreters were also left wondering where his theory fit within the mould.

Robertson and Hayek were the authors of much of the controversy surrounding the semantics of Keynes's contributions in *The Treatise*. Resisting his terminology and twisting it back to ordinary meanings, his opponents thought they spotted inconsistencies. The challenging new value theory was disturbing to the adherents of both the classical and the neo-classical theories. Robertson and Hayek, in an oblique way, were suspicious of Keynes's sympathy with the Ricardian tradition. By hammering away at what they thought was Keynes's splitting of hairs between investment and saving, they forced his theory back to the usual assumption of $S = I$ always, which meant that the second component of Keynes's Fundamental Equation became redundant and that the first part was consistent with the traditional Quantity Theory of Money. They could not therefore see what his fuss of novelty was all about.

Sraffa, another powerful mind, who was discretely in the process of rehabilitating Ricardo's theory of value (which eventually culminated in his *Production of Commodities by Means of Commodities* (1962)), was in a subtle way not interested in Keynes's new theory. Sraffa had an ideologically different agenda from that of Keynes. For Sraffa, Ricardo's is a theory of output that explains how in the long term competitive relative prices determine the distribution of income among the factors of production independently of money and short-term market fluctuations. Indeed, from Sraffa's Ricardian perspective, short-term fluctuations, encapsulated in Keynes's second component of the Fundamental Equation, are irrelevant in the long run; prices are determined solely by the cost of production. Ricardo's theory of value stood on firm ground, as it was consistent with the theory of a cooperative economy, but it was not an applicable monetary theory for the entrepreneurial economy Keynes had in mind.

At the time of the publication of *The Treatise*, Cambridge was entrenched, on the one hand, in the tradition of Marshall, with Pigou and Robertson the dominant intransigent proponents, and on the other hand, with Sraffa and Dobb, the anti-Marshallians, working at demonstrating inconsistencies in the foundations of neo-classical economics. Keynes was in between. Attempting to push on with his own theory, he used both sides as helpful listening points, without giving into either set of staunch canons. Nonetheless, to air and test his controversial thoughts Keynes needed the help of a younger generation, which he hoped would be more open to new ideas than the older one. Richard Kahn and Joan Robinson were among his closest young 'pupils', who, with four others, formed the Circus. Although they were very clever, their knowledge of the doctrines of economics was immature when set against the positions of heavyweights, such as Pigou, Robertson, Hayek and others of their generation. In fact, both Kahn and Robinson were at first pupils of Sraffa, from whom they had learned their anti-Marshallian economics. Kahn, in *The Making of The General Theory* (1984), recalled his having had difficulty in 1928 understanding Marshall (p. 170) and his having found Robertson's *Banking Policy and the Price Level* 'completely unintelligible' (p. 171). It was Sraffa who would help Kahn shortly thereafter begin to grasp the intricacies of Marshall's increasing returns and who was perhaps instrumental in his choice of 'the economics of the short period, under the influence of Marshall' as the topic of his dissertation.

Sraffa's influence on both Joan Robinson and Kahn cannot be underestimated. In Robinson's first major publication, *Imperfect Competition* (1933), there is no mention of Keynes nor are there any references to *The Treatise*. When later in 1936 she presented her proposal to Keynes to publish a popular version of *The General Theory*, he was rather cold to the idea. She nonetheless went ahead and wrote a simplified version, which appeared in 1937. In her 'baby book', as Robertson called it,[2] Keynes's name was not mentioned once in the entire text. The definition of income, on which Keynes had dwelt so much, is hardly nuanced. Her introduction of the discussion of monopoly and her diversions of his theory to frictional unemployment, mobility of labour, and trade and economic national-ism gave a twist of disingenuousness to its being an accessible version of Keynes's theory 'for freshers'.[3] As revealed in her sparse correspondence with Keynes, Joan Robinson was ebullient, quick in forming her opinions, and sometimes in error in Keynes's eyes. On many occasions Keynes felt he had to correct her interpretation of his theory. At the same time he seemed to appreciate her helpful feedback and her fuelling of exchanges in Cambridge and elsewhere.

Joan Robinson was a remarkable, independent, innovative scholar, evolving at the time under the inspiration of various theories, not just that of Keynes. Her tackling economics from different and sometimes incom-patible theoretical frameworks did not make it easy for her own followers. Her influence on subsequent generations created a confusing rift between (Robinsonian) Ricardians, who tried to reconcile Keynes's theory of output with the classical theory of value, and (Robinsonian) Kaleckians, who preferred Kalecki's simpler mark-up price theory – not to mention (Robinsonian) Marxians.[4] Despite her intense involvement in the discus-sion of Keynes's ideas by the Circus, Joan Robinson was too impatient and too distracted to focus on the subtleties of Keynes to appreciate his presenting a whole new paradigm.

Kahn has, on the other hand, been considered the faithful defender of Keynes, for his attempting to fight a way out of the corner into which interpreters had painted his master. In his Mattioli Lectures of 1979, Kahn's assessment of the process of the creation of *The General Theory* and its relation to *The Treatise* raises, however, rather intriguing questions about his own interpretation of Keynes. Kahn does paint Keynes as a remarkable theorist, yet he saw him as 'uncompromising' about the many errors and confusions that he attributes to him (p. 59). Some extracts here might serve as just a few examples of Kahn's opinion of Keynes. Over some 20 pages of the lectures, he noted: Keynes 'did not explain', '[was] not successful', 'insists on symbolic presentation as a reaffirmation of the Quantity Theory of Money', 'was confused', 'most uncompromising', and 'deceived himself into thinking that he had carried the Quantity Theory of Money into the *Treatise*'.[5]

Kahn observed that 'both in the *Treatise* and in the *General Theory* the two [securities and real capital goods] are confused. Don Patinkin agrees with me as to obscurity in the *Treatise*.'[6] Specifically on the marginal propensity to consume, Kahn wrote: 'Keynes did not in any systematic way consider the effect of wealth per head on the propensity to consume' (p. 135); 'Keynes does not mention the Real Balance Effect. Mention of it would have served to reinforce arguments which are already very strong' (p. 135)! On liquidity preference, Kahn noted: 'the origins of the liquidity preference theory of the rate of interest go back to Marshall' (p. 137); 'The distinction between these two motives [precautionary and speculative] is not entirely watertight' (p. 138). Further, 'It is strange that . . . Keynes contemplated no liquid forms of wealth other than cash and fixed-interest securities'; 'In the *Treatise on Money*, Keynes presented a primitive form of liquidity preference theory' (p. 140). On Keynes on the inducement to invest, Kahn wrote: 'The subject is the most important one in the *General Theory*. But this chapter is one of the most confused' (p. 145), 'Keynes failed to mention . . .', 'he was unable of course to suggest how it could be computed otherwise than by empirical observation . . .', and 'Keynes' treatment involves circular argument' (p. 147).

The lectures reveal much more than disagreement and criticism of semantics in Kahn's overall assessment of Keynes's theory. Kahn's interpretation of Keynes deserves a whole study of its own, but the point here is that Kahn's appraisal of Keynes is both intriguing and surprising, especially as coming from one who worked with Keynes almost daily from 1928 to the publication of *The General Theory* in 1936. It appears to suggest that Kahn was not on the same wavelength as Keynes, neither when he was his pupil nor much later. Kahn seemed to have been mesmerized more by a practical, mechanical application of the multiplier than by the fundamental, general theoretical principles at which Keynes was driving. It is interesting to see that Austin Robinson, in reviewing Kahn's book and his comments on how much the Circus contributed to the making of *The General Theory*, came around to accepting Kahn's later position that Keynes was navigating on his own. Austin shared 'Richard Kahn's insistence that the *General Theory* was Keynes's book; great as Kahn's own contribution was, the book is rightly to be regarded as the work of Keynes himself.'[7]

In Kahn's assessment of the making and diffusion of *The General Theory*, although the participation of Harrod and Meade in the debate is briefly identified, there is very little mention of various other proponent participants, such as Lerner, Bryce, Tarshis, and Shackle, among others, who attempted, each in his own way, to elucidate *The General Theory*, either at the time or later. Keynes relied greatly on Harrod's comments on the various drafts of *The General Theory*, but as the correspondence between the two reveals, to Harrod's dismay, Keynes was frustrated with Harrod's having a hard time getting the full story. There is ample evidence in the substantial correspondence that has survived to be published in the *Collected Writings of John Maynard Keynes* that the closest proponents, just like Keynes's critics, had difficulty with his new concepts. It appears that this stemmed largely from their own struggles to pull themselves sufficiently away from the coattails of both classical and neo-classical ideas. This can explain partly the lack of cohesion within the group to come up with a unified synthesis as to what Keynes really meant in *The General Theory*.

It has, for the last 75 years, been taken for granted that the students of Keynes were trying to follow in lock step behind their master, while at the same time correcting him for his 'mistakes' as they went. It is this combination that has cast them in the role of defenders of Keynes's theory, when in fact each had his/her own separate agenda.

The earliest Post Keynesians, just like those opposing Keynes, reinforced the myth that Keynes was confused and kept changing his mind. A casualty of this was that they created the illusion that Keynes had abandoned and moved on beyond *The Treatise* and that therefore this work was unimportant. Subsequent generations of Post Keynesians, taken generally, have not come to realize that *The Treatise* was in fact the backbone of *The General Theory*. If considered at all, it is through secondary interpretations. Contrast Minsky (1975), for example, and his sweeping assertions about *The Treatise*, 'Keynes was concerned mainly with determining the dynamic mechanism by which the quantity theory of money operated. . . . money is a neutral veil', (p. 8) and 'As advanced by Keynes, the short-run mechanism . . . transmits monetary changes to the price level without fundamentally affecting real variables . . .' (p. 9), with Keynes's own analysis of money and general prices:

> the fundamental price-levels can depart from their equilibrium values without any change having occurred in the quantity of money or in the velocities of circulation. It is even conceivable that the cash-deposits may remain the same, the velocities of circulation may remain the same, the volume of monetary transactions may remain the same, and the volume of output may remain the same; and yet the fundamental price-levels may change. (Keynes, CW, vol. V, pp. 146–7)

In fact, Keynes's summation derives from his Fundamental Equation, in which even if its first component remains constant, its second can be changing.

Just as an example, Minsky's representation of *The Treatise* in a few pages of his *John Maynard Keynes* is inconsistent with the ideas of Keynes. Minsky's view, that *The General Theory* '. . . is a break with the fundamental theoretical posture of *A Treatise on Money*, even though both works deal with processes by which observed phenomena – either prices or output – are determined' (Minsky 1976, p. 9), is more in agreement with Hicks's interpretation[8] than with what was intended in either *The Treatise* or *The General Theory*. As a consequence, Minsky confused his misinterpretation for 'muddled' thoughts on the part of Keynes (ibid., p. 69).

In sum, although most of the Post Keynesians of both the earlier and later generations had their heart in the right place and cannot be accused of being anti-Keynes, they nonetheless neglected the importance of *The Treatise* and lacked their own in-depth analysis of the two works together. This was left largely to Keynes's harshest critics (Robertson, Hayek, Hicks, Patinkin, Klein, etc.), who presented the platform on which the Post Keynesians had defensively to react. Their defensive responses in all directions contributed greatly to their inability to establish a unified interpretation of Keynes's theory.

A comprehensive reading and a concordance of the terminologies of *The Treatise* and *The General Theory* reveal striking similarities between the two works, in the sense that there is unity underlying every expression by Keynes of the characteristics of his theory. *The General Theory* is but a portion of the trade cycle that is presented in its entirety in *The Treatise*. The value theory embedded in the Fundamental Equations is a premise of *The General Theory*, in which the wage-unit is the measure of value. The three fundamental concepts that determine employment in *The General Theory* have their genesis in *The Treatise*: (a) income expenditure on consumption goods, (b) inducement to invest, and (c) financial circulation in *The Treatise*, all found their way, albeit with slight modification, into *The General Theory* to become (a) propensity to consume, (b) marginal efficiency of capital, and (c) liquidity preference. The more elaborate discussion of money in *The General Theory* is an extension of a detailed monetary theory in *The Treatise*, with the explicit addition of a psychological attitude towards liquidity, which became the liquidity preference. Finally, both works deal with changes in prices, output, and employment, with the emphasis in *The Treatise* on the impact of prices in the phases of the cycle and in *The General Theory* on employment and output, and wage-units (instead of price level) in a particular phase of the cycle.

Keynes's separation of profit from the cost of production, his concept of user cost, his Fundamental Equations and his wage-unit measure, his partitioning of capital into fixed, working, and liquid capital, his definition of money as State Money, his distinction between financial and physical provisions for the future, which have all evaporated from the discussions and analyses of his thought in the last 75 years, are each and all integral to the understanding of *The General Theory*.

KEYNES'S OVERALL MACROECONOMICS PERSPECTIVE

The well being of a society in terms of both economic and social stability rests to a large extent on an equitable distribution of income. Keynes saw employment as the way to reach that goal, as it sustains a balance between the means and the ends of the various members of society (investors, producers, and labour) who participate in creating wealth. The main concern, perhaps more explicit in *The General Theory* than in *The Treatise*, was to discover the underlying theoretical mechanism which allows for the creation of employment and income. In a monetary market economy, employment requires investment, and incentives to invest depend on profits. Thus, for Keynes aggregate profit, more as means than end, is the starting point of his theory.

Profit Motive and Decision Making in the Determination of Employment

The basic setting of Keynes's theory is different from that of the neo-classical. The latter is a model of a balance of two forces: aggregate demand, consumers' expressing their needs, and aggregate supply, firms' responding to those needs. Keynes's model is also a balance of forces, but tripartite, brought about by the provision of finance, entrepreneurship, and labour, to effect a certain level of employment and income (National Dividend). It is the study of *Effective Demand*.

> . . . the *effective demand* is simply the aggregate income (or proceeds) which the *entrepreneurs* expect to receive, inclusive of the income which they will hand on to the other factors of production, from the amount of current employment which they *decide* to give. (Keynes, CW, vol. VII, p. 55; emphasis added)

It is not the desired needs of consumers that dictate the amount of employment offered, which then translates into employment, production, and income to satisfy those needs, as is the case in the neo-classical approach. In Keynes's monetary market economy, employment and income depend mostly on entrepreneurs who anticipate what they think are the needs of the rest of the community and then commit to the production from which wealth is created. The ensuing income may or may not satisfy all desired needs, and/or may satisfy the needs of some more than others. Unlike the neo-classical model, which is demand driven, Keynes's is production driven, with demand subjugated to supply. Although the purpose of production is the ultimate satisfaction of consumers, in the meantime,

> . . . the entrepreneur (including both the *producer* and the *investor* in this description) has to form the best expectations he can as to what the consumers will be prepared to pay when he is ready to supply them (directly or indirectly) after the elapse of what may be a lengthy period. (ibid., p. 46, emphasis added)

Since there are lags and costs involved in the whole process of investment and production, Keynes relied extensively on the notion of expectations in the entrepreneurs' decision to invest. It is changes in expectation which cause the trade cycle. As Keynes reminded readers in *The General Theory*, those concerns were already dealt with in *The Treatise*:

> a mere change in expectation is capable of producing an oscillation of the same kind of shape as a cyclical movement, . . . which I discussed in my *Treatise on Money* in connection with the building up or the depletion of stocks of working and liquid capital consequent on change. (ibid., pp. 49–50).

In both *The Treatise* and *The General Theory*, profits are the central variable on which the theory is built and through which it is analysed:

> In my *Treatise on Money* the concept of *changes* in the excess of investment over saving, as there defined, was a way of handling *changes in profit*, though I did not in that book distinguish clearly between expected and realised results . . . *the new argument . . . is essentially a development of the old.* (ibid., pp. 77–8, emphasis added)

Consequently, all the policies implied in the two works are geared to impacting profits, in order to effect investment, with the goal of creating employment.

Functions and Remunerations of the Factors of Production

Keynes was primarily interested in 'the behaviour of the economic system as a whole', in which three distinct groups of players participate in the production of value added or 'National Dividend': (a) producers or manufacturers, (b) labourers, and (c) investors or financiers. Figure 12.1 might help visualize their various roles. In a monetary economy, it is the *entrepreneurs*, the producers and investors combined, who, respectively, run and finance production. Their goal is to seek to *maximize* their 'present and prospective *profits*' (ibid., p. 77, emphasis added).

Each group plays a specific role. (a) In their decision to invest, the *producers* are concerned with earning profits, hence with the state of the marginal efficiency of capital (MEC) in relation to the costs of production. To produce output, the producers require the collaboration of both the

Entrepreneurs

Producers
(Production)

Q: Profits
(finance)

E: Community
Income
(labor)

Investors

Workers

LP

Investment

MEC

MPC

O: Output

Intermediary goods or
Investment goods (I)

Final goods or
Consumer goods (C)

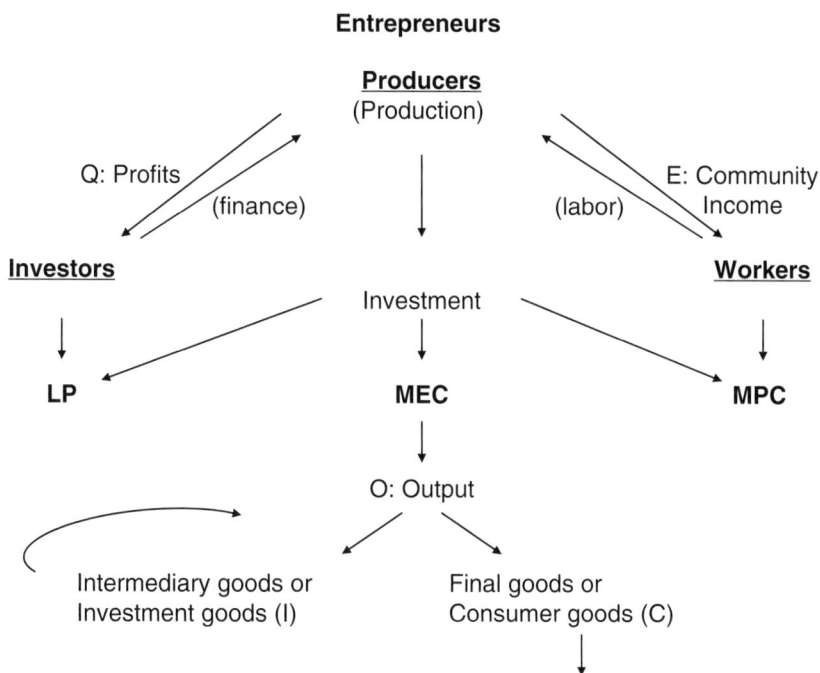

Figure 12.1   Groups of players

labourers, who provide their work, and the financiers, who supply money and credit. (b) While the labourers bargain for the highest wages – save when an economy is at full employment – they have little leverage on the entrepreneurs' decision to invest, even though their propensity to consume out of their income (MPC) is essential in its impact on production, and thus on investment. iii) Investors, who strive for higher returns from their lending, set thereby a threshold for investment and hence for employment and/or production. The investors' liquidity preference (LP) establishes the interest rate against which the marginal efficiency of capital is set and which determines the level of investment of the economic system as a whole.

The entrepreneurs' prime concern, in sum, is the viability of investment to yield profits from production. Aggregate investment is the result of the interaction of three relationships, MEC, MPC, and LP, from which employment and income result.

The whole of Book II of *The General Theory*, which consists of four chapters and comprises almost 10 per cent of the entire work (pp. 37–74), is devoted to 'Definitions and Ideas'. The choice of the units of Keynes's value theory, the meaning of expectations, and the definitions of the incomes of the three groups of players (investors, producers, and labour), of investment and saving, and most importantly of user cost are all laid down and explained precisely,[9] in that order.

Since profits (as remuneration) are the driving force of investment from which the rest of the analysis follows, Keynes began Book II by clarifying what he meant by references to various incomes, namely, the *total income* of the whole economy, the *income of the community*, and the *income of the entrepreneur*. 'The excess of the value of the resulting output over the sum of its factor cost and its user cost is the *profit* or, as we shall call it, the *income of the entrepreneur*' (ibid., p. 23, emphasis added).

Figure 12.2 should help to put in dynamic perspective the various definitions of Keynes's terminologies for the contributions of the factors of production, the circumstances of investment and production, and the means and timing of payments. Production is an ongoing process, thus, at any point in time (T_0, T_1 ... or T_n), there exists a certain amount of stock of capital (G) inherited from the past and a given current level of output (A) available for purchase by consumers and producers. The stock of capital G is made of fixed capital (FK), which consists of machines and equipment, working capital (WK) or goods in progress, and liquid capital (LK) or inventories.[10]

Assume, for the sake of simplicity, an economy with three industries: a furniture manufacturer (F), a power tool industry (D), and a power utility (H). Each industry produces its own final output destined either to be sold to consumers as consumption goods (C) and/or to be sold intra-industry as intermediary goods (I). The power plant can sell its energy as H_0 to consumers for their final consumption and/or as h_0 to the other industries to be used, in the production of power tools and/or furniture. Similarly, the power tool company can sell its screw guns, D_0, directly to hobby consumers and/or to the other two industries, as d_0, to be used to produce tables or power. Furthermore, furniture can be sold as a final consumption good, F_0, or to other industries, as f_0. Keynes called the sum ($F_0+D_0+H_0+f_0+d_0+h_0$) the total output (A) of the whole economy. It is only F_0, D_0, H_0 that is destined to ultimate or final consumption C, while f_0, d_0, h_0 (plus the unsold fraction of F_0, D_0, H_0), which Keynes labelled A_1, is the additional new capital (I). Once I is added to the inherited capital stock, G, that amount of capital stock is available for the next production of goods, $F_1+D_1+H_1+f_1+d_1+h_1$, and so on.

The proceeds from the sale of total output A are the *total income* of the economy.[11] It is the application of a certain level of employment, at T_0, to a given stock of capital G and an amount of 'financial provision for the future', which entrepreneurs are willing to invest in buying 'physical provision for the future', A_1 (ibid., p. 104), which will, in T_1, result in production

Production of final goods A, of consumption goods C, and of investment goods I

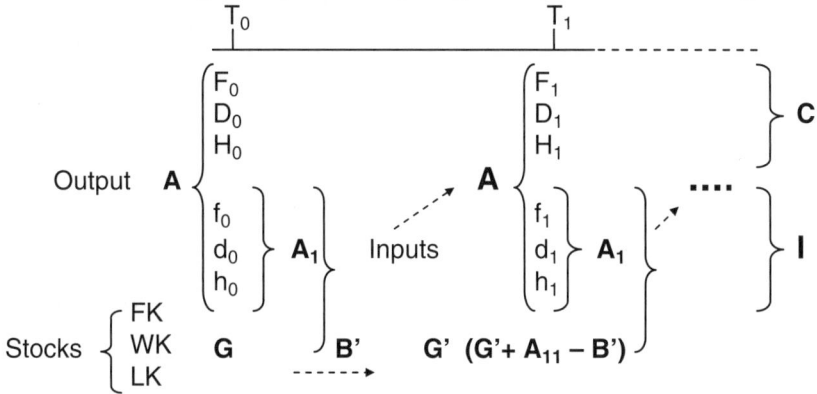

Value terms

A	'sold finished output to consumers or to other entrepreneurs for a certain sum'
G	'capital equipment, which term includes both his stocks of unfinished goods or working capital [WK] and his stocks of finished goods [LK]', and FK
A_1	purchased 'finished output from other entrepreneurs'
B'	'maintenance and improvement'
G'	value of the capital equipment G at the end of the period, if not used
G'−B'	maximum net value that might have been conserved from the previous period
U	user cost, or 'the measure of what has been sacrificed (one way or another) to produce A' $U = (G' - B') - (G - A_1)$
F	*factor cost* of A
V	supplementary cost or 'excess of the expected depreciation over the user cost'

Definitions

A − U	total income (expected proceeds)
A − U −V	*net income*
E = WN	*income of the community*
Q = A − F − U	*income of the entrepreneur or gross profit*
A − A_1	expenditure on *consumption*
A_1 − U	*saving*
A_1 − U − V	net *saving*
A_1 − U	*investment* in addition to capital equipment
A_1 − U − V	net *investment*

A − U = Y = E + Q

$\Delta N = \Delta A_w - \Delta U_w = \Delta Z_w = \Delta \varphi(N)$ Effective Demand Equation

$Z_w = \varphi(N)$, or alternatively $Z = W \varphi(N)$ (where W is the wage-unit and $W Z_w = Z$)

Source: Keynes 1936, Ch. 6.

Figure 12.2 Definition of income, saving and investment

A and yield a return from that investment, net of User Cost U, A_1 − U. Let B be the value of what it takes to maintain and improve the stock of capital, G, inclusive of depreciation and wear and tear, such that at T_1, G becomes G^1. Likewise, A_1 becomes A_{11}, that is to say, the new furniture and power tools bought at T_0 become used furniture and used power tools, as well as the power having been used up in the process, by T_1. User cost U is thus a 'measure of what has been sacrificed (one way or another) to produce A' (ibid., p. 53). Thus, as in *The Treatise*, A_{11} or $A_1 - U$ is the net addition to total capital. Investment, which is described in Keynes's words as 'increment of capital equipment', consists thus 'of fixed capital, working capital or liquid capital' (ibid., p. 75). By definition, since at any point in time all total income, $A - U$, is either sold as C goods, $(A - A_1)$, or finds itself in A_1. If it is not consumed, it must be saved; thus $A_1 - U$ is also saving.

At any point in time, total output supplied in the market is the sum of consumption goods and investment goods. Its total value corresponds to the expected proceeds which producers think (believe) the market will yield from their production. Producers 'entertain' alternative expectations of proceeds and their schedules (ibid., p. 24), which Keynes calls 'Aggregate Demand' (AD). To produce a particular level of output, there is a required amount of employment, whose payment is needed during the process of production, and a required amount of investment on equipment, whose return materializes only after output is ready and sold. 'Aggregate Supply Price' (ASP) corresponds to the cost of the employment that brings about different levels of output for a given technology. Since diminishing efficiency and effort of labour make aggregate cost rise faster than the marginal increase in demand, there is a level of employment for which AD is just equal to the ASP, which is the marginal point beyond which it not worth employing another unit of labour. That intersection is called the 'Effective Demand'

Effective demand relates the income from a given level of employment to the spending on consumption and investment goods from the corresponding level of output. Before turning to the significance of this relationship in terms of the givens and the forward lags, the issue of measurement must be clarified.

Effort in Production and the Importance of 'Wage-unit' as the Measure of Value

In *The Treatise*, Keynes thought that for the General Price Index to have any meaningful economic purpose, it had to be decomposed, and in his discussion of inflation/deflation derived from the Fundamental Equations, he refined that decomposition into separate inflations/deflations: wages, capital, commodities, and profit. Decomposition analysis, although not expressed in those terms, is nonetheless in the background of *The General Theory*. It has been repeatedly asserted, wrongly, that Keynes kept the level of prices constant in *The General Theory*. From the outset of that work, he explained the reasons why a general price index is 'unsatisfactory for the purposes of a causal analysis, which ought to be exact' (ibid., p. 39). As measure of value for all his macroeconomic variables, he chose instead the wage-unit[12] or the money-wage of a unit of labour:[13] 'income measured in wage-units' (p. 79), 'the marginal product to rise in value in terms of the wage-unit' (p. 83), 'consumption in terms of wage-units (C_w)' (p. 90), 'liquidity-preference in terms of wage-units rather than of money' (p. 172), 'effective demand measured in terms of wage-units' (p. 246), 'expenditure in terms of wage-units' (p. 284), and even 'the expected price of a unit of output in terms of the wage-unit' (pp. 283–4). He even defined the general price-level partly, *but not entirely*, in terms of the wage-unit.[14] The main determinant of employment and income, that is, of the level of investment itself, is thus as follows:

> The schedule of the marginal efficiency of capital depends, however, partly on the given factors and partly on the prospective yield of capital-assets of different kinds; whilst the rate of interest depends *partly on* the state of liquidity-preference (i.e. on the liquidity function) and *partly on* the quantity of money measured in terms of wage-units. (ibid., p. 247, emphasis added)

In *The General Theory*, Keynes referred to the 'wage-unit' more than 120 times, and to true inflation throughout. The profession did not know what to make of Keynes's standard of value and chose to ignore it or as in the case of Hicks simply 'to begin by setting out the rest (multiplier, liquidity preference and so on) on the assumption of *fixed* money wages'[15] (Hicks 1974, p. 60). Wages are not fixed, so neither are prices. Inflation becomes of concern when an economy reaches full employment, but that state is rarely attained. Hicks felt he had to twist Keynes's wage-unit analysis into what he 'called the *wage theorem*'[16] (ibid., p. 59). This was tantamount to re-expressing the quantity theory in wage-units, which was not at all the aim of Keynes.

Having made employment dependent on the three factors, LP, MEC and MPC, they too are analysed in terms of wage-units. The wage-unit measurement approach permitted Keynes to express the National Dividend (National Product) as well as remunerations in terms of the quantity of effort put into the production of wealth. Since the purpose of employment is production, which requires effort,[17] labour is rewarded with income,[18] which reflects this effort. The community income, measured in wage-units, reflects the productive effort of the community as a whole. The National Dividend, measured in wage-units and expressed as the number of units of output in terms of effort, is thus shared between those who put in the effort to produce the output and those who supplied the investment. Producers by definition aim to get as much profit as they can, out of the effort put in, in order to have the means for yet higher investment, that is to say, more earnings to be ploughed back into production. Financiers, in *The General Theory*, as owners of the capital-assets, get their income share, also a result of the effort put into production, but not as participants in the effort but as a reward for their risk taken in allocating their liquidity to diverse branches of production. Though finance is vital for production, and is hence remunerated, the financiers do not create added value.

To make a clear distinction between the functions and the remunerations of the producer (manufacturer), investor (capitalist or financier),[19] and labourer, Keynes conceived a theory of an integrated economy[20] in which investment goods (or capital goods in the form of fixed, liquid and working capital) are intermediary goods. They are produced and sold by producers to producers for the ultimate sake of producing final goods. In the aggregate, as intermediary goods (or capital) are produced, they are considered simply as assets owned by the investors, who rent them back to the producers; it is in this sense that it is the shareholders who own the firms. The factor costs to the producer – and in *The General Theory* there is only one factor in the production function – namely, the earnings (E) of labour, are also the earnings of the community, by definition, only the employed members of the community. It is these latter earnings which are available to be spent on consumption and investment goods; this is what is usually written as Y = C + I. Although this is the equilibrium relationship Keynes called the effective demand – Income Y, on the one side, and what is spent on consumption C and on investment goods I, on the other – available and non available items as well as lags are embedded in it. In *The Treatise*, Keynes clearly made distinctions:

> The current output of the community, as distinguished from its money-income, is a flow of goods and services, which consists of two parts – (a) the flow of liquid goods and services which are in a form available for immediate consumption, and (b) the net flow of increments (after allowing for wastage) to capital goods and to loan capital . . . which are not in a form available for consumption. We shall call the former 'liquid' or 'available' output; the latter 'non-available' output . . . (Keynes, CW, vol. V, p. 127)

(These distinctions are kept the same in *The General Theory*.) Further, what is produced as total output will not necessarily correspond at any point in time to total demand, but for that total output to have been produced, it will have required payment corresponding to the cost of the factors of production which realized it:

Thus consumption is governed by the amount of the *available* output (*plus* any drafts on hoards), not by that of the *total* output; whereas – so long as the money rates of remuneration of the factors of production are unchanged – the money income of the community tends to move with the *total* output. (ibid., p. 128, emphasis in original)

On the whole, for an economy, it is the differences in timing between income payments received and that income spent, which cause discrepancies between what is available and what is wanted. It is the shortages and excesses in total output that give rise to profits/losses, relative changes in income distribution, and economic fluctuations.

The Effective Demand Relation and its Policy Implications

The core, interdependent components of Keynes's theory of effective demand, namely money, investment, and consumption,[21] in other words, LP, MEC, and MPC, are all conceived and analysed from the perspective of the firm, where all decisions about investments in the aggregate are made. The simultaneous interaction between these three core, interdependent, aggregate relations depends on both objective[22] and subjective elements. Due to lags between the decisions to invest, to produce and to consume, there are, in addition to the objective elements, the subjective ones, the psychological factors that affect those decisions 'namely, the psychological propensity to consume, the psychological attitude to liquidity and the psychological expectation of future yield from capital-assets' (Keynes, CW, vol. VII, p. 247).

In particular, when evaluating the effective demand, two lags are taken into consideration: i) the lag between the investment in equipment required at the beginning, to start the production process, and the return expected only after the sale takes place, and ii) the lag between, on the one hand, the decision of how much to employ and at what remuneration necessary to bring about a certain level of output, namely the commitment of payment before the start of the process of production, and, on the other hand, the decision to consume or not, which takes place after the production is offered for sale. Unlike perfect foresight found in the neo-classical Keynesian model, for Keynes there is no certainty that investors get their expected return or that producers sell all their output or that the community commits for a fixed amount of consumption. The time lag between investors' spending before their own remuneration and labour's being remunerated before spending introduces a degree of uncertainty in the process of planning and decision making. In *The Treatise*, Keynes expressed the relation between lags and decision making in the use of income as follows:

> At any time, therefore, the community has *two sets of decisions* to make – the one as to what proportion of future income shall be available for consumption and what proportion shall consist of fixed capital, the other as to what proportion of present income shall be consumed productively and what proportion shall be consumed unproductively.[23] (Keynes, CW, vol. V, p. 126; emphasis added)

In *The General Theory* Keynes re-expressed the same distinction, with slightly different implications, between how much is consumed out of a current output and how much is held back for future consumption through allocation for investment:

> The psychological time-preferences of an individual require *two distinct sets of decisions* to carry them out completely. The first . . . determines for each individual how much of his income he will consume and how much he will reserve in *some* form of command over future consumption.
>   . . . there is a further decision which awaits him, namely, in *what form* he will hold the command over future consumption which he has reserved, whether out of his current income or from previous savings. Does he want to hold it in the form of immediate, liquid command (i.e. in money or its equivalent)? Or is he prepared to part with immediate command for a specified or indefinite period, leaving it to future market conditions to determine on what terms he can, if necessary, convert deferred command over specific goods into immediate command over goods in general. (Keynes, CW, vol. VII, p. 166; emphasis added)

For Keynes, the decision not to consume instead of to consume, although it implies saving, does not necessarily mean a postponement of that consumption. His example of an individual deciding to forgo dinner one night (exercising his 'psychological propensity to consume') is to illustrate that the individual's decision does not necessarily mean that he will consume a dinner at a later date to replace that one forgone (ibid., p. 210). This is a good illustration of the point that the propensity to consume does not necessarily convey the same implications as the propensity to save:

> The amounts of aggregate income and of aggregate saving are the *results* of the free choices of individuals whether or not to consume and whether or not to invest; but they are neither of them capable of assuming an independent value resulting from a separate set of decisions taken irrespective of the decisions concerning consumption and investment. In accordance with this principle, the conception of the *propensity to consume* will, in what follows, take the place of the propensity or disposition to save. (ibid., p. 65, emphasis in original)

Furthermore, although the equality between saving and investment is always true, it should be interpreted that since investment must come from somewhere, its source is saving; the amount of investment *causes* the amount of saving[24] and not the other way around.

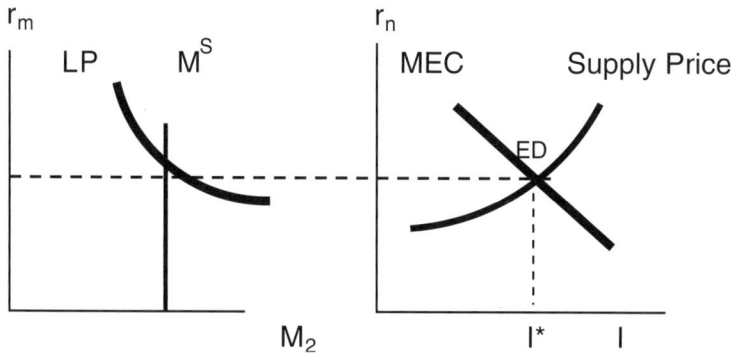

Figure 12.3

Keynes's theory can now be expressed as follows: aggregate demand and aggregate supply price together for given levels of investment determine the level of employment. In Keynes's model, it is the volume of employment and the ensuing level of income and income distribution, which are of prime importance;[25] his policies are about nurturing additional investment and channelling its impact to bring about employment.

The *Effective Demand* Equation in Figure 12.2 in Keynes's notation can also be expressed as:

(a) $E(N) = C(N) + I(r_n, r_m)$[26]

(b) $= P_C C + P_I I$ P_C, actual price of consumer goods
                               P_I, expected price of real assets

First, (a) can be rewritten as $N = f(I)$. This is how Keynes infers the volume of employment from the level of investment, which itself is determined by the intersection of the MEC schedule and the Supply Price curve (Figure 12.3). The MEC curve depicts returns from each additional dollar invested, r_n, and the Supply Price curve depicts the marginal costs of borrowing or the money rate, r_m.[27] As can be seen from Figure 12.3, the liquidity preference and the money supply determine the money rate of interest, r_m, and the corresponding r_n determines the level of Investment I^*.

The level of investment, I^*, can vary for any of the following reasons. Keynes gives three possible ones for shifts in the MEC schedule to occur: (1) changes in prices and wages, (2) changes in technology, and (3) changes in taxes. Shifts in either or both the money supply, M^S, and/or Liquidity Preference curve, LP, can also occur and will affect the interest rate and thus the Supply Price curve.

Thus, for Keynes the level of employment in an economy depends directly on the investment decisions of the entrepreneurs. As has been seen, various factors (technology, prices, taxes, costs, rate of interest, etc.), which impact the intersection of the MEC and the Supply Price curves – the Effective Demand, ED – can shift either one or both curves. It is the fact that the movements of these curves will result in many different levels of employment that rendered Keynes's theory capable of explaining any and all such levels. It should be apparent now that his theory can explain much more than just, as Hicks claimed about the account in *The General Theory*, the special case of an economy in a slump.[28]

Keynes's general theory is more than any Post Keynesian interpretation so far gives it credit of being. It is not just a theory of output, as Ricardian Post Keynesians interpret it. Conceptually it is also very different from the Kaleckian Post Keynesian mark-up price theory. Further, even as labour is an important component, the deficiencies of effective demand have nothing to do with rigidities in the labour market. Moreover, those Post Keynesians who fault Keynes for the lack of a micro-foundation have in fact been seduced by a Walrasian analysis of Keynes, which was not his approach. Keynes's theory is about aggregate entities, although made up of individual elements. Keynes was aware that summation is not an easy task of commensurability and that the interaction between aggregates and their components does not follow the same dynamics.

The prevention of an economy from reaching an adequate level of employment is not the result of labour rigidity, as built into the Keynesian macroeconomic model, but due to the insufficiency of the financial requirements to sustain the marginal efficiency of capital high enough to induce new investment. Fluctuations in a monetary market economy (Keynes's entrepreneurial economy) are the result mainly of changes in entrepreneurs' expectations as they calculate and decide on new additional investment based on their evaluation of the MPC, MEC, and LP, with available finance the *constraining* factor. Money in the form of credit in the hands of investors, subject to speculation, is the root cause of economic instability. Keynes's distinction between the total amount of money provided by the monetary authority and that part of money devoted to speculation marks a clear separation between the banking institution, whose role is to provide the economy with needed liquidity, and the financial institutions, which engage in speculation in the transmission mechanism of that means. It is the latter, which by financial innovation finds ways of expanding or withholding liquidity, when convenient, which causes fluctuation in investment.

CONCLUDING THOUGHTS

For Keynes, it is expected return that determines new investment, and thus employment and income. Aggregate Demand is what entrepreneurs project as to what they think consumer demand would be if they were to hire a certain level of employment. Aggregate supply is the corresponding level of output based on that level of employment. *The General Theory* is therefore a production, not a demand-driven theory of employment. Most of the implied policies of his theory are geared to inducing investment to create employment and income. As employment is created, a more equitable distribution of income ensues.

To Keynes's core theory, income distribution is fundamental whether in the short- or longer-run. It is achieved through the creation of employment, which generates first income and then consumption, and *not the other way around*. Employment depends on new investment. Finance is vital for new investment, which is undertaken by entrepreneurs only when the marginal efficiency of capital warrants it. Keynes's economic policies are designed to improve productive investment through stimulation of aggregate supply. His are economic policies, whether in the form of interest rate changes, and/or credit or tax stimulus, directed only to that production which can generate employment. Credit to consumption (or consumers) is an anathema to Keynes. Increasing effective demand in the form of handouts, at any cost and without limit, as some Post Keynesians advocate, is not Keynes.

NOTES

1. For an account of the participants in early Post Keynesianism, see Harcourt (1985 and 2006) and Pasinetti (2007), and for a more general perspective, see King (2002).
2. Joan Robinson referred to the work herself upon its completion as 'a told-to-the-children book' in a letter to Keynes of 6 March 1937 (Keynes, *Collected Writings* (CW), vol. XIV, p, 148).
3. See Joan Robinson's letter to Keynes of 18 November 1936, where she first broached the topic of her book with Keynes (Keynes, CW, vol. XXIX, pp. 184–5).
4. Not all Post Keynesians followed in Joan Robinson's footsteps. Many, in a subsequent generation, for example, Weintraub, Minsky, Davidson, Asimakopoulos, and Chick, among others, tried to remain close to certain aspects of the text of *The General Theory*, albeit looking at the whole work from a narrower perspective. (*The Treatise* was missing completely from their analysis.) In the 1950s, the discussion as to how to interpret Keynes's aggregate demand and aggregate supply, and his notion of the supply for labour brought Weintraub and some of his followers to put emphasis on the role of the labour market, in particular as found in Chapter 20 of *The General Theory*. See King (1994), for the detailed analysis of that controversy.
5. As found between pages 56 and 76 of the lectures published as *The Making of Keynes' General Theory* (1984).

6. Kahn 1984, p. 71.
7. Robinson 1985, p. 208.
8. The interpretation of Hicks in his review of *The General Theory* would corrupt even the views of Austin Robinson, which still persist: 'Keynes at the time partly accepted our criticism, and as everyone knows moved on from the determination of prices to the determination of output and employment' (Robinson 1985, p. 207).
9. Albeit in cumbersome notation.
10. For more detail about Keynes's classifications of capital, see *The Treatise*, vol. II, Chapters 27, 28, and 29 and Hamouda 2009, Chapter 3.
11. The factor cost of labour or labour cost F or earnings E 'is the wages (and salaries) bill' (Keynes, CW, vol. VII, p. 41); it is the *community income* in the terminology of *The Treatise*.
12. 'If X stands for any quantity measured in terms of money, it will often be convenient to write X_w for the same quantity measured in terms of the wage-unit' (Keynes, CW, vol. VII, p. 41).
13. '. . . if E is the wages (and salaries) bill, W the wage-unit, and N the quantity of employment, $E = N . W$' (Keynes, CW, vol. VII, p. 41).
14. 'Whilst it is for many purposes a very useful first approximation to assume that the rewards of all the factors entering into marginal prime-cost change in the same proportion as the wage-unit, it might be better, perhaps, to take a weighted average of the rewards of the factors entering into marginal prime-cost, and call this the *cost-unit*. The cost-unit, or, subject to the above approximation, the wage-unit, can thus be regarded as the essential standard of value; and the price-level, given the state of technique and equipment, will depend partly on the cost-unit and partly on the scale of output, increasing, where output increases, *more* than in proportion to any increase in the cost-unit, in accordance with the principle of diminishing returns in the short period. We have full employment when output has risen to a level at which the marginal return from a representative unit of the factors of production has fallen to the minimum figure at which a quantity of the factors sufficient to produce this output is available' (Keynes, CW, vol. VII, pp. 302–3).
15. '. . . All expositors of Keynes (including myself) have found this procedure a difficulty . . .' (Hicks 1974, p. 60).
16. 'When there is a general (proportional) rise in money wages, says the theorem, the *normal* effect is that all prices rise in the same proportion – provided that the money supply is increased in the same proportion (whence the rate of interest will be unchanged)' (Hicks 1974, pp. 59–60). See also Kahn 1984, p. 128.
17. '. . . the national income depends on the volume of employment, i.e. on the quantity of effort currently devoted to production . . .' (Keynes, CW, vol. VII, p. 246). Labour means effort; effort means production.
18. For Keynes, labour refers not only to workers, who receive wages, but also to management, supervisors, etc., who receive salaries.
19. In 1934, Keynes expressed his distinctions between these two roles: 'the producer or manufacturer and the investor or capitalist respectively. It is the former who employs labour; he produces goods for sale either to the consumer or the investor; his goods are for sale as soon as they are finished; and his forecast relates to the period which elapses between his decision to employ labour and the sale of his output. The latter does not employ labour but must be conceived as hiring out his capital goods to a producer from one accounting period to the next' (Keynes, CW, vol. XXIX, p. 75).
20. '. . . the employment of a given volume of labour by an entrepreneur involves him in two kinds of expense: first of all, the amounts which he pays out to the factors of production (exclusive of other entrepreneurs) for their current services, which we shall call the *factor cost* of the employment in question; and secondly, the amounts which he pays out to other entrepreneurs for what he has to purchase from them together with the sacrifice which he incurs by employing the equipment instead of leaving it idle, which we shall call the *user cost* of the employment in question' (Keynes, CW, vol. VII, p. 23).

21. This trio is discussed at length in Hamouda 2009.
22. By 'objective' is meant here anything having to do with resources, stocks, technology, and ex-post knowledge of the state of the economy.
23. 'Productive' and 'unproductive' consumption is consumption which leads, respectively, to the creation or not of employment, see Hamouda 2009, Chapter 4.
24. Investment and savings are always equal, $I = S$. S' or ($E - C$ in *The General Theory*) is the savings out of the earnings of the community or voluntary savings (Keynes, CW, XXIX, p. 108). $S - S'$ is involuntary saving. There is no inconsistency between Keynes's assertions in *The Treatise* and *The General Theory*, that $I = S$ always (that investment is always equal to profits and the savings of the community, or S, total savings) and that I is not necessarily equal to S (that investment is not necessarily equal to the saving of the community, S or S'). Notwithstanding the use of different symbols, the two concepts, the identity and the equality, are both consistent features of both *The Treatise* and *The General Theory*.
25. This is unlike the Keynesian model, where income and the corresponding level of prices are the central focus and whereby ensuing policies are assessed in terms of the trade-off between inflation and unemployment.
26. See Keynes, CW, vol. XIII, pp. 483–4.
27. In Keynes, the money rate is the premium that borrowers pay lenders to induce them to part with their liquidity.
28. It could also, as another obvious example, explain the special case of the Classics, the situation where the intersection of MEC and the Supply Price will produce a level of employment N compatible with full employment. Like the instance of the slump, pertinent for the historical circumstances surrounding the writing of *The General Theory*, the full employment case was also important, as Keynes was building a general *General Theory*. It is only at this point, where the real wages are equal to the marginal disutility of labour, that the second Classical postulate holds; it is only in the special case of the Classics that there is no involuntary unemployment.

BIBLIOGRAPHY

Asimakopulos, A. (1983), 'Anticipations of Keynes's General Theory?', *The Canadian Journal of Economics/Revue Canadienne d'Economique*, **16**(3) (August), pp. 517–30.

Asimakopulos, A. (1991), *Keynes's General Theory and Accumulation*, Cambridge: Cambridge University Press.

Cairncross, A. (1983), *The Relationship between Monetary and Fiscal Policy*, London: British Academy.

Cararosa, C. (1984), 'The microfoundations of Keynes's aggregate supply and expected demand analysis: a reply', *Economic Journal*, **94**(376) (December), 941–5.

Chick, V. (1983), *Macroeconomics after Keynes: A Reconsideration of the General Theory*, Oxford: Philip Allan.

Hamouda, O. F. (1991), 'Joan Robinson's Post Keynesianism', in I. Rima (ed.), *The Economics of Joan Robinson*, New York: M. E. Sharpe.

Hamouda, O. F. (1993), *John R. Hicks. The Economist's Economist*, Oxford: Blackwell Publishers.

Hamouda, O. F. (2001), 'The classical classical fallacy', *International Journal of Applied Economics and Econometrics*, **9**(2) (April–June), 147–69.

Hamouda, O. F (2009), *Money, Investment and Consumption: Keynes's Macroeconomics Rethought*, Cheltenham, UK and Northampton, MA, USA: Edward Elgar.

Hamouda, O. F. and B. B. Price (1998), *Keynesianism and the Keynesian Revolution in America*, Cheltenham, UK and Lyme, NH, USA: Edward Elgar.

Harcourt, G. C. (ed.) (1985), *Keynes and his Contemporaries*, New York: St Martin's Press.

Harcourt, G. C. (2006), *The Structure of Post-Keynesian Economics – The Core Contributions of the Pioneers*, Cambridge: Cambridge University Press.

Hayek, F. A. (1931a), *Price and Production*, London: Routledge.

Hayek, F. A. (1931b), 'Reflections on the pure theory of money of Mr. J. M. Keynes', *Economica*, **33** (August), 270–95; reprinted in Bruce Caldwell (ed.), *Contra Keynes and Cambridge. Essays, Correspondence*, vol. 9 of *The Collected Works of F. A. Hayek*, S. Kresge (series ed.), London: Routledge, pp. 121–46.

Hayek, F. A. (1932), 'Reflections on the pure theory of money of Mr. J. M. Keynes (continued)', *Economica*, **35** (February), 22–44; reprinted in Bruce Caldwell (ed.), *Contra Keynes and Cambridge. Essays, Correspondence*, vol. 9 of *The Collected Works of F. A. Hayek*, S. Kresge (series ed.), London: Routledge, pp. 174–97.

Hicks, J. (1935/1982), 'Wages and interest: the dynamic problem', in John R. Hicks (ed.), *Money, Interest and Wages*, Cambridge, MA: Harvard University Press, pp. 64–79.

Hicks, J. (1936/1982), '*The General Theory*: a first impression', in John R. Hicks (ed.), *Money, Interest and* Wages, Cambridge, MA: Harvard University Press, pp. 83–99.

Hicks, J. (1937/1982), 'Mr. Keynes and the classics', in John R. Hicks (ed.), *Money, Interest and Wages*, Cambridge, MA: Harvard University Press, pp. 100–115.

Hicks, J. (1939), *Value and Capital*, Oxford: Clarendon Press.

Hicks, J. (1950), *A Contribution to the Theory of the Trade Cycle*, Oxford: Clarendon.

Hicks, J. (1974), *The Crisis of Keynesian Economics*, Oxford: Blackwell Publishers.

Hicks, J. (1979), 'On Coddington's interpretation: a reply', *Journal of Economic Literature*, **17**(3) (September), 989–75, reprinted in Wood and Woods (eds), *Sir John R. Hicks: Critical Assessments* (1989), vol. III, pp. 209–16.

Hutchison, T. W. (1977), *Keynes versus the 'Keynesians': An Essay in the Thinking of J. M. Keynes and the Accuracy of its Interpretation by his Followers*, London: Institute of Economic Affairs.

Kahn, R. F. (1972), *Selected Essays on Employment and Growth*, Cambridge: Cambridge University Press.

Kahn, R. (1978), 'Some aspects of the development of Keynes's thought', *Journal of Economic Literature*, **16**(2) (June), 545–59.

Kahn, R. F. (1984), *The Making of Keynes' General Theory*, Cambridge: Cambridge University Press.

Kaldor, N. (1983), *Limitations of the 'General Theory'*, London: The British Academy.

Kates, S. (1998), *Say's Law and the Keynesian Revolution: How Macroeconomic Theory Lost its Way*, Cheltenham, UK and Northampton, MA, USA: Edward Elgar.

Keynes, J. M. (1937), 'The "ex-ante" theory of the rate of interest', *Economic Journal*, **47**(188) (December), 663–9.

Keynes, J. M. (1971–1989), *The Collected Writings of John Maynard Keynes*, London: Macmillan and St Martin's Press, for the Royal Economic Society: Vol. V: *A Treatise on Money*, vol. 1 *The Pure Theory of Money*

Vol. VI: *A Treatise on Money*, vol. 2 *The Applied Theory of Money*
Vol. VII: *The General Theory of Employment, Interest, and Money*
Vol. XIII: *The General Theory and After*: pt. 1, *Preparation*
Vol. XIV: *The General Theory and After*: pt. 2, *Defense and Development*
Vol. XXIX: *The General Theory and After: A Supplement*
King, J. (1994), 'Aggregate supply and demand analysis since Keynes: a partial history', *Journal of Post Keynesian Economics*, **17**(1) (Fall), 3–31.
King, J. (2002), *A History of Post Keynesian Economics Since 1936*, Cheltenham, UK and Northampton, MA, USA: Edward Elgar.
Lerner, A. P. (1938), 'Alternative formulations of the theory of interest', *Economic Journal*, **48**(190) (June), 211–30.
Lerner, A. (1974), 'From the *Treatise on Money* to *The General Theory*', *Journal of Economic Literature*, **12**(1) (March), 38–42.
Meade, J. M. (1937), 'A simplified model of Mr. Keynes' system', *The Review of Economic Studies*, **4**(2) (February), 98–107.
Minsky, H. P. (1976), *John Maynard Keynes*, London: Macmillan.
Pasinetti, L. L. (2007), *Keynes and the Cambridge Keynesians: A 'Revolution in Economics' to be Accomplished*, Cambridge: Cambridge University Press.
Pasinetti, L. L. and B. Schefold (eds) (1999), *The Impact of Keynes on Economics in the 20th Century*, Cheltenham, UK and Northampton, MA, USA: Edward Elgar.
Pigou, A. C. (1936), 'Mr. J. M. Keynes' *General Theory of Employment, Interest and Money*', *Economica*, New Series, **3**(10) (May), 115–32.
Robertson, D. H. (1931), 'Mr. Keynes' Theory of Money', *Economic Journal*, **41**(163), (September), pp. 395–411.
Robertson, D. H. (1936), 'Some notes on Mr. Keynes' *General Theory of Employment*', *Quarterly Journal of Economics*, **51**(1) (November), 168–91.
Robertson, D. H. (1938), 'Mr. Keynes and "Finance"', *Economic Journal*, **48**(191) (September), 555–6.
Robertson, D. H. (1956), 'Keynes and supply functions', *Economic Journal*, **66**(263) (September), 485–7.
Robertson, D. H. and H. G. Johnson (1955), 'Keynes and supply functions', *Economic Journal*, **65**(259) (September), 474–8.
Robinson, A. (1985), 'Review of *The Making of Keynes' General Theory By Richard F. Kahn*', *Economic Journal*, **95**(377) (March), pp. 206–8.
Robinson, J. (1933), *The Economics of Imperfect Competition*, London: Macmillan.
Robinson, J. (1937), *Introduction to the Theory of Employment*, London: Macmillan.
Robinson, J. (1979), *The Generalisation of the General Theory, and other Essays*, New York: St Martin's Press.
Robinson, J. (1988), 'What has become of the Keynesian revolution?', in Milo Keynes (ed.), *Essays on John Maynard Keynes*, Cambridge: Cambridge University Press, pp. 123–31
Rymes, T. K. (1989), *Keynes's Lectures, 1932–35, Notes of a Representative Student: A Synthesis of Lecture Notes Taken by Students at Keynes's Lectures in the 1930s Leading Up to the Publication of The General Theory*, Ann Arbor, MI: University of Michigan Press.
Scazzieri, R., A. Sen and S. Zamagni (eds) (2008), *Market, Money and Capital*, Cambridge: Cambridge University Press.

Shackle, G. L. S. (1974), *Keynesian Kaleidics: The Evolution of a General Political Economy*, Edinburgh: Edinburgh University Press.

Sraffa, P. (1962), *Production of Commodities by Means of Commodities. Prelude to a Critique of Economic Theory*, Cambridge: Cambridge University Press.

Tarshis, L. (1939), 'Changes in real and money wages', *Economic Journal*, **49**(193), (March), 150–54.

Tarshis, L. (1941), 'Real and money wage rates: further comment', *Quarterly Journal of Economics*, **55**(4) (August), 691–7.

Torr, C. (1984), 'The microfoundations of Keynes's aggregate supply and expected demand analysis: a comment', *Economic Journal*, **94**(376) (December), 936–40.

Weintraub, S. (1957), 'The micro-foundations of aggregate demand and supply', *Economic Journal*, **67**(267) (September), 455–70.

Wells, P. (1960), 'Keynes' aggregate supply function: a suggested interpretation', *Economic Journal*, **70**(279) (September), 536–42.

Wells, P. (1961), 'Mr. Wells' aggregate supply function – a further comment', *Economic Journal*, **71**(283) (September), 636–7.

Wells, P. (1985), 'The aggregate supply curve: Keynes and downwardly sticky money wages', *Journal of Economic Education*, **16**(4) (Autumn), 297–304.

Wicksell, K. (1907), 'The influence of the rate of interest on prices', *Economic Journal*, **17**(66) (June), 213–20.

Wicksell, K. (1934/1935), *Lectures on Political Economy*, L. Robbins (ed.) and E. Classen (translation), London: Routledge & K. Paul
Vol. I: General Theory
Vol. II: Money

Wicksell, K. (1936), *Interest and Prices*, London: Macmillan.

Wicksell, K. (1997/1999), *Selected Essays in Economics*, Bo Sandelin (ed.) London: Routledge, Vol. I and Vol. II.

Wood, J. C. and Woods, R. N. (eds) (1989), *Sir John R. Hicks: Critical Assessments*, 3 vols., London/New York: Routledge.

13. Money's endogeneity, Keynes's *General Theory* and beyond

Louis-Phillippe Rochon[1]

INTRODUCTION

John Maynard Keynes's *The General Theory of Employment, Interest, and Money* (Keynes, *Collected Writings* (CW), vol. VII) remains one of the most important books written in economics, and certainly ranks as one of the most influential academic books ever written. Its importance cannot be understated, and its influence is felt not only in the area of economic theory, but also policy, and philosophy. It has influenced generations of young scholars and will continue to do so for generations more.

I was first introduced to *The General Theory* as an undergraduate student at the University of Ottawa, while studying with Marc Lavoie, Alain Parguez and Mario Seccareccia, and then at McGill University, under Tom Asimakopulos. In Ottawa, understanding Keynes was necessary in various courses I took. But it is while I was an MA student at McGill that Keynes's *General Theory* was required reading, in Asimakopulos's graduate seminar on Keynes – an endeavour which later became *Keyne's General Theory and Accumulation* (1991). Every week, we read and discussed in detail the content of each chapter, both of *The General Theory* and of Asimakopulos's book. In this sense, I got an early and very distinct education on Keynes and *The General Theory*, not to mention my further studies at the New School with Ed Nell and Tom Palley.

I therefore welcome the opportunity, no less on the 75th anniversary of *The General Theory*, to discuss and reflect on the importance of the book, its lasting relevance today, but also to address some unresolved controversies surrounding some of the more important aspects of the book, or rather, in the context of this contribution, omissions to the book.

The purpose of this contribution honouring Keynes's *General Theory* is to briefly analyse, given the space allotted, whether Keynes had within the confines of his book a theory of endogenous money or whether, as many suspect, Keynes simply assumed the money supply as exogenous and under the control of the central bank.

I will argue that while Keynes did assume an exogenous money supply in *The General Theory*, his analysis is nonetheless consistent with a theory of endogenous money. The problem arises, however, from Keynes's inability to properly analyse the role of banks and that of the central bank in *The General Theory*. We are given a few sentences, scattered throughout the book, but not enough to draw a clear conclusion. We need to go beyond the confines of *The General Theory*, which I will do by looking at his *Economic Journal* articles on the finance motive, published in 1937 and 1939.

Dow (1997, p. 61), whose paper is the inspiration for my own, argues that 'an exploration of Keynes's other writings reveals an understanding of the process of money creation through bank lending, and of the limitations on the scope for control by the monetary authorities'. While I share this view, I disagree with Dow on her analysis contained within *The General Theory*, and also go much further in my conclusion regarding Keynes's position on interest rates. My own view (1999) is that Keynes eventually developed a position that was very close to those held today by Post Keynesians and horizontalists in particular, such as Lavoie (1992) and Moore (1988).

In order to help this analysis, a brief description of what exactly is endogenous money is required. Only then can we compare that to the analytical content of *The General Theory*. My conclusion as to whether Keynes developed a theory of endogenous money both within and after *The General Theory* rests on the analysis presented in the next section.

MONEY'S ENDOGENEITY

The notion of endogenous money has divided heterodox economists for some time. After all, its precise definition has contributed to some fierce debates and disagreements, both in terms of theory but also in terms of policy, although with hindsight, it may have been more a matter of emphasis than fundamental disagreement. Nevertheless, many Post Keynesians propose specific central bank monetary policies based on their specific interpretation of endogeneity. It therefore comes as no surprise that it is also at the heart of a debate over whether Keynes has endogenous money in *The General Theory*, but also in his overall analysis, both before and after *The General Theory*.

We can argue that there are two overall factions among heterodox economists with respect to the definition of endogenous money, each corresponding to a specific relationship within the monetary system. On the one hand, there is an on-going debate between Post Keynesians and circuitists regarding the nature of money (see Deleplace and Nell (1996) and Rochon and Rossi (2003), for a good analysis), and on the other, among Post Keynesians, the so-called horizontalist-structuralist debates which dominated the literature for the greater part of a decade (see Moore (1988); Lavoie (1992, 1996); Rochon (1999); Wray (1990) for a discussion).

This dual approach to the definition of endogenous money is reflected in Lavoie's discussion of the 'two poles of endogeneity' (Lavoie 1984). According to Lavoie, endogeneity of money should be analysed from the point of view of the relationship between banks and bank borrowers, on the one hand, as well as between banks and the central bank, on the other. This corresponds to the generally-agreed principle that loans create deposits which then create reserves.

In general, the debate between circuitists and Post Keynesians deals with the first relationship, whereas the second debate between horizontalists and structuralists deals with the second. In fact, it is perhaps safe to say that in general, the debate between horizontalists and structuralists paid little attention to the first pole of analysis: indeed, this debate was almost entirely about the relationship between banks and the central bank, and the supply of central bank reserves. Are central banks accommodative or not? In the same way, however, circuitists have not paid sufficient attention to the second relationship, although it is certainly implied, hence the often difficult relationship between them and Post Keynesians: indeed, except for a few circuitist authors, the central bank is virtually absent from their analysis.

One of the standing differences between circuitists and Post Keynesians regarding the endogeneity of money therefore is their respective emphasis on the central bank. For the former, the central bank is not required to explain the endogeneity of money since money is endogenous by nature, that is by its very essence, given its relationship to bank debt, which explains why the central bank is virtually absent from their analysis. On the other hand, Post Keynesians have generally insisted on linking endogenous money to a well-developed central bank, as in Chick (1986). In fact, a number of Post Keynesians today still see the money supply as partly endogenous and partly exogenous, depending on the actions of the central bank (see Rochon 1999, for a detailed discussion).

In my opinion, a complete theory of endogenous money should include a full discussion of both poles of endogeneity, to eliminate any possible ambiguities. So while I see money as always endogenous irrespective of central bank actions or the 'stage of banking development', because so many Post Keynesians see central bank actions as tied to the endogenous nature of money, a statement addressing the second pole of endogeneity is important: to wit, central banks always accommodate at the risk of jeopardizing the financial and banking systems. Failing that, we fall into the New Keynesian inconsistency of having banks responding to the demand of credit the supply of which is dictated by the actions of the central bank: central banks affect the price of bank loans, not the quantity.

An ideal definition of endogenous money would merge both approaches together, as is done by Lavoie (1992), Moore (1988), Rochon (1999) and Wray (1990), among others. In this sense, not only is the supply of credit-money – that is resulting from bank credit – demand-determined and endogenous, but so is the supply of central bank reserves. Endogeneity therefore becomes a dual monetary process that involves three groups: bank borrowers, banks and the central bank. The first pole makes clear money's endogeneity given its natural relationship with bank debt, while the second pole adds a vital institutional element that reflects contemporary capitalist systems. Elsewhere (Rochon 1999, p. 63), I have called this a 'revolutionary' definition of endogenous money. Moreover, as will become clear in the next section, this approach will serve us well in analysing Keynes's own analysis of money, and shed some light on the treatment of money in *The General Theory*.

Regarding the first point of analysis between banks and borrowers, it is generally agreed that firms need access to credit in order to proceed with production, that is to pay for the factors of production, but also to purchase capital goods. This applies, as in Keynes as well, equally to the production of investment goods as to consumption goods. Credit is generally required because there exists a discrepancy between the time firms pay for their factors of production and when they receive the proceeds of the sale of their produced goods. This is what circuitists call 'initial finance' (Graziani 1984).

In this sense, the need for credit is associated with the need to enter into a debt relationship with the banking system, as emphasized eloquently by Wray (1990), among others. Money is the physical manifestation of debt: money is debt that circulates freely. Money is therefore created endogenously when banks agree to give firms credit, which is used to remunerate workers. Although linked, there is a difference between credit and money: credit and debt leads to the creation of money. It is therefore more accurate to refer to the supply of credit rather than to the supply of money.

This does not mean of course that banks will automatically grant credit to anyone who demands it. Indeed, banks may and do deny firms credit based on their general perception of the borrower's creditworthiness. In other words, all those deemed creditworthy by the banks will receive credit (see Rochon 2006, for an analysis). This said, the creation of money is certainly credit-led and demand-determined; it can be supply-constrained only in the sense that banks may not want to lend, but not because they cannot lend. This implies therefore that banks are never reserve-constrained, in the sense that the banks' supply of loans does not depend on some *a priori* level of reserves. Hence, there is never any credit rationing taking place, as credit never has to be rationed in the neoclassical sense of a scarce supply of credit, although credit supply can effectively be constrained by the unwillingness of banks to lend, based on their pessimism about future levels of effective demand and their perceived inability of firms to reimburse their debt.

Regarding the second pole of analysis, Post Keynesians have generally emphasized the relationship between banks and central banks. While they did acknowledge that loans created deposits, they concentrated their research principally on the supply of central bank reserves. In this respect, the debate between horizontalists and structuralists essentially discussed whether central banks accommodated fully the reserve needs of commercial banks. Structuralists argued that they did not, and that as a result, the supply curve of money should be viewed as upward sloping, not as horizontal at a given rate of interest. The rate of interest had both endogenous and exogenous features. Horizontalists countered that central banks usually accommodated the needs of banks, but even if they did not, this did not jeopardize the exogenous or administrative nature of the rate of interest (Rochon 1999; Lavoie 1996).

More importantly, structuralists argued that the lack of accommodation on the part of the central bank impacted the ability of banks to lend. In other words, the money supply was both endogenous and exogenous, and central bank reserves were bi-causal (Palley 1996). Horizontalists (and circuitists for that matter) objected to this statement strongly, and argued that central bank reserves were never causal in the determination of the supply of bank credit.

As stated above, both poles are necessary to have a complete theory of endogenous money. In other words, we cannot build a theory of endogenous money with accommodative banks, but a non-accommodative central bank. This is the position of some New Keynesian economists (Kashyap and Stein 1994), who emphasized the money creation ability of banks through the supply of credit, yet somehow retained the exogenous nature of the money supply given the central bank's ability to increase or decrease its supply of high-powered money at will, and how in turn this allowed central banks to influence, albeit indirectly, the supply of bank loans. According to this analysis, central banks are able to influence the creation of money by decreasing its supply of high-powered money to the banking system. In this sense, the money supply was credit-driven, but supply-determined (Rochon 1999). So while New Keynesians (and I believe this analysis applies to the proponents of the New Consensus as well) defend the first pole of analysis, they still draw the money supply curve vertical (as in Blinder 2010).

Finally, there is one more remaining element that needs to be discussed regarding the money's endogeneity and that has to do with the rate of interest. Horizontalists and circuitists argue that the rate of interest is fully exogenous, under the control of the central bank and that, as such, the central bank can have any interest rate it deems appropriate. Structuralists, and I am not sure if this is still correct today, argued that the rate was partly exogenous and partly endogenous, whatever that really meant. Irrespective, there was this view that it was both administered and also determined by market forces.

KEYNES'S ANALYSIS OF MONEY IN *THE GENERAL THEORY*

The above discussion regarding the two poles of endogeneity is a good starting point for the discussion over whether Keynes adopted a theory of endogenous money within *The General Theory* and after. With respect to *The General Theory*, the analysis is challenged by the fact that Keynes discusses very little the role of banks or the central bank. In other words, both poles of analysis are underdeveloped.

In this respect, there has been some discussion regarding the endogeneity of money in *The General Theory*. There are certainly some attempts at interpretation. In doing so, we must distinguish between Keynes's views contained within *The General Theory*, and those which he developed after its publication, especially those concerned with the finance motive (see Rochon 1997).

There are two strong views in dealing with Keynes's treatment of the money supply in *The General Theory*. On the one hand, there are those, for instance Asimakopulos (1991, pp. 86–7) who has argued that 'Keynes assumed in *The General Theory* that the money supply is exogenously determined by the monetary authority, even though he had observed in the *Treatise* . . . that the amount of bank money was very much influenced by the decisions of individuals in the economy'. This view is also defended by Moore (1988).

On the other hand, Dow (1997) has argued that while Keynes did classify in *The General Theory* the money supply as one of his 'exogenous variables', we should not conclude that this means he considered the money supply as exogenous. Rather, she claims, the money supply should be interpreted rather as 'given' by Keynes. Indeed, according to the author:

'Thus the passage should be interpreted as taking the money supply to be given, not exogenous' (Dow 1997, p. 63).

I disagree with the second interpretation. Regarding Dow's assertion, after all, how can the money supply be taken as 'given' when the book is about, as Keynes writes in the preface, 'the forces which determine changes in the scale of output and employment as a whole' (Keynes, CW, vol. VII, p. vii). A theory of endogenous money, as described in the previous section, suggests that when output is changing, so must be the quantity of money since production and output must be financed. So we cannot have a theory of endogenous money where output is changing and the money supply is 'given'. If the money supply is given, then so should be the production level. Hence, it is a difficult argument to reconcile with the overall notion of money's endogeneity. Indeed, as Foster (1986, p. 953) argues, Keynes's analysis in *The General Theory* would require the money supply to be endogenous. This would suggest we cannot take it as 'given'.

Moreover, in Chapter 18, Keynes specifically identifies those variables that 'we usually take as given, which are the independent variables of our system and which are the dependent variables' (Keynes, CW, vol. VII, p. 245). He therefore separates those variables considered 'given' from those he considers 'independent'. Given variables, he writes, 'does not mean that we assume these factors to be constant; but merely that, in this place and context, we are not considering or taking into account the effects and consequences of changes in them' (ibid.). Among the list of those he considers given, he does not mention the money supply. Rather the money supply appears in the list of variables that he specifically considers the 'ultimate independent variables': 'the quantity of money as determined by the action of the central bank' (ibid., p. 247).

It is therefore difficult to accept Dow's argument because (1) it conflicts with the notion of an endogenous money supply; and (2) Keynes separates given variables from independent variables, and does not consider the money supply as one of his given variables. In other words, Keynes had the opportunity of specifying money as given, yet chose not to.

Yet, this does not mean that Keynes believed the money supply was actually exogenous. As stated above, his analysis is consistent with endogenous money. But it does raise the important question of why he accepted the exogeneity of money in *The General Theory*. Was it, as is commonly argued, because he wanted to place effective demand at the heart of his analysis without any further distractions, as is suggested by Robinson (1970)? In other words, this oversight was 'strategic' and 'tactical' (Dow and Dow 1989, p. 149). This may be the case, but irrespective of the reason, his decision to eclipse discussion over the role of the central bank, and keep, as he tells us in the preface to *The General Theory*, the 'technical monetary details . . . into the background' (Keynes, CW, vol. VII, p. vii), has certainly complicated the analysis.

So while this does not mean that Keynes was a fervent defender of the notion of an exogenous money supply, it does suggest that we need to dig deeper in his analysis to see what he believed. On that note, I am in full agreement with Dow (1997, p. 61) when she writes that 'an exploration of Keynes's other writing reveals an understanding of the process of money creation through bank lending, and of the limitations on the scope for control by the monetary authorities', to which I now turn.

Keynes's Analysis Post-General Theory

Keynes's writings on the finance motive after the publication of *The General Theory*, in the *Economic Journal* in 1937 and 1939, are revealing for a number of reasons, and have commanded considerable attention. Here, we find Keynes placing great emphasis on the role of banks. After having said very little about banks or the central bank in *The General Theory*, Keynes now focuses on banks and more specifically their role in the money creation process. There is some initial confusion still, but eventually Keynes arrives at a position certainly compatible with the overall circuitist and Post Keynesian positions. Indeed, Keynes now places banks at the heart of his analysis, claiming in fact that they are 'the key' to understanding the process of production and growth.

Yet, Keynes's analysis with respect to the second pole of analysis remains lacking. Again, he has very little to say about the operations of central banks or their relationship with the banking system: in fact, the central bank is wholly absent. In this sense, it is unclear what Keynes meant to say about the operations of a central bank, and makes the analysis about endogenous money a difficult one. While elsewhere I argued that in his post-*General Theory* articles Keynes developed a theory of endogenous money (Rochon 1999, p. 10), I would be cautious today in reaching such a conclusion. Rather, I would argue that while his post-*General Theory* views on credit and money are considerably more developed than in *The General Theory*, his continued lack of analysis of a central bank muddies the water on whether he truly understood the concept of endogenous money.

As stated above, the notion that loans create money, while necessary, is not a sufficient argument for a theory of endogenous money. We could simply have banks creating money, but still limited by the operations and decisions of the central bank. What is therefore needed to supplement this view is a statement that central banks also supply reserves endogenously, that is high-powered money is not causal in the determination of the supply of bank loans.

Regarding the first pole of analysis, Keynes developed his *General Theory* views considerably. In his post-*General Theory* articles, Keynes elaborates further on the specific role between bank borrowers and the banks, and the demand for credit by the former for the sake of undertaking production and investment. For instance, Keynes argues that because there exists a time lag between the beginning of the production process and the receipt of sale revenues – an 'interregnum' as he calls it – firms must have access to a wage-fund, as well as access to credit to finance part of their investment projects: 'An investment *decision* . . . may sometimes involve a temporary demand for money before it is carried out. . . . *Ex ante* investment is an important, genuine phenomenon, in as much as decisions have to be taken and credit or 'finance' provided well in advance of the actual process of investment' (Keynes, CW, vol. XIV, pp. 207, 216), and that a line of credit is the best way to arrange this finance (ibid., pp. 208, 203). Where this initial finance come from is at first ambiguous in Keynes, although ultimately he argues that the 'finance required during the interregnum between the intention to invest and its achievement is mainly supplied by specialists, in particular by the banks . . . wholly supplied . . . by the banks' (ibid., p. 210) – a situation which he characterizes as 'substantially representative of real life' (ibid., p. 219). Keynes returns to this argument in 1939, in the *Economic Journal*, where he argues: 'It is the role of the credit system to provide the liquid funds which are required first of all by entrepreneurs during the period before they have decided to employ it' (ibid., p. 285).

While the banking system is seen as the purveyor of credit, it is clear that banks will not necessarily supply all credit demanded. As he had argued before, Keynes recognizes there may be a 'fringe of unsatisfied customers' (Keynes, CW, vol. VI, p. 367), that is he argues that banks can 'choose' to 'make the finance available' (Keynes, CW, vol. XIV, p. 210). In this sense, banks have some freedom in supplying the loan to firms.

Moreover, Keynes links the actions of the banking system to the overall growth of the system, that is, 'the pace of economic activity'. Indeed, he argues 'unless the banking system is prepared to augment the supply of money, lack of finance may prove an important obstacle to more than a certain amount of investment decisions being on the tapis at the same time' (ibid., p. 210). Clearly, Keynes rests the primary responsibility for economic activity squarely on the banks. Consider the following: 'The banks hold the key position from a lower to a higher scale of activity' (ibid., p. 222); 'this is why [the banks'] policy is so important in determining the pace at which new investment can proceed' (ibid., p. 219).

So far, therefore, in his post-*General Theory* articles, Keynes advances two key arguments related to the endogeneity of money. First, the banking system is at the centre of the money-creation process. Indeed, he argues forcefully 'too great a press of uncompleted investment decisions is quite capable of exhausting the available finance, if the banking system is unwilling to increase the supply of money. . . . Yet this is only another way of expressing the power of the banks through their control over the supply of money' (ibid., pp. 210–11).

Second, Keynes links the actions of the commercial banks to the pace of economic activity. Banks are special in the sense that their decisions to finance production and investment projects enable the economy to produce and grow.

Yet, regarding the central bank and its relationship with the overall banking system, here again, Keynes has little to nothing to say. This is surely a problematic omission, as discussed earlier. His lack of analysis of the relationship between the central bank and the banking system clouds our analysis and prevents us from reaching a definitive answer to whether he developed a theory of endogenous money. So far, while his arguments and analysis of the relationship between entrepreneurs and banks is well-developed, although still containing some ambiguity, it does provide us with some indication that he understood well, at least the first pole of money's endogeneity. But without a clear statement on the role of the central bank, it is difficult to reach a definitive conclusion.

Nevertheless, Keynes does recognize much later the ability of central banks to administer the rate of interest, and seems to accept the rate of interest as a 'political' or administered rate (Keynes, CW, vol. XXV, p. 149). Yet, these references appear more in correspondence rather than in published articles. For instance, in a 28 May 1936 letter to Hubert Henderson (Keynes, CW, vol. XXIX, p. 222), Keynes writes 'if the supply of money is suitably adjusted, then there is no necessary reason why interest rates need rise during a boom or fall during a depression'. Here he is aware of the role of the monetary authorities. In a 1937 letter to Hicks, he again refers to the 'appropriate' monetary policy that would prevent interest rates from rising (Keynes, CW, vol. XIV, pp. 79–81).

In a letter to Harrod (19 April 1942), Keynes writes that in his view, 'the whole management of the domestic economy depends upon being free to have the appropriate rate of interest without reference to the rates prevailing elsewhere in the world' (Keynes, CW, vol. XXV, p. 149). What is of notice here is the subtle change in language. Whereas before Keynes used to refer to an 'appropriate monetary policy', he now refers to an 'appropriate rate of interest'. Whether intentional or not, it marks a definite progression in his thinking over monetary policy. In 1944, he refers to 'retain[ing] control over our domestic rate of interest' (Keynes, CW, vol. XXVI, p. 16). Finally, in March 1945 (Keynes, CW, vol. XXVII, p. 390)

Keynes says clearly that 'the monetary authorities can have any rate of interest they like . . . They can make both the short and long-term [rate] whatever they like'.

CONCLUSION

The notion that Keynes had a theory of endogenous money within *The General Theory* must be put to rest. It is clear that he regarded the supply of money, not as given, but as exogenous, for whatever reason. To explore the notion that Keynes developed a theory of endogenous money, we must turn to his writings after *The General Theory*, more specifically his writings on the finance motive, which appeared in the *Economic Journal* in 1937 and 1939. Yet even there, there is some ambiguity. To have a complete theory of endogenous money proper, I argue, we should have an explanation of endogeneity at two poles of analysis: between credit borrowers and banks, and between banks and the central bank. Keynes never gave his full attention to the second pole of analysis, at least not in *The General Theory* or in his published writings following it. However, Keynes does give us some indication that he understood the interest-rate setting abilities of central banks. In the end, Keynes's writings show a progression towards a theory of endogenous money which, in the end, is quite analogous to the horizontalist theory that exists today.

NOTE

1. The author would like to thank John Smithin, Sergio Rossi and Claude Gnos for their helpful comments.

BIBLIOGRAPHY

Asimakopulos, A. (1991), *Keynes's General Theory and Accumulation*, Cambridge: Cambridge University Press.

Blinder, A. (2010), 'Quantitative easing: entrance and exit strategies', *Federal Reserve Bank of St. Louis Review*, **92**(6) (November/December), 465–80.

Chick, V. (1986), 'The evolution of the banking system and the theory of saving, investment and interest', *Économies et Sociétés* ('Série Monnaie et Production', 3), **20**(8–9), 111–26, reprinted in P. Arestis and S. C. Dow (eds) (1992), *On Money, Method and Keynes: Selected Essays of Victoria Chick*, London and New York: Macmillan and St Martin's Press, pp. 193–205.

Deleplace, G. and E. Nell (1996), *Money in Motion*, London: Macmillan.

Dow, A. C. and S. C. Dow (1989), 'Endogenous money Creation and idle balances', in J. Pheby (ed.), *New Directions in Post-Keynesian Economics*, Aldershot, UK and Brookfield, VT, USA: Edward Elgar, pp. 147–64.

Dow, S. (1997), 'Endogenous money', in G. Harcourt and P. Riach (eds), *The Second Edition of Keynes's General Theory*, London: Routledge, pp. 43–55.

Foster, G. P. (1986), 'The endogeneity of money and Keynes's general theory', *Journal of Economic Issues*, **20**(4) (December), 953–68.

Gnos, C. (2006), 'French circuit theory', in P. Arestis and M. Sawyer (eds), *A Handbook of Alternative Monetary Economics*, Cheltenham, UK and Northampton, MA, USA: Edward Elgar, pp. 87–104.

Graziani, A. (1984), 'The debate on Keynes's finance motive', *Economic Notes*, **1**(1), 15–33.

Kashyap, A. and J. Stein (1994), 'Monetary policy and bank lending', in N. G. Mankiw (ed.), *Monetary Policy*, Chicago, IL: Chicago University Press.

Keynes, J. M. (1971–1989), *The Collected Writings of John Maynard Keynes*. London: Macmillan/Cambridge University Press for the Royal Economic Society
Vol. VI: *A Treatise on Money. The Applied Theory of Money*
Vol. VII: *The General Theory of Employment, Interest, and Money*
Vol. XIV: *The General Theory and After, Defense and Development*
Vol. XXV: *Activities 1940–44. Shaping the post-War World: The Clearing Union*
Vol. XXVI: *Activities 1940–46. Shaping the post-War World: Bretton Woods*
Vol. XXVII: *Activities 1940–46: Shaping the post-War World*
Vol. XXIX: *The General Theory and After: A Supplement*

Lavoie, M. (1984), 'Un modèle post–Keynésien d'économie monétaire fondé sur la théorie du circuit', *Économies et Sociétés*, **18**(2), 233–58.

Lavoie, M. (1992), *Foundations of Post-Keynesian Economic Analysis*, Aldershot, UK and Brookfield, VT, USA: Edward Elgar.

Lavoie, M. (1996), 'The endogenous supply of credit–money, liquidity preference and the principle of increasing risk: horizontalism versus the loanable funds approach', *Scottish Journal of Political Economy*, **43**(3) (August), 275–300.

Moore, B. (1988), *Horizontalists and Verticalists: The Macroeconomics of Credit–Money*, Cambridge: Cambridge University Press.

Palley, T. (1996), *Post Keynesian Economics: Debt, Distribution, and the Macro Economy*, New York: Palgrave Macmillan.

Robinson, J. (1970), 'Quantity theories old and new: a comment', *Journal of Money, Banking and Credit*, **2**(4) (November), 504–12.

Rochon, L.-P. (1997), 'Keynes's finance motive: a re-assessment. credit, liquidity preference and the rate of interest', *Review of Political Economy*, **9**(3), 277–93.

Rochon, L.-P. (1999), *Credit, Money and Production: An Alternative Post-Keynesian Approach*, Cheltenham, UK, and Northampton, MA, USA: Edward Elgar.

Rochon, L.-P. (2006), 'Endogenous money, central banks and the banking system: Basil Moore and the supply of credit', in M. Setterfield (ed.), *Complexity, Endogenous Money and Macroeconomic Theory: Essays in Honour of Basil J. Moore*, Cheltenham, UK and Northampton, MA, USA: Edward Elgar, pp. 170–86.

Rochon, L.-P. and S. Rossi (2003), *Modern Theories of Money*, Cheltenham, UK and Northampton, MA, USA: Edward Elgar.

Rossi, S. (2007), *Money and Payments in Theory and Practice*, London and New York: Routledge.

Wray, R. (1990), *Money and Credit in Capitalist Economies: The Endogenous Money Approach*, Aldershot, UK and Brookfield, VT, USA: Edward Elgar.

14. Interest and profit

John Smithin[1]

INTRODUCTION

What is the relationship between interest and profit? This question is more likely to arise in the heterodox economic literature, for example, in 'Post Keynesian' economics (Davidson 1996; Mongiovi 1996), than in mainstream analysis. In the standard approach, the rate of interest is often identified with the return to capital, so that a high rate of interest means the same thing as a high rate of return to capital. For policymakers and market participants, however, this is highly confusing when applied to practical discussions of monetary policy. In a practical context, the more usual argument is that higher interest rates will tend to *reduce* profitability by causing an economic downturn. The reason for the inconsistency seems to be a combination of ontological uncertainty about *both* concepts, interest and profit, and the reflexive use by most economists of competitive marginalist analysis, even in the *macroeconomic* context, in which demand constraints are pervasive and the existence of large imperfectly competitive firms cannot be ignored (Kaldor 1983, 1985). Even Keynes in *The General Theory* (1936, pp. 135–46), though he had a clearer idea than most of the difference, was guilty of this error in developing the concept of the 'marginal efficiency of capital' (MEC). Nonetheless, discussions within Keynesian and Post Keynesian economics have been helpful in trying to sort out the confusion. At least in these schools of thought the rate of interest on money is seen as specifically a *monetary* phenomenon and therefore as different in kind from a surplus over production costs.

From the point of view of business the real rate of interest on money is mainly a cost factor, not a measurement of the profitability of enterprise. For this and other reasons, including the inherent limitations to 'effective demand', there is therefore an *inverse* relation between the real interest rate on money and entrepreneurial profit. Income distribution is the primary channel through which monetary policy affects the economy, and higher real interest rates, for example, will have a direct negative impact on both real wages and entrepreneurial profit. A main conclusion is that profit as such is essentially in the nature of 'differential rent'. This term, however, is applied to the specific characteristics of each business *firm*, including demand conditions, rather than plots of land or individual pieces of machinery. The profit share in gross domestic product (GDP) is determined by (a) considerations of 'effective demand', as Keynes did try to argue in the 1930s, and (b) the bargaining power of the main players in 'the struggle over income distribution' – business itself, labour, and the financial interests (which, confusingly, are also often called 'rentier' interests).[2]

ALTERNATIVE THEORIES OF PROFIT

As suggested, the orthodox neoclassical theory of economics is not much help in discussing profit. In the 'best developed model of the economy' in this tradition (Hahn 1983, p. 1), there is no profit at all in equilibrium. Total income is distributed between wage earners and a rental return to different types of purely physical capital as such. Nothing remains as a surplus over and above the costs of production, and nothing is left recognizable as profit in the accounting sense. It is allowed that 'short-run' profit may accrue to a firm in 'disequilibrium', if it gets into a temporary position with some sort of monopolistic advantage before competing firms can enter the market. In fact, it is *only* such fleeting situations that are supposed to provide the incentive for firms to engage in productive activity at all. In the long-run all short-run profits are 'competed away', allowing the firm only to cover the costs of production.

As neoclassical theory is silent on the question of profit, it is necessary to turn back to older sources, such as the Marxian and 'classical' theories discussed more than 50 years ago in an important, but now neglected, article by Kaldor (1955/56). In that same paper, Kaldor also put forward what he described as a 'Keynesian' (demand side) theory of income distribution, although the genuinely Keynesian credentials of this are dubious. The next section of the paper, therefore, follows Kaldor only to the extent of discussing the Marxian and classical theories respectively. The third section then puts forward a synthetic theory of real profit that addresses the flaws in the older theories, and also brings the argument back to Keynes by introducing what some modern writers have called 'Keynes-Kalecki' elements. Once again, however, the reference to Kalecki has mainly to do with issues on the supply side of the economy and the determination of the mark-up (Kalecki 1971, pp. 43–61), rather than Kalecki's own attempt (similar to Kaldor's) to modify Keynesian demand side theory (ibid., pp. 1–14). The Keynesian theory of effective demand is retained in its original form, which, in turn, helps to clarify the interest-profit distinction.

SURPLUS VALUE AND CLASSICAL THEORIES OF PROFIT

In addition to Kaldor's paper, clear expositions of Marx's theory of 'surplus value' are found in Sweezy (1942, pp. 56–71) and Rima (1996, pp. 220–43). The reason it is now worth re-examining the Marxian view, or some features of it, in spite of the obvious anti-capitalist bias, is that it does address the question of the existence and origins of profit, a subject that orthodox economics (supposedly the staunch defender of capitalism) studiously avoids.

Marx used the term value in a specific sense. He adhered to a strict version of the labour theory of value, whereby the value of any commodity is given by the amount of 'socially necessary' labour time that went into its production. This was a major issue in the development of Marxian political economy, and caused the long-running debate on the 'transformation problem' of how to reconcile 'values', defined in these terms, with the 'prices' observed in the empirical world. However, the validity or otherwise of the labour theory of value is not an important issue for the main questions in debate here. It would always be possible to substitute what Ingham (2004, p. 202) perceptively calls a 'social theory of value' at any point in the discussion. The original Marxian concept of value is therefore mentioned here only for the sake of completeness and the historical record. With this caveat, recall that in Marx the expression for total value is given by a formula such as:

$$y = s + c + v \qquad\qquad 14.1$$

where y stands for 'total value' (meaning either the value of aggregate output, or that of an individual firm) and s, c and v stand for 'surplus value', 'constant capital' and 'variable capital'.

Constant capital accounts for the amount of materials and physical capital equipment that are 'used up' in the production process (originally measured as 'stored-up labour time'), that is, outlays on raw materials plus depreciation. Variable capital, meanwhile, is 'the value of the outlay on wages and salaries' (Sweezy 1942, p. 63). The trick in Marxian political economy is the argument that the value of the variable capital needed to sustain the workforce will be less than the total value created during the working day. For example, during an eight-hour day the time necessary to produce the equivalent in goods and services of the wage bill may be only five hours. What is produced in the remaining three hours becomes surplus value, the s term in equation (1), and goes to the employer as profit.

In many ways, as Sweezy (ibid.) pointed out long ago, equation (1) is just an accounting identity, similar to the modern concept of GDP, or to an income statement for a firm. It adds the wage bill, v, depreciation, c, and the profit or surplus, s. It is true that from the perspective of a pre-Marxian classical economist there would be one obvious omission – that no allowance is made for ground rent. However, Marx was aware of this and made the explicit assumption that ground rent is zero (ibid., p. 67). Moreover, this was not unreasonable by the time Marx (1867) was writing, compared with the eras of Adam Smith (1776) or David Ricardo (1817). There is also another omission, however, this time from the standpoint of a modern monetary economist that is more serious on general theoretical grounds. There is no mention in the formula $s + c + v$ of interest on money as anything separate from the profit or surplus. If production takes time, however, and taking a long position in goods, in this way, is surely an essential feature of capitalism, then there should also be an interest charge on *both* constant capital and variable capital. This was not taken into account at least in the original version of the Marxian scheme in Vol. I of *Das Kapital*.

Another key variable in Marx was the 'rate of exploitation' or 'rate of surplus value' (Sweezy 1942, p. 64). This gives the ratio of surplus value to the value of variable capital (three hours to five hours in our example). If the symbol s' stands for the rate of surplus value:

$$s' = s/v \qquad\qquad 14.2$$

The overall rate of profit, p, is then given by the ratio of surplus value to total capital:

$$p = s'/(c + v) \qquad\qquad 14.3$$

Equation (3) implicitly defines profit as a percentage of the total value of capital 'used up' in the production process rather than as the total value of capital employed (probably the more usual definition). However, Marx could get round this with no real loss of generality simply by assuming that all capital 'turns over' exactly once during the production period (ibid., pp. 67–8). In other words, the depreciation rate is assumed to be 100 per cent.

The point at which Marx does get into difficulties, however, is not in defining a rate of profit for each individual enterprise, or in working out the average mark-up for the economy as a whole, but in the simultaneous insistence that the process of competition must 'equalize' the rate of profit across all enterprises (Rima 1996, pp. 233–5). This is what caused confusion in the Marxian scheme between values defined in terms of their labour inputs and prices observed in the actual economy. The point is that the ratio of constant capital to total capital, a ratio Marx calls the 'organic composition of capital', is bound to differ between industries depending on their technical requirements. Therefore, if the rate of profit is to be equalized between those same industries, the prices charged by them must differ from their supposed values in equation (1). From the point of view of a workable theory of profit the problem is not with the logic of equations (1) through (3), but with this additional assumption that rates of profit between different industries and firms are equalized. How is this supposed to happen? The standard answer, noted by Rima is that:

> economy-wide equalization is brought about by inter-industry capital movements. If the rate of profit is above average in . . . (some) . . . industries . . . capital will tend to be attracted from industries . . . where the rate of profit is lower than average, until the average is . . . (the same) . . . for all. (ibid., pp. 234–5)

This is obviously not an idea unique to Marxism but is taken directly from classical economics, and *still* appears in mainstream textbooks to this day. There is always, however, a sense of confusion as to exactly what this 'capital', flowing from one place to another, is supposed to be (Smithin 2009, pp. 95–6). If the notion of capital is meant to involve specific items of physical plant, equipment and machinery, then the image of these things being 'attracted to', or 'flowing from', one industry to another is a problem. It is possible to imagine an individual machine being unbolted from one location, sold second-hand, and moved to another, but even then it would have to be used for a somewhat similar purpose to its original function. It is not possible to visualize a broad mass of physical things being switched effortlessly from one purpose to another. It is really only capital in the sense of *money itself* that can move from one industry to another with any degree of fluency. *Constant* capital though presumably does consist mostly of physical things such as machines and plant, and this must cast doubt on the existence of any smooth mechanism to equalize industrial profit rates. (It also illustrates that a 100 per cent depreciation rate, even if not significant for purpose of working out the equations, should not be taken seriously as a description of the actual world). The same sort of argument applies to the sociologist's concept of 'human capital', things like experience and expertise gained in a particular firm or industry.

For a concrete example involving both types of capital, imagine an entrepreneur who builds a hotel in a vacation resort that is popular for a time, but then becomes unfashionable. Profits fall, and on the standard argument, capital will then flow out of that enterprise and find its way to some more profitable location. But, how can this happen? The building is where it is. It cannot get up and walk away. Nor can the entrepreneur effectively try to turn the physical capital into money as an alternative exit strategy. Who would now want to buy the building, except at a vastly reduced price? Also, as far as human capital is concerned, it may be that this particular entrepreneur is well suited to be a hotelier, and would not be as effective doing anything else. It remains true that no new hotels will be built in the area, and any new *money* that is available will go somewhere else. It might still be said therefore, that in the 'very long run' there would be a *tendency* towards that re-allocation of society's total resources claimed as the main advantage the market system. If the discussion of surplus value or profit is to have any empirical validity, however, we cannot reasonably be talking only about an underlying trend or tendency that, in practice, can never reach final fruition before some other change happens to disturb or reverse it. In a real world situation the mere fact that one resort or one industry is declining while elsewhere another is thriving, will never achieve the literal equalization of profit rates in any finite period of time. What, after all, is a rational business strategy for the stranded hotelier? It may be simply to stay in business and take whatever lower profits are on offer, as long as they are on offer, rather than sell up and lose everything. It may even be reasonable to invest still *more* in a declining asset (for example, refurbish the hotel and try to drive out the remaining competitors on the beach), and so make the best of a bad situation.

What occurs in reality is simply that for long periods of time some industries with low profits co-exist with other industries with high profits. There are bound to be different profit performances within the same industry also, due to the different abilities of the personnel and the different qualities, age, and efficiency of the equipment. This is the empirical situation documented by countless studies of industrial organization. There is no reason to expect the equalization of profit rates across the board in *any* concrete state of the world. How, though, would it be possible to capture this reality in economic theory, and yet still use the device of equilibrium modelling for heuristic purposes? Conceptually, a 'finite horizon equilibrium' would have to exist, involving imperfect competition and different profit rates in each industry, that stays in place until some new innovation or divestment occurs. Even with no profit equalization, however, the same *interest rate* should prevail everywhere, because money itself can be moved around more easily.

It is not easy to arrive at the correct terminology to describe the finite horizon equilibrium. We might think of it, for example, as simply a 'long-run' equilibrium in the restricted sense that this term is used in intermediate textbooks, as opposed to the 'very long run' equilibrium just mentioned. A problem with this, however, would be the overtones of the standard neoclassical growth model, which would be better to avoid.

Another alternative is to use the expression 'medium run' from more recent mainstream economics (Blanchard 2000; Solow 2000), and think of the time horizon in that literature as the empirical counterpart to our theoretical equilibrium model.[3] In that case, however (and *unlike* in neo-classical economics), it is important to note that there would be no other long run or very long run *except* that realized empirically by the stringing together of the historical sequence of medium run outcomes (Kalecki 1971; Marterbauer and Smithin 2000). This is a key issue in the application of any type of equilibrium theorizing to the actual course of events.

Evidently the transformation problem is made redundant. In such a world, there would be an individual version of equation (3) for every enterprise, defining the rate of profit in that enterprise, and an aggregate version of it, summing up the individual firm equations. The concept is similar to Kalecki's notion of the 'degree of monopoly' (Kalecki 1971, p. 45). From the aggregate equation it would still be possible to make mean-ingful *macroeconomic* statements about the overall profit mark-up, and nothing is lost in terms of the 'vision' of capitalism that can be achieved. Profit is now being re-interpreted as the differential rent of each enterprise. However, this is 'rent' that accrues not merely through the possession of land, or individual pieces of machinery, but from the *totality* of firm spe-cific attributes, including the physical sunk capital, the particular expertise of the management and workforce, *and* the demand conditions for the product.

Meanwhile, Kaldor (1955/56, p. 85) also used Ricardo's famous 'corn model' of rent, profit and wages, to illustrate the pre-Marxian classical theory. In this picture of the world, labour is applied to agricultural land to yield 'corn' (grains such as wheat), supposed to be the only product available in the economy. Production is subject to diminishing returns, and both the average product (AP) and marginal product (MP) of labour are falling. However, it was *not* argued that total employment is deter-mined by any sort of marginalist principle. The real wage, also measured/paid in corn, is taken to be a constant close to the subsistence level, and the demand for labour is therefore *pre-determined* each period by a previ-ously accumulated 'wages fund' of stored-up corn. This fixes the amount of labour demanded at each real wage, the amount of labour actually employed, and the level of output. The only role played by marginalism (a concept that later on came to dominate economics almost completely) is to determine the total of ground rent. This is given by the cumulative difference between the AP and MP of labour applied to intra-marginal land, multiplied by the amount of employment, and goes to the landown-ers. Profit is then whatever is left over for the organizers of production (basically tenant farmers), and is the difference between the MP of labour and the real wage, again multiplied by the amount of employment. In the era of classical economics, this basic theory of profit and rent was made the centrepiece of a series of theoretical propositions about the causes of growth, tax incidence, the merits of free trade versus protection, and so on.

However, from a modern perspective a number of problems come to mind, just as in the Marxian case. Once again, there are questions of whether the profit margin can be expected to persist, the relevance of the emphasis on ground rent, and in a generalized version of the model (one that included industry as well as agriculture), again whether the rate of profit is supposed to be equalized across all sectors. Finally, if applied to a modern financially orientated capitalist system, where would the rate of interest fit it – what role would it be expected to play?

The later (post-Marxian) *neoclassical* economists, whether of the nine-teenth century or their modern descendants, would, of course, have com-pletely rejected the notion of any demand constraint fixing the amount of employment. One of the main tenets of mid-nineteenth century main-stream economics ('political economy' in those days) was a supposedly decisive refutation of the wage fund argument. The idea that demand constraints might limit the amount of employment did not then re-emerge until the advent of Keynesian economics, as late as the mid-twentieth century, when it took a completely different (monetary) form, and was promptly dropped once again, in more recent times, with the resurgence of the neoclassical school (to the point of total domination) in contemporary academia.

The basic argument, illustrated by the theory of perfect competition, is that the typical firm is so small in relation to the market that it simply *believes* it can sell all it wants to at the going price. Therefore, it need never be constrained from employing more labour by fear of a lack of demand or an accumulated wage fund, whether conceived in real or financial terms. Wages are actually thought of as a physical share in the output that will *eventually* be produced, and do not need to be distributed until after the product has been sold (or rather exchanged). Therefore, the position taken by late nineteenth-century neoclassical economists, and (perhaps more surprisingly) in most subsequent mainstream economics for the next 150 years, was that employment will be pushed to the point where the real wage equals the MP of labour. It is in this neoclassical (rather than classical) vision that profit disappears with a final distribution of income ultimately between the two 'primary factors' of wages and ground rent, and no room for any separate accounting for interest on money. This was exactly the description of orthodox theory given by Schumpeter (1934, pp. 3–56), in the famous first chapter of *The Theory of Economic Development*. It is also worth noting, however, that although defending this construct on the grounds that it is a useful starting point, Schumpeter himself was the first to recognize that this would hardly do as a theory of *capitalism*. Commonsense, after all, dictates that the profit motive should take a prominent role. This was why Schumpeter had to go on to develop his own theory of 'creative destruction', to give some sort of account of where profits come from (Collins 1986, pp. 122–3). More recent mainstream theory, however, has had no compunction in generalizing from the classical model to a pure neoclassical one. Instead of having just one variable factor (labour), and one fixed factor (land), later theory dispenses with land altogether, and adds another variable factor, the so-called capital whose reward is also determined by marginal productivity. The result is the now standard theory of distribution based on the 'aggregate production function' and the influential neoclassical growth model descended from Solow (1970) that is still one of the main textbooks topics to this day. The basic idea can also be extended to multiple variable factors to any number desired.

There is, however, an alternative method of modifying the original classical model, based on the questions raised above about the nature of profit and interest, and yet still initially retaining marginalist principles, which may be more instructive (Smithin 2009, pp. 100–1). It has already been argued that interest rates should be sharply distinguished from profit – they are not the same thing. It must also be taken into account that in actual capitalism, money and credit creation are integral parts of the technique by which profits themselves are generated (ibid.). It is not credible therefore despite Schumpeter that interest rates will automatically fall to zero in equilibrium. They could only do so as the result of a deliberate episode of central bank policy. Failing this even in a static circular flow there will be an interest charge on the wage bill, as credit creation and the monetary circuit must continue for the most routine circulation of commodities to occur. It was also argued that it is only money, not physical capital that can flow freely from one use to another. It is the interest rates themselves (with due allowance for the individual 'risk factors' stressed in microeconomic textbooks) *not* profit rates that will be equalized across firms as borrowers. Profit itself will differ between firms and industries because, as explained, there must always in effect be 'fixed factors' in place in every enterprise. Therefore, if we abandon the neoclassical equilibrium in which interest rates do not exist, but continue for the moment to apply marginalist principles (as opposed to Keynesian or classical ones), this would give a level of output/employment at the point where the real wage *inclusive* of the interest charge is equal to the MP of labour (Smithin 1986). The final distribution of income would then be between wages, interest, and 'firm specific profit' – three shares rather than two. There are some similarities of this result to the old Marshallian concept of 'quasi rent' (Keynes 1936, p. 135), but a main difference is that under diminishing returns and marginalism (and even more obviously, in a world of generalized imperfect competition and demand constraints introduced in the next section), this can be thought of as more or less 'permanent' income stream to each firm. As the profit depends explicitly on firm level characteristics, there is no strong tendency for it to be competed away, or for profit to be rapidly equalized amongst firms. The three-fold division of income, while different from the two-fold neoclassical scheme is also different from the three-way split of classical economics. Profit in the new scheme takes the place of 'rent' in the classical one,[4] while interest income, and financial returns generally, take the place of the classical 'profits of stock'. There is no chance of firm specific profit being competed away in the new scheme, any more than there was of rent in the classical framework, but also no chance of the purely interest share being competed away either, as this is fundamentally determined in the financial sector, above all by the policy of the central bank. Note that the category of financial income can also be thought of as incorporating the dividend yields of those shareholders who are *not* the active managers of the firm. These returns can also be regarded in some sense as a mark-up over base interest rates (with appropriate adjustment for the different 'risk' and contractual status of the obligations), as in the concept of the 'equity premium' from theoretical finance. The *true* profit for each firm, however, is the firm specific profit applied to each separate entity. These are sums that are *not* extractable by passive shareholders or bondholders, and remain under the control of the real managers or controllers of the firm, those who might genuinely be called the entrepreneurs. In accounting terms, profit is the residual claim on income, *whether or not* accurately identified as such in the formal rules and regulations. The broadest distribution of income in aggregate therefore (before allowing for taxes and transfer payments) is between wages and rentier/financial incomes, both broadly defined, and entrepreneurial profit, properly so-called.

AN ALTERNATIVE THEORY OF PROFIT

In this section, the objective is to put forward a synthetic theory of profit which will summarize the argument. It will need to be more general, however, in two separate senses, than the discussion so far. First, there is no reason why it should rest on the classical/neoclassical premise of diminishing marginal productivity, or (a slightly different point) on any marginalist principle at all. Second, Keynes (1936) sensed that a 'more general theory' should allow for the presence of *demand constraints* that limit the output of each individual firm, and in aggregate. Equation (14.4) therefore reverts to the Marxian type notation introduced above, but initially values the different components purely in money terms. It also allows for the fact that production takes time (and hence both for an interest charge and the need for entrepreneurs to form expectations) with a one-period production lag (the simplest possible):

$$y^e = s + (1 + i)c + (1 + i)v \qquad\qquad 14.4$$

Given the production lag y^e is the expected money value of output offered for sale one period in future. The terms c and v refer to constant capital and variable capital as before, but are expressed in money terms at the start of the period of production. Both bear an interest charge $(1+i)$, where i is the nominal rate of interest. The expected surplus s is also a sum of money, and the analogue to the Marxian rate of surplus value is now $s' = s/[v(1+i)]$. Next, introduce a new term, $k' = c/v$, related to the organic composition of capital,[5] and equation (14.4) can be re-written as:

$$y^e = (1 + s' + k')(1 + i)v \qquad\qquad 14.5$$

This expresses total *expected* value in money terms as a mark-up over investment in variable capital, also measured in money terms. The mark-up covers three main elements in the accounting scheme, the interest charge, depreciation on fixed (or constant) capital and, once again, what Marx would have called 'exploitation' or surplus value, the net profit.

Equation (14.5) can be rewritten in a more familiar notation. Let Y stand for real output produced in the current period and sold one period in the future, and P for the price level, so that y^e becomes $P_{+1} Y$. Similarly, the money value of variable capital can be identified with the nominal wage bill WN, where W is the nominal wage rate and N is the level of employment. Finally, let the symbol k (different from k') stand for the 'gross entrepreneurial profit share', such that $k = k' + s'$. The newly-defined mark-up factor k includes an allowance both for depreciation on physical capital and the rate of surplus value and is a 'gross' mark-up in that sense, but it is 'net' of the nominal interest charge. From a behavioural perspective it is an advantage that k is the *expected* mark-up or surplus, as this is what is relevant for economic decision-making, but in equilibrium actual and expected k will coincide. Both in equilibrium and out, there always exists a subjective value of k at both the firm level, and (in summation) in aggregate (Kalecki 1971, pp. 47–8). However, this term is not an expected profit *rate*. As previously explained, the latter concept is difficult to define and is hardly meaningful at the aggregate level. It always remains possible for each *firm* to define either an expected (or, eventually, an *ex post*) accounting rate of return for themselves in the course of individual business decision-making, and presumably each will be doing so. In specifying an aggregative behavioural model however, it is important to realize that the mark-up term k itself would be a more useful concept, and could reasonably be employed as an incentive variable (in an aggregate investment function, for example). This is because an increase in k is a prerequisite both for an increase in the rate of surplus value, and *on average* for an overall increase in the various *ex ante* profit rates or rates of return used as individual decision metrics. Each firm is also aware of the depreciation allowances that must be set aside under alternative business plans. With the new notation, equation (14.5) then becomes:

$$P_{+1} Y = (1 + k)(1 + i)WN \qquad 14.6$$

This is the basic value equation now written in standard economic notation, highlighting the role of the gross profit share, the rate of interest, and wages.

Finally, define the term A as the AP of labour, and the relationship between labour inputs and output will be:

$$Y = AN \qquad 14.7$$

Although equation (14.7) only explicitly involves the relation between output and labour input, it by no means ignores the constant capital component (which was also accounted for in defining the profit share). The contributions of the various machines, technical knowledge, raw materials, etc., are rolled up in the term A. What emerges is best described as a 'virtual labour theory of production' rather than a labour theory of value. It is a rival or antidote to the familiar 'AK' model of contemporary neoclassical growth economics (Jones 1998, pp. 148–50). This essentially accepts Keynes's (1936, p. 41) view that in macroeconomics it is best to restrict attention to 'quantities of money-value and quantities of employment' rather than to attempt the quixotic task of trying to give a concrete meaning to notion of the capital stock.

Next, we have to employ the simple mathematical technique of taking logarithms, or 'logs', of each of the variables. The effect is to turn a multiplicative relationship such as XZ (*X times Z*), into a linear one, $lnX + lnZ$ (the log of *X plus* the log of *Z*). It will also mean that any graphs can conveniently be drawn as straight lines. With this technique and combining equations (14.7) and (14.6), we get:[6]

$$lnP+_1 = k + i + lnW - lnA \qquad 14.8$$

Next, subtract the term lnP (log of the price level) from both sides of the equation, to give:

$$lnP+_1 - lnP = k + i + lnW - lnP - lnA \qquad 14.9$$

and, re-arranging:

$$k = lnA - [i - (lnP+_1 - lnP)] - (lnW - lnP) \qquad 14.10$$

The term in square brackets $[i - (lnP+_1 - lnP)]$ is actually the nominal interest rate minus expected inflation, in other words the real interest rate, r. Also, let lower case w stand for the log of the real wage rate ($w = lnW - lnP$) and lower case a for the log of labour productivity ($a = lnA$). Then from (10) the basic theory of profit, essentially an 'adding up' theory in terms of logarithms or percentages, becomes:

$$k = a - r - w \qquad 14.11$$

The gross mark-up or profit share is equal to the (log of) labour productivity, minus the real interest rate, minus the (log) of the real wage rate.

We now turn to some simple graphical analysis to illustrate some of the implications of the theory of equation (14.11). Suppose, in the first instance, that labour productivity can be taken as 'given' for the time being, by whatever stage of technological development the society has reached. The term a will therefore be a constant. This does *not* mean, however, that the capital stock itself, regardless of how this is defined, is supposed to be held constant – an assumption that Keynes (1936, p. 246) misleadingly made in *The General Theory*.[7] Similarly, take it that the real interest rate is determined in the financial sector (ultimately by the policy of the central bank) and that real wages have been determined by some sort of bargaining process, perhaps involving labour unions. or other socio-political factors. It might plausibly be argued, for example, that the real wage rate rises with employment, for example, because the bargaining power of labour increases. In these circumstances the mark-up k is the residual component of income after the other shares have been decided. This is the situation depicted in Figure. 14.1, which graphs the log of output per head, y-n, against the log of employment, n. Taking a cue from Keynesian economics, the actual level of employment is determined by a demand constraint depicted as a vertical line in the figure. As simple as this diagram is, it immediately answers the original question about the relation

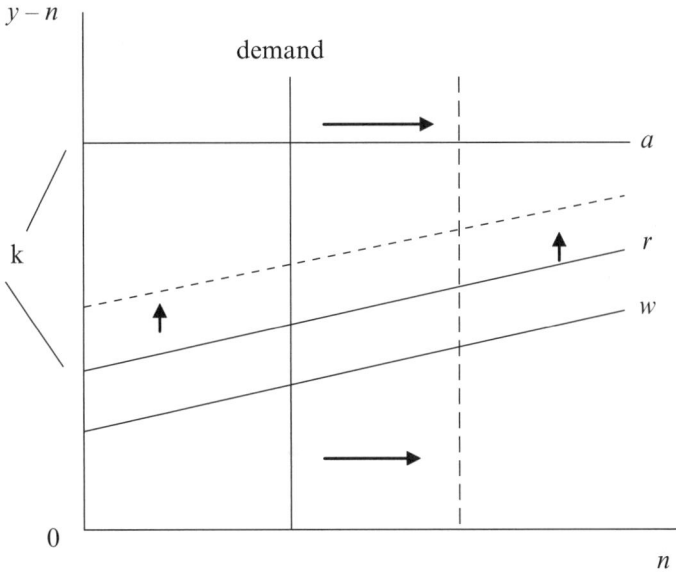

Figure 14.1   Distribution of income between wages, interest and profit

between interest and profit. If there is an increase in real interest rates this will cut into (reduce) the profit share. Conversely, a reduction in interest rates will lead to an increase in profit. With a vertical aggregate demand function there will be no change in output when interest rates change, but things could always have been made somewhat more complicated by making the constraint itself depend on income distribution (for example on k), or on other variables (Atesoglu and Smithin 2007). This is not necessary here as the objective is only to establish the idea of the surplus as the residual claim on income. Meanwhile, as also shown in Figure 14.1, an increase in aggregate demand itself (a relaxation of the demand constraint) increases output and employment in an essentially Keynesian manner, but also reduces the profit share. The reason for this is that real wages are rising as employment rises, but productivity and the real interest charge stay constant. It would not be correct to describe this situation as a 'falling rate of profit', as in Marx. Rather it is the average mark-up or 'average rate of surplus value', that is falling as demand increases and the economy expands. If so, however, presumably with similar effects on the political economy of the system (Smithin 1996).

In the diagram in Figure 14.2, in an obvious next step, the a line, representing the log of the AP of labour is now made downward sloping, which would occur if there was diminishing marginal productivity. This varies

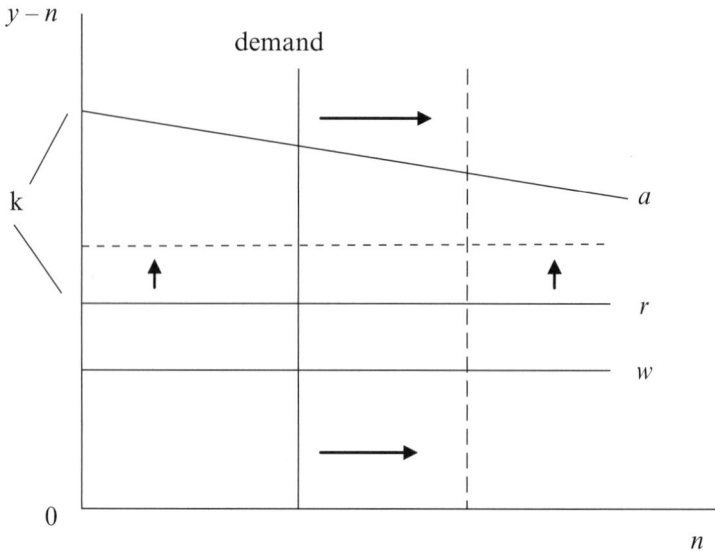

Figure 14.2   Decreasing returns to labor inputs

the technical assumptions about production, but note that the marginal principle itself still plays no role in determining the values of the distributional variables. These are assumed determined by bargaining power as before. For simplicity, the real wage itself is now made a constant (there is a 'target real wage' in wage bargaining), and there is still an interest charge on the wage bill. The main result, of an inverse relationship between real interest rates and profit continues to hold. Also from Figure 14.2, note that even though productivity is now declining as output increases, as long as there is binding demand constraint there is never going to be a point at which the *a* and *r* lines intersect.[8] In such a 'Keynesian' world, it is therefore possible to entirely avoid the confusion about the issue of *causality* between productivity and interest that occurs everywhere else in economics.[9] Once again Keynesian policies will 'work' (that is, a relaxation of the demand constraint will increase employment), but still cause the mark-up and the rate of surplus value to fall.

A final alternative premise considered in Figure 14.3 is some form of *increasing* returns to labour inputs. These might arise, for example, because of economies of scale, a 'learning by doing' effect, or similar. The real wage rate and the real interest rate are again pre-determined by collective bargaining and central bank policy. As shown in Figure 14.3, there is still an inverse relationship between interest rates and profit. Although

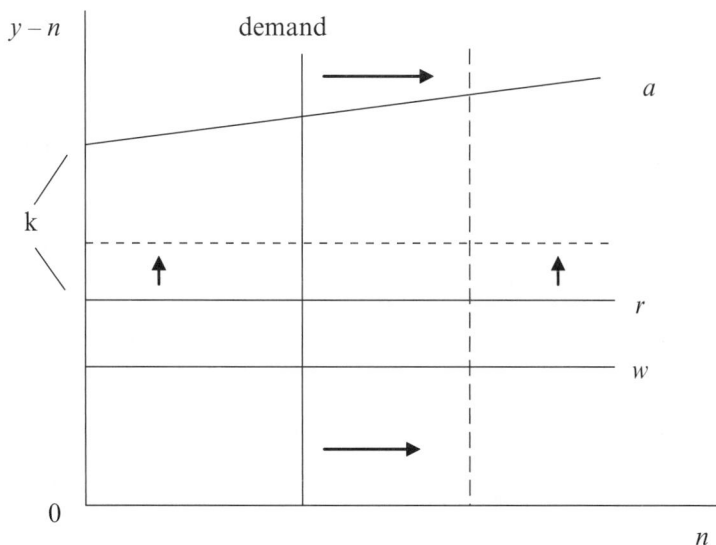

Figure 14.3   Increasing returns to labour inputs

the mark-up now increases with the scale of output, an increase in interest rates reduces its value at each *level* of employment and *vice versa*. If there is a relaxation of the demand constraint (if Keynesian policies arc pursued) in this case there is a *different* result about income distribution than before. An increase in demand will increase output and employment, but will now also allow the mark-up to increase. Because of the increasing returns technology, firms can be *more* profitable if there is an increase in demand, without there being an adverse impact on real wages or the real interest rate. In this situation, 'Keynesian economics' would presumably meet with more favor from the corporate sector than it might do otherwise.

It would clearly be possible to go on to examine other cases each with different technical assumptions about the behaviour of the variables. The exercises already completed, however, establish that the simple expression $k = a - r - w$ provides a flexible tool of analysis for dealing with questions of income distribution between the three key groups of recipients in capitalist economic systems. It was Keynes (1971, CW, vol. IV, pp. 5–32) who long ago characterized these three groups as the 'business class' (merchants, manufacturers and entrepreneurs), the 'investing class' (those who invest in titles to money, or rentiers), and the 'earner' (labour). In the terms used here, business receives entrepreneurial profit k, the investor gets the real interest rate r, and the earner receives the real wage, w.

CONCLUSION

Max Weber's definition of capitalism was '. . . the provision of human needs by the method of enterprise, which is to say, by private businesses seeking profit' (Collins 1986, pp. 21–2). The profit motive is the main principle of capitalism. Every business strives to make profit, and if they fail they literally go 'out of business'. Therefore, it is clear that neoclassical theory, which focuses mainly on market exchange rather than business enterprise, and in which there are no profits, or profits tend to zero, cannot be an adequate theory of capitalism.

Profit is not the same thing as interest on money. Profit is the surplus, whether measured in money or real terms, over and above the costs of production, including the necessary interest and financing costs. It is unlikely that this surplus will be the same in every firm or industry. It will differ according to a variety of circumstances, such as demand conditions, the specialized nature of the physical capital already invested, and the competence and different expertise of the management and workforce. It is therefore unreasonable to expect to see the 'equalization of the rate of profit' among industries or even among different firms in the same industry. There is no effective mechanism to achieve this. The economy-wide *profit share* is therefore simply the aggregate of all of the individual surpluses. On the other hand, *interest rates* can be equalized across a monetary economy as *money* itself can flow freely. The implication is that in the presence of a Keynesian demand constraint there is always an inverse relation between the general level of interest rates and the aggregate mark-up.

Empirically identifying the profit or surplus is complicated by the different accounting rules and regulations in place in different jurisdictions, and by different systems of corporate governance. If, for example, the shareholders of a company are the same persons as those controlling the firm then any dividend payments that they receive may genuinely be counted as part of profit. On the other hand, if the shareholders are purely passive, then the real managers of the firm will see the dividends that they have to pay out as just another element of cost similar to interest payments (albeit with a different contractual status and the addition of some sort of risk premium to the sums disbursed). In this case, we would have to look for the surplus or profit in such areas as retained earnings, the salaries, bonuses and prerequisites of the top management, and possibly also, consumption-type spending by the firm itself (Smithin 2009, p. 107). These, however, are empirical rather than theoretical issues. For them to come up for discussion at all, for there to be any debate about how the surplus is distributed, there must be a profit surplus in existence in the first place.

NOTES

1. I would like to thank Jean-Guy Loranger, John King and Geoff Harcourt for many useful discussions on the topic of this chapter, and the editors of the *Chinese Business Review*, ISSN 1537-1506, David Publishing Company, USA, for permission to reprint previously published material (*Chinese Business Review*, Vol. 8, No. 6, June 2009).
2. Since the early twentieth century, influenced by Keynes (1923, *Collected Writings* (CW), vol. IV, 1936) himself among others, this term has come exclusively to mean the recipients of income from financial assets.
3. According to Solow (2000, p. 137) '. . . (t)here must be a medium run, five-to-ten year time scale at which some . . . transitional model is appropriate'.
4. In the national accounts, any remaining ground rent could be subsumed into that category.
5. This is also similar to the standard economic concept of the capital/labour ratio. If the depreciation rate was less than 100 per cent, k' might be interpreted as the capital/labour ratio multiplied by the depreciation rate. For example, using standard notation, $k' = (K/N)$ where d is the depreciation rate.
6. Equation (8) also uses the accepted approximations that $ln(1 + k) = k$ and $ln(1 + i) = i$.
7. If firms are to expand production at their planned rates, they must be making sufficient investment to keep the a term at the same level in each period.
8. This was already the case in Figure 14.1, when real wages were rising.
9. The usual argument focuses on constant capital rather than variable capital, but the same logic applies.

BIBLIOGRAPHY

Atesoglu, H. S. and J. Smithin (2007), 'Un modelo macroeconomico simple', *Economia Informa*, **346** (May-June), 105–19.

Blanchard, O. J. (2000), 'What do we know about Macroeconomics that Fisher and Wicksell did not', *Quarterly Journal of Economics*, **114**(4), November, pp. 1375–409.

Collins, R. (1986), *Weberian Sociological Theory*, Cambridge: Cambridge University Press.

Davidson, P. (1996), 'In defense of post Keynesian economics: a reply to Mongiovi', in S. Pressman (ed.), *Interactions in Political Economy: Malvern After Ten Years*, London and New York: Routledge, pp. 120–32.

Hahn, F. (1983), *Money and Inflation*, Cambridge, MA: MIT Press.

Ingham, G. (2004), *The Nature of Money*, Cambridge: Polity Press.

Jones, C. I. (1998), *Introduction to Economic Growth*, New York: W.W. Norton and Company.

Kaldor, N. (1955/56), 'Alternative theories of Distribution', *Review of Economic Studies*, **23**(2), 83–100.

Kaldor, N. (1983), 'Keynesian economics after fifty years', in D. Worswick and J. Trevithick (eds), *Keynes and the Modern World*, Cambridge: Cambridge University Press, pp. 1–27.

Kaldor, N. (1985), *Economics without Equilibrium*, Armonk, NY: M.E. Sharpe, Inc.

Kalecki, M. (1971), *Selected Essays on the Dynamics of a Capitalist Economy 1933–1970*, Cambridge: Cambridge University Press.

Keynes, J. M. (1936/1964), *The General Theory of Employment, Interest, and Money*, London, Macmillan.
Keynes, J. M. (1971–1989), *The Collected Writings of John Maynard Keynes*, London: Macmillan/Cambridge University Press for the Royal Economic Society: Vol. IV: *A Tract on Monetary Reform*.
Marterbauer, M. and J. Smithin (2000), 'Fiscal policy in the small open economy within the framework of monetary union', Austrian Institute of Economic Research (WIFO) working paper 137, November, Vienna.
Marx, K. (1867/1976), *Capital: A Critique of Political Economy*, Volume I, London: Pelican Books.
Mongiovi, G. (1996), 'Some critical observations on post Keynesian macroeconomics', in S. Pressman (ed.), *Interactions in Political Economy: Malvern after Ten Years*, London and New York: Routledge, pp. 110–19.
Ricardo, D. (1817/1973), *The Principles of Political Economy and Taxation*, London: J.M Dent & Sons Ltd.
Rima, I. H. (1996), *Development of Economic Analysis*, 6th edn, London: Routledge.
Schumpeter, J. A. (1934 /1983), *The Theory of Economic Development: An Inquiry into Profits, Capital, Credit, Interest, and the Business Cycle*, New Brunswick, NJ: Transactions Publishers.
Smith, A. (1776/1981), *An Inquiry into the Nature and Causes of the Wealth of Nations*, Indianapolis, IN: Liberty Fund.
Smithin, J. (1986), 'The length of the production period and effective stabilization policy', *Journal of Macroeconomics*, **8**(1) (Winter), 55–62.
Smithin, J. (1996), *Macroeconomic Policy and the Future of Capitalism: The Revenge of the Rentiers and the Threat to Prosperity*, Cheltenham, UK and Brookfield, VT, USA: Edward Elgar.
Smithin, J. (2009), *Money, Enterprise and Income Distribution: Towards a Macroeconomic Theory of Capitalism*, London and New York: Routledge.
Solow, R. M. (1970), 'A contribution to the theory of economic growth', in A. Sen (ed.), *Growth Economics,* Harmondsworth: Penguin, pp. 161–92.
Solow, R. (2000), 'Towards a macroeconomics of the medium run', *Journal of Economic Perspectives*, **14**(1) (Winter), 151–8.
Sweezy, P. M (1942/1970), *The Theory of Capitalist Development: Principles of Marxian Political Economy*, New York: Modern Reader Paperbacks.

15. Keynes after 75 years: rethinking money as a public monopoly

L. Randall Wray

INTRODUCTION

In this chapter I first provide an overview of alternative approaches to money, then focus in more detail on two main categories: the orthodox approach to money that views money as an efficiency-enhancing innovation of markets and the Chartalist approach that sees money as a creature of the state. I then move on to a brief examination of the implications of viewing money as a public monopoly. I then link that view back to Keynes, arguing that extending Keynes along these lines would bring his theory up to date.

ALTERNATIVE APPROACHES TO MONEY

No matter how hard macroeconomics tries to keep money in the background, it refuses to play its assigned role as a neutral veil. Indeed, many of the most important debates – including the divisions between schools of thought – were driven by differences of opinion over money's role in the economy. To be sure, postwar IS-LM Keynesians gave monetary policy a backseat, however, insatiable desire for money results in recessionary liquidity traps that can be resolved only through appropriate fiscal expansion. In Milton Friedman's hands, money (and bad monetary policy) was said to be the cause of all inflations and depressions. Robert Lucas claimed monetary surprises led optimizing agents to take extended vacations, standing on line for hand-outs of soup and bread as equilibrium GDP falls until nominal prices adjust.

Turning to the latest fads and fancies, in the New Monetary Consensus, only careful monetary management can align market interest rates with natural rates to achieve potential GDP. Money plays an important role even in Real Business Cycle theory – sort of like the dog that doesn't bark in a detective novel – becoming so irrelevant that one wonders why the representative agent who is optimizing her consumption through time bothers with it. Self-styled 'rigorous' explications invent highly implausible *deus ex machina* requirements, such as 'cash in advance', to find room for money in models that do not need it.

And yet many economists who let money play an explicit and prominent role in their theories are dismissed as 'monetary cranks' and find their names listed in the Palgrave dictionary under that heading. Or they are relegated to the fringes of the discipline in the Austrian school or among the ranks of gold bugs decrying fiat money and calling for a return to sound money.

There are three notable economists who openly embraced money's importance: Marx, Veblen, and Keynes. Each of these, in his own way, argued that money is the *purpose* of production – that the production process itself begins and ends with money (Dillard 1980). Keynes, indeed, called his approach a 'monetary theory of production'. There is a long tradition of followers of that tradition, many of whom fall within the Post Keynesian camp; others include the Circuitistes and the Institutionalists (particularly the American variety – who find a similar approach in Veblen's theory of business enterprise). The best known advocate of this alternative interpretation is Davidson (1978), who focuses on money's 'peculiar' characteristics from Keynes's Chapter 17 and on the importance of decision making in conditions of uncertainty. This is by now so well known among heterodox economists that I do not wish to pursue it further.

Another tradition extends Keynes's analysis to develop an endogenous money approach. Here, Moore (1988) is most representative, who argues that we should think of the supplies of reserves and money as horizontal. Circuitistes have also adopted horizontalism in their analysis of creation and destruction of money at the beginning and end of the circuit, respectively – building on Schumpeter's work, but without the dynamic innovation for which he is justly famous. Again, this literature is well-developed and requires no further comment here (Graziani 1990).

A more recent extension of Keynes has been in the direction of Knapp's state money approach, or what is also called Chartalism (or in the UK, Cartalism). This chapter adopts Chartalism; however, I do not wish to simply repeat work that has been carried on over the past 15 years. Instead, I will argue that if we recognize that the money of account is chosen by the state, and that only the state can issue domestic currency, then we should view 'money' as a public monopoly. We can apply the theory of public monopolies to money to provide an alternative view of its source and importance in the modern economy.

BRIEF OVERVIEW OF THE ARGUMENT: MONEY IS A GOVERNMENT, NOT A PRIVATE, CREATION

In this chapter I argue that the reason both theory and policy get money 'wrong' is because economists and policymakers fail to recognize that money is a public monopoly. In this section I will very quickly contrast the orthodox view that money was an invention of private markets that had relied inconveniently on barter with a Chartalist view that money is a creation of the state.

Much has already been written on this, and I find the Chartalist view to be consistent with the historical record, such as it exists. I admit that there are – and will always be – gaps in our knowledge of money's origins. Hence, it is not my purpose to use historical evidence to challenge orthodoxy. Rather, what follows should be seen as following the spirit of the 'story' of money presented in textbooks – not claiming it to be historically accurate but rather providing a framework for understanding something about money's nature (Innes 1913, 1914).

Conventional wisdom holds that money is a private invention of some clever Robinson Crusoe who tired of the inconveniencies of bartering fish with a short shelf-life for desired coconuts hoarded by Friday. Self-seeking globules of desire continually reduced transactions costs, guided by an invisible hand that selected the commodity with the best characteristics to function as the most efficient medium of exchange. Self-regulating markets maintained a perpetually maximum state of bliss, producing an equilibrium vector of relative prices for all tradables, including the money commodity that serves as a veiling numeraire.

All was fine and dandy until the government interfered, first by reaping seigniorage from monopolized coinage, next by printing too much money to chase the too few goods extant, and finally by efficiency-killing regulation of private financial institutions. Especially in the US, misguided laws and regulations simultaneously led to far too many financial intermediaries but far too little financial intermediation. Chairman Volcker delivered the first blow to restore efficiency by throwing the entire Savings and Loan sector into insolvency, and then freeing thrifts to do anything they damn well pleased. Deregulation morphed into a self-regulation movement in the 1990s on the unassailable logic that rational self-interest would restrain financial institutions from doing anything foolish.

This was all codified in the Basle II agreement that spread Anglo-Saxon 'anything goes' financial practices around the globe. The final nail in the government's coffin would be to tie monetary policy-makers' hands to inflation targeting, and fiscal policy-makers' hands to balanced budgets to preserve the value of money. All of this would lead to the era of the 'great moderation', with financial stability and rising wealth to create the 'ownership society' in which all worthy individuals could share in the bounty of self-regulated, small government, capitalism. (In Euroland, the reins were even tighter, as fiscal policy was irretrievably separated from national currencies by adoption of the euro – creating an additional bulwark against government's natural propensity to create inflation.)

We know how that story turned out. In all important respects we managed to recreate the exact same conditions of 1929 and history repeated itself with the same results. Take John Kenneth Galbraith's *The Great Crash*, change the dates and some of the names and you've got the *post mortem* for our current calamity. (And in Euroland, the results have been even worse, with markets downgrading governments and imposing austerity that is generating violent resistance movements like nothing seen in the West since the 1930s as the Maastricht criteria not only prevent inflation but also any reasoned response to the crisis (Goodhart 1998)).

What is the Keynesian-Institutionalist alternative? Money is not a commodity or a thing. It is an institution, perhaps the most important institution of the capitalist economy. The money of account is social, the unit in which social obligations are denominated. I won't go into pre-history, but following the great numismaticist, Grierson, I trace money to the wergild tradition – that is to say, money came out of the penal system rather than from markets, which is why the words for monetary debts or liabilities are associated with transgressions against individuals and society (Wray 1998, 2004). To conclude, money predates markets, and so does governmental authority. As Karl Polanyi argued, markets never sprang from the minds of higglers and hagglers, but rather were created by government, often to provision armies (Wray 1990). In any case we should look for money's origins in a nonmarket economy, and in institutionalized behaviours that predate markets.

My running hypothesis is that the monetary system, itself, was invented to mobilize resources to serve what government perceived to be the public purpose. If money is a government creation, then we cannot imagine a separation of the economic from the political – and any attempt to separate money from politics is, itself, political. Adopting a gold standard, or a foreign currency standard ('dollarization'), or a Friedmanian money growth rule, or an inflation target is a political act that serves the interests of some privileged group. There is no 'natural' separation of a government and its *fiscus* from its money.

The gold standard was legislated, just as the Federal Reserve Act of 1913 legislated the separation of Treasury and Central Bank functions, and the Balanced Budget Act of 1987 legislated the *ex ante* matching of federal government spending and revenue over a period determined by the heavenly movement of a celestial object. Ditto the myth of the supposed independence of the modern central bank – this is a smokescreen to hide the fact that monetary policy is run for the benefit of particular interest groups (usually, the moneyed ones).

From inception, then, we can suppose that money was created to give authorities command over socially created resources. We can think of money as the currency of taxation, with the money of account denominating one's social liability. Often, it is the tax that monetizes an activity – that puts a money value on it for the purpose of determining the share to render unto Caesar. The sovereign government names what money-denominated thing can be delivered in redemption against one's social obligation or duty to pay taxes. It can then issue the money thing in its own payments. That government money thing is, like all money things, a liability denominated in the state's money of account. And like all money things, it must be redeemed, that is, accepted by its issuer so that the payer dispenses with her obligation to pay.

As Hyman Minsky (1986) always said, anyone can create money (to be more accurate, money-denominated things), the problem lies in getting them accepted. Only the sovereign can impose tax liabilities to ensure its *sovereign* money things will be accepted. To be sure, power is always a continuum and we should not imagine that acceptance of non-sovereign money things is necessarily voluntary. We are admonished by the *good book* to be neither a creditor nor a debtor, but (almost?) all of us are always simultaneously debtors and creditors. Maybe that is what makes us human – or at least members of the same family tree as chimpanzees, who apparently keep careful mental records of liabilities, and refuse to cooperate with those who don't pay off debts (Atwood 2008). This is called reciprocal altruism: if I help you to beat Chimp A senseless, you had better repay your debt when Chimp B attacks me.

Similarly, nonmonetary as well as monetary debts and credits are ubiquitous in human societies; perhaps what sets humans apart from other apes is our ability to denominate credits and debts in a representative, universal money of account. Our penal system moved from 'an eye for an eye' to monetary fees, fines, and taxes – a leap our ape cousins seem unable to make. And our social system created sovereign power – the ability to impose monetary obligations for imagined transgressions – aided and abetted in the West by religion: we are all from birth guilty and only by payment of tithes can we wash ourselves of our 'original sin'. With the rise of democracy, we prefer to believe we impose these obligations on ourselves, accepting taxes as the price of civilization.

MONOPOLY MONEY

In the US, the dollar is our state money of account and high powered money (HPM or coins, green paper money, and bank reserves) is our state monopolized currency. We can make that just a bit broader because US treasuries (bills and bonds) are essentially HPM that pays interest (indeed, treasuries are really reserve deposits at the Fed that pay higher interest than regular reserves), so we will include HPM plus treasuries as the government currency monopoly. One must deliver these in payment of federal taxes, which destroys currency. If government emits more in its payments than it redeems in taxes, currency is accumulated by the nongovernment sector as financial wealth.

We need not go into all the reasons (rational, irrational, productive, fetishistic) that one would want to hoard currency, except to note that a lot of the *nonsovereign* dollar denominated liabilities are made convertible (on demand or under specified circumstances) to US currency. Hence, it is handy for many economic units to keep currency close at hand to convert their liabilities to currency. Obviously, banks are the best example because demand deposits are convertible on demand.

Since government is the only issuer of currency, like any monopoly government can set the terms on which it is willing to supply it. If you have something to sell that the government would like to have – an hour of labour, a bomb, a vote – government offers a price that you can accept or refuse. Your power to refuse, however, is not unlimited. When you are dying of thirst, the monopoly water supplier has substantial pricing power. The government that imposes a head tax can set the price of whatever it is you will sell to government to obtain the means of tax payment so that you can keep your head on your shoulders or yourself out of jail. Since government is the only source of the currency required to pay taxes, and since at least some people do have to pay taxes, government has pricing power – that is, can set the conditions according to which it will supply the currency.

Just as a water monopolist does not let the market determine an equilibrium price for water, the money monopolist should not let the market determine the conditions on which money is supplied. Rather, the best way to operate a money monopoly is to set the 'price' and let the 'quantity' float – just like the water monopolist does.

My favourite example is Minsky's universal employer of last resort (ELR) programme in which the federal government offers to pay a basic wage and benefit package (say $12 per hour plus usual benefits), and then hires all who are ready and willing to work for that compensation (Wray 1998). The 'price' (labour compensation) is fixed, and the 'quantity' (number employed) floats in a countercyclical manner. With ELR, we achieve full employment (as normally defined) with greater stability of wages, and as government spending on the programme moves countercyclically, we also get greater stability of income (and thus of consumption and production).

Unfortunately, government usually does not recognize it operates a monopoly money, believing that it must pay 'market determined' prices – whatever that might mean. Unemployment and inflation are the results of this misunderstanding.

LEVERAGING MONOPOLY MONEY

Following Minsky, I have said anyone can create money. I can issue IOUs denominated in the dollar, and perhaps I can make my IOUs acceptable by agreeing to redeem them on demand for US government currency. The conventional fear is that I will issue so much money that it will cause inflation, hence orthodox economists advocate a money growth rate rule (central bank control over reserves determines private money creation given the deposit multiplier) (Wray 1990). But it is far more likely that if I issue too many IOUs, they will be presented for redemption. Soon I run out of the currency with which I promised to redeem my IOUs, and am forced to default, ruining my creditors. That is the nutshell history of most private money creation until the twentieth century – and it remains a relevant story even today. In other words, 'markets' would work far better than many free marketers believe, with redemptions limiting expansion of private money things long before they cause inflation.

But we have always anointed some institutions – banks – with a special relationship, allowing them to act as intermediaries between the government and the nongovernment sectors. Most importantly, government makes and receives payments through banks. Hence, when you receive your Social Security payment it takes the form of a credit to your bank account; you pay taxes through a debit to that account. Banks, in turn, clear accounts with the government and with each other using reserve accounts (currency) at the Fed, which was specifically created in 1913 to ensure clearing at par. To strengthen that promise, we introduced deposit insurance so that for most purposes, bank money functions like government money. We can think of that as leveraging monopoly money – since ultimately it is backed by currency used to clear accounts.

Here's the rub. Bank money is privately created when a bank buys an asset – which could be your mortgage IOU backed by your home, or a firm's IOU backed by commercial real estate, or a local government's IOU backed by prospective tax revenues. But it can also buy one of those complex sliced and diced and securitized toxic waste assets that created all the trouble since 2007. A clever and ethically challenged banker will buy completely fictitious 'assets' and pay himself huge bonuses for non-existent profits while making uncollectible 'loans' to all of his deadbeat relatives.

The bank money he creates while running the bank into the ground is as good as the government money the Treasury creates serving the public interest. And that crooked banker will happily pay outrageous prices for assets, or lend to his family, friends and fellow frauds so that they can pay outrageous prices, fueling asset price inflation. This generates nice virtuous cycles in the form of bubbles that attract more money until the inevitable bust. I won't go into output price inflation except to note that asset price bubbles can fuel spending on consumption and investment goods, spilling-over into commodities prices, so on some conditions there can be a link between asset and output price inflations.

The amazing thing is that the free marketers want to 'free' the 'private' financial institutions but advocate reining-in government on the argument that excessive issue of money by government is inflationary. Yet we have effectively given banks the power to issue government money (since banks have access to the central bank and treasury), and if we do not constrain what they purchase they will fuel speculative bubbles. By removing government regulation and supervision, we invite private banks to use the public monetary system to pursue private interests.

Again, we know how that story ends since we have got both the 1930s and the late 2000s experiences as evidence. Unbridled lending for speculative purposes invites excess and rewards fraud, and is inevitably followed by a crash. That, of course, does not mean that government spending cannot also be too large, or even that its regulation cannot be too constrictive. Finding exactly the right government stance, with it spending just the right amount to move resources to the public sector while leaving sufficient resources for the private purpose and with it regulating just the right amount to let financial institutions finance private activity at a scale commensurate with those left-over resources, is not easy.

To come to a conclusion for this section: the primary purpose of the monetary monopoly is to mobilize resources for the public purpose. There is no reason why private, for-profit institutions cannot play a role in this endeavour. But there is also no reason to believe that self-regulated private undertakers will pursue the public purpose. Indeed, we probably could go farther and assert that both theory and experience tell us precisely the opposite: the best strategy for a profit-seeking firm with market power rarely coincides with the best policy from the public interest perspective. And in the case of money, it is even worse because private financial institutions compete with one another in a manner that is financially desta-bilizing: by increasing leverage, lowering underwriting standards, increas-ing risk, and driving asset price bubbles. Unlike my ELR example above, private lending and spending are strongly pro-cyclical.

These apprehensions are in addition to the usual arguments about the characteristics of public goods and bads that make it difficult for the profit-seeker to capture external benefits, and for the market to force the producer to internalize costs. For this reason, we need to analyse money and banking from the perspective of regulating a monopoly – and not just any monopoly but rather the monopoly of the most important institution of our society.

KEYNES AND CHARTAL MONEY

Many Post Keynesians turn to Chapter 17 for the 'essential proper-ties' that make money special (Kregel 1976). Keynes argues that part of money's peculiarity arises from the fact that it has a very small 'elastic-ity of production', meaning that 'the response of the quantity of labour applied to producing it to a rise in the quantity of labour which a unit of it will command' is minuscule (Keynes 1964, p. 230). By this, Keynes was not arguing for a fixed quantity of money in the face of rising demand for money, but rather saying that an increase of liquidity preference cannot keep labour employed in the production of money. This is why Keynes argues that 'unemployment develops, that is to say, because people want the moon; – men cannot be employed when the object of desire (i.e. money) is something which cannot be produced and the demand for which cannot be readily choked off' (ibid., p. 235).

He concluded that the existence of money is the cause of unemploy-ment, because 'in the absence of money . . . the rates of interest would only reach equilibrium when there is full employment' (ibid.). If money is the ultimate cause of unemployment, why are economies organized around its use? Orthodoxy argues that money originated to reduce transactions costs, in contradiction to Keynes's proposition that money prevents the economy from operating at its efficient, full capacity, level. That is, money causes one of the most important inefficiencies there is: failure to achieve full employment.

Keynes clearly thought that money serves a more fundamental purpose than to 'lubricate' the market mechanism. In *The General Theory* he explicitly advanced 'the Theory of the Monetary Economy' (ibid., p. 293). In his preparation of *The General Theory*, Keynes spoke of the 'monetary theory of production', that would deal

> with an economy in which money plays a part of its own . . . so that the course
> of events cannot be predicted, either in the long period or in the short, without
> a knowledge of the behaviour of money between the first state and the last.
> And it is this which we ought to mean when we speak of a monetary economy.
> (Keynes, CW, vol. 13, pp. 408–9)

Long before he wrote *The General Theory*, Keynes tried to explain
money's nature and origins (Ingham 2000). For example, in the *Treatise*,
he argued the

> money of account comes into existence along with debts, which are contracts
> for deferred payment, and price lists, which are offers of contracts for sale or
> purchase. . . . [and] can only be expressed in terms of a money of account.
> (Keynes 1976, vol. I, p. 3)

He distinguished between 'money and money of account by saying that
the money of account is the description or title and the money is the thing
which answers to the description' (ibid.). Further, the state

> claims the right to determine what thing corresponds to the name, and to vary
> its declaration from time to time – when, that is to say, it claims the right to
> re-edit the dictionary. This right is claimed by all modern States and has been
> so claimed for some four thousand years at least. It is when this stage in the
> evolution of money has been reached that Knapp's chartalism – the doctrine
> that money is peculiarly a creation of the State – is fully realized. (ibid., p. 4)

Finally,

> the age of chartalist or State money was reached when the State claimed the
> right to declare what thing should answer as money to the current money of
> account – when it claimed the right not only to enforce the dictionary but also
> to write the dictionary. To-day all civilised money is, beyond possibility of
> dispute, chartalist. (ibid.)

That is a clear endorsement of Knapp's (1924) state money approach. But
he seems to have adopted this view much earlier – perhaps long before
he read Knapp (which was translated in 1924) – in his 1914 review of an
article by A. Mitchell Innes, where he approvingly noted Innes's rejection
of the story of the evolution of money from early commodity moneys to
credit and fiat money (Keynes 1914, p. 420; Innes 1913). Like Knapp,
Innes argued the state 'enforces the dictionary' by imposing a tax in the
money of account and ensures that the money it issues – denominated in
its own money of account – is generally accepted by agreeing to accept it
in tax payments (Innes 1913, p. 398). In his review, Keynes concluded 'Mr.
Innes's development of this thesis is of unquestionable interest. . . . [T]he

main historical conclusions which he seeks to drive home have, I think, much foundation' (Keynes 1914, p. 421).

Innes insisted that even state money (what Keynes calls 'money proper') is debt, and it shares with all debt the promise that it must be accepted by its issuer. According to Innes, this is the 'very nature of credit throughout the world', which is 'the right of the holder of the credit (the creditor) to hand back to the issuer of the debt (the debtor) the latter's acknowledgment or obligation' (Innes 1914, p. 161). Yet, government money is different, because it is 'redeemable by the mechanism of taxation' (ibid., p. 151): '[I]t is the tax which imparts to the obligation its "value". . . . A dollar of money is a dollar, not because of the material of which it is made, but because of the dollar of tax which is imposed to redeem it' (ibid., p. 152). What 'stands behind' currency is the state's obligation to accept it in payment of taxes.

When a bank makes a loan, it accepts an IOU and issues its own IOU; the bank's debtor clears his IOU by delivering the bank's IOU, which it must accept. All modern banking systems include a clearing house so that a bank's debtor can deliver the liability of any bank – and banks use currency (central bank reserves) to clear among each other. Likewise, as Keynes noted, tax liabilities are met by delivering bank liabilities, with the central bank clearing accounts between private banks and the treasury. There is a hierarchy of monies, with bank liabilities used by the non-government sector and with government liabilities used for net clearing among banks and with the government (Bell 2001). Given this arrangement, banks must hold reserves for clearing (as in the USA), or have ready access to them (as in countries like Canada, where the central bank offers overdraft facilities and banks attempt to hold zero net reserve balances). Ultimately, a central bank cannot refuse to provide reserves for clearing if it wishes to maintain an orderly payments system with par clearing. Further, as Moore (1988) insists, to hit its interest rate target the central bank must accommodate the demand for reserves.

POLICY IMPLICATIONS IN LIGHT OF THE GLOBAL FINANCIAL CRISIS

The Marx-Veblen-Keynes monetary theory of production asserts that money is the *object* of production – it is not merely the way we measure the value of output, nor even something we hold in the presence of uncertainty. It is because money does not take any particular commodity form that it can be the purpose of production of all particular commodities. It is the general representation of value – it buys all commodities and all commodities buy (or, at least attempt to buy) money. Commodities obtain their value – they *become* commodities – by exchanging for the universal representation of social value, money. By the same token, obtaining money allows us access to all commodities that are trying to buy money.

This presents the possibility of disappointment: the fruits of production can enter the market but fail to buy money, which can lead to a decision to cease production and to default on monetary obligations. Goodhart (2008) argues the reason orthodoxy cannot find a role for money or financial institutions in its rigorous models is because default is ruled out by assumption. All IOUs are equally safe because all promises are always kept as debts are always paid. This means anyone can borrow at the risk-free interest rate and that any seller would accept a buyer's IOU; there is no need for cash and never any liquidity constraint. Nor would we need specialists such as banks to assess credit-worthiness, nor deposit insurance, nor a central bank to act as lender of last resort. Almost all interesting questions about money, financial institutions, and monetary policy are left out if we ignore liquidity and default risk.

Default risk on a bank's IOUs is small (and nonexistent in the case of government guaranteed deposits), hence bank liabilities are widely accepted. Banks specialize in underwriting (assessing credit-worthiness of) 'borrowers' – those whose IOUs they hold. Not only do banks intermediate between government and its taxpayers but they also intermediate by accepting borrowers' IOUs and issuing their own IOUs. The IOUs they hold generally have higher default risk (except in the case of government debt) and are less liquid than the IOUs they issue. For this service, they earn profits, in large part determined by their ability to charge a higher interest rate on the IOUs they hold than the rate they pay on their own. The image of a debt pyramid is useful – those lower in the pyramid use the IOUs issued by entities higher in the pyramid to make payments and to retire debt.

When a crisis hits, this is manifested as a 'run' to the safest liabilities – those highest in the pyramid. The intense demand for 'money' raises its subjective return while lowering the demand for other financial and real assets. As Keynes said, unemployment results because everyone wants 'the moon' – money. In a crisis, only government can swim against the tide, offering its liabilities. The first line of defence is the central bank, which lends reserves without limit to financial institutions facing a run on their own liabilities. This allows banks to convert deposits as necessary, and to 'refinance' their positions in longer term assets by borrowing at the central bank.

The second line of defence is central bank purchases of illiquid and risky financial assets the nongovernment sector is trying to unload. This prevents what Irving Fisher called a 'debt deflation' process as 'fire sales' of assets drive their prices ever lower. There are obvious incentive problems: if market participants know that the central bank will always bail-out markets by purchasing overpriced assets when a bubble collapses, they will be tempted to pursue speculative excesses in a boom.

The third line of defence is fiscal, as the sovereign government spends by issuing currency – simultaneously satisfying liquidity preference and propping up aggregate demand. Again, incentives are affected as markets might come to expect such a response.

When the global financial crisis hit in 2007, many of the central banks of the biggest economies acted as lenders of last resort, and several moved on to massive purchases of assets to prop up prices. Financial markets had become huge, many times greater than total global GDP. To really make a difference in a market like securitized US mortgages, the Fed had to lend, buy, and guarantee many trillions of dollars worth of liabilities. In doing so, it had to pick 'winners' and punish 'losers' – deciding which financial institutions and instruments to save, and which would be allowed to fail. The problem was not that the Fed could not 'afford' to lend or purchase on the necessary scale to save every market participant, it was a question about the wisdom of doing so. In addition to central bank actions, treasuries around the world also engaged in fiscal stimulus – although on a much smaller scale.

As of the beginning of 2011 it is too early to say whether the interventions have been sufficient to save the global financial system. But it is clear that even if the scale of intervention was large enough, many potential problems were created with respect to incentives, transparency of central bank activities, and democratic accountability.

Further, the central banks were not able to prevent deep and lasting downturns with tremendous growth of unemployment. While governments also typically used treasury spending and tax cuts to provide fiscal stimulus, the scale was too small to prevent the worst calamity since the Great Depression. For the most part, timidity was due to fears of afford-ability and size of deficits. The difference between the actions of central banks and treasuries is remarkable – the size of interventions by central banks was essentially limited only by their own discretion, while fiscal interventions were limited by budgets approved by elected representatives. When Chairman Bernanke was asked by Congress where the Fed gets all the money it used for bailouts, he responded (quite correctly) that it is simply a matter of crediting bank accounts with Fed liabilities – something that faces no inherent limit.

Yet, when President Obama had to defend his administration against charges that it ought to do more about unemployment, he claimed the US government had 'run out of money'. Supposedly, government can always 'afford' to buy more financial assets from banks, but it cannot 'afford' to buy more products of industry, nor could it 'afford' to hire more workers. And, yet, operationally, these activities are 'financed' in the same way – by crediting banks accounts with government liabilities.

In truth, a sovereign government cannot run out of its own liabilities. If there are banks that want to sell bad assets to the central bank, it can buy them by crediting bank accounts with reserves. If there are unemployed workers who want to work for a wage, government can hire them by crediting bank accounts. There may be reasons why hiring unemployed labour, or buying output from private firms, is not desired in a slump, but 'affordability' is not a legitimate excuse when offered by a sovereign government that issues its own nonconvertible monopoly currency. And it cannot be a matter of insufficient demand for the currency – unemployment and unsold goods are together strong evidence of an unmet demand for the currency – a demand that can be easily met by the monopoly supplier of currency.

Understanding how a monopoly money works would advance public policy formation a great deal. Affordability is never the issue; rather, the real debate should be over the proper role of government: how it should use the monetary system to achieve the public purpose.

BIBLIOGRAPHY

Atwood, M. (2008), *Payback: Debt and the Shadow Side of Wealth*, Toronto: Anansi Press.

Bell, S. (2001), 'The role of the state and the hierarchy of money', *Cambridge Journal of Economics*, **25**(2) (March), 149–63.

Davidson, P. (1978), *Money and the Real World*, London: Macmillan.

Dillard, D. (1980), 'A monetary theory of production: Keynes and the institutionalists', *Journal of Economic Issues*, **14**(2) (June), 255–73.

Goodhart, C. A. E. (1998), 'Two concepts of money: implications for the analysis of optimal currency areas', *European Journal of Political Economy*, **14**(3) (August), 407–32.

Goodhart, C. A. E. (2008), 'Money and default', in M. Forstater and L. R. Wray (eds), *Keynes for the Twenty-First Century: The Continuing Relevance of the General Theory*, New York: Palgrave Macmillan, pp. 213–23.

Graziani, A. (1990), 'The theory of the monetary circuit', *Economies et Societes*, series no. 7, June.

Ingham, G. (2000), '"Babylonian madness": on the sociological and historical "origins" of money', in J. Smithin (ed.), *What is Money?*, New York: Routledge, pp. 16–41.

Innes, A. M. (1913), 'What is money?', *Banking Law Journal*, **30**(5) (May), 377–408, reprinted in L. R. Wray (ed.), *Credit and State Theories of Money*, Cheltenham, UK and Northampton, MA, USA: Edward Elgar (2004), pp. 14–49.

Innes, A. M. (1914), 'The credit theory of money', *Banking Law Journal*, **31**(2) (February), 151–68, in L. R. Wray (ed.), *Credit and State Theories of Money*, Cheltenham, UK and Northampton, MA, USA: Edward Elgar, pp. 50–78.

Keynes, J. M. (1914), 'What is money?', *Economic Journal*, **24**(95) (September), 419–21.

Keynes, J. M. (1964), *The General Theory of Employment, Interest, and Money*, New York: Harcourt Brace Jovanovich.

Keynes, J. M. (1971–1989), *The Collected Writings of John Maynard Keynes*, London: Macmillan and Cambridge University Press for the Royal Economic Society

Vol. IV: *A Tract on Monetary Reform*, 1971

Vol. XIII: *The General Theory and After. Part I Preparation*, 1973

Vol. XIV: *The General Theory and After. Part II Defense and Development*, 1973

Vol. XXVIII: *Social, Political and Literary Writings*, 1982

Keynes, J. M. (1976), *A Treatise on Money*. Volumes I and II, New York: Harcourt, Brace & Co.

Knapp, G. F. (1924), *The State Theory of Money*, Clifton, NY: Augustus M. Kelley.

Kregel, J. A. (1976), 'Economic methodology in the face of uncertainty: the modeling methods of Keynes and the post Keynesians', *Economic Journal*, **86**(34) (June), 209–25.

Minsky, H. P. (1986), *Stabilizing an Unstable Economy*, New Haven, CT: Yale University Press.

Moore, B. J. (1988), *Horizontalists and Verticalists: The Macroeconomics of Credit Money*, Cambridge: Cambridge University Press.

Wray, L. R. (1990), *Money and Credit in Capitalist Economies: The Endogenous Money Approach*, Aldershot, UK and Brookfield, VT, USA: Edward Elgar.

Wray, L. R. (1998), *Understanding Modern Money: The Key to Full Employment and Price Stability*, Cheltenham, UK and Lyme, NH, USA: Edward Elgar.

Wray, L. R. (2004), *Credit and State Theories of Money: The Contributions of A. Mitchell Innes*, Cheltenham, UK and Northampton, MA, USA: Edward Elgar.

Name index

Subject index